LIBRARY OF NEW TESTAMENT STUDIES

317

formerly the Journal for the Study of the New Testament Supplement series

Editor
Mark Goodacre

PAUL'S USE OF THE OLD TESTAMENT IN ROMANS 9.10-18

An Intertextual and Theological Exegesis

BRIAN J. ABASCIANO

t &t clark

Published by T&T Clark International
A Continuum imprint
The Tower Building, 11 York Road, London SE1 7NX
80 Maiden Lane, Suite 704, New York, NY 10038

www.continuumbooks.com

British Library Cataloguing-in-Publication Data
A catalogue record for this book is available from the British Library

ISBN: HB: 978-0-567-03103-7

Typeset by Free Range Book Design & Production Limited
Printed and bound in Great Britain

To Bob Lovejoy, beloved and faithful man of God and pastor, mentor, friend, and treasured co-worker in the gospel

And to Paula Lovejoy, faithful servant of the Lord and beloved minister of God to our family, godly wife, mother and teacher of many children in the Lord, and encourager of God's people

CONTENTS

ACKNOWLEDGMENTS

I wish to thank the many people who have helped to make this book possible in one way or another. I am grateful to T&T Clark for accepting this work for publication, and to Senior Editor Dominic Mattos for his patience in waiting for me to submit the manuscript. I am also grateful to those who have read portions of the manuscript and provided helpful comments: Desmond Alexander, Bob Chisholm, Luke Gowdy, Ben Henshaw, Bill Klein, Bob Lovejoy, Tom McCall, and above all, Paul Ellingworth, who supervised most of my doctoral research, which was published in my first book, and has continued to provide feedback on my continuing scholarly work. His responsiveness to my requests for his reading and commenting on my work is amazing and greatly appreciated. I would also like to thank Michael Segal for answering my questions about *Jubilees* 48.17, and Laura Whitney of Andover-Harvard Theological Library for her helpfulness with my use of the library.

I continue to experience God's blessing in the privilege of pastoring at Faith Community Church (FCC) in Hampton, New Hampshire, which has remained an ideal situation in which to research and write while also providing for my family, serving my Lord, and fulfilling his call on my life. I thank and praise God for our church family, which has loved and cared for us in so many ways and is the type of godly community the New Testament calls the Church to be. Their prayers for us are precious in the sight of God and of us, and to them we owe a continuing debt. Indeed, the many prayers that have gone up before the throne of God for this book from members of FCC are partly responsible for its completion and any articulation of truth its pages may hold. This book is dedicated to my co-pastor, Bob Lovejoy, and his wife, Paula. They are a great blessing to us and so many. Their love and faithfulness to the Lord and his people are inspiring and a great example to the Church at large. Bob mentored me in ministry and raised me up to pastor alongside him. And now he has helped support my scholarship by not only praying for me and working together with me in the ministry, but also taking on extra ministry responsibility in the last months of my work on this book when I devoted extra, focused time to its completion.

I am overflowing with thankfulness for my wife Valerie, who is, as I often say, the best woman in the world. Her constant friendship, help and support are invaluable gifts, as are our children Noah, Jacynth, Benaiah and Hannah. Valerie is a great wife and mother, and the children are great kids. I thank and praise God for my family. It is simply wonderful, a great joy. I wish to thank them for their patience and sacrifice for any time we have missed as a family because of my work on this book.

But more than anything, I am thankful to and for God, who is the faithful Father of the heavenly lights and the source of every good and perfect gift (Jas 1.17). He has blessed me with every spiritual blessing in Christ (Eph. 1.3), 'who loved me and gave himself for me' (Gal. 2.20). To the triune God 'be the glory forever! Amen' (Rom. 11.36).

Brian Abasciano
Hampton, NH
October 2010

ABBREVIATIONS

AB	Anchor Bible
ABS	Archaeology and Biblical Studies
AGJU	Arbeiten zur Geschichte des antiken Judentums und des Urchristentums
AnBib	Analecta biblica
ANTC	Abingdon New Testament Commentaries
ATJ	*Ashland Theological Journal*
BBR	*Bulletin for Biblical Research*
BDAG	W. Bauer, F. W. Danker, W. F. Arndt and F. W. Gingrich, *A Greek–English Lexicon of the New Testament and Other Early Christian Literature* (Chicago: University of Chicago Press, 3rd edn, 2000)
BDB	F. Brown, S. R. Driver and C. A. Briggs, *A Hebrew and English Lexicon of the Old Testament* (Oxford: Clarendon Press, 1907)
BDF	F. Blass, A. Debrunner and R. W. Funk, *A Greek Grammar of the New Testament and Other Early Christian Literature* (Cambridge: CUP, 1961)
BECNT	Baker Exegetical Commentary on the New Testament
BEvT	Beiträge zur evangelischen Theologie
BHT	Beiträge zur historischen Theologie
Bib	*Biblica*
BNTC	Black's New Testament Commentaries
BRev	*Bible Review*
Bsac	*Bibliotheca Sacra*
BSC	Bible Student's Commentary
BWANT	Beiträge zur Wissenschaft vom Alten und Neuen Testament Neunte Folge
CBAA	Catholic Biblical Association of America
CBC	Cambridge Bible Commentary
CBQ	*Catholic Biblical Quarterly*
CBQMS	*Catholic Biblical Quarterly*, Monograph Series
CCEL	Christian Classics Ethereal Library
CPNIVC	College Press NIV Commentary
CUP	Cambridge University Press
DJG	J. B. Green, S. McKnight and I. H. Marshall, *Dictionary of Jesus and the Gospels* (Downer's Grove: InterVarsity Press (IVP), 1992)

DNTB	C. A. Evans and S. E. Porter (eds), *Dictionary of New Testament Background* (Downer's Grove: IVP, 2000)
DOTP	T. D. Alexander and D. W. Baker (eds), *Dictionary of the Old Testament: Pentateuch* (Downer's Grove: IVP, 2003)
DPL	G. Hawthorne, R. P. Martin, and D. G. Reid (eds), *Dictionary of Paul and His Letters* (Downers Grove: IVP, 1993)
DSB	Daily Study Bible
ESV	English Standard Version Bible
ETR	*Etudes théologiques et religieuses*
EvQ	*Evangelical Quarterly*
FOTL	The Forms of the Old Testament Literature
FRLANT	Forschungen zur Religion und Literatur des Alten und Neuen Testaments
GKC	*Gesenius' Hebrew Grammar* (ed. E. Kautzsch, rev. and trans. A. E. Cowley; Oxford: Clarendon Press, 1910)
HALOT	L. Koehler and W. Baumgartner et al. (eds), *The Hebrew and Aramaic Lexicon of the Old Testament Study Edition* (ed. and trans. M. E. J. Richardson; 2 vols; Leiden: Brill, 2001)
HSMM	Harvard Semitic Museum Monographs
IBC	Interpretation: A Bible Commentary for Teaching and Preaching
ICC	International Critical Commentary
ISBE	G. Bromiley (ed.), *The International Standard Bible Encyclopedia* (4 vols; Grand Rapids: Eerdmans, rev. edn, 1979–88)
ISFCJ	International Studies in Formative Christianity and Judaism
ITC	International Theological Commentary
IVPNTC	InterVarsity Press New Testament Commentary
JBQ	*Jewish Bible Quarterly*
JETS	*Journal of the Evangelical Theological Society*
JPSTC	Jewish Publication Society Torah Commentary
JSJSup	*Journal for the Study of Judaism*, Supplement Series
JSNT	*Journal for the Study of the New Testament*
JSNTSup	*Journal for the Study of the New Testament*, Supplement Series
JSOT	*Journal for the Study of the Old Testament*
JSOTSup	*Journal for the Study of the Old Testament*, Supplement Series
JSPSup	*Journal for the Study of the Pseudepigrapha*, Supplement Series
JSS	*Journal of Semitic Studies*
LCL	Loeb Classical Library
LNTS	Library of New Testament Studies
LSJ	H. G. Liddell, R. Scott and H. S. Jones, *Greek–English Lexicon* (Oxford: Clarendon Press, 9th edn, 1968)
NAC	New American Commentary
NASB	New American Standard Bible®

NBD2	J. D. Douglas, N. Hillyer et al. (eds), *New Bible Dictionary* (Wheaton: Tyndale House, 2nd edn, 1982)
NCB	New Century Bible
NETS	A. Pietersma and B. G. Wright (eds), *New English Translation of the Septuagint* (Oxford: OUP, 2007).
NIB	New Interpreter's Bible
NIBCNT	New International Biblical Commentary on the New Testament
NIBCOT	New International Biblical Commentary on the Old Testament
NICNT	New International Commentary on the New Testament
NICOT	New International Commentary on the Old Testament
NIDNTT	C. Brown (ed.), *The New International Dictionary of New Testament Theology* (3 vols; Exeter: Paternoster Press, 1975)
NIDOTTE	W. A. VanGemeren (ed.), *New International Dictionary of Old Testament Theology and Exegesis* (5 vols; Grand Rapids: Zondervan, 1997)
NIGTC	New International Greek Testament Commentary
NIVAC	New International Version Application Commentary
NovTSup	*Novum Testamentum*, Supplements
NRSV	New Revised Standard Version Bible
NTC	New Testament Commentary
NTS	*New Testament Studies*
OBO	Orbis biblicus et orientalis
OTP	J. H. Charlesworth (ed.), *The Old Testament Pseudepigrapha* (2 vols; New York: Doubleday, 1983–85)
OTL	Old Testament Library
OUP	Oxford University Press
PBM	Paternoster Biblical Monographs
PBTM	Paternoster Biblical and Theological Monographs
PNTC	Pillar New Testament Commentary
RHBC	Randall House Bible Commentary
RSPT	*Revue des sciences philosophiques et théologiques*
SAP	Sheffield Academic Press
SB	Subsidia Biblica
SBEC	Studies in the Bible and Early Christianity
SBL	Society of Biblical Literature
SBLDS	Society of Biblical Literature Dissertation Series
SBLSCS	Society of Biblical Literature Septuagint and Cognate Studies
SBLSS	Society of Biblical Literature Semeia Studies
SCS	Septuagint Commentary Series
SJLA	Studies in Judaism in Late Antiquity
SJT	*Scottish Journal of Theology*
SNTSMS	Society for New Testament Studies Monograph Series
SPIB	Scripta Pontificii Instituti Biblici
Str-B	H. L. Strack and P. Billerbeck, *Kommentar zum Neuen Testament aus Talmud und Midrasch* (6 vols; Munich,

	1922–61)
TAB	The Aramaic Bible
TDNT	G. Kittel and G. Friedrich (eds), *Theological Dictionary of the New Testament* (trans. G. W. Bromiley; 10 vols; Grand Rapids: Eerdmans, 1964–76)
TDOT	G. J. Botterweck and H. Ringgren (eds), *Theological Dictionary of the Old Testament* (Grand Rapids: Eerdmans, 1974–)
TJ	*Trinity Journal*
TOTC	Tyndale Old Testament Commentaries
TPI	Trinity Press International
TWOT	R. L. Harris, G. L. Archer Jr and B. K. Waltke (eds), *Theological Wordbook of the Old Testament* (2 vols; Chicago: Moody, 1980)
TynBul	*Tyndale Bulletin*
VT	*Vetus Testamentum*
WBC	Word Biblical Commentary
WUNT	Wissenschaftliche Untersuchungen zum Neuen Testament
ZTK	*Zeitschrift für Theologie und Kirche*

Chapter 1

INTRODUCTION

This investigation continues the intertextual exegesis of Romans 9 begun in my previous volume,[1] picking up where that study left off. The first volume covered the first nine verses of Romans 9 (9.1-9), whereas the present volume covers the next nine verses (9.10-18). A projected third volume is to cover the rest of the chapter (9.19-33). The reasons, goals and approach of this investigation are covered in the introduction to the first volume, so there is no need to address those matters here.

But perhaps it is worth recalling what we mean by 'intertextual exegesis'. The term refers to standard grammatical-historical exegesis of a New Testament text – in this case, Romans 9 – that alludes to the Old Testament, informed by a detailed analysis of the author's use of Scripture. Such analysis involves exegeting the Old Testament text in its original context, surveying the history of its interpretation in Judaism and Christianity prior to and roughly contemporaneous with Paul, and comparing its extant relevant textual traditions to the form of Paul's quotation. Hence, we will subject the Old Testament background of Paul's discourse in Rom. 9.10-18 to this sort of analysis, specifically Gen. 25.23; Mal. 1.2-3; Exod. 33.19b; and Exod. 9.16.[2] We will then bring the results of that research to bear on the exegesis of Rom. 9.10-18. Specifically, we will cover the intertextual background material for Rom. 9.10-13 in chapters 2–4, culminating in our exegesis of the passage in Chapter 5. Then we will cover the intertextual background material for Rom. 9.14-18 in chapters 6–7, culminating in our exegesis of the passage in Chapter 8. Finally, Chapter 9 will bring the investigation to a close with some brief concluding reflections.

Romans 9 is notorious for content that is rife with controversial theological subjects such as election and divine hardening of human beings. That is one

---

1. B. J. Abasciano, *Paul's Use of the Old Testament in Romans 9.1-9: An Intertextual and Theological Exegesis* (JSNTSup/LNTS, 301; London: T&T Clark, 2005). One reviewer complained that the book references the doctoral dissertation on which it is based too much, which was only available at the University of Aberdeen's library. Happily, the dissertation is now available on the internet, at http://evangelicalarminians.org/Abasciano-Pauls-Use-of-the-Old-Testament-in-Romans-9.1-9-An-Intertextual-and-Theological-Exegesis.

2. The exegesis of Exod. 33.19 and its context has already been conducted in ibid., 46–72, with focused exegesis of 33.19 on pp. 65–69. Therefore, this investigation omits a full exegesis of this text and refers readers to the one already provided in my previous volume.

thing that makes the passage such an exciting one to study. In our exegesis of 9.1-9, we began to delve into these issues substantially. But now, in 9.10-18, we plunge into them with greater focus and intensity because, as Paul's argument progresses, he addresses them with greater precision and depth.

Chapter 2

GENESIS 25.23 IN ITS OLD TESTAMENT CONTEXT

Genesis 25.23, the first Old Testament passage that Paul quotes in Rom. 9.10-18, is situated in the larger passage of Gen. 25.19-34,[1] which may be divided into three basic sections:

(1) 25.19-26   The birth and destiny of Jacob/Israel and Esau/Edom.
(2) 25.27-28   The character of Jacob and Esau.
(3) 25.29-34   Esau despises/sells his birthright to Jacob.[2]

This larger passage serves as a preface to the Jacob cycle of Genesis (roughly 25.19–35.29), introducing its main themes.[3] The Jacob cycle itself is part of the patriarchal history of Genesis (chs 12–50), which develops the book's main plot of God's covenantal promises to Abraham and their fulfilment, summed up by Gen. 12.1-3.[4] The portion of this saga most directly under consideration here, Gen. 25.19-34, echoes a number of features of the Abraham cycle (11.27–25.11) as it prepares the audience for the story of the people of Israel's origin in their forefather, Jacob, emphasizing the continuity between Abraham and Jacob and that the line of promise runs through Jacob.[5] Accordingly, Wenham has perceptively pointed out that the oracle of 25.23 parallels the programmatic promises to Abraham in 12.1-3, fulfilling a similarly programmatic role for Jacob's story.[6] Indeed, 25.23

---

1.   Most interpreters take 25.19-34 as a unit (G. J. Wenham, *Genesis 16–50* (WBC, 2; Dallas: Word, 1994), 172).

2.   Ibid., 172, also divides the passage into these three basic sections, but provides a more detailed outline. For an even more detailed outline, see G. W. Coats, *Genesis with an Introduction to Narrative Literature* (FOTL, 1; Grand Rapids: Eerdmans, 1983), 183–86.

3.   See e.g., Wenham, *Genesis*, 172–73.

4.   L. A. Turner, 'Genesis, Book of', *DOTP*, 350–59 (353), observes that the scholarly consensus regards the divine promises and blessings recorded in Genesis as the book's central core. We need not concern ourselves with the source criticism of Genesis since, inter alia, Paul and his contemporaries would have approached the text in its final form; cf. Abasciano, *Romans 9.1-9*, 46. For a recent overview of pentateuchal source criticism and its present state, see D. W. Baker, 'Source Criticism', *DOTP*, 798–805.

5.   Cf. Wenham, *Genesis*, 173.

6.   Ibid., 173, 180. K. A. Mathews, *Genesis 11:27–50:26* (NAC, 1B; Nashville: Broadman & Holman, 2005), 385, and J. P. Fokkelman, *Narrative Art in Genesis: Specimens*

joins 12.1-3 in embodying the theme of the entire Pentateuch and even the rest of the Old Testament.[7]

2.1. *Genesis 25.19-26*

Chapter 25.19a stands as a heading over the entire main Jacob cycle: 'These are the generations [תולדת] of Isaac, the son of Abraham'.[8] The recurring תולדת headings in Genesis normally refer to the lives of the children of the specific patriarchs they mention.[9] Interestingly, there is no תולדת of Abraham in Genesis, that is, there is not a substantial focus on Isaac's story.[10] This has the effect of highlighting Jacob as the chosen heir of the covenant promises to Abraham by bringing out the connection between Abraham and Jacob more directly,[11] a natural focus for a work that had Israel as its audience.

This is not to say that Isaac is unimportant. He is, after all, the promised seed of Abraham (25.19b). He is the carrier of the covenant promises to Abraham and must also produce offspring to carry on the promises if YHWH is to remain faithful to them. So 25.20 records Isaac's marriage to Rebekah at the age of 40. The reference to Rebekah's homeland (Paddan-Aram) and her brother Laban prepare the reader for the later narration of Jacob's journey to that place and his dealings with Laban.[12]

But just as with Abraham and Sarah, the fulfilment of YHWH's covenant word of promise was endangered by infertility – Rebekah was barren (25.21). For this reason, Isaac prayed on her behalf. Then YHWH granted Isaac's request so that Rebekah conceived. The recording of Rebekah's barrenness and its resolution by the hand of YHWH displays the role of YHWH in the granting of offspring to the chosen covenant head and thus his faithfulness to his covenant promise as well as his sovereignty over the fulfilment of the divine plan. Isaac was wholly dependent on YHWH and his will for the attainment of the blessings for which he longed.[13] All of vv. 19-21 lead to the momentous conception that will carry on the Abrahamic covenant and its promises.

But Rebekah's was a problem pregnancy: 'the children struggled together within her' (25.22), so much so that Rebekah questioned why she was

of Stylistic and Structural Analysis (Assen/Amsterdam: Van Gorcum, 1975), 93, find 25.23 to be the centre of a chiasm encompassing 25.20-26.

7.   For Gen. 12.1-3 as the theme of the Pentateuch, see e.g., Wenham, *Genesis*, 173.

8.   Unless otherwise noted, all translations of Scripture in this investigation are the author's.

9.   J. H. Walton, *Genesis* (NIVAC; Grand Rapids: Zondervan, 2001), 548.

10.   Ibid. The latter statement of this point is commonly observed in one way or another by commentators.

11.   This also helps to explain the unusual reference to the father (Abraham) of the subject (Isaac) of the תולדת formula in 25.19 noted by Wenham, *Genesis*, 174.

12.   Cf. ibid.

13.   Cf. J. Calvin, *Genesis* (ed./trans. J. K. King; Geneva Commentary; 2 vols in 1; repr., Edinburgh: Banner of Truth, 1965), 2.40–41; C. F. Keil, *The Pentateuch* (trans. J. Martin; Commentary on the Old Testament, 1; 3 vols in 1; repr., Grand Rapids: Eerdmans, 1973), 1.267.

experiencing such distress and went to inquire of YHWH.[14] The answer
he provides sets the course of her children's lives, and indeed, of salvation
history itself. A prophetic oracle, it comes in poetic verse: 'And YHWH said
to her',

> Two nations are in your womb.
> And two peoples from your belly will be divided.
> And one people will be stronger than the other people.
> And the older will serve the younger. (25.23)

As already mentioned, the oracle is programmatic for the whole passage
(25.19-34), the story of Jacob chronicled in Genesis, and salvation history.
It essentially records the election of the people Israel in their eponymous
ancestor.

The oracle unfolds in successive lines of synthetic parallelism,[15] each one
developing the previous one with greater specificity.[16] The first line reveals at
least that two distinct nations would descend from the offspring of Rebekah's
pregnancy,[17] but in the context of the oracle it also means that she is carrying
twins, each the corporate head of a nation/people that will descend from
him. It is important to recognize that the oracle is primarily corporate in its
significance and emphasis. The first three lines speak of nations and peoples,
requiring that the older (רב) and younger (צעיר) of the final line also refer
primarily to the peoples respectively represented by the twins. But this does
not mean that the individuals to whom Rebekah will give birth (Jacob and
Esau) are not in view at all. They are very much in view, but primarily as
the corporate representatives of their descendants. This is an example of
the ancient and scriptural principle of corporate solidarity/representation in
which the individual head of a group is identified with the group, represents

---

14.   The verb for 'struggle' here, רצץ, suggests a vigorous clashing; see e.g., Wenham,
Genesis, 175. The precise meaning of Rebekah's question is unclear because of an elliptical
construction (אִם־כֵּן לָמָּה זֶּה). Another common option besides that represented above is to
take (with the Syriac text) Rebekah to ask why she is alive, but as D. Kidner, *Genesis: An
Introduction and Commentary* (TOTC, 1; London: Tyndale, 1967), 151, comments, this is
'hardly convincing'. H. C. Leupold, *Exposition of Genesis*, II (Grand Rapids: Baker Book
House, 1942), 703, suggests more plausibly if not convincingly that Rebekah asks what her
destiny will be in relation to her pregnancy, though this is close to the interpretation adopted
above, which is supported by the LXX (ἵνα τί μοι τοῦτο). The text does not specify how
Rebekah sought the Lord, but consultation of a prophet (perhaps Abraham?) is the most
likely assumed scenario; cf. Wenham, 175.
15.   On synthetic parallelism in Hebrew poetry, see e.g., W. S. LaSor, 'Poetry, Hebrew',
ISBE, 3.891–98 (893).
16.   Cf. Fokkelman, *Genesis*, 89.
17.   Wenham, *Genesis*, 175, 179, is probably correct that the first line does not in
itself imply twins, though his reasoning is suspect. Indeed, the whole oracle is cryptic like
a good deal of prophecy, which only becomes clear with fulfilment. Nevertheless, given
her participation in the original milieu of the oracle, it is certainly possible that Rebekah
(whether one thinks of actual history or only the story world of Genesis) would have grasped
its meaning. In any case, our focus in interpretation is to try and unpack the text's full
meaning in its context.

it and sums it up in himself.[18] What is true of the corporate representative also becomes true of the group generally. His name, identity and inheritance, for example, belong to them.

The second line of the oracle reveals that the two peoples represented by the twins would be in conflict with one another from their inception in accordance with the conflict between the twins that began in the womb. The nature of the struggle between Jacob and Esau is not yet stated, but it will become clear in the ensuing narrative that it first and foremost concerns the family headship and inheritance. But the primary reference is to the struggle for dominance between the nations that would descend from these two brothers, Israel and Edom, as a result of the twins' conflict. The third line simply informs us that one of these brothers and his people would be stronger than the other and presumably prevail.

The final line, which Paul quotes in Rom. 9.12, forms the oracle's climax by identifying which brother/people would prevail – the younger (and therefore his people). Thus, the final line essentially sums up the whole oracle and becomes the main point of the passage to this point. By saying that the older would serve the younger,[19] YHWH indicates that the younger brother would be granted the headship of the family and its inheritance. This would include headship of the Abrahamic covenant passed through Isaac along

---

18.   On this concept, see the references in B. J. Abasciano, 'Corporate Election in Romans 9: A Reply to Thomas Schreiner', *JETS* 49/2 (June 2006), 351–71 (355 n. 17); henceforth, 'Election'.

19.   R. C. Heard, *Dynamics of Diselection: Ambiguity in Genesis 12–36 and Ethnic Boundaries in Post-Exilic Judah* (SBLSS, 39; Atlanta: SBL, 2001), 98–101, demonstrates the surprising facts that the final line of 25.23 is actually ambiguous in itself grammatically and normal Hebrew word order would favour 'the younger' (צעיר) as the subject. But the immediate context as well as the book of Genesis and the rest of the Bible make the standard interpretation certain as evidenced by the fact that רב has almost universally been interpreted as the subject throughout history (see ch. 4.5 below for possible exceptions); Heard himself furnishes a lengthy list of representatives of the standard view and cites no contrary example. This offers an implicit critique both of Heard's method of seeking any possible ambiguity in a passage and of his conclusion that 'the narrator leaves a great number of characterizational decisions in readers' hands' (183). Human language often contains ambiguity by its nature despite authors' intentions to be clear. Moreover, ambiguity frequently results from an author's assumption of what will be clear to his readers. This is partly why the work of interpretation is not for the faint of heart and is ill served by methodologies that ascribe meaning to the reader's activity. It also militates against the thesis of O. T. Allis, 'The Birth-Oracle to Rebekah (Gen. XXV.23): A Study in the Interpretation of Prophecy', *EvQ* 11.2 (1939), 97–117, that the oracle was intentionally ambiguous as originally pronounced to test those originally involved. Allis offers a more detailed treatment of the oracle's ambiguity and makes a more compelling case with the suggestion of a motive for it. However, he must resort to speculation concerning a number of issues that the text is silent about and overlooks that Genesis was written for an audience that would have taken the oracle's meaning for granted. Moreover, Rebekah might be expected to have understood more than is revealed by the mere words of the oracle (see n. 17 above). Allis admits that the traditional interpretation is ultimately correct (e.g., 110).

with its priceless promises.[20] The covenant and its promises would now pass through the younger brother to his descendants.

This is a reversal of the ancient law of primogeniture, which gave family headship and a double portion of the family inheritance to the firstborn male.[21] But this is a familiar pattern in Genesis. God is repeatedly portrayed as choosing the younger/weaker over the older/stronger for blessing and as the instrument through which the advancement of his plan will take place contrary to human expectations and values.[22] The point of these reversals appears to be that YHWH is sovereign over both his plan to redeem and bless humanity and the covenant through which it is to be accomplished.[23] It is his prerogative to choose who the covenant head is and thus who his covenant people are as well as the way in which he will fulfil his promises to Abraham.

Accordingly, in addition to the concept of corporate representation, we also have the related Old Testament concept of corporate election at work in this passage.[24] The descendants of Jacob, who is later to be renamed Israel by YHWH (32.28; 35.10), are chosen as YHWH's covenant people as a consequence of their identification with Jacob/Israel, whose name they bear. At the same time, the descendants of Esau, who comes to be called Edom

---

20.   Indeed, עבד ('to serve') is often used in the OT to signify covenantal service/ subjection. This service was frequently political since ancient Near Eastern suzerain-vassal treaties/covenants typically required service/subjection from the vassal king and his nation. Hence, according to *HALOT*, 773, עבד often means 'to serve politically', a meaning it finds in Gen. 25.23. On the rich wordplay in this last line, which embodies the reversals it predicts, see R. J. D. Knauth, 'Esau, Edomites', *DOTP*, 219–24 (220–21). For the probable ancient Near Eastern background behind the use of רַב (older) and צָעִיר (younger) along with inheritance rights and their reversal, see E. A. Speiser, *Genesis* (AB, 1; New York: Doubleday, 1964), 194–95, who seems to represent the consensus in applying ANE background to the sale of Esau's birthright. V. P. Hamilton, *The Book of Genesis* (NICOT; 2 vols; Grand Rapids: Eerdmans, 1990/1995), 2.184, questions the applicability of this background and notes controversy over the question.

21.   Cf. e.g., Keil, *Pentateuch*, 268–69; N. M. Sarna, *Genesis* (JPSTC; Philadelphia: JPS, 1989), 181; Kidner, *Genesis*, 152; R. O. Rigsby, 'Jacob', *DOTB*, 461–67 (462); and more generally, J. M. Wilson and R. K. Harrison, 'Birthright', *ISBE*, 1.515–16. Walton, *Genesis*, 558, curiously separates Esau's birthright/inheritance from the covenant and land promise. His observation that Isaac owned no land is irrelevant since all of Isaac's inheritance, including his inheritance from the Lord with its covenant and promise of land, would pass to his descendants as made clear by the promises (e.g., Gen. 15.13-16; 17.1-22; 22.15-18; 26.3-5).

22.   See esp. J. H. Sailhamer, 'Genesis', in F. E. Gaebelein (ed.), *The Expositor's Bible Commentary*, II (Grand Rapids: Zondervan, 1990), 1–284 (182–83), who lists a number of reversals in Genesis.

23.   A point made frequently by interpreters in one way or another; see e.g., ibid., 183.

24.   On corporate election, see Abasciano, 'Election'; idem, Romans 9.1-9, 185–89 (cf. 41–44); idem, 'Clearing Up Misconceptions about Corporate Election', *ATJ* 41 (2009), 59–90 (henceforth, 'Misconceptions'). One might question whether Gen. 25.23 really indicates divine election when it could just as well be merely a prediction; see e.g., J. G. Janzen, *Abraham and All the Families of the Earth: A Commentary on the Book of Genesis 12–50* (ITC; Grand Rapids/Edinburgh: Eerdmans/Handsel, 1993), 95. But it cannot be doubted that Genesis and the rest of the Bible – especially Paul – view Jacob as freely chosen by God.

(25.30), are excluded from the covenant along with the rest of the world as a result of their identification with Esau (or lack of identification with Jacob!), whose name they bear. But this exclusion is not absolute. The purpose of the covenant was ultimately to include all the nations of the world in its blessings through connection with the covenant head/people (12.3; 18.18; 22.18; 26.4; 28.14).[25] Therefore, ideally, individual Edomites could eventually gain access to the covenant and its blessings by joining the covenant people.

The corporate focus of the oracle and its last line demands a primary application to the peoples Israel and Edom. In addition to indicating that Israel would be the chosen covenant people, it also implies the accompanying general political/military dominance of Israel over Edom. Whereas Esau never literally served Jacob, and indeed Genesis reports that Jacob and Esau eventually reconciled even as it depicts Jacob as ultimately bowing down to Esau and calling him his lord (33.1-15; 35.28-29),[26] Edom did become a prime enemy of Israel and was subjugated to her over much of the history of their relations.[27] Although Edom did sometimes gain the upper hand, 'in the long and bitter struggle between these two peoples, the descendants of Jacob finally triumphed'.[28]

Rebekah did indeed bear twins (25.24). The older came out covered with red hair,[29] leading his parents to name him Esau (עֵשָׂו; 25.25), which sounds a little like the Hebrew word for hair (שֵׂעָר) and the name of the land of Seir (שֵׂעִיר), which Esau and his descendants would eventually inhabit. When the younger came out, his hand was grasping Esau's heel (עָקֵב), leading his parents to name him Jacob (יַעֲקֹב), a name related to the Hebrew word for heel and capable of meaning 'he grasps the heel/supplants' or 'may he (God)

25   See Abasciano, *Romans 9.1-9*, 153–54, 210–11, 221. Of course, there is debate over the precise import of the blessing of the world in Abraham/Isaac/Jacob, but we are fortunate to know Paul's view of the matter. For him, the nations of the world would be included in the covenant through faith-union with Jesus Christ, the supreme seed of Abraham and covenant head (Rom. 4; Gal. 3–4).

26.   See Knauth, 'Esau', 222. It is also worth noting that despite the oracle, God blessed Esau (33.9; 36.6-7; cf. Knauth) much as he did the similarly rejected Ishmael; cf. Abasciano, *Romans 9.1-9*, 168–69, 193–95. The motif of covenantal rejection of the firstborn is a significant undercurrent in Genesis, spawning some detailed attention, the most extensive studies probably being those of R. Syrén, *The Forsaken First-Born: A Study of a Recurrent Motif in the Patriarchal Narratives* (JSOTSup, 133; Sheffield: SAP, 1993) and (thematically more general) Heard, *Diselection*.

27.   For helpful overviews, see Knauth, 'Esau', 222; G. C. Aalders, *Genesis*, II (trans. W. Heynen; BSC; Grand Rapids: Zondervan, 1981), 79–80.

28.   Aalders, *Genesis*, 80.

29.   Scholars differ on whether Esau's complexion or his hair is red, but the text specifically links his hairiness with his redness; cf. Heard, *Diselection*, 102, though he argues that Esau was not born hairy, showing no awareness, however, of the possibility that Esau's hair was red. This description of Esau at his birth already pictures him as wild and perhaps unsavoury since hairiness appears to have been associated with wildness/incivility and red hair was particularly scorned in ancient times (see Wenham, *Genesis*, 176, citing Vawter; Sarna, *Genesis*, 180). Interestingly, both Hamilton, *Genesis*, 183, and Sarna observe that a ruddy complexion was considered indicative of heroic stature.

protect' (25.26).[30] The fact that Isaac was 60 years old when the twins were born (25.26) means that he and Rebekah suffered the agony of infertility for 20 years (cf. 25.20) with much of the challenge to faith that similar circumstances posed for Isaac's parents, Abraham and Sarah.

2.2. *Genesis 25.27-28*

Verses 27-28 describe the characters of the grown-up Jacob and Esau along with the respective attitudes of each parent towards each son. Esau was a man of the field, skilled at hunting, which won his father's love (over Jacob) because of his taste for the meat Esau provided for him. Jacob on the other hand is said to be a cultured man (אִישׁ תָּם)[31] who dwelled in tents, preferring to stay at home and (probably) work as a shepherd.[32] The contrast between the two men represents Esau as a rugged, primal type, and Jacob as a more mature, sophisticated personality. The characterization will be played out in the following verses and their story of Jacob supplanting Esau in the rights of the firstborn. As for Rebekah, we are told that she loved Jacob (over Esau). But unlike the case of Isaac's preferential love of Esau, we are given no reason for Rebekah's preferential love of Jacob. Presumably, the main reason is the oracle that she received.[33]

2.3. *Genesis 25.29-34*

These verses now report the initial fulfilment of the oracle of 25.23 in a terse style.[34] Virtually every line adds pertinent information to the story, building to a climax until the rights of the firstborn are transferred from Esau to Jacob – thus making Esau Jacob's slave in principle – and Esau is denounced

30.   On the meaning of the name, see esp. A. R. Millard, 'Jacob', *ISBE*, 4.948–55 (948). The name is almost certainly a shortened form of the name Jacob-el.

31.   Cf. *HALOT*, 1742–43. The meaning of תָּם here has been very puzzling to interpreters because of its usual meaning of 'complete/perfect' and use as a designation of the 'highest moral approbation' when the context shows Jacob to be less than upright (see Wenham, *Genesis*, 177). Nevertheless, the term does suggest some sort of positive characterization of Jacob here (see below). Most scholars seem to opt for a meaning of 'quiet, simple' or the like.

32.   Commentators commonly link Jacob's tent-dwelling here to shepherding; see e.g., Wenham, *Genesis*, 177.

33.   Cf. J. C. L. Gibson, *Genesis*, II (DSB; Philadelphia: Westminster, 1982), 138; Calvin, *Genesis*, 2.50, who are among those who note this connection; cf. Janzen, *Genesis*, 96. For other possible reasons for Rebekah's love, see Calvin, ibid.; Leupold, *Genesis*, 710. There are a number of questions related to 25.19-34 that the text does not directly address, such as why Rebekah loved Jacob and whether Rebekah told Isaac about the oracle. Gibson and Janzen tend to raise such questions more than others. The text's silence about many of these details calls our attention all the more to the details it does relay.

34.   As for structure, Fokkelman, *Genesis*, 95–97, is notable for the chiasm he has suggested.

for despising his birthright. The story is relatively straightforward. Jacob had cooked stew, and Esau came in from the field exhausted (25.29). So Esau politely but crudely asked Jacob for some of the stew, identifying it only by its red colour (אָדֹם), bringing him to be called by the name Edom (אֱדוֹם), which sounds like the word for red in Hebrew (25.30). Matching Esau's brusqueness, Jacob demanded that he first sell his birthright to Jacob. 'The way Jacob states his demand suggests long premeditation and a ruthless exploitation of his brother's moment of weakness'.[35]

Esau's response reveals that he did not value his birthright, which, as mentioned earlier, included headship of the family and its inheritance along with ownership of a double portion of the inheritance:[36] 'Behold, I am going to die. So what is this to me – the right of the firstborn?' (25.32). Jacob then demanded that Esau swear to give him the birthright in exchange for the stew (25.33a). 'So he swore to him and sold his birthright to Jacob. Then Jacob gave bread and lentil stew to Esau. And he ate and drank and got up and left. Thus Esau despised the right of the firstborn' (25.33b-34). Despite his claim, Esau was obviously not on the verge of death, but he esteemed his birthright so lightly that he sold it for a bowl of lentil stew to satisfy the sensual desire of the moment. Even the way his behaviour is reported, with a rapid succession of verbs describing basic physical activity, suggests a coarseness and vulgarity to Esau's actions in relation to the birthright and its blessings.[37]

The final sentence of the passage gives the author's assessment of the episode: 'Esau despised the birthright'. As the text's own interpretation, this judgment represents the main point of 25.29-34. Interestingly, 'Though Jacob has been portrayed as heartlessly exploitive',[38] the narrator does not explicitly condemn him. This does not in any way suggest that Jacob's actions are to be

---

35.   Wenham, *Genesis*, 178.

36.   Ibid. (citing Tsevat), among others, holds that Esau only sold his inheritance to his father's property, not his rank or position. But Gen. 27 does not demand this view as Tsevat contends; cf. K. Walton, *Thou Traveller Unknown: The Presence and Absence of God in the Jacob Narrative* (PBTM; Carlisle: Paternoster, 2003), 22, against Tsevat. The patriarchal blessing is obviously typically part of the privileges of the firstborn, though the father of the family could divert the right of the firstborn or parts of it to another son if he so chose (see n. 21 above; Gen. 48.13-22; 49.3-4; 1 Chron. 5.1-2; 26.10; Wilson and Harrison, 'Birthright'). It could be that Isaac sought to restore the birthright (or part of it) to Esau through the blessing the blessing he intended for him. There are just too many unanswered questions regarding a host of issues that bear on the relationship between the birthright of Gen. 25 and the blessing of Gen. 27 to establish a fundamental separation between them. Kidner, *Genesis*, 155, represents just one plausible approach to Gen. 27 that views the birthright and the blessing as intertwined. In contrast to Wenham et al., C. Westermann, *Genesis 12–36: A Commentary* (trans. J. J. Scullion; Minneapolis: Augsburg, 1985), 418, thinks the birthright does not refer to property rights, but to general priority. The wisest approach would seem to be to take the birthright as generally encompassing all the privileges typically associated with the firstborn but subject to the father's reassignment in whole or in part. As for what Paul's view likely was, it is instructive to note that Heb. 12.16-17 essentially equates the birthright and the blessing.

37   Cf. Speiser, *Genesis*, 195.

38.   Wenham, *Genesis*, 178.

commended, though his esteem of the birthright is surely approved implicitly. As many commentators have pointed out, that his actions were reprehensible goes without saying. Moreover, 'The subsequent stories will show how Jacob had to pay for the enmity he had stirred up'.[39] Nevertheless, Esau's despising of his birthright is clearly presented as the greater sin. The question to be answered is, why does the author stress this point? The answer to this question is tied up with the relationship of 25.29-34 to the other sections of the broader passage.

2.4. *The Logical Structure of Genesis 25.19-34*

The oracle of 25.23, summed up by its last line – 'The older will serve the younger' – provides the main thrust of 25.19-26. Formally, there is a progression of thought from the oracle proclaiming the twins' birth and destiny to the reporting of their actual birth and its circumstances (25.24-26). These latter verses further testify to the faithfulness of God's word of promise as the completion of the pregnancy which already so testified. They also bring beginning fulfilment to the oracle. But because of its divine character, its prominence in the narrative, and its programmatic function, the birth oracle remains central to the section in which it is found. The case is much the same with the report of the twins' characters when they are grown, found in the next section, 25.27-28. There is some further progression in thought from the oracle with muffled intimations of its fulfilment that also set the scene for the story of its first full-blown fulfilment. But 25.27-28 is still a stepping-stone on the way to the oracle's fulfilment.

This leads us to the oracle's first substantial fulfilment, 25.29-34, and the question of how it is to be related to the oracle. More specifically, we must address how the oracle's summary proclamation, 'The older will serve the younger', relates to the main point of 25.29-34, 'Esau despised the right of the firstborn'. The answer to this is the same as the answer to the question of why the author stresses Esau's guilt in the selling of his birthright. There are three main options.

The first option is that the oracle is causative. In its most extreme form, this view would take YHWH's prophetic word to Rebekah to actually cause all the specific circumstances that lead to its fulfilment. This amounts to an absolute divine predestination of all aspects of the events described including Jacob's deplorable exploitation of his brother and Esau's despising of his birthright. But this interpretation has no real support in the text and is frankly counterintuitive as evidenced by the fact that few if any interpreters of this text have suggested it even though it is demanded on some level by certain theological traditions.[40] It is a possible

---

39. Ibid., 178–79.

40. Calvin may approach this position in viewing God as leaving Esau to his own natural disposition but disposing Jacob to himself through election (see Walton, *Traveller*, 26; cf. the recent view, similar to Calvin, of E. R. Clendenen, 'Malachi', in R. A. Taylor and

logical connection that must rely on a broader theological/philosophical system.

Nevertheless, there is surely a measure of causality in the oracle's function, though not in specific relation to Esau's despising of his birthright. YHWH chose Jacob to possess the Abrahamic covenant and blessing despite Esau's 'natural right' to it. So when Jacob takes possession of the birthright by shamefully exploiting his brother, it is clearly God's will that Jacob possess the birthright, though it is equally clear that YHWH in no way condones either Jacob's or Esau's actions. In typical fashion, YHWH is able to sovereignly bring about his will even through sinful choices and actions that he did not directly cause or engineer.[41] While this establishes a causal connection between the divine decree that the older would serve the younger and the transferal of Esau's birthright to Jacob, it leaves the specific connection between the decree and the text's own emphasis on Esau's guilt in the matter unspecified.

The second option for interpreting this connection is the opposite of the first, maintaining that Esau's, and to a greater or lesser extent, Jacob's, actions are causative. This appears to be the approach, in one way or another, of most interpreters who suggest a connection.[42] Although Jacob's actions are reprehensible, they still show a laudable cherishing of the birthright and the blessings of God associated with it.[43] Esau, on the other hand, is portrayed as treating it all with vile contempt. So it is a logical if not necessary deduction that the record of Jacob's esteem and especially Esau's contempt for the birthright has been attached to the oracle of Jacob's election in order to indicate that Esau was unfit to be the covenant head and Jacob more suitable for the privilege. In other words, Esau was rejected from the covenant because of his impiety while Jacob was chosen as the heir to the covenant because of his relatively greater piety. The application of the term תם to Jacob (25.27), which is usually a very positive term for moral uprightness, supports this view.

But even though Esau's actions reveal him to be unsuitable as the covenant heir, Jacob's uncharitable behaviour hardly commends him for the privilege. Moreover, Genesis' picture of Jacob and Esau is more complex than this view would suggest. Esau is actually portrayed somewhat positively overall and

E. R. Clendenen, *Haggai, Malachi* (NAC, 21A; Nashville: Broadman & Holman, 2004), 203–496 (257–58)), but even he does not specifically attribute all the twins' actions to God, at least in his Genesis commentary.

41.   For an excellent concise treatment of God's sovereignty as contained in the Pentateuch along these lines, see J. N. Oswalt, 'Theology of the Pentateuch', *DOTP*, 845–59 (853–54). In specific relation to Gen. 25.19-34, cf. Walton, *Traveller*, 25–27, though he overemphasizes paradox.

42.   See e.g., Keil, *Pentateuch*, 269; Walton, *Genesis*, 558; Leupold, *Genesis*, 714–15; cf. Janzen, *Genesis*, 98. Against it, see Calvin, *Genesis*, 2.51–52, who noted the popularity of this view. According to Walton, *Traveller*, 26, this tends to be the approach of traditional Jewish interpretation.

43.   See Calvin, *Genesis*, 2.50–55, for a very positive (in fact, unduly so) view of Jacob's actions in this account. But even he admits Jacob's actions to be inhumane.

Jacob as frequently deceitful, conniving and underhanded.[44] Neither Jacob nor Esau was worthy of covenant heirship, and Jacob does not ultimately prove himself to be any worthier than Esau.[45]

The third option for relating the oracle to Esau's selling/despising of the birthright is as a sort of justification for God's choice without identifying a basis for it, bearing some similarity to the view just discussed. It takes seriously the text's emphasis on Esau's guilt, but it avoids the pitfalls of exaggerating Jacob's worthiness, caricaturing Esau's impiety, or suggesting that Jacob was chosen by default. John Sailhamer's articulation of this view deserves to be quoted at length:

> The story of Esau's rejection of his birthright is purposefully attached to the end of the narrative that introduces the motif of the older serving the younger. It is a narrative example that God's choice of Jacob over Esau did not run contrary to the wishes of either of the two brothers. It is clear from the narrative that Esau was one who 'despised' his birthright, while Jacob is portrayed as one who would go to great lengths to gain it. The importance of the contrast between the two brothers can best be seen in the fact that the writer himself explicitly states the point of the narrative in the conclusion of the story: 'So Esau despised his birthright' (v.34). In few cases in Genesis do we find such a clear and forthright statement of the writer's own understanding of the sense of the individual stories. We are left with no doubt that the writer saw in this story of Jacob's trickery a larger lesson, that Esau, though he had the right of the firstborn, did not value it over a small bowl of soup. Thus, when in God's plan Esau lost his birthright and consequently his blessing, there was no injustice dealt him. The narrative has shown that he did not want the birthright. He despised it.[46]

Thus, the main point of 25.19-34 as a whole comes to be YHWH's election of Jacob (and his descendants) and its justification (not cause) based on the despising of the birthright and covenant blessings by the original heir.[47] This does not mean that YHWH's choice needed to be justified or that he would have been bound to choose Esau if he proved more pious. Rather, YHWH's right to choose who would carry on the Abrahamic covenant with its promises, already indisputable, receives additional justification from Esau's casting aside of the privilege. All of this emphasizes God's grace in election. As Wenham has said, 'God chooses the patriarchs not because they are

44. See Knauth, 'Esau', 222–23. Indeed, these facts have precipitated defences of Esau's character such as E. Neufeld, 'In Defense of Esau', *JBQ* 20.1 (Fall 1991), 43–49; J. Stiebert, 'The Maligned Patriarch: Prophetic Ideology and the "Bad Press" of Esau', in A. G. Hunter and P. R. Davies (eds), *Sense and Sensitivity: Essays on Reading the Bible in Memory of Robert Carroll* (FS Robert Carroll; JSOTSup, 348; London/New York: SAP, 2002), 33–48.

45. Nevertheless, it may be that we are to view Jacob's regard for the covenant inheritance as revealing some level of faith in the covenant promises on his part, however erring and twisted in its expression, that motivated but did not compel the Lord, in his foreknowledge, to choose him as the covenant head/heir over Esau, who despised these blessings.

46. Sailhamer, 'Genesis', 183–84.

47. Hence, the text is not as unapologetic as W. Brueggemann, *Genesis* (IBC; Atlanta: John Knox, 1982), 217, claims.

particularly loveable characters but because of his declared intention that in them all the families of the earth should find blessing. So the patriarchs emerge from Scripture not as lily-white heroes but as real men of flesh and blood, red in tooth and claw'.[48] Nothing in Jacob or Esau could lay meritorious claim on covenant heirship.

2.5. *Jacob and Esau in the Rest of the Old Testament*

Outside of Genesis, the only significant references to Jacob and Esau together as individuals occur in Josh. 24.4 and Hosea 12.4 (12.3, Eng.).[49] In the former, YHWH states, 'I gave Jacob and Esau to Isaac. And I gave Mount Seir to Esau to possess it. But Jacob and his sons went down to Egypt'. In the following verses, YHWH then goes on to recount the history of Israel up through the conquest and the time of Joshua. It is significant that this reference comes as part of a renewal of the covenant. For the covenant with YHWH essentially sums up Israel's inheritance. While YHWH did bless Esau and his descendants with a land of their own, Jacob, and especially his descendants, were to follow the difficult but supremely rewarding path of covenant relationship with YHWH (which did, of course, ultimately include land), which would take them into slavery in Egypt and eventual deliverance, all in fulfilment of God's covenant with Abraham (Gen. 15.13-14). Their utmost portion was to be YHWH's own people. The covenant renewal led by Joshua called Israel to total commitment to YHWH and his covenant, to make a choice for or against him (Josh. 24.18-28). Israel agreed to serve YHWH alone as God, though Joshua warned them that they would come to harm if they failed in their commitment.

After Hos. 12.3 (12.2, Eng.) announces YHWH's intention to punish the people of Israel (referred to corporately as 'Jacob' in accordance with the concepts of corporate solidarity and representation) for their ways, Hos. 12.4 immediately turns to Jacob's prenatal grasping of his brother's heel. It is difficult to know whether this behaviour is looked upon positively or negatively. Hosea 12.3 would suggest the former while 12.5-6 would suggest the latter. Either way, Jacob's example is set forth as an inducement to Israel to repent (12.7). It may be that the reference is negative, exemplifying Israel's corrupt, devious character from its beginning, and that the following lines turn to positive examples from Jacob's life, a sequence that calls Israel to turn from its unfaithful behaviour to covenant loyalty just as YHWH worked in Jacob's life to turn him from being a deceiver to a man of faith.[50] But most significantly for considering Gen. 25.23 in Rom. 9.12, Hos. 12.4 looks upon

---

48.   Wenham, *Genesis*, 181.

49.   B. K.-H. Park, 'God's Sovereign Election and Rejection: Paul's Use of the Old Testament in Romans 9:10-13' (unpublished masters thesis; Gordon-Conwell Theological Seminary, 1992), 41. See also 1 Chron. 1.34.

50.   On the metamorphosis of Jacob's character as a major concern of Genesis' Jacob narrative, see Mathews, *Genesis*, 371.

Jacob's behaviour as negative (or positive) on some level while already in the womb. This accords with the emphasis on God's grace in choosing Jacob we have had occasion to note in Gen. 25.19-34.

Three points stand out for special mention concerning references to Jacob and Esau outside of Genesis. First, the names usually carry a corporate significance, either referring directly to the nations descended from these patriarchs (Israel/Edom), or referring to the patriarch in his capacity as father of the nation.[51] Second, Esau/Edom comes to be a symbol of the nations and of Israel's enemies.[52] Third and relatedly, Esau/Edom comes under severe condemnation in the Prophets, who depict the nation 'in an overwhelmingly negative and morally deficient way'.[53]

51.   Cf. Park, 'Sovereign', 42.

52.   See e.g., B. Dicou, *Edom, Israel's Brother and Antagonist: The Role of Edom in Biblical Prophecy and Story* (JSOTSup, 169; Sheffield: SAP, 1994); B. C. Cresson, 'The Condemnation of Edom in Postexilic Judaism', in J. M. Efird (ed.), *The Use of the Old Testament in the New and Other Essays* (FS W. F. Stinespring; Durham: Duke University Press, 1972), 125–48 (136–48, passim); R. L. Smith, *Micah–Malachi* (WBC, 32; Waco: Word Books, 1984), 305–06. Dicou argues that Esau/Edom already had this role in Genesis.

53.   Stiebert, 'Maligned', 42. For a brief overview of the prophetic view, see Stiebert, 38–41; B. Glazier-McDonald, 'Edom in the Prophetical Corpus', in D. V. Edelman (ed.), *You Shall Not Abhor an Edomite for He is Your Brother: Edom and Seir in History and Tradition* (ABS, 3; Atlanta: Scholars Press, 1995), 23–32; Cresson, 'Condemnation', 133–48. For a more detailed analysis, see Dicou, *Edom*, 20–114.

Chapter 3

MALACHI 1.2-3 IN ITS OLD TESTAMENT CONTEXT

The book of Malachi calls Israel back to covenant faithfulness.[1] In the prophet's estimation, the post-exilic restoration community doubted the Lord's own covenant love and faithfulness, falling into widespread violation of the covenant stipulations.[2] Hence, as the Lord's covenant messenger, the prophet assures Israel of God's covenant love and faithfulness as well as his firm commitment both to save and bless those who are faithful to him and to curse the faithless/wicked.[3] At the same time he challenges Israel's sinful, blasphemous attitudes toward the Lord, including arrogance and contempt in addition to charges of divine unfaithfulness and injustice.

Malachi 1.2-3, Paul's second Old Testament quotation in Rom. 9.10-18, appears in Malachi's introductory oracle (1.2-5), which plays a programmatic role in the book's structure and message, 'establishing the context (covenant relationship with Yahweh), tone (judgment), and style (hortatory discourse) of the oracles'.[4] Indeed, the thesis statement of the book may be found in 1.2's declaration of love for Jacob/Israel,[5] part of which Paul quotes in Rom. 9.13. The pericope epitomizes Malachi's basic and somewhat unique disputational rhetorical style in which he (1) makes a statement that indicts or contradicts (even if only implicitly) attitude(s) and/or action(s) of the audience; (2) states an objection from the audience in the form of a question(s); and (3) refutes the objection and substantiates the original statement.[6]

1.   Cf. A. E. Hill, *Malachi: A New Translation with Introduction and Commentary* (AB, 25D; New York: Doubleday, 1998), 42.

2.   Cf. ibid., 43. The precise date of Malachi is not necessary to determine for our purposes. It is enough to recognize with the vast majority of scholars that the book was written in the fifth century BCE after the rebuilding of the Temple and reflects general conditions addressed by Ezra and Nehemiah.

3.   Cf. Clendenen, 'Malachi', 232.

4.   Hill, *Malachi*, 34. Cf. e.g., Clendenen, 'Malachi', 232; P. A. Verhoef, *The Books of Haggai and Malachi* (NICOT; Grand Rapids: Eerdmans, 1987), 194–95; A. J. Botha, 'Die belang van Maleagi 1:2–5 vir die verstaan van die boek', *Skrif en Kerk* 21 (2000), 495–506.

5.   See Hill, *Malachi*, 150.

6.   On the prophetic disputation speech in Malachi, see e.g., ibid., 34–37; Clendenen, 'Malachi', 218–21 (who doubts the form's interpretive usefulness). Perhaps D. F. Murray best sums up the aspects of the disputation form as thesis, counterthesis, and dispute (cited by

Malachi 1.2a contains the original disputational statement of the section: '"I have loved you," says YHWH'. The sense of this statement is that YHWH has loved Israel over the course of her history into the present, the best understanding of the Hebrew perfect אֲהַבְתִּי in this context.[7] That is, YHWH chose Israel as his covenant people, establishing and maintaining a familial relationship of mutual obligation in which YHWH was committed to grant affection, care, protection, discipline and blessing whereas his people were required to respond in kind with affection, trust and obedience.[8] The covenantal orientation of YHWH's love is widely recognized in these verses.[9] This first statement of it is broad and rich, summing up YHWH's covenant commitments to his people. Thus, the declaration of 1.2a is tantamount to claiming that YHWH has been faithful to his covenant with Israel and remains so. It serves as the basic main point of 1.2-5, which the rest of the passage corroborates.

Malachi 1.2b ('But you say, "How have you loved us"'?) voices the people's attitude that called forth this insistence on YHWH's love, formally functioning as an objection to the truth of that statement. Israel in the time of Malachi had grown skeptical of YHWH's covenant love because, as Pieter Verhoef has observed, 'Their expectations of a glorious renewal of their national life after the return from exile had been disappointed. The promised kingdom of the Messiah had still not dawned. Israel as a nation was not delivered and glorified. They still remained under Persian rule (1:8) and were suffering from pests and plagues (2:17; 3:11, 12)'.[10] What is more, they believed that they saw the righteous suffering and the wicked prospering, and concluded that YHWH was unjust and that there was no benefit in serving him (2.17; 3.13-15). In short, they believed they saw no evidence of the fulfilment of YHWH's covenant promises.

So in 1.2c-5, YHWH proceeds to disabuse Israel of this heinous, dangerous notion by pointing to his sovereign and free election of them as his own people in their patronymic ancestor Jacob and his very observable destruction of their most hated of enemies.[11] The opening question is a rhetorical one expecting a positive answer, drawing attention to the fact that the patriarchs Jacob and Esau were brothers with no ostensible reason for the former to be preferred over the latter: 'Was not Esau Jacob's brother'? (1.2c).[12]

Hill, 35, and Clendenen, 219). D. K. Stuart, 'Malachi', in T. E. McComiskey (ed.), *The Minor Prophets: An Exegetical and Expository Commentary*, III (Grand Rapids: Baker, 1998), 1245–1396 (1248), adds implication (e.g., Mal. 1:5) as a fourth element of the form.

7.   So e.g., Verhoef, *Malachi*, 193 n. 1, 195.

8.   Cf. Abasciano, *Romans 9.1-9*, 122.

9.   See e.g., Hill, *Malachi*, 146–47, 150–52, 165; Clendenen, 'Malachi', 247; Verhoef, *Malachi*, 196–97; Smith, *Malachi*, 305.

10.   Verhoef, *Malachi*, 198; see also Hill, *Malachi*, 42, 146, 163–64.

11.   The rest of the book goes on to detail inter alia how Israel's own actions were responsible for her miserable state.

12.   J. Morison, *Exposition of the Ninth Chapter of the Epistle to the Romans: A New Edition, Re-written, to which is Added an Exposition of the Tenth Chapter* (London: Hodder and Stoughton, 1888), 82–94, makes a good case for there being no reference to

Indeed, there would be reason to prefer Esau as the older twin, possessor of the birthright. The statement that Paul quotes in Rom. 9.13 follows as an adversative which stands despite the brotherhood of the twins: 'Yet I loved Jacob, but Esau I hated' (1.2d-3a).

This assertion pithily sums up the way in which YHWH had loved Israel. It is phrased again in covenant terminology like the initial declaration of YHWH's love. But this time, the same term for love (אהב) especially stresses covenantal election, for it is contrasted with שנא ('to hate'), alludes to the election of Jacob over Esau as the head of the Abrahamic covenant (Gen. 25.23 etc.) and addresses the question of how YHWH has loved Israel. The covenant terminology of love and hate here, then, means, 'I chose Jacob as my covenant partner, but I rejected Esau as my covenant partner'.[13]

This refers, as just mentioned, to the election of Jacob over Esau as the head of the Abrahamic covenant, most directly stated by Gen. 25.23.[14] As in Gen. 25.23, the election of Mal. 1.2-3 is primarily corporate,[15] a point established not only by the fact that Malachi alludes to Gen. 25.23, but also by the corporate use in the Old Testament of the names Jacob and Esau to refer to the nations Israel and Edom respectively (see Obadiah for example) evidenced here with Esau/Edom, and especially by the fact that Jacob's

the individuals Jacob and Esau here, pointing out that the verse could readily be translated with the present tense ('Is not Esau Jacob's brother'?) and refer patronymically to the peoples designated by these patriarchs as often in the OT. But every patronymic use of these names has its basis in the peoples' identification with their respective patriarch, leaving him in the background even if remotely. So it may be that there is no substantial reference to the individual patriarchs here. It is a question of emphasis. My interpretation above takes its cue from Malachi's seeming emphasis on the entire history of YHWH's dealing with Israel. In any case, the passage does primarily have the peoples in view; see below.

13.   Cf. e.g., Hill, *Malachi*, 165–67; Verhoef, *Malachi*, 199–202; Smith, *Malachi*, 305; Stuart, 'Malachi', 1283. The common observation that the collocated language of love and hate can refer to relative degrees of love so that hate means 'to love less' does not really apply here. We are dealing with 'technical terminology from ancient Near Eastern covenants' (J. N. Pohlig, *An Exegetical Summary of Malachi* (Dallas: Summer Institute of Linguistics, 1998), 24). At the same time, the covenantal terminology does suggest that the term 'hate' implies no personal animosity here (cf. J. G. Baldwin, *Haggai, Zecharaiah, Malachi: An Introduction and Commentary* (TOTC, 24; Leicester: IVP, 1972), 223). Nevertheless, it must later take on personal animosity when it turns to judgment in the following clauses.

14.   On which, see ch. 2 above.

15.   See the discussion of corporate election in ch. 2.1 above. Clendenen, 'Malachi', 256–57, and B. Glazier-McDonald, *Malachi: The Divine Messenger* (SBLDS, 98; Atlanta: Scholar's Press, 1987), 34, represent two common and opposite misconceptions about the corporate orientation of this passage. Clendenen believes that individual election is equally present since the individuals Jacob and Esau are named. But this misses their roles as corporate representatives of their descendants. Their individual election/diselection entailed the election/diselection of the peoples identified with them, which is the focus of concern. Glazier-McDonald, on the other hand, claims that individuals are not in view, but nations. But this also misses the roles of the individuals Jacob and Esau as corporate representatives. The most accurate course is to recognize that the election in view is primarily corporate in that the covenant people's election is based on its identification with the elect individual corporate head.

election is set forth as the way in which YHWH had loved *Israel*. That is, Jacob's election was Israel's election; the people are elected as a consequence of their identification with Jacob. Thus, the assertion that YHWH loved Jacob means that he chose Israel as his covenant people.

On the other hand, the assertion that YHWH hated Esau means that the nation of Edom is not in covenant with YHWH, who therefore has no special obligation towards them. There is no explicit commitment on his part that would temper his divine judgment against them for any wickedness they might have committed. Moreover, insofar as they are enemies of his covenant people, they are his enemies and will suffer his wrath for any wrongs against Israel. This is important in the present context since Edom had come to be regarded as Israel's archenemy, the symbol of the Gentile world (see 2.1.e above), due in the post-exilic era especially to Edom's participation in Babylon's destruction of Jerusalem (587 BCE) and occupation of Judean villages.[16] Edom's status as Israel's enemy partly explains why YHWH's destruction of Edom is an expression of his love for Israel.

In 1.3b-4, YHWH continues by describing the results of his hatred of (i.e., lack of covenant commitment to) Edom: 'and I have made his mountains a desolation, and his inheritance a wilderness for jackals. Though Edom says, "We have been shattered, but we will rebuild the ruins," thus says YHWH of hosts, "They themselves may build, but I myself will tear down." So they will call them, "territory of wickedness" and "the people whom YHWH has cursed forever."' Because Edom had wronged YHWH's own people inter alia, and because YHWH had no covenant commitment to Edom, he had destroyed their land and permanently ended their existence as a nation. Though they would try to return to their land and rebuild, YHWH would prevent them from succeeding and they would perpetually bear the humiliation and consequences of their wickedness.[17]

Herein lies one of the key differences between YHWH's love and hate. It is not that YHWH punishes only those who are not in covenant relationship with him. Indeed, his covenant with Israel demanded punishment for ongoing sin. But the punishment of his covenant people is corrective discipline with the hope of eventual restoration whereas his judgment upon those outside the covenant carries no hope for restoration.[18] Nevertheless, '"the lesson on love is a warning, and the example of Edom a threat" ... [God] is free to elect (love) and reject (hate) apart from any conditions or considerations'.[19] Therefore, Israel cannot take its election for granted by ignoring its covenant obligations. YHWH is Lord of the covenant and determines who his covenant people are.

16. See e.g., Hill, *Malachi*, 151; Glazier-McDonald, 'Edom', 24, 27–29; Stuart, 'Malachi', 1287–88.

17. Edom's ultimate downfall appears to have resulted from the gradual Nabatean Arab invasion, which was in full swing by Malachi's time and saw the Nabateans firmly established by no later than 312 BCE (see Glazier-McDonald, *Malachi*, 35–41; Hill, ibid.; cf. Stuart, ibid.).

18. Cf. Clendenen, 'Malachi', 253.

19. Hill, *Malachi*, 167, citing P. C. Craigie.

However, it is important to remember that these matters are corporately oriented. The same sort of observations we made concerning the corporate election of Jacob in Gen. 25.23 apply here.[20] Edom's exclusion from a covenant relationship with YHWH applies to them as a nation. Any Edomite could enter the covenant and enjoy its blessings by joining the elect people and keeping the covenant.[21] But in doing so, he would have to effectively cease being an Edomite and become an Israelite, essentially identifying with the covenant head of YHWH's choosing. Moreover, Israelites who were unfaithful to the covenant would be cut off from it – as Malachi testifies throughout the book – while the covenant aimed ultimately to include all the nations of the world in its blessings through connection with the covenant head/people.

These observations render the traditional question of whether the election referred to by Malachi concerns historical roles or salvation almost irrelevant. For the real teeth of the question come from the assumption that a soteriological interest would indicate an unconditional election/predestination of individuals unto salvation or damnation respectively, which many find theologically and morally repugnant even as others are driven to defend such a doctrine. But the above considerations would suggest that even if YHWH's love/hatred entails salvation/damnation, the election and rejection in view are neither absolute nor unconditional on the individual level. And indeed, it would seem that the election of Mal. 1.2-3 involves both historical role and salvation, for it is difficult to sever Israel's election from YHWH's salvation and blessing. Salvation, life and blessing of every sort were promised in the covenant. The results of the rejection of Mal. 1.3 similarly appear to involve ultimate destruction (however Malachi may conceive of it) as the punishment for unrepentant wickedness (cf. especially 3.14–4.3). However, this rejection does not exactly parallel Israel's election unto salvation as a rejection unto damnation. Divine retribution for wrongs committed against the covenant people and irreversible catastrophic judgment upon sin are the conditional (on guilt) consequence of Edom's diselection, not its content or purpose.

Verse 5 now presents what the results of this permanent decimation of Edom will be: 'Therefore, your eyes will see, and you yourselves will say, "Great is YHWH from above [מֵעַל] the territory of Israel!"' Malachi prophesies that when Israel sees that the destruction of Edom is permanent, then they will consequently recognize and confess YHWH's greatness, that is, his power, supremacy, love and covenant faithfulness. There is some question of whether the preposition מֵעַל means 'above'[22] or 'beyond'.[23] Either makes good sense in this context. The focus on YHWH's love of Israel favours the former while the attention to his sovereign dealings with Edom and the

20.   See ch. 2.1 above.
21.   Cf. rightly, Clendenen, 'Malachi', 252, though Clendenen fails to grasp the proper relationship between corporate and individual election.
22.   So e.g., Verhoef, *Malachi*, 206.
23.   So e.g., Stuart, 'Malachi', 1292, and most translations.

book's universalistic concerns (e.g., 1.11, 14) favour the latter.[24] Perhaps the wisest course would be to acknowledge all of these aspects of the text while recognizing that YHWH's love for Israel is the dominant theme. This has led me to take מֵעַל as incorporating both concepts and to translate מֵעַל literally ('from above'),[25] yielding a picture of YHWH as lovingly and protectively hovering over Israel first and foremost, and then dealing with the nations from that position for the good of his beloved people. The sense of the exclamation is then, 'Great is YHWH *above and beyond* the territory of Israel'!'[26] YHWH is sovereign over Israel and the nations. As Hill, who translates 'above', admits, 'implicit in Malachi's allusion to the "Zion tradition" of the Psalter is the de facto rule over all the nations by Yahweh from his holy habitation in Jerusalem'.[27]

As the result of YHWH's dealings with Israel and Edom, the envisioned recognition of YHWH's greatness by Israel functions as the climax of the passage and receives the stress of vv. 1.2c-5. However, as the concrete affirmation of YHWH's love and faithfulness based on its undeniable demonstration described in 1.2c-4, the declaration of v. 5 also supports the content of 1.2c-4. It substantiates those verses and functions quasi-metonymically for their content.

In any case, 1.2c-5 supports the declaration of YHWH's love for Israel in 1.2a by answering the objection to it given in 1.2b, demonstrating the way in which YHWH had loved Israel. He had chosen Israel as his covenant people rather than Edom, Israel's archenemy and the representative of all the enemies of God and his people. Therefore he had restored and blessed Israel after punishing them for their sin whereas he put a permanent end to Edom for their sin.[28] His covenant love and commitment to Israel moved YHWH to be gracious to her and to wipe out her enemy. His love is proven both by the contrast in his treatment of the two peoples and by his opposition to those who would oppose his people.

---

24.   See Hill, *Malachi*, 161–62, for a convenient description of the reasoning of the two main positions.

25.   Cf. HALOT, 827 (8a).

26.   The LXX's ὑπεράνω supports the meaning of 'above' for מֵעַל, but Stuart, 'Malachi', 1292, claims that '"above and beyond" can also be the sense of the Septuagint'.

27.   Hill, *Malachi*, 162.

28.   The restoration of Israel is surely evoked by this passage in contrast to Edom's permanent destruction (see e.g., ibid., 168). Indeed, some of the prophets connect Edom's destruction with the restoration of Israel (see Glazier-McDonald, 'Edom', 31–32; Verhoef, *Malachi*, 202), a tradition probably assumed here.

Chapter 4

INTERPRETIVE TRADITIONS SURROUNDING
GENESIS 25.23 AND MALACHI 1.2-3

Having exegeted Gen. 25.23 and Mal. 1.2-3 in their original contexts, it
is now time to turn to ancient interpretive traditions surrounding these
passages, which we will consider together because of the inherently close
connection of these passages in the Old Testament itself. Due to the large
amount of material that could be regarded as relevant to these passages, we
can only consider what we find to be the most pertinent.[1]

4.1. *Jubilees*

There is no quotation of Gen. 25.23 in the second-century BCE book of
Jubilees, but there are some passages in the book that relate to the broader
context of this verse and the concept of Jacob's election over Esau embedded
in it. Not surprisingly, these are also germane to the Jewish interpretive
background of Mal. 1.2-3. The first appears in *Jub.* 19.13-31. Verses 13-14
record the birth and subsequent character of Jacob and Esau corresponding
roughly to Gen. 25.24-27. Already in these verses the goodness of Jacob
and the wickedness of Esau are emphasized.[2] Jacob is described as smooth,
upright, and literate,[3] but Esau as fierce, rustic, hairy, illiterate and warring.
   Jubilees 19.15-31 then appears to expand at length on Gen. 25.28's
affirmation of Rebekah's preferential love for Jacob in contrast to Isaac's love
for Esau by describing Abraham's similar preferential love for Jacob over
Esau.[4] Abraham's exalted status in Jewish tradition gives his view of Jacob

   1.   For helpful surveys of interpretive traditions related to the relationship between
Jacob and Esau, see Park, 'Sovereign', 46–49, and esp. J. L. Kugel, *Traditions of the Bible:
A Guide to the Bible as It Was at the Start of the Common Era* (Cambridge, MA/London:
Harvard University Press, 1998), 352–89.
   2.   Cf. J. C. Endres, *Biblical Interpretation in the Book of Jubilees* (CBQMS, 18;
Washington, DC: CBAA, 1987), 22–24.
   3.   Jacob's literacy here is meant to depict him as learned in godly knowledge (Kugel,
Traditions, 354; Endres, *Jubilees*, 24).
   4.   As Kugel, *Traditions*, 354 n. 3, and Endres, *Jubilees*, 25, see it, *Jub.* 19.15
substitutes Abraham for Gen. 25.28's Rebekah. Endres further observes that even Isaac's
reason for preferring Esau is omitted.

and Esau an aura of divine approval so that his view virtually represents the divine view in the text. Abraham's love for Jacob over Esau here is based on Esau's deeds (of wickedness presumably) and Jacob's election as the one through whom the promises to Abraham would be fulfilled. '[I]n Jacob a name and seed would be named for' Abraham (19.16).[5] This uses the same language spoken of Isaac as the chosen seed in 16.16b,[6] a loose citation of Gen. 21.12, a biblical passage that Paul quotes in Rom. 9.7 only shortly before his quotation of Gen. 25.23. Indeed, *Jub.* 16.17-18 go on to specify that one of Isaac's sons (not yet named) would become the chosen seed whose descendants would be God's special people while all other descendants of Abraham would be 'counted with the nations', that is, they would be identified with the Gentiles in exclusion from the covenant and its blessings.

The language of name and seed is based on the foundational promises to Abraham in 12.22-24 (Gen. 12.1-3). Abraham's name/glory/heritage would be established through Isaac and then through one of his sons and that son's descendants. Now in 19.15-31 Abraham himself identifies Jacob as the covenant heir and head, indicating that he and his descendants would receive every blessing God had promised Abraham.[7] Jacob's is a corporate election, for he is chosen 'as a people' (19.18). Abraham also pronounces blessing upon Jacob, saying among other things, 'And may the spirit of Mastema [i.e., Satan] not rule over you or over your seed in order to remove you from following the Lord who is your God henceforth and forever and may the Lord God be for you and for the people a father always and may you be a firstborn son' (19.28-29). Here we see the presumption that following the Lord is part of the essence of being the covenant people and a concern that this people would persevere in this sacred obligation against supernatural opposition. More directly related to Gen. 25.19-34, we can see that the right of the firstborn is a matter of status that encompasses all the blessings of the covenant. Perhaps the most striking aspect of this whole passage is its extremely positive view of Jacob along with its negative view of Esau.

Jubilees 24.3-7 records the episode of Esau's sale of his birthright to Jacob in a straightforward way, including the comment that Esau despised his birthright (24.6). The only aspect of the passage worth noting for our purposes is the summary statement of the results of the episode found in v. 7: 'And Jacob became the older one but Esau was lowered from his seniority'. Here again we can see that the author of *Jubilees* viewed the birthright as an issue of status, which presumably entailed various privileges, rather than simply as representative of certain limited rights (cf. 19.29 treated above; 37.2-3).

The relationship between Jacob and Esau is the dominant theme of *Jubilees* 35–38. One of the most prominent features of the text's presentation

---

5.   Unless otherwise noted, quotations of *Jubilees* in this investigation are from O. S. Wintermute, 'Jubilees: A New Translation and Introduction', *OTP*, 2.35–142.

6.   See Abasciano, *Romans 9.1-9*, 170–72, on *Jub.* 16.16b-18.

7.   See Endres, *Jubilees*, 26–27, for Gen. 13.16 and its blessing of Abraham as the basis of *Jub.* 19.21b-23, and additional related biblical background.

is the goodness/righteousness of Jacob over against the wickedness of Esau. The contrast is pervasive in these chapters. Jacob himself claims, 'And you, mother, know from the day I was born until this day all of my deeds and everything which is in my heart, that I always think of good for everyone' (35.3). As for Rebekah, 'she said, "My son, all my days I have never seen against you anything perverse but only uprightness"' (35.6). To Isaac, she asserted that Esau's inclination had 'been evil since his youth' and that there was 'no goodness in him' (35.9). Indeed, 'he is bitter against you because you blessed Jacob, your perfect and upright son, because he has no evil but only goodness' (35.12). Thus Rebekah attributes Jacob's reception of the blessing, which fulfils the Gen. 25.23 birth oracle in principle, to Jacob's uprightness. As for Isaac's part, he agreed with her assessment of the two brothers:

> I know and see the deeds of Jacob, who is with us, that with all his heart he is honoring us. And I first loved Esau more than Jacob because he was born first, but now I love Jacob more than Esau because he has increasingly made his deeds evil. And he has no righteousness because all of his ways are injustice and violence ... And neither he nor his seed is to be saved for they will be destroyed from the earth, and they will be uprooted from under heaven since he has forsaken the God of Abraham ... (35.13-14)

Rebekah then elicits promises from both Jacob and Esau that they would love one another and do no harm to each other. Later Isaac commands them to do the same, binding them under oath and prescribing eternal damnation for the one who would harm his brother (36.4-11). This spells out the doom of Esau, for his sons prevail upon him to lead them in attacking Jacob after the death of Isaac (chs 37–38; cf. *T. Jud.* 9). But Jacob kills Esau and his forces utterly defeat those of Esau, resulting in the perpetual servitude of Esau's descendants to Israel.

The texts we have surveyed from *Jubilees* so far make it clear that Jacob was chosen as the covenant heir because of his goodness and that Esau was rejected because of his wickedness, at least from the human side, which very likely is to be thought of as the divine perspective because of the godly individuals who articulate this viewpoint. Be that as it may, one final passage for our consideration does unquestionably give the corroborating divine perspective. *Jubilees* 15.30 tells us, 'For the Lord did not draw Ishmael and his sons and his brothers and Esau near to himself, and he did not elect them because they are the sons of Abraham, for he knew them. But he chose Israel that they might be a people for himself'. It is apparently the Lord's knowledge of Esau's character as wicked that served as the basis of his covenantal rejection of him.

Intriguingly, 15.30-32 connects the themes of the nations and predestination with the election of Israel and the rejection of Ishmael and Esau, all themes that are highly relevant to Romans 9. We have already discussed *Jub.* 15.30-32 in a precursor volume and will not repeat that entire discussion, to which I would direct the reader,[8] but need only restate some of our conclusions and

8.   See Abasciano, *Romans 9.1-9*, 173.

make a couple of new observations. We found that in *Jubilees* (a) Ishmael and Esau are regarded as part of the nations/Gentiles, and (b) God causes spirits to lead the nations astray from him while protecting and blessing Israel, though this determinism is neither absolute (at least in the case of Israel) nor unconditional. Nevertheless, *Jubilees* holds out little hope for the salvation of Gentiles. As for the election of Israel, it is clearly a corporate matter. It is obviously assumed that the corporate election of Israel is in the individual Jacob, but its corporate nature comes out all the more clearly when the text contrasts the rejection of Ishmael and Esau with the election of the people Israel and omits mention of Jacob.

4.2. *Pseudo-Philo/Liber Antiquitatum Biblicarum*

Pseudo-Philo paraphrases Mal. 1.2-3 in *LAB* 32.5: 'And God loved Jacob, but he hated Esau because of his deeds'.[9] Interestingly, this paraphrase appears in a concise narration of events related to the birth of Jacob and Esau (32.5-6), establishing a link for the author between Mal. 1.2-3 and the context of Gen. 25.23. The author seems to apply these prophetic words especially to the individuals Jacob and Esau. However, a corporate application is probably not far from view since this is presented as the history of Israel. Indeed, earlier in the chapter the election of Israel as a nation is equated with the election of Abraham, who is identified as the father of the nation (32.1). In any case, Ps.-Philo does not state what the Lord's love and hatred mean, though this is probably assumed to be obvious for the audience from Genesis. The most important element of this allusion is the addition of a reason for the Lord's hatred of Esau – his deeds, which are presumably wicked, agreeing with *Jubilees*' point of view.

4.3. *4 Ezra*

In my previous volume, we saw that *4 Ezra* contains a number of similarities to Romans 9.[10] One of the most pertinent is that both are concerned with theodicy vis-à-vis the faithfulness of God's word to and election of Israel in light of their hopelessly cursed state and destiny. It is in presenting this problem that the main character of *4 Ezra* refers to the election of Jacob over Esau (3.16):

> And when they [earth's inhabitants] were committing iniquity before you, you chose for yourself one of them, whose name was Abraham; you loved him, and to him alone you revealed the end of the times, secretly by night. You made an everlasting covenant with him, and promised him that you would never forsake his descendants;

9.   All quotations of *LAB* are from D. J. Harrington, 'Pseudo-Philo: A New Translation and Introduction', *OTP*, 2.297–377; italics removed from above quotation. For introductory literature on *LAB*, see Abasciano, *Romans 9.1-9*, 74 n. 101.
10.   See Abasciano, *Romans 9.1-9*, 81–83, 158–61.

and you gave him Isaac, and to Isaac you gave Jacob and Esau. You set apart Jacob
for yourself, but Esau you rejected; and Jacob became a great multitude. (3.13-16)[11]

The purpose of the reference to Jacob's election and Esau's rejection, along
with that to the election of Abraham and the promise to him, is to set up the
problem of Israel's lack of experience of the blessings appropriate to her elect
status. This is very similar to Paul's procedure in Rom. 9.1-5. Indeed, just as
Paul counts the glory of God and the giving of the Law to Israel as among the
privileges of election (Rom. 9.4),[12] so Ezra links them to the choice of Jacob
and his descendants over Esau (*4 Ezra* 3.17-19). Part of the problem for Ezra
as he expresses it to God is,

> Yet you did not take away their [Israel's] evil heart from them, so that your law might
> produce fruit in them. For the first Adam, burdened with an evil heart, transgressed
> and was overcome, as were also all who were descended from him. Thus the disease
> became permanent; the law was in the hearts of the people along with the evil root;
> but what was good departed, and the evil remained. (3.20-22)

Thus Ezra bemoans the inability of Israel to meet God's demands with a view
toward questioning God's righteousness in his treatment of Israel.[13] This is
striking in light of the motif of the hardening of Israel in Romans 9–11.

However, it is critical to understand that the character Ezra undergoes
a conversion of thought over the course of the book through his dialogue
with the angel Uriel, whose views represent the ultimate viewpoint of *4 Ezra*
and its author.[14] The immediate divine answer Ezra receives concerning
Israel's situation is that God's ways are inscrutable (4.1-25; cf. Rom. 9.19-
21).[15] Nonetheless, the deeper answer he eventually receives is that God's
ways are justified because humans have freely chosen their way (7:10-16,
21-22, 72-74, 127-31; 8:56-60; 9:7-12).[16] The divine perspective offers
a corrective to the pre-conversion Ezra's theology of the evil heart as the

11.   All quotations from *4 Ezra* in this investigation are from the NRSV unless otherwise
noted. Interestingly, M. E. Stone, *Fourth Ezra: A Commentary on the Book of Fourth Ezra*
(Hermeneia; Minneapolis: Fortress, 1990), 71, notes that the latter part of 3.15 adapts Josh.
24.3-4, which we saw earlier is one of only two places outside of Genesis in which Jacob and
Esau are mentioned together as individuals.

12.   See Abasciano, *Romans 9.1-9*, 124–27, 131–32.

13.   We should note that Ezra does not limit the evil inclination to Israel, but his main
concern at this point is Israel's perplexing condition in light of her elect status. Indeed,
he finds Israel to be more righteous than the Gentiles and finds it all the more troubling
that Israel's judgment includes subjection to the Gentiles (3.28-36). It is also interesting to
observe Ezra's apparent belief that Adam was sinful from the beginning, virtually destined
to sin, though as Stone, *Ezra*, 63, observes, the book 'carefully avoids directly attributing the
creation of this evil inclination to God'. He suggests this is due to the author's conception of
free will (64).

14.   See B. W. Longenecker, *Eschatology and the Covenant: A Comparison of 4 Ezra
and Romans 1–11* (JSNTSup, 57; Sheffield: JSOT, 1991), 148–50. Cf. Stone, *Ezra*, 24–33.

15.   To borrow the title of the section assigned to it by B. M. Metzger, 'The Fourth
Book of Ezra: A New Translation and Introduction', *OTP*, 1.517–59 (529).

16.   See Abasciano, *Romans 9.1-9*, 158–60.

determining factor in human behaviour. At the same time, both of these perspectives are important as potential background for Romans 9–11, for the author of *4 Ezra* probably sought to correct views actually present in his environment.[17]

The other reference to Jacob and Esau in *4 Ezra* occurs in 6.7-10. Ezra asks the Lord,

> 'What will be the dividing of the times? Or when will be the end of the first age and the beginning of the age that follows'? He said to me, 'From Abraham to Abraham, because from him were born Jacob and Esau, for Jacob's hand held Esau's heel from the beginning. For Esau is the end of this age, and Jacob is the beginning of the age that follows. For the end of a man is his heel, and the beginning of a man is his hand; between the heel and the hand seek for nothing else, Ezra'!'[18]

Here Esau is associated with the present (evil) age while Jacob is associated with the (righteous) age to come, yet another instance of a thoroughly negative evaluation of the former and a generally positive evaluation of the latter. This is reminiscent of Philo's treatment of Ishmael as representative of that which is inferior and must give way to that which is perfect and complete (*Sobr.* 8ff.; *Cher.* 3–10; cf. *Poster. C.* 130–31).[19] Since the present age in *4 Ezra* is also associated with the rule of Rome (ch. 12),[20] it would appear that Esau is (again) associated with ungodly Gentiles, who persecute the people of God. The point of the text seems to be that the true people of God will triumph over the ungodly (i.e., Rome) in the eschaton, which is the next event in the divine plan, answering the challenge to God's faithfulness posed by Israel's present humiliation.[21]

Two observations should be kept in mind concerning the point of this text just stated. First, the true Israel in *4 Ezra* is eventually equated not with ethnic Israel, but with anyone (including Gentiles) and only those who are righteous by works.[22] Second, the text links the prenatal activity of Jacob and Esau with the order of eschatological events, which many scholars find to be a major concern of Romans 9–11.[23]

---

17.   Longenecker, *Eschatology*, 148–50, regards Ezra's pre-conversion understanding of the means of salvation (ethnocentric, gracious covenantalism) as representative of mainstream first-century Judaism, which the book seeks to correct.

18.   Stone's (*Ezra*, 143–44) translation.

19.   See Abasciano, *Romans 9.1-9*, 174–75.

20.   Cf. Metzger, 'Ezra', 521, 550 n. b; Kugel, 'Traditions', 358; Stone, *Ezra*, 160–61.

21.   Cf. D. Aschoff, 'Maior Minori Serviet: Zur Wirkungsgeschichte eines Genesisverses (Gen 25,23)', in M. Becker and W. Fenske (eds), *Das Ende der Tage und die Gegenwart des Heils: Begegnungen mit dem Neuen Testament und seiner Umwelt* (Festschrift H.-W. Kuhn; AGJU, 44; Leiden: Brill, 1999), 281–304 (288), who sees this as the author's attempt to comfort his readers suffering under Roman rule with the hope of the vindication of Israel's election.

22.   Longenecker, *Eschatology*, 152–53, 274ff.

23.   See e.g., J. D. G. Dunn, *Romans* (WBC, 38; 2 vols; Dallas: Word, 1988), 677.

4.4. *Philo*

Perhaps the most characteristic feature of Philo's treatment of Jacob and Esau is his consistent and thoroughgoing depiction of Jacob as (wholly) good and Esau as (wholly) wicked.[24] The two are complete opposites.[25] Not surprisingly, for Philo their character and deeds serve as the basis of Jacob's election and Esau's rejection.[26] This point is actually part of Philo's interpretation of Gen. 25.23.

Philo provides an exposition of Gen. 25.23 in *Quaest. in Gen.* 4.157. He begins by noting the primarily corporate orientation of the oracle and the brothers' roles as national patriarchs. With the second line of the oracle he observes the opposition between the two peoples, attributing it to their respective characters, 'since one of them desires wickedness, and the other virtue'.[27] He then cites the third line of the oracle thus: 'and people will surpass people in excellence', and comments that this shows that

> equals should not be mixed and put together with unequals ... it is necessary for one of the two to surpass the other and to increase, and for the other to decrease and to diminish ... the good man shall surpass the bad, and the righteous the unrighteous, and the temperate man the intemperate. For one of them is heavenly and worthy of the divine light, and the other is earthy and corruptible and like darkness.

As for the critical final line of the oracle, which Paul quotes in Rom. 9.12, Philo interprets it similarly to mean that 'the younger [i.e., virtue/Jacob] is the ruler and sovereign of the elder [i.e., evil/Esau] by the law of nature', though good is younger in time than evil in the human race in that evil is present in human beings from the beginning, but good must be acquired. Thus Philo appears to have interpreted Gen. 25.23 as declaring God's election and rejection based upon the moral characters of Jacob and Esau.

Strikingly, Philo also quotes Gen. 25.23 in connection with the idea of predestination in *Leg. All.* 3.88. The larger context treats predestination and foreknowledge (*Leg. All.* 3.65–106)[28] in an overall exposition of Gen. 3.14, the Lord's curse upon the serpent, that turns to various biblical examples of the phenomenon. Philo is concerned to explain why God 'curses the serpent without allowing him to make any defense' (3.65).[29] His answer is that the

24.   See e.g., *Leg. All.* 2.59; 3.2; *Sacr.* 4; 81; 135; *Det. Pot. Ins.* 45; *Ebr.* 9; *Migr. Abr.* 153; *Congr.* 61–62; 129; *Fug.* 23–27; 42–43; *Praem. Poen.* 59–60; *Quaest. in Gen.* 4.155, 162–74, 203–06, and further below.

25.   See esp. *Sacr.* 135; *Ebr.* 9; *Quaest. in Gen.* 4.155, 157, 162, 206; *Congr.* 129.

26.   See *Sacr.* 16–18; 119–20; 135; *Sobr.* 26; *Rer. Div. Her.* 252; *Congr.* 175–76; *Fug.* 39–40; *Quaest. in Gen.* 4.157, 166; cf. *Virt.* 208–10.

27.   Unless otherwise noted, all translations of Philo in this investigation have been taken from LCL.

28.   On Philo's use of Scripture in *Leg. All.* 3.65–106, see P. Borgen, *Philo of Alexandria: An Exegete for His Time* (NovTSup, 86; Leiden: Brill, 1997), 51–56, which I have also found helpful for guidance through Philo's discussion.

29.   Yonge's translation; all translations by Yonge in this investigation have been taken from C. D. Yonge (trans.), *The Works of Philo: New Updated Edition Complete and*

serpent, which represents pleasure, is intrinsically and wholly evil. Therefore, God is right to foreordain curse upon it (3.68). The case is similar with God's judgment of Er 'without bringing an open charge against him' (3.69). God knew him to be evil and therefore slew him. Er represents the body for Philo, and Er's case serves to call the reader to disregard the body but nurture his soul and virtue, bringing him to perfection and divine approval.

Interestingly, in this context Philo asserts that 'it was requisite for the manifestation of the better things, that there should also be a subordinate creation of the inferior things, through the power of the same goodness which was the cause of all, which is God' (3.73).[30] This idea is similar to what some believe Paul argues in Rom. 9.22-23.[31] However, for Philo it does not refer to God's creation of some people as superior/inferior, but to his creation of animate/inanimate things. In light of the larger context, it would seem that this principle also applies to the creation of both good and evil in the soul of each person (3.75-76, 91, 104).

Philo then turns to predestination in relation to good people (with some contrasting negative examples) in 3.77-106,[32] asserting that God gives 'pre-eminent honour to virtuous natures without any visible cause; not alleging any action of theirs before the praises of them which he utters' (3.77).[33] He offers Noah as an example, who proved to be praiseworthy only after he found grace before God. This point leads Philo to emphasize the grace of God (3.77-78), a concept that is of great importance to Paul. With the example of Melchizedek, Philo begins to verge on a sort of unconditional positive predestination in advancing the idea that God made Melchizedek king and priest because he created him worthy (3.79). God did not predetermine his actions, but he did apparently predetermine his character. Yet ultimately, Melchizedek does not appear to function as a type of the individual person but as a symbol of reason.

Isaac presents a better possibility for an example of pure, positive predestination: 'But there are some persons whom, even before their creation, God creates and disposes excellently; respecting whom he determines beforehand that they shall have a most excellent inheritance' (3.85).[34] But even here, it seems to be an exceptional action and not a standard divine practice. Elsewhere Philo fully affirms human free will and rejects the idea of predetermined reprobation (*Abr.* 127; *Deus Imm.* 45–50).[35] Nevertheless, the example of Isaac leads into

Unabridged in One Volume (Peabody, MA: Hendrickson, 1993).

30. Yonge's translation.
31. See e.g., J. Piper, *The Justification of God: An Exegetical and Theological Study of Romans 9:1–23* (Grand Rapids: Baker, 2nd edn, 1993), 214–16.
32. Borgen, *Philo*, 51.
33. Yonge's translation.
34. Ibid.
35. But J. M. G. Barclay, '"By the grace of God I am what I am": Grace and Agency in Philo and Paul', in J. M. G. Barclay and S. Gathercole (eds), *Divine and Human Agency in Paul and His Cultural Environment* (LNTS, 335; London: T&T Clark, 2006), 140–57 (145–46), has drawn attention to a preserved fragment from Philo's lost *Legum Allegoriae* Book 4 that appears to profess a strong divine determinism. Yet Philo's comments in *Deus*

consideration of Jacob, Esau and Gen. 25.23 in what could be construed as an affirmation of unconditional double predestination:

> Once again, of Jacob and Esau, when still in the womb, God declares that the one is a ruler and leader and master, but that Esau is a subject and a slave. For God the Maker of living beings knoweth well the different pieces of his own handiwork, even before He has thoroughly chiselled and consummated them, and the faculties which they are to display at a later time, in a word their deeds and experiences [Philo then grounds this point with a quotation of Gen 25.23] ... For in God's judgement that which is base and irrational is by nature a slave, but that which is of fine character and endowed with reason and better is princely and free. And this not only when either is full-grown in soul, but even if their development is still uncertain. For it is universally the case that even a slight breath of virtue is an evidence not of liberty merely but of leadership and sovereignty, and on the other hand that the most casual beginning of wickedness enslaves the reasoning faculty, even if its offspring have not yet come forth fully developed. (3.88-89)

But notice that God's predestination in the case of Jacob and Esau is based on his foreknowledge of their actions and experiences. This raises the question for us of whether this foreknowledge is itself based on God's creative predetermination of their characters or rather on a divine ability to foreknow free human acts and events. Unfortunately, Philo does not address this question clearly here, but the latter appears to be his position.

Certainly, Philo grounds God's foreknowledge of human actions in his identity as Creator. But this foreknowledge seems to arise from the Creator knowing his own work well rather than predetermining how his human creatures will be or act. Philo's belief in human free will mentioned above agrees with this assessment, as does his use of predetermined judgment upon Er/evil to encourage godly pursuit mentioned earlier. Moreover, his remarks in 3.89 also point in this direction since there may be doubt about whether a soul will go the way of virtue or vice, though the dominance of either is enough to judge the soul as master or slave even though the characteristic may be slight. Finally, the overall discussion in *Leg. All.* 3.65–106 aims to show that God has created two different natures,[36] good and evil, which apparently exist in each person and must be chosen between.

Thus in the conclusion of his discussion (3.104–06) Philo reasons, 'Seeing then that we have found two natures created, undergoing moulding, and chiselled into full relief by God's hands, the one essentially hurtful, blameworthy, and accursed, the other beneficial and praiseworthy ... let us

Imm. 45–50 are even clearer and stronger in favour of human free will, in which he grounds moral responsibility. Interestingly, Philo considers Deut. 30:15 in both places. If Philo's comments in these passages can be reconciled, those that might appear to affirm absolute divine determinism are more easily reconciled into a view that allows for relative human freedom within God's sovereignty (thus incompatible with absolute determinism) than vice versa.

36.   Borgen, *Philo*, 53. Cf. *Sacr.* 4, where Philo interprets the conception of Jacob and Esau as the conception of good and evil, and their prenatal activity to be the beginning of the conflict between them.

offer a noble and suitable prayer ...'. So the creation of these two opposing natures in the human soul calls for prayer to God essentially to foster the one and bind the other. This leads Philo, based on Deut. 34.12 and 32.34-35, to consider God's sovereignty over the bestowal of good and evil upon people, and God's good and merciful character that prefers to bestow good and to give opportunity for repentance to those who sin (3.105–06). All of this suggests that Philo does not see a person's character and destiny as absolutely fixed by God, but conceives of two differing natures whose characters and destinies have been predestined and that people must (constantly) choose between. This calls for prayer to go the right way in reliance upon God's goodness, grace and mercy, which point to the possibility of repentance when one has chosen the wrong way.

Borgen has pointed out that, in addition to citing Gen. 25.23 amidst a list of biblical examples, both Philo and Paul picture God as a modeller in clay.[37] We might add that in the context of their respective discussions both refer to other passages that come from similar scriptural contexts.[38] Borgen concludes that Philo and Paul drew 'on a common expository tradition of Gen 25:23'.[39] But this conclusion may be overdrawn. While there are striking similarities between Philo's and Paul's use of Gen. 25.23, there are also profound differences that indicate they are not using the same specific interpretive tradition. It would be fair to say that they both draw on a traditional approach to Gen. 25.23 that applied the text to divine sovereignty and predestination. But beyond that, Paul interprets this text very differently from Philo, a point for which substantiation must be left to our treatment of Paul's use of Gen. 25.23 in the next chapter. As for Philo, he interpreted Gen. 25.23 along with much of Judaism as the divine declaration of Jacob's election and Esau's rejection based on their moral characters.

Philo's assessment of the brothers' characters plays into another point that has some parallel to Romans 9. Klaus Haacker has drawn attention to the fact that both Philo and Paul deny physical descent as determinative for the blessing of God.[40] He cites *Virt.* 207–10 and *Praem. Poen.* 58–60, which speak of Jacob and Esau.[41] The former passage appears as proof in a larger discussion arguing that noble ancestry is neither supreme nor the sufficient cause of blessing, but that actual nobility or virtue is (*Virt.* 187–227). According to Philo, Esau's life 'stands recorded as the clearest proof that to those who are unworthy of nobility, nobility is of no value' (*Virt.* 210). Citing *Praem. Poen.* 152, Haacker insightfully observes that this notion opens the door to the inclusion of Gentiles in the blessing of God.[42]

---

37. Borgen, *Philo*, 54–56.
38. Philo quotes Exod. 33.13 (*Leg. All.* 3.101) and Deut. 32.34-35 (*Leg. All.* 3.105), while Paul alludes to Exod. 32.32 (Rom. 9.3), Exod. 33.19 (Rom. 9.15) and the Song of Moses (Deut. 32), which plays an important role in Rom. 9–11.
39. Borgen, *Philo*, 56.
40. K. Haacker, 'Die Geschichtstheologie von Röm 9–11 im Lichte philonischer Schriftauslegung', *NTS* 43 (1997), 209–22 (211–16).
41. Ibid., 212–13.
42. Ibid., 216–17.

The similarity and difference between Pauline and Philonic thought are obvious.[43] Paul and Philo agree that physical descent does not guarantee God's blessing and that Gentiles can obtain it. But they part company over what does confer divine approval. For Philo, it is virtue. For Paul, it is the call of God and faith in Christ.

4.5. Rabbinic Literature[44]

As with earlier written Jewish tradition, rabbinic literature is marked by a tendency to view Jacob as exceedingly good and Esau as extremely evil. Indeed, Jacob's goodness and Esau's wickedness along with their conflict was believed to have begun in the womb.[45] Jacob attempted to get out of the womb to go to synagogues while Esau attempted to go to idol-temples (*Gen. R.* 63.6 on Gen. 25.22). They quarrelled in the womb over spiritual matters such as the existence of the world to come, asserted by Jacob and denied by Esau.[46] In fact, they fought in the womb over who would be born first and possess the birthright, Jacob yielding to Esau because he threatened to kill their mother.[47] Another tradition has it that Esau emerged first from the womb as part of the offensive matter (*Gen. R.* 63.8 on Gen. 25.25). But yet another tradition hastens to point out that it was actually Jacob who was conceived first (*Gen. R.* 63.8 on Gen. 25.25).

Rabbinic interpretation of Gen 25.23 itself continues in the same spirit. The two nations embodied in Jacob and Esau and carried in Rebekah's womb were Israel and Rome (the supreme Gentile nation) respectively, the former marked by the Torah and the latter marked by sin.[48] As in *4 Ezra* 6.7-10, the Gentiles, headed by Rome, may rule now, but Jacob/Israel will eventually triumph.[49] The association of Jacob with Israel and Esau with Gentiles helps to explain *Gen. R.* 63.7's interpretation of Gen 25.23b as indicating that Jacob was actually born circumcised whereas other sources assert that

43.   Cf. ibid., 213–17, on this.

44.   Though containing some idiosyncrasies, Josephus' (*Ant.* 1.257–58; 2.2–3) account of matters related to Gen. 25.23 is relatively straightforward, requiring no comment. Concerning rabbinic literature, it should be kept in mind that these materials as we have them were codified after the first century, though they may well preserve more ancient traditions that provide background to the NT; for our approach to them, see Abasciano, *Romans 9.1-9*, 12–13. It should also be remembered that Jewish traditions are not uniform. Citation of any one tradition makes no claim for overall Jewish tradition unless so indicated. For collections of rabbinic traditions related to Gen. 25.19-34, see *Gen. R.* 63.1–14; L. Ginzberg, *The Legends of the Jews* (7 vols; Philadelphia: Jewish Publication Society, 1909–38), 1.311–21.

45.   *Gen. R.* 63.6; Ginzberg, *Legends*, 1.313.

46.   Ginzberg, ibid.

47.   Ibid., 1.313–14.

48.   Ibid., 1.314; cf. *Gen. R.* 63.7, 9–10. The targums speak of peoples or nations in the first line of Gen. 25.23, but then speak of kingdoms throughout the rest of the oracle.

49.   Ginzberg, *Legends*, 1.314; *Gen. R.* 63.9; cf. the marginal reading of *Targ. Ps.-J.* Gen. 25.23.

Esau was born with the figure of a serpent upon him, symbolizing 'all that is wicked and hated by God', and remained uncircumcised.[50] Strikingly, *Gen R.* 63.7 cites Mal. 1.3 in its treatment of Gen 25.23 just as Paul does in Rom. 9.10-13.

The portion of Gen. 25.23 that Paul quotes receives a fascinating interpretation in some sources. *Gen R.* 63.7 paraphrases the line: 'If he [Jacob] is deserving, he [Esau] shall serve him; if not, he [Esau] shall enslave him'.[51] *Targum Pseudo-Jonathan* Gen. 25.23 is similar, but omits direct reference to Esau ruling while specifying what would make the younger (representing Israel) deserving: 'and the older shall be subjected to the younger if the children of the younger keep the commandments of the Law'.[52] Two points stand out for mention. First, the targum presents a corporate perspective of Jacob, applying the oracle's significance primarily to his children. Second, the prophecy and any election it may invoke are strictly conditional on the works/worthiness of Jacob and Esau and/or their descendants, most sharply stated by the midrash. This interpretation is probably based on the ambiguity of the oracle's wording noted earlier.[53] It may have been proposed to account for Gentile domination over Israel. It certainly held out substantial motivation for Jews to pursue faithfulness to the Law. Its emphasis on the conditional nature of the oracle is complemented by *Targ. Ps.-J.* Gen. 25.21, which maintains that Isaac changed the Lord's intention and decree by his prayers for Rebekah to conceive. Yet we do get a hint of some sort of divine predestination in *Gen. R.* 63.8 and its treatment of Gen. 25.25, where we are told that Esau was destined to be scattered like chaff, though it is then said by another tradition that this destiny is due to their (Edom's) attack on the noble ones (Israel). Then again, in a pair of traditions that evoke the calling/naming theme of Romans 9, God is said to declare that he created Esau for nought; he is a swine that has been named, whereas the firstborn is named Israel.

The degree of goodness attributed to Jacob and of wickedness attributed to Esau is truly remarkable. In fact, *Gen. R.* 63.2 claims that Abraham's life was saved because of Jacob's merit.[54] Jacob was righteous (*Gen. R.* 63.8–9), perfect in good works (the targums on Gen. 25.27), devoted to worship and the study of Torah (*Gen. R.* 63.6, 10, 13; the targums on Gen. 25.27) and

50. Ibid., 315.
51. Translation from the midrash in this investigation come from H. Freedman and M. Simon (eds), *The Midrash Rabbah* (5 vols; London/Jerusalem/New York: Soncino, new edn, 1977); brackets here original.
52. All translations of *Targum Pseudo-Jonathan* Genesis in this investigation are from M. Maher, *Targum Pseudo-Jonathan: Genesis: Translated, with Introduction and Notes* (TAB, 1b; Collegeville, MN: The Liturgical Press, 1992), 90.
53. See n. 19 in ch. 2 above. Ginzberg, *Legends*, 5.273 n. 21, notes that *Midrash ha-Gadol* explicitly calls attention to the ambiguity of Genesis' language.
54. Indeed, while many traditions throughout rabbinic literature in general regard Abraham as the greatest of the patriarchs, many attribute this status to Jacob instead; see Ginzberg, *Legends*, 5.274–76 n. 35. On the other hand, Esau's ignomiy matches Jacob's exalted status in Jewish tradition in its use of Esau/Edom as the type of the enemies of God and his people; see Ginzberg, 5.272 n. 21.

dedicated to turning others to God.[55] But Esau was wicked, murderous, deceitful, immoral, oppressive, blaspheming and disgraceful (*Gen. R.* 63.8, 10, 13–14; *Targ. Ps.-J.* Gen. 25.27-28). He was so bad that God took Abraham's life early to spare him the distress of seeing his grandson's great wickedness (*Gen. R.* 63.12). 'The day Abraham died, Jacob boiled dishes of lentils and went to comfort his father. Esau came from the country, and he was exhausted because he had committed five transgressions that day: he had practiced idolatry; he had gone into a betrothed maiden; he had denied the life of the world to come, and had despised the birthright' (*Targ. Ps.-J.* Gen. 25.29; cf. *Gen. R.* 63.12). The reason why Esau sold the birthright was because he did not believe in the world to come (*Targ. Ps.-J.* Gen. 25.32). Indeed, his selling/despising of the birthright was a renunciation of his share in the world to come and a claiming of this world.[56] As a result of his choice, God declared Esau and his descendants despised, wicked and cut off.[57] *Genesis Rabbah* 63.14 applies Mal. 1.4 at this point, which is directly connected to verses that Paul quotes in relation to Gen. 25.23 in Rom. 9.10-13.

As for Jacob's part, his motives were pure in wresting the birthright from Esau. He knew that the wicked Esau should not be the one to offer the sacrificial service, which was part of the birthright, and he desired to offer this worship to the Lord.[58] Moreover, he wanted to protect Esau and deprive him of the means for wickedness.[59] Indeed, he took the birthright because Esau did not want it, and he fairly disclosed the value of the birthright before making the deal.[60] 'Though no blame can attach to Jacob for all this, yet he secured the birthright from him by cunning, and therefore the descendants of Jacob had to serve the descendants of Esau'.[61] This final comment brings us back to Paul's quotation of Gen 25.23d. It again likely reveals a conditional view of that divine decree and an attempt to come to terms with Gentile domination over the people of God.[62]

---

55.   See Ginzberg, *Legends*, 1.314, for this last quality.

56.   Ibid., 5.277 n. 43; cf. *Gen. R.* 63.14; *Targ. Ps.-J.* Gen. 25.32-34; *Targ. Neof.* Gen. 25.34.

57.   Ginzberg, *Legends*, 1.321; *Gen. R.* 63.14. M. A. Seifrid, 'Romans', in G. K. Beale and D. A. Carson (eds), *Commentary on the New Testament Use of the Old Testament* (Grand Rapids: Baker Academic, 2007), 607–94 (640), adds *b. Yoma* 38b and *b. Meg.* 6a as affirming Jacob's righteousness and Esau's wickedness as the cause of their election or rejection, and further cites Str-B, 3.267–78.

58.   *Gen. R.* 63.13; Ginzberg, *Legends*, 1.320.

59.   Ginzberg, *Legends*, 5.277 n. 44; cf. Philo, *Quaest. in Gen.* 4.172.

60.   Ginzberg, *Legends*, 1.320.

61.   Ibid., 1.321.

62.   It could reflect a reading of the oracle with 'the younger' as subject, but that seems less likely in view of Israel's self-conscious identity as the people of God and other rabbinic tradition mentioned earlier and in line with our view above. This statement is tied to one of the few aspects of rabbinic tradition that is actually positive towards Esau, on which see ibid., 5.278 n. 51.

4.6. *Hebrews*

We now turn to consider the non-Pauline writings of the New Testament, where the only substantial allusion to Gen. 25.19-34 occurs in Heb. 12.16-17, which alludes to Esau's sale of his birthright as part of an exhortation to pursue peace and sanctification (12.14-17):

> Pursue peace with all, and the sanctification without which no one will see the Lord, seeing to it that no one is falling short of the grace of God; that no root of bitterness, growing up, causes trouble, and through it many be defiled; that no one be a fornicator or godless person like Esau, who, in exchange for a single meal, gave up his own birthright. For you know that even afterwards, when he was desiring to inherit the blessing, he was rejected, for he did not find a place for repentance even though he sought it with tears.

This passage fits squarely into the author's overarching purpose in the epistle of warning his audience against the doomed course of apostasy. The peace and sanctification of the church community were to be sought through guarding against this terrible possibility, which excludes those who forsake Christ from the grace of God, defiles the community and is equivalent to trading salvation for the cheap and fleeting pleasures of sin. The example of Esau serves to illustrate the danger of forsaking or compromising the Christian hope and the serious, spiritually fatal consequences this incurs. He is a type of those who commit apostasy while the birthright of Genesis 25 and the blessing of Genesis 27, essentially equated by the author, are a type of the Christian inheritance.

There are several points worth noting about Hebrews' use of Esau vis-à-vis Rom. 9.10-13. First, the birthright is viewed as having to do with salvation, supporting (though by no means conclusively) the contention that Paul's argument in Romans 9 also concerns salvation and not merely historical roles. Second, in harmony with Jewish tradition generally, Hebrews views Esau as godless. His loss of the birthright/blessing was due to his own wickedness, reflecting the viewpoint of Genesis itself (25.34). Third and relatedly, Hebrews' use of Esau and the selling of his birthright as a type of apostasy to dissuade his Christian readers from following suit suggests a non-deterministic reading of Gen. 25.19-34. The author of Hebrews does not seem to hold any sort of doctrine of double predestination. Quite to the contrary, he saw Esau as truly possessing the birthright and then renouncing it, a type of Christians who truly possess salvation in Christ but then renounce it to irremediable condemnation. Nevertheless, fourth, the use of Esau as a type means that the author did not necessarily believe Esau himself to be eternally condemned or evil over his whole lifetime. He isolates a specific instance in Esau's life that provides a good example of shortsightedly giving up the blessing of God for inferior assets.

4.7. Summary/Conclusion

Interpretive traditions surrounding Gen. 25.21-23 and Mal. 1.2-3 in literature prior to and roughly contemporaneous with Paul largely looked upon Jacob as exceedingly good and Esau as exceedingly evil. Indeed, their respective characters and deeds are often considered to be the reason for God's election of Jacob and rejection of Esau. The election associated with these passages was conceived of as corporate while Esau was frequently grouped with the Gentiles and even considered representative of them. Moreover, many of the themes found in Romans 9–11 also appear in connection with the interpretive traditions we have surveyed. Ancient interpreters addressed the themes of predestination, theodicy, the faithfulness of God to his word to and election of Israel, Israel's inability to obey God's Law, divine sovereignty, foreknowledge, human free will, the order of eschatological events, conditionality in Israel's enjoyment of the benefits of election, the possibility of man changing God's intention, apostasy and the eternal inheritance.

Chapter 5

NOT BY WORKS, BUT BY THE ONE WHO CALLS: ROMANS 9.10-13

Having analyzed the two Old Testament quotations Paul offers in Rom. 9.10-13 in their original contexts and having surveyed ancient interpretive traditions surrounding these passages, we will now compare the forms of Paul's quotations with their Old Testament wording and then seek to draw on what is relevant from our research to elucidate what Paul has written in Rom. 9.10-13.

5.1. *Textual Comparison of Romans 9.12 and Genesis 25.23*

A textual comparison of Rom. 9.12 and Gen. 25.23 reveals that Rom. 9.12 reproduces Gen. 25.23 LXX exactly, itself a close translation of the Hebrew.

Rom. 9.12   ὁ μείζων δουλεύσει τῷ ἐλάσσονι
Gen. 25.23 LXX   ὁ μείζων δουλεύσει τῷ ἐλάσσονι
Gen. 25.23 MT   רַב יַעֲבֹד צָעִיר

Indeed, the LXX of Genesis generally follows a Hebrew text very similar to the MT,[1] with Gen. 25.19-34 being no exception. Besides what we have already noted in our exegesis of this passage, there are only two points in the LXX's translation that merit attention for our purposes.[2] First, it renders תם of 25.27 with ἄπλαστος, which probably means something like 'genuine' in this context,[3] an ironic choice in light of Jacob's actual character. If we were correct to join HALOT in taking תם to mean something like 'cultured' in 25.27, then the LXX is even more positive towards Jacob here, providing more support for those who think that Genesis presents Jacob's uprightness as part of the ground of his election. Second, it translates בזה ('to despise') with φαυλίζω ('to treat/regard as cheap'). There is not much difference between the two, but the latter is slightly interpretive, clarifying how Esau

---

1.   See J. W. Wevers, *Notes on the Greek Text of Genesis* (SBLSCS, 35; Atlanta: Scholars Press, 1993), xiii; Hamilton, *Genesis*, 1.74.
2.   For detailed treatment of the LXX translation, see Wevers, *Genesis*, 389–97.
3.   Cf. ibid., 394; LSJ, s.v.

despised his birthright and bringing out what is fully implied by בזה – Esau counted his birthright as worthless.

5.2. *Textual Comparison of Romans 9.13 and Malachi 1.2-3*

We now turn to a textual comparison of Rom. 9.13 and Mal. 1.2-3, which reveals Paul's formal quotation to be slightly loose.[4]

Rom. 9.13	τὸν Ἰακὼβ ἠγάπησα, τὸν δὲ Ἠσαῦ ἐμίσησα
Mal. 1.2-3 LXX	καὶ ἠγάπησα τὸν Ἰακὼβ τὸν δὲ Ἠσαῦ ἐμίσησα
Mal. 1.2-3 MT	וָאֹהַב אֶת־יַעֲקֹב וְאֶת־עֵשָׂו שָׂנֵאתִי

The LXX translates the Hebrew very closely.[5] But Paul has omitted the Septuagint's καί and moved τὸν Ἰακώβ to the beginning of the clause. There is very little difference in meaning between Paul and the LXX. The omission of καί is inconsequential and to be expected in a quotation of this sort in order to fit the quotation more smoothly into the syntax of the epistolary context.[6] The shift of τὸν Ἰακώβ, however, does give greater stress to 'Jacob' in the clause and makes both clauses of the quotation parallel. This has the effect of emphasizing the parallel character of the divine treatment of Jacob and Esau, and thus complements Paul's point of a sovereign election. But contrary to Stanley's claims,[7] the change neither heightens the contrast between Jacob and Esau nor alters the depiction of God's hatred of Esau. For Malachi's statement is structured chiastically in both the MT and the LXX, presenting the contrast just as fully, and the context in Malachi does not actually stress God's hatred of Esau over his love of Jacob.[8] The change in word order also creates a chiasm with Rom. 9.12's citation of Gen. 25.23 (elder/younger/ Jacob/Esau), reinforcing the connection between the two citations.[9] Despite the slightness of the difference between Paul and the LXX, it seems most likely that he purposely altered the latter to communicate his point most effectively

4. This of course assumes that Paul is quoting the LXX. It is certainly possible that he translated the Hebrew himself or quoted from a Greek text no longer extant, but given his frequent use of the LXX, it is simplest to assume his use of it when his quotation basically conforms to it and there is no competition from Hebrew mss. For the terminology and classification of quotations used in this investigation, see Abasciano, *Romans 9.1-9*, 16.

5. The LXX of Malachi generally follows closely a Hebrew *Vorlage* reflected by the MT (Verhoef, *Malachi*, 169). The LXX of Mal. 1.2-5 does not differ from the Hebrew in any way that requires comment for our purposes.

6. Cf. C. D. Stanley, *Paul and the Language of Scripture: Citation Technique in the Pauline Epistles and Contemporary Literature* (SNTSMS, 69; Cambridge: CUP, 1992), 105. He observes that Paul frequently omits introductory particles.

7. Ibid., 106.

8. See the exegesis in ch. 3 above. Stanley, ibid., has been misled by the greater amount of space devoted to the description of God's hatred of Esau in Malachi and missed the logic and intent of the passage.

9. J. G. Lodge, *Romans 9–11: A Reader-Response Analysis* (ISFCJ, 6; Atlanta: Scholars Press, 1996), 63; cf. Stanley, ibid.

rather than offering mere stylistic difference or accidentally misquoting his intertext, all of which are theoretically possible.

5.3. *Intertextual Exegesis of Romans 9.10-13*

Finally, having examined material relevant to the Old Testament background of Paul's discourse in Rom. 9.10-13, we are now ready to begin our direct exegesis of the passage.

5.3.a. *The Argument of Romans 9.1-9*

It is important to keep in mind that the exegesis of Rom. 9.10ff. that we are picking up here is a continuation of the exegesis of Rom. 9.1-9 laid out in my previous volume. In brief,[10] that study found that in Romans 9–11 Paul was concerned to unite a predominantly Gentile Roman church containing a substantial minority of Jews behind his gospel for his future mission to Spain along with its Jew-prioritizing methodology. Toward this end Paul defends the gospel he has presented in Romans 1–8 against its most compelling objection – that it would render God unfaithful to his covenant promises to Israel since the vast majority of Jews have not received the fulfilment of those promises even though the promises have been realized in the elect messianic community, the Church of Jews and Gentiles. So after exulting in the Church's possession of all the blessings of God for his chosen people (Romans 8), Paul declares his profound grief over the cursed state of his fellow Jews (9.1-3), who are separated from Christ and therefore cut off from the covenant and its promises, their election nullified and they devoted to destruction under the eschatological wrath of God (9.3). As the clarifying, climactic expression of Paul's immense grief, 9.3 stands as the main point of 9.1-5 with its allusion to Moses' intercession on behalf of idolatrous Israel in Exod. 32.32. Romans 9.4-5 then ground Paul's grief by revealing that the (Jewish) people who have been excluded from the covenant and its blessings are the very people to whom the promises most properly belong as the historic bearers of the divine election. This is all the more tragic following on the heels of Romans 8, since mostly Gentiles are participating in the eschatological fulfilment of the name and blessings of election.

Having raised the problem of God's faithfulness in Rom. 9.1-5, Paul then states his main thesis for all of chs 9–11 in 9.6a: the promises of God to Israel have not failed. Romans 9.6b-9 ground this programmatic statement. More specifically, 9.6b provides what also turns out to be a programmatic statement, which Paul fleshes out over much of the rest of chs 9–11, to the effect that

---

10. Here I can provide only a bare sketch of the basic meaning and logical flow of Rom. 9.1-9 with a view toward setting the context for an exegesis of 9.10-18, leaving out much of Paul's intention. For a full account of the meaning of this passage, see Abasciano, *Romans 9.1-9*.

not all ethnic Israelites are part of the true Israel, to whom the covenant promises were actually made. The point is stated more clearly though again negatively in 9.7a, and stated positively through the quotation of Gen. 21.12 in 9.7b. As the positive statement of Paul's point and his chief scriptural proof text, Gen. 21.12/Rom. 9.7b becomes the thrust of Paul's argument to this point. It speaks of the calling of God's covenant people as his naming/identification of them as his own, the true heir to the covenant promises. Romans 9.8 then gives an interpretation of 9.7b, summing up and explaining all of 9.6b-7, becoming Paul's practical main point in support of 9.6a. That point is that God does not (nor did he ever) regard mere physical descendants of Abraham ('children of the flesh') as heir to the covenant promises, but he regards those who believe the promises ('children of the promise') as the true heir to them (i.e., the true Israel).[11] That is, as it pertains to the present time of eschatological fulfilment, all and only those who believe in Christ are regarded as God's covenant people to whom the promises were made. Finally, 9.9 supports Paul's interpretation of Gen. 21.12 in 9.8 by quotation of Gen. 18.10, 14, showing that Isaac and the covenantal descendants of Abraham represented by him would be identified through promise rather than ancestry. Thus, Paul's response to the charge against God's faithfulness so far is that God never guaranteed enjoyment of the promises to ethnic Israel, but only to spiritual Israel, which means, in the context of Romans, all who believe in Christ.

---

11.   τὰ τέκνα τῆς ἐπαγγελίας is a rich designation that speaks of more than believing or inheriting the promise. But this is the practical main thrust of the phrase in the context of Romans. For a full treatment of the phrase, see ibid., 196–98. The concept of faith is conspicuously absent from Piper's (*Justification*, 68–70) interpretation of this phrase as is any meaningful reference to Romans 4, which Paul echoes in the view of many scholars (e.g., Dunn, *Romans*, 541; D. J. Moo, *The Epistle to the Romans* (NICNT; Grand Rapids: Eerdmans, 1996), 577) based on substantial linguistic/thematic links. This is curious since faith is so foundational to the Galatian texts Piper discusses. Moreover, while giving attention to Rom 2.25-29 is valid, Piper errs in treating it as more important than Romans 4 based on structure when the latter is far more relevant in content. It is ironic that Piper draws the following point out of the former – 'The saving spiritual reality depends on a "counting" or "reckoning" which God performs, not man' – when the latter makes it clear that the reckoning God performs is a response to the faith of man. (Besides, even Rom. 2.25-29 presupposes faith in those whose hearts therefore become circumcised by the Spirit, since the Spirit is received by faith; see T. R. Schreiner, 'Did Paul Believe in Justification by Works? Another Look at Romans 2', *BBR* 3 (1993), 131–158 (147–55).) What is striking about each of the texts Piper highlights is that they deal with the inclusion of Gentiles in the true Israel, militating against his approach to Romans 9, which is based to no small degree on construing 9.6-13 to address inner-Jewish election rather than, as I would argue, election of ethnic Israel vs the Church.

5.3.b. *Introducing the Case of Rebekah (Romans 9.10 and Beyond)*

Romans 9.10-13 continues Paul's argument by offering a further example to support the contention of 9.8[12] that only those who believe in Christ are the covenant seed of Abraham, to whom the promises were made: 'And not only [this], but [there was] also Rebekah, having sexual intercourse with one man, Isaac our father. For not yet having been born, nor having done anything good or evil, in order that the purpose of God in election would continue not by works, but by the one who calls, it was said to her, "The older will serve the younger", just as it is written, "Jacob I loved, but Esau I hated"'. As is widely recognized, Paul's syntax is difficult in 9.10-12.[13] Some take Ῥεβέκκα as a pendent nominative or a nominative absolute picked up by 12b's αὐτῇ, and vv. 11-12a intervening as a parenthesis.[14] Many others think Paul does not grammatically complete the sentence begun in 9.10 while completing its thought in 12b along with that of 11-12a, which is understood as a sort of parenthesis.[15] But with such difficult syntax, it would seem best to follow, with many others, the simplest route of taking 9.10 as elliptical, requiring that a finite verb be supplied,[16] not a rare phenomenon.[17] Indeed, the fact that Paul begins v. 10 with the admittedly elliptical expression οὐ μόνον δέ, ἀλλὰ καί encourages this approach.[18] But the question becomes, what is to be supplied? A variety of suggestions have been made. But again, with such uncertainty,

12. Cf. C. E. B. Cranfield, *A Critical and Exegetical Commentary on the Epistle to the Romans* (ICC; 2 vols; Edinburgh: T&T Clark, 1975–79), 476. A. Reichert, *Der Römerbrief als Gratwanderung: Eine Untersuchung zur Abfassungsproblematik* (FRLANT, 194; Göttingen: Vandenhoeck & Ruprecht, 2001), 197, misses this logical flow in the text, viewing the main thrust of 9.10-13 as the *Leitthesis* of all of 9.6b-13 (cf. H.-M. Lübking, *Paulus und Israel im Römerbrief: Eine Untersuchung zu Römer 9–11* (Frankfurt: Lang, 1986), 65, who views 9.10-13 as a continuing clarification of 9.6-9). E. Brandenburger, 'Paulinische Schriftauslegung in der Kontroverse um das Verheissungswort Gottes (Röm 9)', *ZTK* 82 (1985), 1–47 (22), is wiser to find in 9:8 'Der paulinische Deutungsschlüssel'. Like most scholars, W. Schmithals, *Der Römerbrief: Ein Kommentar* (Gütersloh: Gütersloher, 1988), 344, recognizes that 9.10-13 continues the argument of 9.6-9, but then he curiously misses the specific connection between the two sections, taking the predestinarian theme of 9.10-13 as independent of the promise theme of 9.6-9 (345).

13. Thankfully, even though Paul's syntax is unclear, resulting in disagreement over the precise meaning of what he says, his overall meaning is relatively clear (cf. C. Hodge, *Commentary on the Epistle to the Romans* (Grand Rapids: Eerdmans, rev. edn, 1886), 308), as evidenced by widespread agreement concerning much of its import.

14. See e.g., J. A. Fitzmyer, *Romans: A New Translation with Introduction and Commentary* (AB, 33; New York: Doubleday, 1993), 561–62. J. Murray, *The Epistle to the Romans* (NICNT; 2 vols in 1; Grand Rapids: Eerdmans, 1959–65), 2.14, understands a nominative absolute without 9.11 as a parenthesis, but as syntactically connected to 9.12.

15. See e.g., Cranfield, *Romans*, 477.

16. See e.g., Piper, *Justification*, 51 n. 10; R. Jewett, *Romans: A Commentary* (Hermeneia; Minneapolis: Fortress, 2007), 577. Moo, *Romans*, 579 n. 44, identifies this as the most common translational approach.

17. On which, see BDF, §§ 479–81.

18. The unique character of this instance notwithstanding; on this and the formula generally, see ibid., § 479.1.

simplicity seems the wisest road. And the simplest and most common verb implied by ellipses is a form of εἰμί. Therefore, I suggest that 9.10 is best taken with ἦν supplied, yielding the translation given above. οὐ μόνον δέ refers elliptically to the case of Sarah and Isaac alluded to in 9.7-9,[19] while Ῥεβέκκα functions as a predicate nominative.[20]

οὐ μόνον δέ, ἀλλὰ καί (9.10) does not in itself indicate that Paul's argument is progressing to a stronger example of his point,[21] but merely that he is adding something – in this case, an example – to his argument. The construction focuses attention on the case now to be presented by de-emphasizing the previous example, and thus provides a transition that suggests the weight of a mounting argument. Moreover, by connecting the example of Rebekah so tightly to that of Sarah, Paul indicates that this new example supports the same point that the previous one does, that is, 9.8, which in turn ultimately supports the faithfulness of God (9.6a).

Understood intertextually,[22] the content of 9.10-13 does reveal that Paul now produces an even stronger proof for his point that covenant heirship has always depended on God's call and promise rather than ancestry (see below). The attributive participial phrase ἐξ ἑνὸς κοίτην ἔχουσα tells us that Rebekah had sexual intercourse with one man,[23] leaving the reader to surmise based on the Old Testament background that she was therefore pregnant by one man. Some interpreters argue that κοίτη refers to semen here, and that Paul therefore indicates that Rebekah received one emission

19.   For other options regarding the referent(s) of οὐ μόνον δέ, see John Calvin, *Commentaries on the Epistle of Paul the Apostle to the Romans* (ed./trans. J. Owen; Grand Rapids: Eerdmans, c1947), 348 n. 1 (editor's note).

20.   This appears to be the approach of the NASB. If this be thought impossible because there is no apposite noun, then as many have done, a verb can be supplied for which Ῥεβέκκα functions as subject. Murray's (*Romans*, 2.14 n. 18) suggestion of a nominative absolute that introduces what follows is not much different from my suggestion, and is quite simple and reasonable. These types of approaches avoid the difficulty of taking 9.11-12a as a parenthesis when these vv. are anything but parenthetical logically (see below). Nevertheless, while this weighs against 11-12a as a parenthesis, it is not a definitive point since there can be a difference between grammatical and logical function. Indeed, E. Käsemann, *Commentary on Romans* (trans. G. W. Bromiley; Grand Rapids: Eerdmans, 1980), 263–64, and U. Wilckens, *Der Brief an die Römer*, II: Röm 6–11 (EKKNT, 2; Zürich: Benziger/Neukirchen: Neukirchener Verlag, 1980), 194, affirm a parenthesis and find Paul's main point in it.

21.   Contra what Moo, *Romans*, 579, and Dunn, *Romans*, 542, imply.

22.   It should be noted that it is only through knowledge of the OT background that one can understand how the case of Rebekah provides an even more solid proof for Paul's case, testifying to his assumption of a biblically knowledgeable audience.

23.   The preposition ἐκ is used to identify from whom one receives sexual intercourse. English idiom prefers 'with'. The argument that ἐκ supports the meaning of 'semen' for κοίτη (so e.g., Cranfield, *Romans*, 477) is weak, since it could just as well indicate by whom conception took place or as I have taken it. The position of some that Paul explicitly – though it is obviously implicit – refers to one act of intercourse by ἐξ ἑνός (so J. Cottrell, *Romans*, II (CPNIVC; Joplin: College Press, 1998), 78, and apparently Dunn, *Romans*, 542) is untenable since Ἰσαάκ is in apposition to ἑνός.

of semen from one man.[24] But this is all but impossible. κοίτη never denotes semen by itself, but only in combination with the genitive σπέρματος.[25] It is almost universally agreed that Paul's language refers explicitly to conception, and the lexicons are largely agreed that κοίτην ἔχειν is an idiom for conception/being pregnant. However, Rom. 9.10 appears to be the only instance of this phrase,[26] and that is exceedingly slim evidence upon which to establish an idiom. The judgment that this phrase means 'to conceive' seems to be driven by concern to clarify Paul's language and the fact that Paul clearly refers to the conception of Jacob and Esau. But as we have already seen, and will continue to see, Paul speaks elliptically in these verses. So we should resist the temptation to make Paul's language clearer and more explicit than it is, and adopt a standard meaning for κοίτη that fits this context – 'sexual intercourse'.[27]

Virtually all commentators observe in some way that the case of Rebekah Paul now introduces is immune to any objections that could be raised against his previous example of Sarah, Isaac and Ishmael. The latter two were of course Abraham's sons, but they had different mothers, and Ishmael was the son of Sarah's slave. So it could be argued that there was a significant ancestral difference between the two sons that accounted for God's choice of Isaac over Ishmael as the covenant seed/heir and head, contradicting Paul's argument against ancestry as the defining characteristic of God's people. But there was no such difference between Rebekah's sons. They had the same mother and father. What is more, they were twins, conceived at the same time with no substantive difference between them that could demand the divine favour for one over the other.

Yet much of this lies in the unspoken details of Paul's intertextual allusion. He does not state that this next example eliminates any difficulties with the last one. Nor does he explicitly state that Rebekah conceived twins. He appears to assume this knowledge on the part of his audience, expecting his allusion to point them back to the Old Testament context, through which they could most fully understand his argument.

Paul identifies the father of Rebekah's children as Ἰσαὰκ τοῦ πατρὸς ἡμῶν ('Isaac our father') by placing the designation in apposition to ἑνός. The fact that he calls Isaac *our* father is significant in this context, which fits into a larger purpose of uniting Jews and Gentiles in the Roman church. Although most interpreters think that Paul is here identifying himself with the Jewish people ethnically (cf. 9.3), and means something like, 'Isaac is the father of us

24. See e.g., Cranfield, ibid.
25. It is widely held that κοίτη can denote semen by itself based on the singular instance of LXX Num. 5.20. But upon closer inspection, it is far more likely that it refers to sexual intercourse there, since that is an established meaning of the word, the LXX follows the Hebrew closely there, and the Hebrew word the LXX translates (שְׁכָבְתּ) means just this in Num. 5.20 (see *HALOT*, 1488).
26. Rom. 9.10 is the only instance cited by the lexicons.
27. Cf. A. T. Hanson, *Studies in Paul's Technique and Theology* (London: SPCK, 1974), 87–88.

Jews',[28] it is more likely that he identifies Isaac as the father of all who believe in Christ, whether Jew or Gentile.[29] For in ch. 4 Paul argued that Abraham is only the father of Jews and Gentiles who believe in Christ, and here in Romans 9, he has referred to Isaac as head of the Abrahamic covenant through whom Abraham's covenant seed are identified (9.7). Moreover, Paul is in the midst of defending God's rejection of ethnic Israel and naming of those who believe in Christ (the children of the promise) as his covenant people, the same basic issue argued in ch. 4 and reflected elsewhere in Romans (e.g., 2.28–3.31). Furthermore, Paul is addressing a predominantly Gentile church and speaks similarly to another Gentile church in 1 Cor. 10.1, identifying ancient Israel as their (and his) fathers.[30] Finally, this best fits in with the purpose of Romans 9–11 mentioned above. The reference to Isaac as the father of all Christians confirms our interpretation of Romans 9 thus far.

5.3.c. *The Grammar and Structure of Romans 9.11-12*

Romans 9.11-13 now explain the significance of the case of Rebekah and her pregnancy for Paul's argument. Many take the γάρ of 9.11 to relate to an unspoken thought as is often (though not most often) the case with this conjunction, some taking it as causal/substantiating[31] and others as explanatory,[32] depending on what thought is supplied. But if our reading of Paul's syntax is correct (see 5.3.b above), then it is unnecessary to supply an unstated thought, and an explanatory γάρ becomes most likely in order to segue into Paul's explanation of his Old Testament allusion/proof. The fact that vv. 11-12 do undeniably explain the import of Rebekah's situation for Paul supports this approach as does the resulting fact that the semantic thrust of 9.10-13 lies in these verses. Thus, with γάρ, Paul moves to the heart of his point concerning Rebekah and her sons.

---

28.   See e.g., Moo, *Romans*, 579 n. 45. Jewett's (*Romans*, 578) support for this position does not hold, for even though the context concerns 'Jewish unbelief in the messianic fulfilment', this theme is set against Gentile faith in Christ and inclusion in the people of God, and the main theme is actually God's faithfulness to his promises to Israel, which have been fulfilled in Christ and in which Gentiles participate.

29.   Cf. F. Godet, *Commentary on St. Paul's Epistle to the Romans* (trans. A. Cusin and T. W. Chambers; New York: Funk & Wagnalls, 1883), 348; Seifrid, 'Romans', 640. Lodge, *Romans 9–11*, 61, describes both options. Wilckens, *Römer*, 194 n. 859, seems to take this of all ethnic Jews and Christians, contra Käsemann, whom he cites as taking it of Jewish Christians.

30.   See Abasciano, *Romans 9.1-9*, 113.

31.   So W. Sanday and A. C. Headlam, *A Critical and Exegetical Commentary on the Epistle to the Romans* (ICC; New York: Charles Scribner's Sons, 5th edn, 1902), 244; Moo, *Romans*, 580 n. 48; Hodge, *Romans*, 308.

32.   So Cranfield, *Romans*, 477.

He begins with a genitive absolute describing the circumstances in which the divine word was spoken to Rebekah about her children.[33] It was before Jacob and Esau were born, and therefore, before they did anything good or evil,[34] that God declared who would be the covenant head and heir.[35] Paul does not explicitly express the subject of the genitive absolute participles (γεννηθέντων/πραξάντων), creating another ellipsis. But anyone familiar with the scriptural background would immediately know that Paul speaks of Rebekah's twin children, Jacob and Esau.[36] As Wilckens observes, 'Paul writes for readers who know the Bible',[37] yet another indication that Paul's allusions point back to their original contexts and that he intended his discourse to be most fully understood against the Old Testament background.

The basic scriptural fact Paul calls attention to is the detail that the oracle came to Rebekah when the twins were not yet born (9.11a). Paul then presumably infers from this that the children had not yet done anything good or evil (11b).[38] Next, he gives an interpretation of these facts in the purpose clause of 9.11c-12b (ἵνα ... καλοῦντος). The structure of 9.11-12 is arresting in that Paul piles up clauses that look forward to the main verb (ἐρρέθη) of the sentence. It is not surprising to find a genitive absolute at the beginning of a sentence, but it is unusual for a final clause to appear before the main verb. When it does, the purpose clause receives emphasis. Combined with the genitive absolutes in 9.11, there is a piling up of clauses here that draws extra attention to the almost stuttering beginning of the sentence, laying heavy stress on the purpose clause as the interpretation of the circumstances

33.   This genitive absolute is one of attendant circumstances, the construction's standard usage. It most likely carries a temporal significance (*when* not born etc.) as is also typical of the construction. Piper's (*Justification*, 51) assertion that the genitive absolute clauses are adversative is possible, but unlikely. Besides consideration of standard usage, Paul's logic does not emphasize discrepancy between the twins' state and the timing of the divine oracle, but these facts themselves and their proper interpretation. In any case, the meaning is much the same.

34.   Although the variant κακόν has good external support, φαῦλον has fair support and internal considerations demand that the former be rejected as the substitution of a more typical word for an irregular one (so e.g., Cranfield, *Romans*, 477). Dunn, *Romans*, 542, suggests Paul chose φαῦλος over his more usual κακός to strike 'a deeper note of "good-for-nothingness"'.

35.   Cf. Moo, *Romans*, 580, though his description of Paul's syntax does not seem to cohere with his own translation or with his citation of Cranfield and Dunn.

36.   Scholars typically suggest that υἱῶν is the implied subject of the two participles.

37.   Approvingly cited by Dunn, *Romans*, 542.

38.   Moo, *Romans*, 580, describes the flow of thought (though not the syntax) accurately. Piper, *Justification*, 51, on the other hand, mistakenly argues that 9.11b does not stress the timing of God's determination relative to the twins' behavior, but that it was not based on their behaviour, on the assumption that the former is already implicit in 11a and would therefore be redundant. But this is specious reasoning since he argues that 12a-b makes the same point, which would be redundant. At this point, Paul is laying out the facts, specifically the timing/circumstances of the divine oracle, which he goes on to interpret in 11c-12b. Nevertheless, Piper's basic instincts are right in that Paul interprets the timing of the oracle to mean that God's determination was not mandated by their behaviour.

in which (described by the genitive absolutes) the divine word of election was spoken (related in 12c-d). Grammatically, the genitive absolutes are unrelated to the rest of the sentence. But logically, they obviously relate to the annunciation of the oracle in 12c-d (ἐρρέθη αὐτῇ ...) while the ἵνα clause depends directly on ἐρρέθη.[39] Thus, the whole focus of Paul's argument in 9.10-13 comes to concentrate on the purpose clause of 9.11c-12b.[40] This is his interpretation of the case of Rebekah, Jacob and Esau. It is the main point in 9.10-13.

That it is, is confirmed by the great importance exegetes have found in the subject of 9.11c-12b, the key phrase ἡ κατ' ἐκλογὴν πρόθεσις τοῦ θεοῦ. Indeed, according to Piper, the meaning of the purpose spoken of in 9.11c is 'the key exegetical question forcing itself on us from the context' and 'of tremendous doctrinal significance'.[41] Sanday and Headlam go so far as to say, 'These words are the key to chaps. ix–xi and suggest the solution of the problem before St. Paul'.[42] It is curious, therefore, that interpreters have not given more detailed attention to the precise meaning and grammatical options for the phrase.

5.3.d. *The Purpose of God in Election (Romans 9.11c-12b)*

The vast majority of translations and commentators rightly translate πρόθεσις as 'purpose' here. The word refers to goal or aim, that which someone intends to accomplish.[43] Here, it is God's purpose that concerns the apostle, as is

39.   Cf. Cranfield, *Romans*, 477–78.
40.   Cf. Wilckens, *Römer*, 194.
41.   Piper, *Justification*, 50.
42.   Sanday/Headlam, *Romans*, 244. Cf. C. K. Barrett, *A Commentary on the Epistle to the Romans* (BNTC; London: A & C Black, 2nd edn, 1991), 170–71; O. Kuss, *Der Römerbrief*, III, (Regensburg: Pustet, 1978), 706–07; U. Luz, *Das Geschichtsverständnis des Paulus* (BevT, 49; Munich: Kaiser, 1968), 71. More broadly, Lübking, *Paulus*, 65, views 9.10-13 as the key to interpreting 9.6-13.
43.   The word can also mean 'plan', which is obviously very similar to 'purpose'. Moo, *Romans*, 580, actually defines purpose here as 'a predetermined plan'. But in English, the word 'plan' suggests a detailed scheme through which one accomplishes a higher purpose, and therefore does not fit the sweeping character of Paul's argument or the divine will as well. But 'plan' as a detailed scheme would work fine if equated with the overarching purpose of God as in Rom. 8.28-30. On Paul's distinctive use of this word, see Sanday/Headlam, ibid., who go so far as to say that it is a technical Pauline term for the 'purpose of God for the salvation of mankind'. G. Maier, *Mensch und freier Wille nach den jüdischen Religionspartien zwischen Ben Sira und Paulus* (WUNT, 12; Tübingen: Mohr Siebeck, 1971), 359–62, argues that ἐκλογή and πρόθεσις were Pharisaic technical terms for free will and predestination respectively, and that in using them, Paul invokes the debate in ancient Judaism over determinism and free will. But this proposal is overdrawn. Maier himself acknowledges (362) the speculative nature of his suggestion that Paul's πρόθεσις τοῦ θεοῦ is meant to render the Hebrew for God's predestining plan (אל המשבת) used at Qumran. Moreover, his proposal concerning ἐκλογή relies on two occurrences of the word in which it refers to free choice in a theological context (*Pss. Sol.* 9.4; Josephus, *War* 2.165), a rather slim basis on which to establish a word as technical terminology (Jewett, *Romans*, 578,

indicated by the possessive genitive τοῦ θεοῦ. But the real difficulty comes in determining the significance of the qualifying prepositional phrase κατ᾽ ἐκλογήν, which relates purpose to election in some way.

5.3.d.1. *The Significance of κατ᾽ ἐκλογήν*

First, we should note that κατ᾽ ἐκλογήν is in the attributive position. Some assume that this requires taking the phrase adjectivally so that God's purpose is described as an electing purpose.[44] But this is not a necessary conclusion. In the attributive position, κατά with a noun in the accusative case can function as an adjective or a genitive.[45] Even if it is taken as adjectival, there is more than one possibility for what an electing purpose might mean. It could mean, as Piper assumes, (1) a purpose to elect.[46] That is, election is the purpose in view. Alternatively, an electing purpose could be (2) a purpose that pertains to election,[47] or it could be a purpose that elects, which could be construed as (1) above, or (3) as a purpose that elects as a means to fulfilling its intention.[48] This last adjectival option happens to coincide with what is probably the most common scholarly assessment of the phrase, which takes it to mean (4) 'the purpose of God which operates by selection'.[49] This view seems to be based on the very common use of κατά as a marker of norm ('according to'),

---

accepts Maier's claim too easily). There are further problems with the details of his case (see e.g., B. Mayer, *Unter Gottes Heilsratschluss: Prädestinationsaussagen bei Paulus* (Würzburg: Echter, 1974), 179–80), but suffice to say here, that even if his purported background is allowed, it is still an open question as to its significance for Paul's argument, with various reasonable possibilities besides Maier's view presenting themselves. The important thing is to determine what Paul actually argues rather than letting such an uncertain background unduly influence our interpretation, bringing us back to the matter at hand – exegesis of the text.

44. Piper, *Justification*, 53.
45. BDAG, 513. Cf. BDF, § 224; M. Zerwick, *Biblical Greek: Illustrated by Examples* (ed./trans. J. Smith; SPIB, 114; Rome: SPIB, 1963), § 130. Both BDAG and Zerwick cite Rom. 9.11 as an example of the genitive sense of the construction. For the various uses of κατά mentioned in the following discussion, see BDAG, 511–13.
46. See Piper, *Justification*, 53. That Piper misses the genitival option severely weakens his treatment of the phrase, which is so critical for his interpretation of Romans 9. That he simply assumes one possible sense of the adjectival option weakens it doubly. Cranfield, *Romans*, 478, interprets similarly. For ease of reference, the various options for the meaning of ἡ κατ᾽ ἐκλογὴν πρόθεσις τοῦ θεοῦ will be numbered when introduced.
47. So Hodge, *Romans*, 309. This seems to be based on the κατά of reference, which could also be used to understand the phrase the same way, but non-adjectivally. This could be the basis of Fitzmyer's (*Romans*, 562) and the NIV's translation that speak of God's purpose 'in election'.
48. See Barrett, *Romans*, 170–71; B. Byrne, *Romans* (Sacra Pagina, 6; Collegeville, MN: Liturgical Press, 1996), 291, 294–95.
49. BDAG, 306; cf. 869. On this interpretation, the phrase is often translated as 'the purpose of God according to election'. Besides Barrett and Byrne (see previous note), representatives of this view include Moo, *Romans*, 581 n. 53; Sanday/Headlam, *Romans*, 244; M. Black, *Romans* (NCB; London: Marshall Morgan and Scott, 1973), 132; Lodge, *Romans 9–11*, 62. It is unclear whether these interpreters understand κατ᾽ ἐκλογήν adjectivally or not; they do not state that it is adjectival.

which can also lead to viewing the phrase in question as meaning (5) 'the purpose based on/determined by election'.[50]

As for the genitival option, it may involve a genitive that is either (6) subjective ('the purpose election accomplishes') or (7) possessive ('election's purpose').[51] But these are roughly equivalent, speaking of God's purpose for election, and so that which he intends to accomplish through it. Significantly, these are also roughly equivalent to options 2–4 above. Each implies the others, making election the means to the fulfilment of God's purpose. Hence, we are left with three main grammatically grounded options for the meaning of the phrase under discussion: (a) election = God's purpose ((1) above); (b) election is the basis and determiner of God's purpose ((5) above); (c) election as the means to fulfilling God's purpose ((2)–(4) and (6)–(7) above).[52]

The most likely of these options is (c) on both grammatical and contextual grounds.[53] As we have seen, ἡ κατ' ἐκλογὴν πρόθεσις τοῦ θεοῦ is grammatically ambiguous. But most of the grammatical options converge to yield the same basic meaning, which suggests this is the most obvious and natural meaning and the one Paul would intend when using such an ambiguous construction. Option (b) is rather awkward (inspiring few supporters), which may be seen in Murray's explanation of it as meaning a purpose 'which springs from election and fulfils its design',[54] making God's purpose fulfil election's purpose. It is much simpler, clearer and straightforward to say that election fulfils God's purpose. As for (a), it is myopic in its restriction of God's purpose to election (contrast Rom. 8.28-30 with its similar wording and portrayal of God's grand purpose of salvation leading eventually to the argument of Romans 9–11) and its failure to grasp the depth and grand, sweeping nature of Paul's argument, not to mention specific connections to the immediate context and the backdrop of the epistle as a whole.[55]

---

50.   So Murray, *Romans*, 2.15, who translates as in the previous note, and also regards κατ' ἐκλογήν as adjectival. View (4) above can also construe κατά to indicate basis, but more weakly, in the sense that the purpose is based on election because it relies on election for its fulfilment.

51.   BDF, § 224; Zerwick, *Greek*, § 130.

52.   Cf. incisively, Moo, *Romans*, 581 n. 53.

53.   It can be artificial to specify one particular grammatical meaning for every construction since grammatical features can bear more than one function. This is especially so when several options carry the same basic meaning. Living language does not necessarily fit into neat grammatical categories. Nevertheless, if pushed to specify here, I would say that I follow BDAG and Zerwick (see n. 45 above) in taking κατ' ἐκλογήν to function as a genitive. More specifically, I read a possessive genitive with a strong implication that election is the means by which God's purpose is accomplished, not only because this is intrinsic to such a genitive in this context, but also because this would be suggested by the common use of κατά to indicate norm, basically combining views 5 and 7. My translation at the beginning of 5.3.b above ('the purpose of God in election') is not based on a κατά of reference, but is my attempt to concisely convey that Paul speaks of the purpose God accomplishes through election.

54.   Murray, *Romans*, 2.15, though Murray is quite right that supratemporality does not rule out the prospect of logical priority.

55.   See below on the more specific meaning of the phrase. The difference between (a)

By placing κατ' ἐκλογήν in the attributive position, Paul accomplishes two things. First, if we are correct to read the phrase as a circumlocution for a possessive genitive, he avoids an awkward and confusing doubling of genitives in connection with τοῦ θεοῦ.[56] Second, he focuses attention on God's purpose rather than election itself, as κατ' ἐκλογήν modifies πρόθεσις.[57] This is crucial to see since it provides the proper orientation to Paul's rhetoric at this point while many interpreters mistakenly focus on election itself. It is easy to see how this would happen, for Paul does make a point about election, but this is part of a larger point about the purpose of election. We must keep this in mind if we want to follow Paul's argument rightly.

5.3.d.2. *Identifying God's Purpose*

To follow Paul's argument, we must now ask, what is the purpose of election that Paul speaks about? It is none other than God's purpose to bless the world in Abraham.[58] This is suggested by three weighty considerations. The first is the broader context of Romans, which is very concerned to argue for the inclusion of Gentiles in the covenant people of God; indeed, to argue that all and only those who believe in Christ, whether Jew or Gentile, are regarded as the covenant seed of Abraham and heirs of the Abrahamic covenant promises. Romans 3–4, which happen to be widely regarded as significantly linked to ch. 9,[59] are especially connected to this theme. Romans 8 again raises the themes of sonship and heirship as it describes the glorious blessings to which sons/ believers in Christ are heirs, who are said to be 'called according to [God's] purpose' in 8.28, which (a) is the only other occurrence of πρόθεσις in the epistle, (b) uses a somewhat similar (κατά) construction as 9.11, and (c) invokes one of the key concepts of 9.11's context, that of call. Not insignificantly, it is this line of thought that leads directly into the argument of Romans 9–11.

and (c) is the difference between Paul answering the objection to God's faithfulness by simply stating that God has determined to elect unconditionally or sovereignly vs going back to the very purpose God has in electing at all.

56. If κατά indicates something other than a genitive sense, then Paul avoids the probable attachment of the κατά phrase to the verb μένω, keeping it as descriptive of God's purpose.

57. This is true despite the general agreement of the grammars that the first attributive position places greater stress on the adjective than on the substantive, for this refers to an emphasis of description rather than topic, with the attributive identifying what is most distinctive about the substantive in the synchronic perspective of the author, leaving the topic of discourse to be the substantive as inseparably qualified by the attributive. Moreover, as we have argued, the κατά phrase in Rom. 9.11 functions as a genitive. Nevertheless, its placement in the attributive position still makes it subordinate. In any event, a possessive genitive would also keep πρόθεσις as superordinate.

58. See Abasciano, *Romans 9.1-9*, 153–54, 211, 221–22; idem, 'Election', 363; Sanday/Headlam, *Romans*, 244, 250; Byrne, *Romans*, 294; F. J. Leenhardt, *The Epistle to the Romans: A Commentary* (London: Lutterworth, 1961), 248–49, 251; J. R. Edwards, *Romans* (NIBCNT; Peabody: Hendrickson, 1992), 233; P. J. Achtemeier, *Romans* (IBC; Atlanta: John Knox, 1985), 157; Cottrell, *Romans*, 80. Cf. Moo, *Romans*, 580–81.

59. See B. J. Abasciano, 'Paul's Use of the Old Testament in Romans 9:1-9: An Intertextual and Theological Exegesis' (PhD thesis; University of Aberdeen, 2004), 84.

Second, the Old Testament background of Rom. 9.7-9 identifies the divine purpose of Abraham's election to be the blessing of all the nations of the world in Abraham and/or his seed.[60] This is consistently affirmed in the patriarchal narratives of Genesis (12.3; 18.18; 22.18; 26.4; 28.14), to which Paul repeatedly alludes in Rom. 9.6-13. Most significantly, Gen. 18.18-19 does so, a passage that is directly connected to Gen. 18.10, 14, which is cited in Rom. 9.9.[61] Finally, the immediate context of Rom. 9.11 also favours the same view of God's purpose. For as we have seen, Rom. 9.10-13 with its main point, stated by the purpose clause of 9.11c-12b, supports 9.8 and its insistence that it is not those who are ethnically Jewish, but those who believe in Jesus that are regarded as the seed of Abraham, heirs to the covenant promises.

5.3.d.3. *The Means and Basis of Fulfilling God's Purpose*
The point Paul wants to make about this divine purpose of blessing the world, based on the timing of the announcement of God's choice of Jacob over Esau as the heir of the covenant, is expressed by the phrase οὐκ ἐξ ἔργων ἀλλ᾽ ἐκ τοῦ καλοῦντος, which 'draws out the implication of the genitive absolute with which v. 11 began'.[62] By choosing Jacob before either of the twins did anything, whether good or bad, God ensured that his purpose 'would continue not by works, but by the one who calls'. There is a question about precisely what this phrase modifies, whether the preceding verb (μένῃ), the succeeding verb (ἐρρέθη), or the whole sentence.[63] It reads most naturally with μένῃ since it follows it immediately[64] and most clearly brings out Paul's point here in conjunction with this verb, given that the purpose clause begun in v. 11 presents Paul's interpretation of the circumstances he invokes and the prepositional phrase in question is commonly regarded as most explicitly conveying the real essence of Paul's point. But fortunately, as Piper states,

---

60.   See again, Abasciano, *Romans 9.1-9*, 153–54, 211, 221–22.
61.   Ibid.
62.   Cranfield, *Romans*, 478.
63.   See Piper, *Justification*, 51–52, for a convenient listing of the options with representative supporters.
64.   Though the phrase immediately precedes ἐρρέθη, all things being equal, it is more natural to take it with what it immediately follows, since taking it with what it precedes would require recognizing that it does not modify what precedes it, suspending the natural flow of the text, in order to then attach it to what follows. Stöckhardt's contention that this would yield 'a very awkward construction and thought connection' (cited by ibid., n. 11) is surprising, since the construction is no more awkward than the alternative, and it fits the thought of the passage perfectly (see below). Cf. the similar construction in Rom. 8.12, 20. To refer the phrase generally to the whole of vv. 11-12 is even more unlikely, for it leaves the phrase with no direct grammatical connection. Moo's (*Romans*, 582 n. 57) application of it directly to ἐκλογήν is yet more unlikely since it arbitrarily sets aside the phrase's admitted grammatical connection. While this is not egregious, since the fulfilment of God's purpose based on his call implies that the election employed by that purpose has the same basis, it does, like so many, illegitimately focus attention on election when Paul focuses on God's purpose and its fulfilment.

there is no substantial difference between these three views.[65] On any view, both the fulfilment of God's purpose and the declaration of the election that accomplishes that purpose (along with the election itself) are achieved by means of and on the basis of God's sovereign call rather than human works.[66]

Commentators commonly point out that 9.11's μένη furnishes a contrasting parallel to 9.6's ἐκπέπτωκεν, which speaks of the falling of God's promises. Thus, μένη refers to the standing firm of God's word/promises/purpose, amounting to the fulfilment of the same. Paul asserts that God announced his choice of Jacob over Esau before birth in order that his purpose to bless the world would be accomplished not on the basis of human works, but by God on the basis of his own will and calling. But what does the means/basis of fulfilling God's purpose to bless the world matter for its fulfilment and how does the sovereign election of Jacob establish this? There is much to explore in answering these questions.

5.3.d.3.a. *The Epistolary Background of Romans 9.11c-12b and its Implications for Exegesis*

Paul's language here continues to recall his argument in chs 3–4, and it is therefore crucial to keep this background in mind when interpreting what he says now. Accordingly, some exegetes have inferred that Paul now implicitly invokes his works/faith contrast so central to the argument of those chapters.[67] Barrett comments insightfully, 'Works and calling are coordinated here, just

---

65. Piper, *Justification*, 52.

66. In the phrase, ἐκ is best taken as indicating means, basis and underlying principle; see BDAG, 297 (3e, f, i), for these uses of ἐκ, which probably combine here.

67. In addition to those cited by Moo, *Romans*, 583 n. 60, see also Barrett, *Romans*, 171; Black, *Romans*, 132; Brandenburger, 'Schriftauslegung', 34–35; Schmithals, *Römerbrief*, 347. Cf. those who at least imply that Paul is invoking his doctrine of justification argued for in those same chapters (noted by H. Räisänen, 'Römer 9–11: Analyse eines geistigen Ringens', *ANRW* 2.25.4 (1987), 2891–939 (2899), as the usual interpretation): Käsemann, *Romans*, 264 (and those he cites); Dunn, *Romans*, 543–44; Byrne, *Romans*, 292; T. R. Schreiner, *Romans* (BECNT, 6; Grand Rapids: Baker, 1998), 499; Fitzmyer, *Romans*, 562 (seemingly); Luz, *Geschichtsverständnis*, 72; R. Schmitt, *Gottesgerechtigkeit-Heilsgeschichte-Israel in der Theologie des Paulus* (Frankfurt: Lang, 1984), 72; Wilckens, *Römer*, 194. Against it, see Moo (seemingly); H. Hübner, *Gottes Ich und Israel: Zum Schriftgebrauch des Paulus in Römer 9–11* (Göttingen: Vandenhoeck & Ruprecht, 1984), 24–25; Räisänen, 'Römer 9–11', 2899–900; idem, 'Faith, Works and Election in Romans 9: A Response to Stephen Westerholm', in J. D. G. Dunn (ed.), *Paul and the Mosaic Law* (WUNT, 89; Tübingen: Mohr-Siebeck, 1996), 239–46 (240–41). That Hübner and Räisänen find Paul's language here to be in tension with what he has written elsewhere in the epistle is probably an indication that they have misunderstood Paul and that the majority is correct to find allusion to justification by faith here rather than that Paul has contradicted himself (cf. more generally F. Refoulé, 'Unité de l'Épître aux Romains et histoire du salut', *RSPT* 71 (1987) 219–42, who believes the view of Abrahamic descent in Rom. 9 is incompatible with that of Rom. 4, and advances the outlandish suggestion that Rom. 9–11 is an interpolation into Romans), a conclusion that is only strengthened by Räisänen's ('Faith', 240) resort to urging us to distinguish somehow between what Paul '"really" has in mind' from the way he argues his case.

as, earlier in the epistle, works and faith are coordinate. Evidently calling and faith correspond ... Not works but faith leads to justification; not works but God's call admits to the promise. These are different ways of expressing the same truth'.[68] This is exactly right. And it is another indication of the close connection of Romans 9–11 to the preceding chapters of the epistle argued for in my previous volume.[69] Indeed, in harmony with our view of Romans 9–11 as partially a defence of the gospel Paul laid out earlier in the letter,[70] it suggests that Paul is here defending God's right to name/regard those who believe in Christ rather than ethnic/Law-keeping Jews as his covenant people/ the seed of Abraham, a point confirmed by the role of 9.10-13 and its main point of 9.11c-12b as a ground for 9.8. This is another way of saying that Paul is defending his doctrine of justification by faith, which has to do with, inter alia, the question of how God's people are identified.

In view of the invocation of Paul's earlier argument for justification by faith, his 'not by works' language here almost certainly has special (but not exclusive) reference to the works of the Law by which no one will be justified. This is not to say that 'works' here is merely shorthand for the fuller phrase 'works of the Law',[71] but that the latter is 'simply a subset of the'[72] former yet would be the natural focus of concern from the broader category for Paul and his readers in the context of Romans and the early church. Moo is surely correct to argue that Paul speaks of any human deeds, based on the fact that Paul draws his point from the pre-Law era and specifically refers to doing anything good or bad.[73] But the unavoidable main application of this principle for Paul and his audience would be to the works of the Law, just as, in Romans 3–4, Paul argued from the pre-Law era of Abraham and a concomitant general 'not by works' principle against justification by works of the Law.[74]

Also as in Romans 3–4, Jewish ethnicity and works are here closely linked. As Murray says, '"Not of works" and "not of natural descent" are

68.   Barrett, ibid.

69.   See Abasciano, *Romans 9.1-9*, 34–36, and passim; and more extensively, idem, 'Romans 9:1-9', 80–87, and passim.

70.   See Abasciano, *Romans 9.1-9*, 29–32.

71.   Contra Dunn, *Romans*, 543. Even N. T. Wright, 'Romans', in L. E. Keck (ed.), *The New Interpreter's Bible*, X (NIB, 10; Nashville: Abingdon, 2002), 393–770 (637), admits that the emphasis here is on doing good, though he thinks Paul still had in mind the rabbinic idea that the patriarchs obeyed the Torah before it was given.

72.   Moo, *Romans*, 582 n. 55.

73.   Ibid.

74.   S. Grindheim's (*The Crux of Election* (WUNT, 2.202; Tübingen: Mohr Siebeck, 2005), 144 n. 31) objection to this sort of point fails to reckon with the idea that a general works principle is necessarily applicable to any sort of works, including works of the Law. On the other hand, M. Cranford, 'Election and Ethnicity: Paul's View of Israel in Romans 9.1-13', *JSNT* 50 (1993), 27–41 (39–40), goes too far the other way by restricting Paul's language here to the keeping of the Law 'as an external identifier of covenant membership', even if this is its practical emphasis. Wright, 'Romans', 637, and J. R. Wagner, *Heralds of the Good News: Isaiah and Paul 'in Concert' in the Letter to the Romans* (NovTSup 101; Leiden: Brill, 2002), 50 n. 22, strike a balance somewhat similar to ours.

correlative and point to the same principle. Thus the apostle can adduce the one in an argument that is mainly concerned with the other without any sense of incongruity'.[75] This is because Paul's 'of the Law' terminology in Romans 3–4 connotes ethnicity as well as Law-keeping. Those who keep the whole Jewish Law, including its prime boundary markers of circumcision, food laws and Sabbath, are either ethnic Jews or proselytes to Judaism. The two concepts of total Law-keeping and Jewishness are virtually inseparable. But Paul here insists that the fulfilment of God's purpose for election does not rest on Jewish Law-keeping (or works of any kind), but on his own will concerning whom he will call/identify as his own people. That will, Paul has argued in Romans, is to reckon/call those who believe in Jesus as the seed of Abraham. God has sovereignly determined that faith in Christ is the basis for participation in the covenant and that unbelief is the basis for exclusion from the covenant.

5.3.d.3.b. *Faith as a Basis/Condition for Election*
But this makes faith a condition of election on some level, a view that has been strongly opposed by some as a likely implication in this context. The objections that have been raised, however, are not compelling.[76] The first is basically an argument from silence and therefore somewhat weak. Schreiner and Moo make much of the fact that Paul does not explicitly identify faith as the basis of election.[77] But this ignores the importance of context for establishing meaning, the organic connection of Romans 9–11 to the preceding chapters of Romans and its role in a unified, unfolding argument, and Paul's evocative language so far in Romans 9 generally and at this point specifically.[78] Our exegesis of Rom. 9.1-9 has shown that faith is very much at issue in this precise context,[79] especially in 9.8, which, as we have repeatedly mentioned, 9.11c-12b supports. The fact that so many interpreters – including

75. Murray, *Romans*, 2.14. So there is both support for and opposition to the New Perspective in Rom. 9.11-12. There is opposition in the fact that Paul does specifically oppose a notion of general works-righteousness. Yet there is support in that the focus of Paul's concern seems to be a more specific, ethnocentric form of works-righteousness.

76. It should be noted that the following discussion is conducted from the perspective that the election in view in Romans 9 is primarily corporate. Therefore, when I speak of faith as the basis of election, on the individual level, I refer to the basis (in the sense of condition) upon which an individual participates in Christ/the elect people and his/its election. On the corporate level, I refer to the basis upon which the Church participates in Christ and his election. I have already advocated this view of Romans 9 (see ch. 2 n. 24 above), and will take it up again shortly in relation to 9.10-13.

77. Schreiner, *Romans*, 500; Moo, *Romans*, 583. Cf. similarly Hübner, *Schriftgebrauch*, 24–25; Räisänen, 'Römer 9–11', 2899–900; idem, 'Faith', 240–41.

78. The point also stands against those who maintain or imply that since Paul does not explicitly identify the basis of election, no conclusion can be drawn from this context (e.g., Sanday/Headlam, *Romans*, 245; Fitzmyer, *Romans*, 562). The important question is whether the context and other interpretive data provide the basis for a conclusion.

79. See Abasciano, *Romans 9.1-9*. Note also 9.30-33, which serves as a concluding summary to the argument of ch. 9 and makes clear that Paul was addressing works vs justification by faith.

Schreiner – find reference to Paul's doctrine of justification in 9.12 should be evidence enough that it is simplistic to argue that the idea of faith cannot be implicit because the word is not mentioned. To admit that Paul's doctrine of justification is implicit here demands that one admit that faith is implicit here also, since his doctrine is justification *by faith*.[80]

Moreover, it is usually ill advised to base our judgment about what an author means by imposing our own view of what we think he should have said to communicate his point. Indeed, it is invalid to demand that if faith as the basis of election is implicit in the present context, then Paul must state this explicitly, precisely because the point is implicit. Paul is defending the point that participation in the covenant and its promises is based on faith in Christ (9.8). The point is assumed and the argument is focused on its defence.[81] It has already been established in Romans; chs 9–11 then defend God's faithfulness against the objection that if Paul's gospel is true, God is unfaithful because ethnic Israel does not receive what was promised to her. In the immediate context, the point about faith has been essentially restated in 9.8. Besides, it is stated explicitly in the concluding summary of Romans 9 provided by 9.30-33.

Both Schreiner and Moo acknowledge that faith cannot be ruled out as a basis of election in principle based on Paul's anti-works language here.[82] To do so would be to make faith a work when Paul sharply opposes faith and works. But in a second major argument against the line of interpretation we offer, they, along with Piper,[83] do argue or imply that God's call precludes faith as a basis for election. But this is based on an erroneous view of God's call as an effectual summons that produces faith. Rather, we have seen that God's call in Paul's thought is actually an effectual naming/declaration based on faith, a point established particularly clearly by Romans 9.[84] Thus, Piper's attempt to restrict faith to justification is unsuccessful not to mention

80.   The critical question then concerns the nature of Paul's concept of calling and its relationship to faith; see below.

81.   This vitiates Moo's claim that Paul would have explicitly cited faith as the basis of election in response to the charge of injustice introduced by 9.14. For faith's role as the basis of election is part of the very point at issue! On the specific logical connection of 9.14 to 9.10-13, see ch. 8 below.

82.   Schreiner, *Romans*, 500; Moo, *Romans*, 583.

83.   Piper, *Justification*, 53.

84.   See Abasciano, *Romans 9.1-9*, 198–208. Now we can add that 9.11-12 specifically portrays God's call as a declaration/identification of Jacob's elect status rather than a summons to it. Granted, one could point out that this call was not based on faith. But we will see that Jacob's election does not serve as a type of individual election. Curiously, Moo, *Romans*, 54 n. 82, 531 n. 126, refers readers to W. W. Klein, 'Paul's Use of *KALEIN*: A Proposal', *JETS* 27/1 (March 1984), 53–64, on the concept of effectual calling in Paul, who argues for the very type of understanding I advocate. B. R. Gaventa, 'On the Calling-Into-Being of Israel: Romans 9:6-29', in F. Wilk and J. R. Wagner (eds), *Between Gospel and Election: Explorations in the Interpretation of Romans 9–11* (WUNT, 257; Tübingen: Mohr Siebeck, 2010), 255–69, suffers from a failure to recognize the naming sense of calling. She rightly emphasizes that the divine call is creative, but misses that the call that creates the people of God is the designation of a people as God's own, which is indeed selective.

reductionistic, missing faith's intimate interconnection with other aspects of Paul's theology. Indeed, the declarative nature of calling makes for significant overlap with justification, for these both involve the divine declaration of the righteous/elect status of believers. Moreover, although Piper asserts that, 'The counterpart to works in conjunction with election (as opposed to justification) is always God's own call (Rom 9:12b) or his own grace (Rom 11:6)',[85] in the very place Paul links grace, faith and calling, he says that it is faith that makes heirship of the promises, that is, elect status, according to grace (Rom 4.16-17). That is, he grounds grace in faith. What is more, 4.17 grounds calling in faith as well.[86] As a result of Abraham's faith, God establishes Gentiles who imitate his faith as part of Abraham's covenant seed, 'calling the things not existing as existing', just as the indisputably naming call of God in Rom. 9.25-26 calls 'the one [who was] not my people, "my people"' and 'sons of the living God', and calls 'the one not beloved, "my beloved"', also referring to Gentiles who are said shortly thereafter to attain righteousness by faith in contrast to Israel who failed to attain righteousness because they pursued it by works rather than faith (9.30-32).

So Paul's calling language strongly supports faith as the assumed basis of election in 9.12. But it must be remembered that this is *assumed* by Paul's

---

85. Piper, *Justification*, 53.

86. Piper's (ibid.) appeal to Rom. 8.29-30 as establishing that calling is prior to justification *without basis in faith* is rather weak, since inter alia there is nothing about Rom. 8.29-30 that separates faith from calling or demands that calling and justification be separated in actual time (cf. the typical Calvinist understanding of foreknowledge and predestination in these verses). Nevertheless, I would revise my claim (Abasciano, *Romans 9.1-9*, 219) that justification results in calling. Rather, the two concepts are closely related, touching on the same reality, with calling logically prior, though minimally so. Calling refers to the naming of a people as God's own (i.e., his son), while justification refers to the declaration of his people's right relationship with him. Both are contingent on faith. Piper's appeal (cf. similarly Schreiner, *Romans*, 508) to Rom. 9.16 as excluding faith (construed as a type of willing) as a basis for the bestowal of God's mercy is also unwarranted. The verse and its genitive constructions are open to more than one interpretation (Piper himself (155 n. 4) acknowledges with respect to 9.16 that, 'The genitive is a *very* flexible case and must derive its nuance of meaning from the *immediate* context'; emphasis original). I would argue that 9.16 is better understood, as our exegesis of Romans 9 to this point would suggest, to assert that 'the decision concerning who God grants his mercy to rests with him (and the stipulations he chooses to lay down) rather than with the will or effort of man' (Abasciano, 'Election', 359). Paul argues in 9.16 that God has the right to dispense mercy as he sees fit, defending God's specific choice to regard only those who believe in Jesus (the children of the promise) as the covenant seed of Abraham. On the other hand, Piper's view runs into serious (though not necessarily impossible) difficulty. For he would have to acknowledge that repentance and faith are conditions for the bestowal of God's mercy on some level in Pauline theology. Granting this, Piper would then have to explain how it is that what are admittedly conditions are not really conditions. I suspect that an attempt to answer this objection would lead to qualifications that would have to read a lot of theology into the verse in order to make it bear the weight Piper wants to place on it, and either beg the question at issue or contradict the assertion that 9.16 necessarily excludes the possibility that God could sovereignly establish faith as the basis of election. For exegesis of 9.16, see ch. 8 below.

argument. His real concern at this point is to provide the basis for this basis of election. That is, in 9.10-13, he is showing how it is and why it is that God can and does call only those who believe in Christ as his people. He is defending the justice of the faith-based call of God, which is precisely why he contrasts God's call rather than faith to works.[87]

5.3.d.3.c. *The Significance of the Means and Basis of the Fulfilment of God's Purpose*

We can now answer the vital question of the significance that the basis of the fulfilment of God's purpose to bless the world has for the accomplishment of this specific purpose. In the words of Rom. 4.16-17, God's purpose to bless the world must be fulfilled by God's call, which is based on faith, rather than by works,

> in order that [heirship of the promise to inherit the world for Abraham and his seed would be][88] according to grace, so that the promise would be certain to all the seed, not to the [believing] one of the Law only, but also to the [Gentile] one of the faith of Abraham, who is the father of all of us – just as it is written, 'I have made you a father of many nations' – before whom he believed, God, the one who gives life to the dead and calls the things not existing as existing.

In other words, basing God's purpose to bless the world on his call rather than on works/ethnicity for its fulfilment makes that fulfilment possible, for it enables God to include Gentiles in the blessings of Abraham. If it was fulfilled by works/ethnicity, then Gentiles would be excluded, and God's purpose and promises would fall to the ground. 'For if those of the Law are heirs, faith has been invalidated and the promise has been nullified' (Rom. 4.14). We can now see one important way that 9.10-13 supports 9.8's contention that only those who believe in Christ are regarded as Abraham's seed, which in turn supports the assertion that God's purpose and promises have not failed (9.6a). It is by this principle of call/faith/grace that these can be accomplished. But how does the sovereign election of Jacob establish this? [89] With this

---

87.   Hence, Moo's (*Romans*, 583) contention (along with the similar positions of Hübner and Räisänen; see n. 67 above) that the contrast between human and divine activity excludes any human action from the basis of election is off target. Nevertheless, there is some truth in this in that Paul wants to preserve the divine sovereignty over election and its basis (as Wilckens, *Römer*, 196, observes, while Paul gives attention to faith as the criteria for obtaining the promise, 9.6ff. concentrates on the freedom of the divine election). But this in no way excludes all human participation.

88.   I have supplied the ellipsis of 4.16b from 4.13.

89.   I prefer to speak of Jacob's call/election as sovereign rather than unconditional in this context, meaning that Paul depicts God as free in his call/election, i.e., not *constrained* in his choice by anything outside of his own will, which allows that he could sovereignly choose to act based on any sort of condition he desires. Cf. Godet, *Romans*, 348–49; K. Berger, 'Abraham in den paulinischen Hauptbriefen', *MTZ* 17 (1966), 47–89 (83); F. Siegert, *Argumentation bei Paulus: gezeigt an Röm 9–11* (WUNT, 34; Tübingen: Mohr Siebeck, 1985), 127. F. L. Forlines, *Romans* (RHBC; Nashville: Randall House, 1987), 258, is correct to point out that, 'The fact that God's choice of Jacob was made before he was born does not within itself prove that God's choice was not by works. God in his foreknowledge could

question in mind, we now proceed to analyze Paul's quotations of Gen. 25.23 and Mal. 1.2-3.

5.3.e. *Paul's Quotation of Genesis 25.23 (Romans 9.12c)*

Paul has been alluding to Gen. 25.21ff. since v. 10, but now he finally quotes Gen. 25.23 in Rom. 9.12b ('it was said to her,[90] "The older will serve the younger"'). Like the other texts from the Abraham cycle of Genesis to which Paul has alluded in Rom. 9.6-9,[91] this one is well fitted to support his argument for the faithfulness of God. The patriarchal narrative of Genesis is largely about this very theme. It concentrates on God's covenant promises, which are constantly threatened, and their fulfilment. Genesis 25.19-34 plays its role in this scheme by showing the advancement of the process of fulfilling the promises to Abraham through Jacob, overcoming the dire threat of infertility and identifying the seed through whom fulfilment would continue.

Paul shows interpretive perspicacity by quoting the heart of the entire passage, the climactic, representative line of the oracle of Gen. 25.23. It is part of the main point of 25.19-34 and is programmatic for the pericope as

---

have chosen Jacob on the basis of works if He had desired to do so'. Indeed, some have astutely argued that Paul here counters a certain stream of Jewish theology, which we have thoroughly documented in ch. 4 above, that took Jacob's election to have rested on God's foreknowledge of his works (see Dunn, *Romans*, 543–44; Moo, *Romans*, 583 n. 60). Even Qumran evidences belief in election based on foreknowledge of righteous and moral character and reprobation based on wicked deeds (Grindheim, *Election*, 64 n. 109). In any case, the evidence shows contemplation of God's foreknowledge to be a significant factor in first-century thought about the basis of election. Similarly, some ancient Jewish tradition viewed Jacob as good and Esau as evil already in the womb (see ch. 4.5-6 above). Indeed, Hos. 12.4 views Jacob's behaviour in the womb as negative (a passage Siegert, ibid., notes Paul does not mention). All of this suggests that Paul was not arguing that the fact of the prenatal divine decision necessarily proves that God acted unconditionally, but that his choice was not constrained, since the twins had not actually done anything that could be thought to constrain his decision. His comments provide an interpretation of the divine purpose for the timing of the announcement of Jacob's election rather than an assertion of arbitrariness. The interpretation he provides denies works as a basis of election and highlights God's freedom to decide whom he will designate as his covenant people (which would entail any conditions he set for membership in the elect people). This might then tie in with Genesis' (not to mention Hebrews') strong emphasis on Esau's perversity in the despising of his birthright, and allow for the possibility that Paul could have read Genesis to imply the election of Jacob based on – but not required by – his fledgling faith in the covenant promises; cf. n. 45 in ch. 2 above. I am genuinely torn between the two options for whether Paul's argument *demands* the unconditional election of Jacob, and lean toward the conclusion that it does not. But thankfully, *the issue makes no impact on our broader exegesis because of the nature of Jacob's election as the corporate representative of God's people*; see below. In principle, I would have no problem describing Jacob's election here as unconditional and would happily grant the point for the sake of argument.

90. The omission of αὐτῇ in some mss is likely due to parablepsis facilitated by homoeoteleuton with the preceding word (ἐρρέθη).

91. See Abasciano, *Romans 9.1-9*.

well as for the whole Jacob cycle and beyond, paralleling the programmatic promises to Abraham in 12.1-3. It is also ideal to make the point Paul wishes to make about God's sovereignty over covenantal election and the fulfilment of its purpose, articulating as it does, the free divine determination of the covenant seed of Abraham, who represents and embodies the covenant people, a freedom highlighted by the divine reversal of the natural order of election/inheritance, the law of primogeniture.[92] Paul does seem to be countering a prevalent theological conviction among Jews, which we have looked at in detail and that took Jacob's election and Esau's rejection to have rested on their works.[93] The salvation-historical observation that Paul makes gets to the core of Israel's election – for Jacob's election is the election of Israel – and destroys any notion that God is bound to call/name the seed of Abraham based on ethnicity or Law-keeping.

5.3.e.1. *The Corporate Nature of Election*

This brings us to the vexed question of the nature of the election Paul has in view in Romans 9. I have already argued with reference to Rom. 9.1-9 that he had a corporate concept of election to salvation in mind.[94] Paul's use of Gen 25.23 confirms this conclusion. As we saw in our exegesis of this text, Jacob was chosen as the covenant heir and representative/head, entailing the covenant membership/election of those who are identified with him and therefore bear his name, Jacob/Israel. Thus, 'The covenant representative on the one hand and the people/nation of Israel on the other hand are the focus of the divine covenantal election, and individuals are elect only as members of the elect people'.[95] Although in the Old Testament context the normal mode of inclusion in the elect people was by birth, Genesis itself, not to mention Paul, looks toward the inclusion of the nations in the covenant and

---

92.   Grindheim, *Election*, 145, observes that 'there is a certain logic to God's choice, the logic of a reversal of values'. I would add that this makes God's choice conditional. If God's choice follows a logic that chooses that which is not excellent, then that choice is conditioned on the character of what is chosen.

93.   See n. 89 above.

94.   See n. 24 in ch. 2 above; since the main issues and resources are covered by the references there, we will not cover the same ground here, but focus on the contribution of Rom. 9.10-13. The recognition that corporate election is to salvation avoids one of the primary objections to the corporate view of election. For a critique of my view and my response, see T. R. Schreiner, 'Corporate and Individual Election in Romans 9: A Response to Brian Abasciano', *JETS* 49/2 (June 2006), 373–86, and Abasciano, 'Misconceptions'. It should be noted that it is not that the election in the OT texts Paul quotes is specifically unto salvation absolutely (see Abasciano, *Romans 9.1-9*, 99, and the excursus below), but many commentators have gone astray in claiming that the OT election of Israel was restricted to temporal blessing or service; see ch. 3 above and Abasciano, *Romans 9.1-9*, esp. 89–142. The promises of the Old Covenant were conditional on faith. But all in the New Covenant believe. Moreover, Paul undoubtedly saw its election as the fulfilment of the Old Covenant election and promises. In any case, Paul at the very least applies the election of Jacob/Israel to the salvific election of the New Covenant; cf. Piper, *Justification*, 64.

95.   Abasciano, 'Election', 353.

its blessings through connection with the covenant head/people.[96] Indeed, in the Old Testament, foreign individuals, who were not originally members of the elect people, could join the chosen people and become part of the elect, while individuals who apostatized could be cut off from the elect people, demonstrating that the locus of election was the covenant community and that individuals found their election through membership in the elect people. This clears away one of the main objections to the corporate view of election in Romans 9, viz., that Paul is concerned about 'how individual Israelites were accursed'.[97] For the locus of election remained corporate even as individuals could be either cut off from or incorporated into the elect people (cf. Rom. 11.17-24).

Without question, the words Paul quotes carry a primarily corporate significance in their original context: 'Two nations are in your womb. And two peoples from your belly will be divided. And one people will be stronger than the other people. And the older will serve the younger' (Gen. 25.23). Yet, as we noted earlier, this does not exclude reference to the individuals Jacob and Esau altogether. They are in view as the corporate representatives of their respective peoples, who then share in the name, identity and inheritance of their respective corporate heads.[98] But the focus is unquestionably upon the peoples and their destinies rather than the individuals Jacob and Esau.

What is imperative to see in relation to the nature of the election Paul envisions in Rom. 9.10-13 is that the significance of the individual Jacob's election for Israel was that they were elect by virtue of their identification with him. Their election was 'in him', and thus intrinsically consequent upon his. This dispels another of the main objections to taking election as corporate in these verses – that the individuals Jacob and Esau are obviously in view to one degree or another, and therefore so is individual election (of individuals as autonomous entities).[99] This objection fails to apprehend

96. See n. 25 in ch. 2 above.

97. Piper, *Justification*, 66. It is questionable that Paul's focus is on individuals at all (see Abasciano, *Romans 9.1-9*, 185–89; C. Müller, *Gottes Gerechtigkeit und Gottes Volk: Eine Untersuchung zu Römer 9-11* (FRLANT, 86; Göttingen: Vandenhoeck & Ruprecht, 1964), 75), but the question is irrelevant in light of the present argument.

98. Cf. Hübner, *Schriftgebrauch*, 33 n. 74a, though he (along with Maier, *Mensch*, 357–58) does not grasp how this undercuts a doctrine of individualistic election, unlike Mayer, *Prädestinationsaussagen*, 181–86, 213. Puzzlingly, Luz, *Geschichtsverständnis*, 70, denies a primary reference to Jacob and Esau as representatives of peoples on the apparent basis that Paul refers primarily to the OT story; but it is this very story that highlights Jacob and Esau's representative roles.

99. What I would call individualistic election to distinguish it from the fact that corporate election encompasses individual election in that individuals are elect as part of the people. For representatives of individualistic election in Malachi and/or Paul, see e.g., Clendenen, 'Malachi', 256; Hodge, *Romans*, 310–12, who argued in the nineteenth century the basic points that have become the standard objections to corporate election; Murray, *Romans*, 2.15–19; Moo, *Romans*, 585; more recently, R. H. Bell, *The Irrevocable Call of God* (WUNT, 184; Tübingen: Mohr Siebeck, 2005), 211–12. Bell's argument that Paul only quotes the words he does in order to cast aside their original meaning runs aground on the

the relationship between the election of the corporate representative and his people. The corporate representative's election is unique, entailing the election of all who are identified with him. Its significance was never that each individual member of the elect people was chosen as an individual to become part of the elect people in the same manner as the corporate head was chosen. Rather, the individual possesses elect status as a consequence of membership in the elect people/identification with the corporate representative. In the case of the divine covenantal election, God chooses his people by his choice of the covenant head.

A great obstacle to the view that Paul is teaching direct election of individuals as individuals to become part of his people and receive salvation is the fact that the corporate view is the view of the Old Testament generally and the texts Paul interprets in Romans 9 specifically as well as the standard view of Judaism in Paul's day. Moo, an outspoken advocate of individual election, admits as much and concedes, 'We would expect Paul to be thinking of "election" here in the same terms, an expectation that seems to be confirmed by the OT texts that Paul quotes'.[100] This is exactly right. As I have argued elsewhere, the burden of proof lies squarely upon those who would argue that Paul departs from the standard biblical and Jewish concept of election.[101] Therefore, it is an insuperable problem for the individual election view that everything Paul says here in Romans 9 fits comfortably into the view of corporate election, which could speak of the inclusion or exclusion of individuals vis-à-vis the covenant without shifting the locus of election itself to the individual.[102] Indeed, Paul's olive tree metaphor in Rom. 11.17-24 evidences the view of corporate election perfectly. Individuals get grafted into the elect people (the olive tree) and participate in election and its

evidence we have seen that Paul's quotations of the OT have been functioning as pointers to their original contexts, a view of Paul's practice in general that Bell himself defends and provides evidence for in *Provoked to Jealousy: The Origin and Purpose of the Jealousy Motif in Romans 9–11* (WUNT, 2.63; Tübingen: Mohr Siebeck, 1994). Of course, some deny that individuals are in view at all; see e.g., Morison, *Exposition*, 72–82; L. Morris, *The Epistle to the Romans* (Grand Rapids: Eerdmans, 1988), 356–57; Cranford, 'Election', 39, who also cites W. S. Campbell; S. Lyonnet, 'Le rôle d'Israël dans l'histoire du salut selon Rom 9–11' in S. Lyonnet, *Etudes sur l'Epître aux Romains* (AnBib, 120; Rome: Editrice Pontifico Istituto Biblico, 1989), 264–73 (266); J. Munck, *Christ and Israel: An Interpretation of Romans 9–11* (Philadelphia: Fortress, 1967), 38, 42.

100.   Moo, ibid.; cf. idem, 'The Theology of Romans 9–11: A Response to E. Elizabeth Johnson', in D. M. Hay and E. E. Johnson (eds), *Pauline Theology III: Romans* (Minneapolis: Fortress, 1995), 240–58 (254). Of course, Moo goes on to explain why he thinks Paul unexpectedly speaks of individual election, but all of his arguments falter upon the view presented here. Astonishingly, Schreiner, 'Response', 375–78, untenably rejects the very concept of a primarily corporate election in the OT held by most scholars, and thus, in light of his contention that corporate election necessitates individualistic individual election, implies that the OT contains a full-blown view of individual election. See Abasciano, 'Misconceptions', section III.5, for critique.

101.   See Abasciano, *Romans 9.1-9*, 187; idem, 'Election', 371.

102.   Thus, there is little warrant for Käsemann's (*Romans*, 264) claim that Paul disregarded the context of his quotation and made Jacob and Esau timeless types of individual election and rejection respectively.

blessings by faith or get cut off from God's chosen people and their blessings because of unbelief, while the focus of election clearly remains the corporate people of God, which spans salvation history.[103] The natural understanding of Jacob's election in a first-century context would have led readers to apply Paul's example to the character of the corporate election of God's people rather than to the individual. Advocates of individual election in Romans 9 appear to have jumped to applying election directly to individuals because of individualistic assumptions foreign to Paul and his socio-historical milieu.

Thus, Paul's argument based on Jacob and Esau is salvation-historical. Based on the circumstances of their conception and the timing of the divine call/proclamation of Jacob's election as the covenant heir, Paul concludes that the election of God's people was not dictated by any distinctive of either twin, but by the sovereign will and call of God. Generally speaking, by basing the foundational election of his people on his sovereign call rather than some meritorious distinctive of Jacob or de-meritorious distinctive of Esau, God ensured that he remained free to choose who his people are according to his own good pleasure. More specifically, he ensured that he remained free to choose the head/mediator of his covenant for any (or no) reason whatsoever, and thereby to choose similarly who his people are. Most specifically in the context of Paul's argument, God's sovereign call of Jacob and his descendants ensured that he could call only those who believe in Jesus Christ seed of Abraham if he so chose, that is, regard them as his covenant people, and thereby fulfil his purpose of blessing the whole world in Abraham, for Israel's election depended wholly on his sovereign will from the beginning and therefore remained subject to the dictates of his own will.

Excursus 5.1: The Theological Substructure of Paul's Doctrine of Election

Paul's doctrine of election is Christocentric. He believed Christ to be *the* seed of Abraham, the true Israel and embodiment of the covenant people of God, who was the heir to the Abrahamic covenant promises (Gal. 3.16)[104] and the mediator and head of the New Covenant (1 Cor. 11.25; 2 Cor. 3.6), which is essentially the fulfilment of the Abrahamic covenant. By believing in Christ, Christians come to be 'in Christ' and therefore share in his identity as the covenant representative. Consequently, they are also the seed of Abraham and sons of God – that is, the elect people of God – through faith in Christ.[105]

---

103. Cf. the OT background of Rom 9.3 in Exod. 32.31-33 and its corporate election from which individuals could be severed (see Abasciano, *Romans 9.1-9*, 56–57, 104–05).

104. Much of this paragraph is a reworking of Abasciano, 'Election', 355, which see for documentation. Much of its thought is also drawn from Romans 4 and Galatians 3–4, which I will not generally continue to cite in this section. It is worth noting that N. T. Wright's (*The Climax of the Covenant: Christ and the Law in Pauline Theology* (Edinburgh: T&T Clark, 1991), 162–68) masterful treatment of Gal. 3.15-18 and its incorporative conceptual matrix links the text strongly to Rom. 4.13-18, which we have found to be important background for Romans 9.

105. In relation to Rom. 9.10-13 specifically, cf. Barrett, *Romans*, 171.

Thus, Christ fulfils the election of Abraham/Isaac/Jacob/Israel and every promise of God is fulfilled in him (2 Cor. 1.19). God's sovereign freedom over the election of the covenant head guarantees his sovereign freedom over the election of the covenant people. Just as individual Israelites were elected as a consequence of their identification with Jacob, individual Christians are elected as a consequence of their identification with Christ through faith.[106] As Eph. 1.4 puts it, God chose the Church *in Christ*. The 'in Christ' phrase indicates covenant identification and solidarity with Christ as the corporate head/representative, and therefore implies covenant membership as well. As a result of faith-union with Christ, Christians share in Christ's election.

Paul argues in Romans 4 and 9 that it was never ancestry or works, but always faith that was the means by which God's people could possess the blessings of the covenant. However, this does not make for an election within the elect people or a difference between national corporate election and individual election per se.[107] The national election was meant to provide salvation for the members of the covenant as they trusted in the Lord and his covenant promises. But as we saw in Rom. 9.1-9, Paul reveals that unbelieving Jews are only nominally part of the elect people, possessing the blessings of election outwardly, but not truly.[108] In order to remain in the covenant truly, Jews had to believe in Christ. Otherwise, they are cut off from the chosen people. At the same time, Gentiles may be incorporated into the elect people by faith and Jews can also be incorporated back into the elect people by faith (11.17-24; cf. Eph. 2.11-22). Thus, the Church is the continuation and fulfilment of Old Testament Israel, but only because it is in Christ, who is himself the true Israel and its fulfilment.

***

5.3.e.2. *The Typological Import of Genesis 25.23*
The fact that Paul's argument is salvation-historical does not prevent it from also being typological. Indeed, the election of Jacob over Esau does appear in Paul's rhetoric to be a salvation-historical reality that has been recapitulated in Christ and the New Covenant, and thus is a type of the eschatological events wrought in Christ. But rather than being a type of the election of the individual Christian, it is a type of the election of God's people, just as the primary significance of Jacob's election was the election of the people of God in him. Through the metalepsis created by Paul's allusions to Genesis 25, Paul appears typologically to assign unbelieving ethnic Israel to the place of Esau, the elder descendant of Abraham with natural right to the inheritance of the

---

106. Cf. the similar dynamic we saw in Rom. 9.3 in light of its OT background. Just as God had reconstituted the covenant with Israel to be fundamentally with Moses, and then with Israel by virtue of its identification with him, so Paul saw Christ as the New Moses with whom God had principally made the New Covenant, and then with the Church by virtue of its identification with him by faith (see Abasciano, *Romans 9.1-9*, 63, 70, 108–09).

107. See Abasciano, *Romans 9.1-9*, 99.

108. See ibid., esp. 118–21.

covenant household who is sovereignly rejected as the heir of the covenant in favour of the younger descendant who had no natural right to it according to the ancient law of primogeniture.[109]

The Church fulfils the role of Jacob in Paul's scheme. While the Church is composed of both Jews and Gentiles, part of the pathos of the situation Paul addresses in Romans 9–11 is that the Church is composed of mostly Gentiles. So one could speak loosely of God now choosing the Gentiles,[110] who like Jacob were not naturally covenant heirs, rather than ethnic Israel, who like Esau were naturally covenant heirs. As Paul says later in the chapter, God has now identified some from among the Gentiles as part of his people, calling 'the one who was not my people, "my people"', (9.24-25). That is, Gentiles, who did not pursue righteousness, obtained it by faith, while ethnic Israel, who pursued righteousness by the Law rather than faith, did not obtain it (9.30-32). It is this dynamic that calls God's faithfulness into question. So Paul argues for God's sovereign right to name whomever he will as his people, which would include whatever basis if any he might choose for that call.

Paul has just argued similarly from the case of Isaac and Ishmael (9.6-9).[111] Just as with Ishmael, the case of Esau also displays a measure of blessing bestowed upon the rejected physical seed despite his rejected status, foreshadowing God's blessing upon ethnic Israel despite her rejected status as described in Romans, not least in chs 9–11. However, this motif is much less intertextually pronounced in the case of Esau since his blessing is not directly attached in Genesis to Paul's actual quotation and the verbal blessing he does receive is quite minimal (Gen. 27.39-40). Still, the narrative does reveal significant blessing for Esau in great prosperity and Jacob's submissive posture towards him (33.1-15).

Interestingly, both Ishmael and Esau were associated with the Gentiles in Jewish tradition.[112] Esau particularly came to be a symbol of all the enemies of God and his people. Thus, Paul has again classed ethnic Israel with the Gentiles in his argument in Romans 9. As offensive as this must have been to his countrymen, it also contained a silver lining of hope because cursed ethnic Israel could get back into the covenant along with the Gentiles by faith in accordance with the divine purpose of including all the nations in the covenant and its blessings. This is part of the goal of Paul's ministry revealed in Romans 11 – to bring Israel to faith in Christ, and therefore to salvation.

5.3.e.3. *Echoes of the Justification of God*
It is remarkable that the main point of Gen. 25.19-34 is the election of Jacob and his descendants over Esau and his descendants, and its justification based on the despising of the birthright by the natural heir. For this mirrors

---

109. Cf. the emphasis of D. J.-S. Chae, *Paul as Apostle to the Gentiles: His Apostolic Self-Awareness and Its Influence on the Soteriological Argument in Romans* (PBTM; Carlisle: Paternoster, 1997), 230–32.

110. Cf. ibid.

111. See Abasciano, *Romans 9.1-9*, 118–21.

112. Ibid., 194–95; see also ch. 4 above.

the situation Paul addresses very closely in accordance with the typology just discussed. The remarkable factor we turn our attention to now is the prominent validating point of the Genesis narrative vis-à-vis the validating concern of Paul's own argument.[113] Paul is defending God's faithfulness to his promises to Israel in light of his expulsion of ethnic Israel from the covenant and its inheritance.

The transumption supports Paul's argument similarly, highlighting Israel's own guilt for bringing about their cursed state. Just as Esau despised his birthright/inheritance, carelessly relinquishing it, so ethnic Israel has despised its inheritance of the Abrahamic promises, carelessly casting it aside by their rejection of Christ, who encompasses all of Israel's privileges and the promises made to her (cf. 9.1-5). Therefore, God cannot be considered unfaithful for cutting ethnic Israel off from the covenant promises. They have spurned his Messiah, who carries the fulfilment of the promises. Indeed, they have spurned God himself in the person of the Messiah, 'who is over all, God blessed forever' (9.5). God already had the sovereign right to regard whoever he wanted as his people. But Israel's actions justify God's choice all the more. Paul's use of Gen. 25.23 joins with his use of Gen. 18.10, 14 in Rom. 9.9 in anticipating the focus of the next major segment of his argument in 9.14ff. – theodicy and the justice of God in his rejection of ethnic Israel and election of the Church.[114] But before he addresses that concern, he has one more piece of evidence to add in order to buttress his argument in Rom. 9.10-12, a quotation of Mal. 1.2-3.

5.3.f. *Paul's Quotation of Malachi 1.2-3 (Romans 9.13)*

Paul introduces his quotation of Mal. 1.2-3 with his most typical introductory quotation formula in Romans, καθὼς γέγραπται,[115] which he regularly uses to corroborate what he says.[116] He now quotes Mal. 1.2-3 in corroboration of his interpretation of Gen. 25.21-23. But how does it corroborate his point? It expresses 'the same truth as the words from Genesis', upon which Paul's

---

113. Cf. e.g. Piper's (*Justification*) characterization of Paul's argument in the title of his study.

114. Cf. Abasciano, *Romans 9.1-9*, 208–13, 230.

115. The external support in favour of καθώς rather than καθάπερ, read only by B, is overwhelming.

116. This standard use of the formula weighs against the more specific view that 9.13 grounds the election and rejection of 9.11-12 in God's love and hatred respectively, popular in the time of Sanday/Headlam, *Romans*, 246; considered and rejected by Cranfield, *Romans*, 480; cf. Moo, *Romans*, 584 (though he seems to go on and unwittingly contradict his agreement with Cranfield in the next breath); seemingly advocated recently by Schreiner, *Romans*, 501. It also fails to reckon with the OT background informing the meaning of love and hatred. Contra Hübner, *Schriftgebrauch*, 29–30, who seems to measure Paul's intertextual activity with an unwarranted formal rigidity, Paul does seem to be concerned to allude to various sections of the OT as was common among ancient Jews (see Abasciano, ibid., 39–40, and references there; cf. Schmithals, *Römerbrief*, 345). But this does not conflict with Hübner's observation that Paul was concerned to confirm his argument by repetition. Indeed, this would appear to be part of the rationale for the Jewish practice.

point (9.11c-12b) is based, 'but expressing it more clearly and pointedly'.[117] Both passages demonstrate that the divine election was not constrained by any human work, but was a matter of God's sovereign call. Attending to the original context of this quotation will give us greater insight into its meaning and Paul's argument.

5.3.f.1. *Remarkable Contextual Correspondence and Salvation-historical Continuity*

It is again striking how well suited Paul's intertextual activity is to his argument for the covenant faithfulness of God to his promises to Israel and his freedom in election.[118] For Mal. 1.2-3 addresses these very issues along with related ones of concern to Paul's discourse. First, Paul shows biblical and interpretive sensitivity by linking Mal. 1.2-3 to Gen. 25.23, since the former appears to allude to the latter. Second, the book of Malachi is actually addressed to a practically apostate Israel that challenged the covenant faithfulness and justice of God, believing they saw no evidence of the fulfilment of YHWH's covenant promises. The prophet refutes and rebukes these blasphemous attitudes and assures Israel of God's covenant love and faithfulness as well as his firm commitment both to save and bless those who are faithful to him and to curse the faithless/wicked. Third, the section of Malachi (1.2-5) from which Paul quotes addresses these issues programmatically, and some of the words he quotes essentially encapsulate the main thesis statement of the entire book. Indeed, in its original context Paul's quotation is actually a declaration of God's covenant faithfulness to Israel. This can hardly be a coincidence.

Just as Malachi defended God's covenant faithfulness and promises in his capacity as God's covenant messenger against doubting challenges, so does Paul in his capacity as God's New Covenant messenger.[119] Indeed, Paul proclaims the fulfilment of God's covenant promises to Israel in his gospel. Just as Malachi held out the promise of salvation to the faithful and the threat of covenant curse to the unfaithful in Israel, so Paul holds out the promise of salvation to Jews (not to mention Gentiles) who believe his gospel and the threat of covenant curse to those who do not (cf. e.g., Rom. 9.3, 30-33; 10.8-13; 11.17-24).[120] It would seem that Paul envisions a genuine salvation-historical continuity between his own ministry and that of Malachi. At the very least, he applies Malachi's invocation of the salvation-historical event of the election of Jacob/Israel over Esau/Edom to the election of the Church and rejection of unbelieving ethnic Israel.[121] Concordantly, it is likely that

---

117. Cranfield, ibid. T. H. Tobin's (*Paul's Rhetoric in Its Contexts: The Argument of Romans* (Peabody: Hendrickson Publishers, 2004), 329) assertion that the quotation plays no real role in Paul's interpretation is almost shocking.

118. Cf. F. Thielman, 'Unexpected Mercy: Echoes of a Biblical Motif in Romans 9–11', *SJT* 47 (1994), 169–81 (175).

119. On Paul's role as a prophet/covenant messenger, see Abasciano, *Romans 9.1-9*, 41, 209, and references there.

120. Cf. the typological significance of Paul's ministry suggested by his use of Exodus 32–34 in Romans 9 and elsewhere discussed in ibid., 108–15.

121. Cf. Hübner, *Schriftgebrauch*, 28; Räisänen, 'Römer 9–11', 2901 n. 56.

Paul continues the Jacob/Church–Esau/Jews typology we observed in his use of Gen. 25.23. In fact, this is almost certain since he cites Malachi as a corroboration of his interpretation of Genesis.

5.3.f.2. *God's Love and Hatred in Intertextual Perspective*

There has been much discussion of what Paul means by God's love and hatred in this quotation. Some argue that the language of love and hate occur here in Semitic idiom referring to relative degrees of love so that hate means 'to love less'.[122] While there is such a Semitic idiom (see e.g., Luke 14.26), the Old Testament background is determinative here. The love and hate of Mal. 1.2-3 refer to the covenantal election of Jacob and his people (love) and the covenantal rejection of Esau and his people (hate) respectively.[123] If there were any doubt about the significance of the Old Testament background in Rom. 9.13, relating it to the immediate context in Romans places this interpretation beyond all serious doubt, as Paul explicitly mentions election in relation to Jacob and Esau.[124]

The covenantal significance of the love/hate terminology of Rom. 9.13 suggests that God's hatred of Esau entails no personal animosity towards him or his descendants.[125] Nonetheless, this lack of covenant commitment leaves Edom the people open to God's irremediable personal animosity and judgment for any wickedness they might perpetrate. Presumably, the same is true for all who are not in covenant with the Lord, especially in light of Esau's/Edom's role in biblical and Jewish thought as a symbol of the nations and the enemies of God and his people. The astonishing thing in Paul's argument is that he is applying this status to ethnic Israel as a whole. They have been separated from Christ and therefore the New Covenant (9.1-5). They have been cut off from the covenant people of God (11.17-24; cf. 9.6-9). They are now counted with Esau and the nations.

The Church of Jesus Christ, on the other hand, is the recipient of God's covenantal love/election, and therefore his salvation. It is they who are the children of the promise (9.8), those who will receive its fulfilment. Immediately before the words Paul quotes, Malachi drew attention to Jacob and Esau's brotherhood and basic equality in eligibility for covenant headship/inheritance; indeed, Esau's elder-superiority could not lie far from view. The definitive difference between them along with their respective peoples vis-à-vis covenant inheritance lay in God's sovereign choice. Neither could justly lay claim to the privilege as an inalienable right. It was God's right to name whoever he wanted as his covenant partner, and to remain sovereign over the covenant people and their identity. We saw that this partly served as

---

122. See e.g., Hodge, *Romans*, 312; Morison, *Exposition*, 90–91; Byrne, *Romans*, 295.

123. See ch. 3 above.

124. That Paul speaks of election and rejection appears to be the consensus among contemporary interpreters; see e.g., Cranfield, *Romans*, 480; Moo, *Romans*, 587.

125. A common observation; see e.g., Moo, ibid. For an argument for reference to full-fledged hatred, see Murray, *Romans*, 2.21–24, who misses the covenantal significance of the language.

a warning to the erring Israel of Malachi's day. Through Paul's rhetoric, it sounded a note of warning for the Israel of his own day too, buttressing his interpretation of Jacob's election and its application to the present stage of salvation history as well as some of the rationale for his own ministry.

5.3.f.3. *Further Insights into the Corporate Election of Romans 9*

Paul and Malachi certainly agree in their interpretation of Gen. 25.23 as showing God's sovereignty over election. They also agree in their conception of election as corporate. All along in our analysis of Romans 9 we have seen that Paul and the texts he is interpreting hold a corporate view of election. We have just seen this very clearly in Gen 25.23 and Paul's use of it. We may now observe it in Mal. 1.2-3, further confirming our assessment of the concept in Romans 9 and Paul's theology.

We have already laid out the concept of corporate election in our previous volume and in our exegesis of Gen. 25.21-23, Mal. 1.2-3 and Rom. 9.12 in the present volume. So there is no need to go over it again. But it may be helpful to make a few observations regarding Mal. 1.2-3 and its significance for Paul's argument in this regard. First, it is very clear that Malachi conceives of election as primarily corporate. Second, one of the features of the text that shows this so clearly – that YHWH loved/chose Israel as his covenant partner by choosing Jacob – supplies hard evidence of a point we made earlier that militates against the concept of individualistic election in Malachi and Paul, viz., that the consequence of the individual election of the covenant head is the corporate covenantal election of the people identified with him.

Third, the corporate orientation of the election and rejection described in Mal. 1.2-3 left election and rejection open on the individual level. Any Edomite could enter the covenant and enjoy its blessings by joining the elect people, identifying with the covenant head of YHWH's choosing, while any Israelite could be cut off from the covenant people for unrepentant unfaithfulness. In the time of the New Covenant as proclaimed by Paul's gospel, Jesus Christ is now the covenant head and mediator of God's choosing that all must identify with through faith in order to be incorporated into the covenant people and share in the covenant promises. Jews who do not believe have been cut off from the elect people.

Fourth and relatedly, the covenantal significance of the Lord's love/election and hate/rejection reveals that the two are not completely antithetically parallel. While the purpose of the former was to bestow blessing, the purpose of the latter was not to effect condemnation. Rather, condemnation is the consequence of sin when there is no divine covenant commitment. The flip side of this is that God's covenant commitment includes corrective discipline for his people, which ties into a general theme of Romans that we have seen exhibited in Rom. 9.1-12 – a special measure of blessing upon ethnic Israel as the nominal but rejected bearers of the covenant and a commitment to work towards their restoration to covenant privilege (through the gospel).

All of this carries far-reaching implications for assessment of the bearing of Romans 9 on the doctrines of election and predestination. Far from supporting a notion of unconditional individual election or predestination, as has been argued by some interpreters, the Old Testament background of Rom. 9.10-13 and Paul's appropriation of it suggest that Paul viewed these concepts corporately. God chose a people for salvation and the inheritance of the covenant promises. Individuals share in the election and destiny of the elect people as a consequence of membership in that people, not as the result of some sort of arbitrary divine assignment to the group. What Paul has argued in Romans and will continue to argue in vv. 9–11 is that membership in that people comes by faith in Jesus Christ.

5.3.f.4. *Intertextual Insights into God's Sovereignty over Election, the Jews, and the Gentiles*

But this is not to deny that Paul stresses the sovereignty of God over election in these verses. In harmony with Mal. 1.2-3, he surely does, so as to defend God's right to name who he chooses as his people, and more specifically, to justify God's rejection of unbelieving Jews and naming of only those who believe in Jesus as his people, whether Jew or Gentile. Indeed, Paul's conviction concerning God's sovereignty appears to be partially rooted in the context of his Malachi quotation, which affirms God's sovereignty over both Israel and the Gentiles.[126]

But the parallel runs deeper. Not only is God presented as sovereign over both Israel and the Gentiles, but he also declares that his sovereign dealings with the Gentiles will glorify him and move Israel to acknowledge his greatness and covenant faithfulness (cf. Rom. 9.17, where God's sovereign dealings with Pharaoh proclaim his glory throughout the earth). This may have provided some inspiration to Paul for his conviction that God's gracious dealings with the Gentiles through his own ministry might provoke Israel to come to faith in Christ and be grafted back into the people of God (Rom. 11.11-32). But this prospect faces the difficulty that, in the immediate Malachi context, it is God's destruction of Gentile Edom that will bring Israel to see his faithful love. However, the important point for Paul may lie in the fact that it is God's sovereign activity with the Gentiles that will impact Israel, as his focus on God's sovereignty would suggest.

But if Paul is continuing his Jacob/Church–Esau/Jews typology, as he almost certainly is, then that would place the Church in the role of (true) Israel (God's covenant people) and unbelieving ethnic Israel in the role of Esau (rejected as God's covenant people). Could it be that we are also to understand that Mal. 1.2-3 suggested to Paul that God's judgment on unbelieving ethnic Israel (Esau) would be used of God to bring the Gentiles to see God's greatness and believe that he had fulfilled his covenant promises to his people? It would seem so, since Paul goes on to argue that God's rejection of Israel is the means by which he would bring the Gentiles into reconciliation with God and enjoyment of his salvation and blessing (11.11-15, 30).[127] It

---

126.   Cf. Chae's (*Paul*, 232) recognition of the ethnic concerns of the Malachi context.
127.   The problem with this is that it looks at the Gentiles as already God's people when the salvation-historical reality described by Paul in Romans 11 actually envisages Gentiles

would appear that Mal. 1.2-3 provides some of the scriptural basis for Paul's conviction that God's judgment of unbelieving ethnic Israel would bring Gentiles to faith and that his merciful treatment of the Gentiles would bring Jews to faith, summed up in 11:30-31.

One might wish to question this suggested meaning-effect because it could look as if we are assigning contradictory symbolic/typological meanings to Jacob and Esau in an arbitrary way to squeeze out of Paul's quotation as much meaning as possible. But I would counter that it is actually Paul's paradoxical, but ultimately coherent, view of Israel and his perception of the movement of salvation history that account for the polyvalent nature of this symbolism/typology. As we have seen earlier in Romans 9, Paul regarded unbelieving ethnic Israel as possessing the name and prerogatives of the covenant people outwardly, but not fully and truly (Rom. 9.1-9).[128] They were from Israel but not Israel, Jews outwardly but not inwardly, circumcised but uncircumcised, cut off from their own olive tree. In the time of Paul's ministry, many Jews had gone from being members of God's people to be being excluded from his people, while many Gentiles had gone from not being God's people to being God's people in Christ (cf. e.g., 9.24-26). Therefore, depending on what aspect of the present salvation-historical epoch is being considered, one could look at either the Jews or Gentiles as typified by either Jacob or Esau. Just as we saw that Paul could use Ishmael as a type of both non-believing Israel and Gentiles in their common plight of separation from God, so now he can use Jacob on the one hand and Esau on the other as types of Jews and Gentiles as God's covenant people and those rejected from the covenant respectively as these types are applicable to either group in accordance with whatever position they hold at any given time, whether looked at as unbelievers separated from Christ or as believers in covenantal union with him.[129]

The basic facts support our contention. The Malachi context speaks of God's sovereign dealings with those who are not in covenant relationship with him bringing his covenant people to see and acknowledge his greatness and faithfulness. In Romans 9–11 Paul views the Jews and the Gentiles separately, sometimes in the role typified by Jacob (chosen) and sometimes in the role typified by Esau (rejected), though the dominant motif is as we find it here in 9.13, that of the Church in the place of Jacob and unbelieving Jews in the place of Esau. In this way, Paul can cite Mal. 1.2-3 in partial anticipation

---

as coming to faith so as to *become* God's people. However, typology does not necessitate exact correspondence in every detail, but operates on relevant perceived correspondences. It is typical of typology that there are elements of continuity and discontinuity present in that which is parallel. Moreover, true parallelism may often be found at a more general level of description that articulates the relevant perceived correpsondence. Paul seems to have found a pattern in salvation history now recapitulated and escalated in the time of eschatological fulfilment. The general similarity here between the OT and NT contexts seems strong enough to render this meaning-effect probable.

128. See Abasciano, *Romans 9.1-9*, esp. 118–21.

129. See Abasciano, *Romans 9.1-9*, 194–95, on Paul's metaleptical use of Ishmael in 9.7.

of the argument he will make in ch. 11 that God's treatment of each group is intended to lead the other to faith and salvation.

5.4. *Summary/Conclusion*

Romans 9.10-13 continues Paul's argument begun in 9.1-9 concerning God's faithfulness to his promises to Israel. More specifically, these verses add to the support Paul adduced from Gen. 18.10, 14 for the contention of Rom. 9.8 that only those who believe in Christ are the covenant seed of Abraham, to whom the promises were made. Romans 9.8 is the practical main point of 9.7-9, supporting the programmatic statement of 9.6b that 'not all who are from Israel are Israel', which in turn grounds Paul's assertion that God's word has not failed in 9.6a, the thesis statement of all of Romans 9–11.

In 9.10-13, Paul adds to his support for the claim that only those who believe in Christ are *rightful* heirs of the covenant promises by furnishing an even stronger example than that of Sarah, Isaac and Ishmael of the principle that covenant heirship has always depended on God's call and promise rather than ancestry – the example of Rebekah, Jacob and Esau. This example is stronger than the previous one because Jacob and Esau were basically equal in terms of ancestral descent. In fact, Esau had a natural advantage as the firstborn; according to the ancient law of primogeniture, he had the natural right to inherit the covenant and its promises. But God sovereignly chose Jacob over Esau for the privilege, as was his divine right, a right that was underscored by the prenatal timing of the announcement of God's choice. Indeed, Paul argues that the purpose of God in announcing his choice before the twins were born was to ensure that the fulfilment of his purpose to bless the world would proceed on the basis of his sovereign right to name whoever he wants as his covenant people rather than on the basis of human works or ancestry. It is this purpose statement, found in 9.11c-12b, that (1) presents Paul's interpretation of the Old Testament texts to which he alludes, (2) is the main point of vv. 10-13, and thus (3) serves as the essence of 10-13's support of the principle enunciated in 9.8 that only those who believe in Christ are rightful covenant heirs.

Defending God's right to name his people based on faith rather than works/ancestry, Paul explains in 9.10-13 how God could justly do so as well as why he acts in this way. God retains the right to choose who his people are according to his own good pleasure (for any or no reason whatsoever) because the election of his people depended wholly on his sovereign will from the beginning through his election of Jacob, the covenant head, and therefore remained subject to the dictates of his own will. Consequently, he is able to call only those who believe in Jesus Christ the seed of Abraham if he so chooses. Basing the fulfilment of God's purpose to bless the world on his sovereign call rather than on works/ethnicity makes that fulfilment possible, for it enables God to call his people based on faith rather than works/ethnicity and thereby include Gentiles in the blessings of Abraham.

We have found that, just as in Rom. 9.1-9, many of the themes that Paul addresses in Romans 9 are also present in ancient interpretive traditions surrounding the texts he cites in 9.10-13.[130] But Paul's argumentation is thoroughly based on Scripture in these verses. Indeed, it assumes knowledge of its biblical background on the part of Paul's audience, pointing readers to the original contexts of his intertexts. Those contexts hold vital information for a full understanding of Paul's discourse. They even appear to have guided his view of the current events of salvation history.

It is remarkable how closely the texts to which Paul alludes match his argument. As he faces a challenge to God's faithfulness to both his covenant promises and his election of his people, he turns to two texts that deal with these very themes. The first, Gen. 25.21-23 and its context, is fundamental. It is in fact ideal to make Paul's point that God is rightfully sovereign over covenantal election and the fulfilment of its purpose (and therefore just in his calling of the Church and rejection of unbelieving ethnic Israel), for it describes the free divine determination of the identity of the covenant seed of Abraham in Jacob in violation of the natural order of election/inheritance, countering a prevalent theological conviction among Jews that took Jacob's election and Esau's rejection to have rested on their works.

Paul's argument is salvation-historical. He has appealed to the foundational election of God's people in Jacob to establish that God is indeed free to name whoever he wants as his people. Since the election of the covenant people is entailed in and dependent on the election of the covenant head with whom they are identified, the implications of the circumstances of Jacob's election as the covenant head and heir apply also to the election of the covenant people. Indeed, the oracle Paul quotes from Gen. 25.23 applied primarily to the people who would bear Jacob's election and is most naturally understood as bearing this connotation in Paul's argument as well, in harmony with the corporate orientation of his perspective in Romans, especially chs 9–11.[131] Moreover, in showing that Jacob's election as the covenant head was entirely at God's sovereign discretion, he showed that God was free to transfer the covenant headship to Christ in the time of eschatological fulfilment and thereby choose as his covenant people all who identify with him.

Paul's argument is also typological. But his typology is totally grounded in his salvation-historical observations.[132] The foundational corporate election of God's people in Jacob rather than Esau has been recapitulated in the election of the Church rather than ethnic Israel. Just as Isaac served as a type of the Church and Ishmael served as a type of unbelieving ethnic Israel in 9.7-9, so Paul has now placed the Church, consisting mostly of Gentiles, in the role of Jacob on the one hand, and unbelieving ethnic Israel in the place of Esau on the other hand. Ethnic Israel had the prior and natural right to the covenantal

---

130. See the summary in ch. 4.7 above.

131. On Paul's corporate perspective in Romans, see ibid., passim (e.g., 41-44, 218, 224-25).

132. But this is to be expected, since typology is normally regarded as grounded in history; see ibid., 228 n. 26.

inheritance as the historic people of God while the Gentiles had no such right as those without covenantal status. But God has again sovereignly restricted the covenant seed of Abraham, this time by choosing Christ as the covenant seed/head/representative and thereby limiting covenantal election of Jews to those who believe in Christ and paradoxically opening the covenant to the whole world of both Jews and Gentiles, admitting any who will believe.

This all involves the familiar Old Testament motif of 'the displaced firstborn'.[133] But it is more than that. Paul's metalepses also evoke a less prominent motif present in the Old Testament background to which he alludes – that of continued blessing and care for the displaced firstborn along with the possibility of his reinclusion. We saw this playing out in Paul's allusion to Isaac and Ishmael in 9.7-9. Now it suggests itself again from the texts Paul cites in vv. 10-13, anticipating Paul's stress later in Romans 9–11 on God's continued care and blessing for ethnic Israel despite her present rejected status.

A particularly striking aspect of both Paul's Jacob/Esau typology as it appears in his argument and the original Old Testament context from which he draws it is that the main point of Gen. 25.19-34 includes not only the election of Jacob and his descendants over Esau and his descendants, but also the justification of this election based on the despising of the birthright by the natural heir. It would seem that in Paul's view, just as Esau despised his birthright/inheritance, carelessly relinquishing it, so ethnic Israel has despised its inheritance of the Abrahamic promises, carelessly casting it aside by their rejection of Christ, who encompasses all of Israel's privileges and the promises made to her (cf. 9.1-5). Therefore, God cannot be considered unfaithful for cutting ethnic Israel off from the covenant promises even apart from his sovereign right in election. This focus on justifying God and his covenant faithfulness in both Genesis and Malachi contributes to the same phenomenon in Paul's argument here in 9.10-13, but also points forward to the next stage of the argument in 9.14-18 as he takes up even more directly the question of God's righteousness ('Is there unrighteousness with God'?; 9.14) in relation to his rejection of ethnic Israel and election of the Church.

The second text Paul cites is Mal. 1.2-3. Much of what we have been saying applies to Paul's quotation of Malachi as well as his quotation of Genesis,[134] for the Malachi text itself alludes to the Genesis text and embodies much of its thrust, especially understood in context. But it also matches Paul's argument in a way that is distinctive and arresting in its own right. Malachi directly addresses the issues of the covenant faithfulness of God to his promises to Israel and his freedom in election in response to a doubting challenge, the very issues Paul is addressing in Romans 9–11, also in response to a doubting challenge. Just as Malachi, in his capacity as God's covenant messenger, held out the promise of salvation to the faithful and the threat of covenant curse to the unfaithful in Israel, so Paul, in his capacity as God's

133. Cf. n. 26 in ch. 2 above.
134. Note that I have implied as much by speaking at times generally of 'the texts to which Paul alludes', etc.

New Covenant messenger, holds out the promise of salvation to Jews (not to mention Gentiles) who believe his gospel and the threat of covenant curse to those who do not.

Paul continues his Jacob/Church–Esau/Jews typology with his quotation of Mal. 1.2-3. Astonishingly, it is now the Church of Jews and mostly Gentiles that is loved (which equates to chosen covenantally) by God and unbelieving Jews who are hated (which equates to rejected covenantally), classed with the Gentiles. But it was God who sovereignly chose Jacob as the covenant head and heir, and it remained his right to name whoever he wanted as his covenant partner, and thereby to continue as sovereign over the covenant people and their identity. This sovereignty over election of the people of God served as a warning to the erring Israel of both Malachi's and Paul's times. They should not dare to presume upon his grace, for it is his sovereign decision to cut off from his people those who do not believe and to graft into his people those who do believe, whether Jews or Gentiles.

Indeed, the Malachi passage testifies that God is sovereign over both Israel and the Gentiles, contributing to Paul's stress on God's sovereignty in Romans 9. Moreover, Mal. 1.2-3 also appears to contribute to Paul's conception of some of the specific details of the outworking of God's sovereign dealings with Israel and the nations, namely, his conviction that God's judgment of unbelieving ethnic Israel would bring Gentiles to faith and that his merciful treatment of the Gentiles would provoke Jews to jealousy and faith. For God declares in Mal. 1.2-5 that his sovereign dealings with Edom, representative of the nations, would bring his people to glorify him and to acknowledge his greatness and covenant faithfulness, a point that can be applied by way of general analogy to the Gentiles as God's people and ethnic Israel as not God's people or vice versa.

We have found that a concept of corporate election emanating from the Old Testament texts Paul quotes thoroughly pervades the argument of Rom. 9.10-13, supporting our previous conclusions about Paul's concept of election drawn from Rom. 9.1-9. Though some have argued that these verses articulate a notion of unconditional individual election or predestination, the Old Testament background of Rom. 9.10-13 and Paul's appropriation of it suggest that Paul viewed these concepts corporately. God chose a people for salvation and the inheritance of the covenant promises. Individuals share in the election and destiny of the elect people as a consequence of membership in that people (ultimately, through identification with the covenant head/representative), not as the result of some sort of arbitrary divine assignment to the group. What Paul has argued in Romans and will continue to argue in chs 9–11 is that membership in that people comes by faith in Jesus Christ.

Indeed, just as in the Old Testament context divine election and rejection were neither absolute nor unconditional on the individual level, but individual Edomites could join the elect people and individual Israelites could be cut off from the elect people for unrepentant unfaithfulness, so Paul affirms that those who do not continue to believe in Christ will be cut off while those who believe will be grafted into God's people (11.17-24). Thus, Paul holds out hope that God's merciful treatment of the Gentiles will provoke the Jews to jealousy and faith in Christ (11.11-24).[135] But he has much to say before he arrives at that part of his argument. We must now attend to the Old Testament background of the next immediate stage of his presentation.

135. Indeed, 11.7-24 supports this corporate understanding of the elect as focused in Christ and therefore referring only to those who are actually in Christ (rather than referring to those who have been chosen to believe and therefore specifically applying to certain unbelievers who will eventually believe), for as Luke Gowdy has pointed out to me in personal correspondence, in 11.7, 'the rest' are not elect. But Paul believed that more from 'the rest' would eventually believe, requiring us to conclude that the elect in 11.7ff. is a dynamic term that allows for departure from and entry into the elect as portrayed in the olive tree metaphor.

Chapter 6

EXODUS 9.16 IN ITS OLD TESTAMENT CONTEXT WITH SPECIAL
ATTENTION TO THE HARDENING OF PHARAOH'S HEART

Exodus 9.16, the fourth and final Old Testament text Paul quotes in Rom.
9.10-18, is situated within a wide swath of material in the book of Exodus
that stretches from 1.1 to 15.21 and reports the basic events of the exodus
from Egypt.[1] It begins by describing the woeful plight of Israel under Egyptian
bondage and oppression (chs 1–2), setting the stage for the needed deliverance
by YHWH, upon which the narrative comes to focus at length. Moses, the
deliverer YHWH would choose, is then introduced along with the divine call
for him to go to Pharaoh and deliver Israel, and preparations for him to do
so, including instructions and the appointment of his brother Aaron as his
spokesman in response to Moses' reluctance to go as YHWH's spokesman
(chs 2–4). After going to the people of Israel and gaining their support (4.27-
31), Moses and Aaron went to Pharaoh and presented YHWH's demand that
he let Israel go to celebrate a feast to him in the wilderness (5.1-3). Pharaoh
responded by defiantly refusing to let the people go and harshly increasing
their oppression (5.2-23). YHWH then responded in turn by sending Moses
back to Pharaoh to charge him again to let the people go. Upon continued
refusal, YHWH struck Egypt with plague after plague, sometimes giving
relief from one in response to temporary capitulation from Pharaoh only
to be followed by another of typically greater intensity[2] when Pharaoh

1.   Remember that I omitted a detailed exegesis of Paul's third Old Testament
quotation in Rom. 9.10-18 (Exod. 33.19b cited in Rom. 9.15) in this investigation because
I have provided one in my previous volume; see Abasciano, *Romans 9.1-9*, 46–72 (esp. 65–
69). Exodus can be divided in various ways, but it can scarcely be denied that the material
in 1.1–15.21 relates to the exodus proper. Differing approaches are quite understandable
given the various valid ways to look at the organization of the book, whether from the
perspective of: the deliverance (as we have done; cf. P. Enns, *Exodus* (NIVAC; Grand Rapids:
Zondervan, 2000), 33; W. Brueggemann, 'The Book of Exodus: Introduction, Commentary,
and Reflections', in L. E. Keck et al. (eds), *The New Interpreter's Bible*, I (NIB, 1; Nashville:
Abingdon, 1994), 675–982 (687–88)), or Sinai (D. K. Stuart, *Exodus* (NAC, 2; Nashville:
Broadman & Holman, 2006), 19–22), or where Israel was located (J. I. Durham, *Exodus*
(WBC, 3; Waco: Word, 1987), vii–x), or various themes (R. C. Bailey, *Exodus* (The College
Press NIV Commentary; Joplin, MO: College Press, 2007), 27), etc.
2.   On the increasing intensity of the plagues, see Stuart, *Exodus*, 187, who later notes
that this has been observed by virtually all commentators (200).

renewed his refusal to let YHWH's people go, until the final, deadly plague on the firstborn leading to Pharaoh actually sending Israel out of the land (chs 6–13). But after letting Israel go, 'the heart of Pharaoh and his servants was turned against the people' (14.5). So the Egyptians went after Israel, presumably to re-enslave them, resulting in the Egyptians' destruction in the Red Sea by YHWH's miraculous intervention (chs 14–15).[3]

Perhaps the most striking feature of the exodus narrative is the theme of the hardening of Pharaoh's heart. It is pervasive in chapters 4–14, undoubtedly integral to the main thrust of the entire narrative. Yet it raises troubling and thorny questions about God's justice and sovereignty, and human free will and responsibility. It is a classic biblical and theological problem that has drawn an enormous amount of attention and spawned a vast literature. At various points the text relates that YHWH hardened Pharaoh's heart, which kept him from capitulating to YHWH's demand to release his people and so resulted in further plagues falling on Egypt, climaxing in the horrific slaying of all the firstborn of Egypt, not to mention the destruction of the Egyptian army that followed upon further hardening of Pharaoh's heart for that very purpose. This theme gains even greater importance due to Paul's appeal to it in Romans 9 in defence of God's sovereign freedom in election. Therefore, we will give special attention to it in our exegesis of Exod. 9.16 and its context.

One important consideration in approaching the narrative of Exodus 1–15 that goes a long way in ameliorating the difficulties raised by the hardening theme is that YHWH's acts in liberating his people are a response to the Pharaonic and Egyptian oppression of Israel (2.23-25; 3.7-9, 16-17; 4.31; 6.2-8). At the least, the divine hardening of Pharaoh's heart is a judgment upon Pharaoh and his people for their oppression of God's people. We will leave the support and details of this perspective to emerge from our exegesis of the text, turning for the moment to a related detail that is also important to have in mind as one approaches the exodus story, namely that it is the continuation of the story begun in Genesis. Paul would certainly have read Exodus in this way without concern for the text's tradition-historical prehistory, literary sources or redactional stages, and without any question as to its historicity. Just as with our exegesis of Exodus 32–34, we must treat chapters 1–15 as a unity, focusing on its final narrative form and the theology encompassed therein as well as interpreting the parts of these chapters with reference to (roughly in decreasing order of importance) one another, the entire book of Exodus, the Pentateuch and the whole of the Old Testament.[4]

As the continuation of the story of Genesis, the exodus narrative relates the continuation of YHWH's fulfilment of the Abrahamic covenant. Indeed, it was in the context of officially making that covenant that YHWH informed Abraham that his descendants would be enslaved and oppressed in a foreign land, but that YHWH would judge the nation of their oppressors and that they would (therefore) come out of that nation, and with great possessions

---

3.   Here I have provided a broad outline of 1–15.21. A more detailed outline will emerge in our detailed exegesis of the text.

4.   See Abasciano, *Romans 9.1-9*, 46–47; cf. Piper, *Justification*, 160.

at that (Gen. 15.13-14). The narrative portrays YHWH as coming to deliver his people in fulfilment of his covenant promises, a theme that goes hand in hand with the text's most prominent concern to condemn idolatry and reveal YHWH as the incomparably great and uniquely sovereign God. Both themes combine to reveal the character and glory of YHWH, who alone is to be trusted for well-being, an observation that intimates the purpose of the narrative – to encourage Israel to flee idolatry, trust in the Lord alone, and be faithful to the covenant.

Edward Meadors has provided a helpful summary of the exodus story that incorporates these themes as well as the other main theme we have identified, the hardening of Pharaoh's heart:

> Exodus tells the story of what happened when a powerful pagan king challenged Yahweh's covenant with his people Israel. In this story the hardening of Pharaoh's heart is a theological phenomenon that sets in motion God's covenant promise to Abraham to 'curse those who curse you' (Gen 12:3). Pharaoh's hardening and the attendant plagues against Egypt stem from Pharaoh's oppression of Israel and his refusal to let God's people go. Pharaoh's hardening also assists Yahweh's ultimate covenant purpose by prolonging the public display of his absolute power (Exod 4:21; 9:13-17; 10:1) and his commitment to preserve the covenant people (Exod 4:22-23). In this course of events Pharaoh epitomizes the consequence awaiting all human obstacles to the covenant plan of God. The plagues demonstrate the impotence of idolatry and polytheism ... In the end Pharaoh emerges as the archetypal hardened sinner – a classic foil to the character of faithful obedience Yahweh desires in his people Israel.[5]
>   ... Exodus exposes as powerless *all* of Egypt's gods, including Pharaoh, through the plagues and through Pharaoh's hardening. Through plagues God displays that he alone is all-powerful and that covenant with him is the only means of true deliverance. It is in Israel's best interest to remain faithful to him, because he is the only living God.[6]

6.1. *Exodus 1.1-22*[7]

Exodus opens with a report of the household leaders who came to Egypt with Jacob from the Promised Land, the total number of persons in the company and the passing of that generation (1.1-6). This report establishes Exodus as the direct continuation of the story of Genesis, which may be summed up briefly as YHWH undertaking to restore blessing to the world by choosing one man, Abraham (and his descendants), with whom to enter into covenant, making covenant promises to him, and beginning to fulfil those promises.

---

5.   E. P. Meadors, *Idolatry and the Hardening of the Heart: A Study in Biblical Theology* (New York/London: T&T Clark, 2006), 17.
6.   Ibid., 18.
7.   While the main headings given throughout our exegesis will provide an outline of Exod. 1–15, it should be noted that this outline does not necessarily represent the natural flow of the text, but breaks the text up into sections that will most helpfully facilitate our exegesis with its specific concern to understand Paul's use of 9.16 and the hardening theme in Rom. 9.

Exodus continues the story of the process of the fulfilment of the covenant promises of God.

Verse 7 then reports the first word of further fulfilment, the multiplication of Abraham's descendants: 'But the sons of Israel were fruitful, and teemed, and multiplied, and were exceedingly numerous, so that the land was filled with them' (cf. Gen. 12.2; 15.5; 17.4-6; 18.18; 22.17; 26.4; 28.14; 35.11; 46.3).[8] Given the obvious note of fulfilment in v. 7 of the covenantal promise of numerous descendants, it is surprising that more commentators do not mention it.[9] But the allusion can hardly be doubted. Not only is the promise issued repeatedly in Genesis, but it is also issued in the same general context as YHWH's announcement to Abraham that Israel would be enslaved and oppressed in a foreign land, but that they would escape to the Promised Land (Gen. 15.5, 13-16), and then finally repeated as a promise to be fulfilled specifically in Egypt in conjunction with YHWH's promise to bring Israel back to the Promised Land (46.3-5).[10] Hence, the fulfilment of numerous progeny also points forward to the future fulfilment of the promise of land.[11] Taken with what follows, it also points to the future fulfilment of the promise of deliverance.

But even though many commentators fail to observe this important implication of the text, most do recognize an allusion to the creation story of Genesis with its divine blessing of fruitfulness upon humanity (Gen. 1.28), a theme that comes to expression time and again in Genesis, beginning again with the re-creation described after the flood (9.1, 7) and continued by the patriarchal promises mentioned above.[12] Indeed, God's creational intention to bless all of humanity on the one hand and his blessing of fruitfulness on his chosen people on the other hand come together in the conception that

8.   Brueggemann, 'Exodus', 694, goes so far as to say that 1.7 'provides a summary to the book of Genesis'.

9.   Those who do note this include: C. Houtman, *Exodus* (trans. J. Rebel and S. Woudstra; Historical Commentary on the Old Testament; 3 vols; Kampen: Kok, 1993–96), 1.233; T. E. Fretheim, *Exodus* (IBC; Louisville: John Knox, 1991), 24–25; B. S. Childs, *The Book of Exodus: A Critical, Theological Commentary* (OTL; Philadelphia: Westminster, 1974), 2–3; Durham, *Exodus*, 5; and most emphatically, L. Eslinger, 'Freedom or Knowledge? Perspective and Purpose in the Exodus Narrative (Exodus 1–15)', *JSOT* 52 (1991), 43–60 (53). Strangely, E. Kellenberger, *Die Verstockung Pharaos: Exegetische und auslegungsgeschichtliche Untersuchungen zu Exodus 1–15* (BWANT, 171; Stuttgart: Kohlhammer, 2006), 120, is uncertain about the tie to Genesis because he does not find the wording to be exactly the same. Not only is this an overly restrictive criterion that is insensitive to the overall developing Pentateuchal narrative, but 1.7, 9 do use language that was part of God's promise in Genesis of numerous descendants to the patriarchs.

10.   Gen. 46.3's reference to a 'great [גָּדוֹל] nation' surely includes the notion of numerous descendants; see e.g., Wenham, *Genesis*, 441.

11.   Durham, *Exodus*, 5.

12.   This is part of a larger creational concern for the blessing of fruitfulness upon all life, but there is a special concern for the fruitfulness of humanity as the image of God and apex of creation ordained to rule over all other life. Stuart, *Exodus*, 61, stresses that Genesis teaches an ongoing creation; he asserts that Exod. 1.7 shows 'that Israel was in itself a fulfilment of the creation commands'.

after sin arose in the world, YHWH undertook to mediate to all humanity the blessing he originally intended for them through his covenantal blessing of his chosen people (cf. Gen. 12.3; 22.18; 26.4; 28.14). Terence Fretheim has captured this aspect of the text's meaning well:

> Verse 7 connects not only with historical promises but also with the creation/re-creation accounts of Gen. 1:28 and 9:1, 7 ... God's intentions in creation are being realized in this family; what is happening is in tune with God's creational purposes. This is a microcosmic fulfillment of God's macrocosmic design for the world (cf. 40:34-38). Israel is God's starting point for realizing the divine intentions for all.[13]

But the population explosion of Exod. 1.7 is obviously more than a natural and automatic outworking of YHWH's creational intentions. The verse records a *supernatural* blessing of fruitfulness by packing 'into the verse about every possible way of saying that the Israelites rapidly increased in number'.[14] This is, as we have stressed, a fulfilment of God's covenant promises to his people.

It is ironic then that it is actually this supernatural blessing that provokes the oppression and enslavement that Israel came to suffer at the hands of the Egyptians. Exodus 1.8-22 report the harsh and oppressive Egyptian response to Israel's extraordinary growth. The Pharaoh

> said to his people, 'Behold, the people of the sons of Israel are too numerous and mighty for us. Come, let us deal shrewdly with him, lest he multiply and it be, if war breaks out, that he himself joins with those who hate us, and fights against us and departs from the land'. So they appointed slave-gang overseers in order to afflict him in their burdens. And he built cities of storage for Pharaoh, Pithom and Raamses. But the more they afflicted him, the more he multiplied and the more he spread. So they were in dread because of the sons of Israel. Therefore the Egyptians harshly made the sons of Israel labour as slaves. Thus they made their lives bitter with hard labour in mortar and in bricks and with all kinds of labour in the field, all their labour which they laboured among them in severity. (1.9-14)

As severe as this treatment of the Israelites is portrayed, the narrator relates that Pharaoh took the oppression of the Israelites to an even more ruthless level when they continued to multiply – he commanded that the Hebrew midwives kill any Hebrew boys born; and when they did not cooperate, he commanded the Egyptian people to carry out the heinous policy of infanticide (1.15-22).

6.2. *Exodus 2.1-22*

Having intimated through the total effect of the story to this point that God would deliver his people from slavery and oppression in fulfilment of his covenant promise, the narrative now begins to tell about the origins and

---

13. Fretheim, *Genesis*, 25; emphasis removed; cf. Durham, *Exodus*, 5.
14. Stuart, *Genesis*, 61.

development of the man that YHWH would choose as deliverer – Moses. He is presented as one who emerges out of the oppression from which he will deliver his people,[15] himself saved from Pharaoh's murderous edict by a series of 'fortuitous' ironies that leave little doubt that he was actually saved by the hand of providence (2.1-10) despite the fact that God is not mentioned in the narrative about Moses' early life (2.1-22).[16] Indeed, as John Durham comments, 'The omission of any reference to God in these verses [2.1-10] is surely intentional. The author is involving the reader in the conclusion of faith which such a narrative must inevitably suggest'.[17]

The story proceeds to a time when Moses, now grown up, definitively identified himself with the people of Israel and their oppression by killing an Egyptian who was beating a fellow Hebrew (2.11-12). But the episode, which gives a glimpse of the beginnings of Moses' delivering role, amounts to something of a false start as Moses meets with rejection at his involvement in the affairs of his own people (2.14)[18] and must flee for his life from Pharaoh when the matter is discovered (2.15). But this brings him to a place (Midian) where his penchant for saving others meets with success. When he saw the daughters of the priest of Midian (Reuel/Jethro) being harassed by shepherds, he drove the shepherds away and served the women by watering their flock (2.16-17), leading to his incorporation into the priest's family and the beginning of his own by marriage to Reuel's daughter Zipporah, followed by the siring of his first son (2.18-22).

All of this brings Moses to the place where he will meet YHWH and receive the call to deliver Israel.[19] Chapter 2 'present[s] us with an exceptional deliverer, exceptionally prepared, in the setting of a persecution precipitated by God's fulfilment of the first half of his promise [progeny], and in anticipation of his fulfilment of the second half of that promise [land]'.[20] The chapter's overarching theme is 'the preparation of the deliverer for his task, itself based, as are the themes of multiplication and oppression, upon the

15.   Durham, *Exodus*, 15.
16.   See ibid., 15, 17; Fretheim, *Exodus*, 37–38, who also details most helpfully the many ironies in Moses' early life and salvation.
17.   Durham, *Exodus*, 17; cf. Fretheim, *Exodus*, 37–40; Childs, *Exodus*, 19.
18.   Enns, *Exodus*, 80–81, points out that the rejection of Moses at this point introduces 'two interconnected themes that recur throughout the Pentateuch: Israel's rebellion and the rejection of Moses' (80).
19.   Durham, *Exodus*, 21, mentions that commentators have often proposed that the literary function of 2.11-22 is to place Moses for theophany and call, though he rightly thinks there is more to the section than that. However, it is unclear whether his suggestion is correct that part of the point of Moses' trip to Midian was to join a people (Reuel and his family) who worship the God of his fathers (22, 24). There is debate over whether the priest is to be considered a worshipper of YHWH or of another god(s). In favour of the former, see e.g. ibid., 244; against it and in favour of the latter, see e.g. Stuart, 100 n. 148, 101, 411–13. J. K. Bruckner, *Exodus* (NIBCOT, 2; Peabody: Hendrickson, 2008), 165, who offers a mediating position, probably has it right that Reuel/Jethro is to be taken as a worshipper of the Creator God prior to his full conversion, which brought him to recognize that God as YHWH. But it may be that he worshipped other gods as well.
20.   Durham, *Exodus*, 15.

theological foundation of the promise of God to the fathers'.[21] In this state of preparation to receive the call of God, Moses has come to embody 'Israel in his own life experience' – at odds with the Egyptians and oppressed by them, 'fleeing from Egypt to the wilderness, where he encounters God at Sinai', a sojourner in a foreign land.[22]

6.3. *Exodus 2.23-25*

Exodus 2.23-25 is an important transitional section that functions as a literary hinge, concluding the previous sections (1.1–2.22) and pointing forward to what is to come.[23] It reaches back to the previous narrative by recalling the miserable state of Israel under Egyptian oppression. It also updates a thread of the earlier narrative by reporting the death of the Pharaoh who sought Moses' death, removing a major impediment to the narrative moving forward through the chosen deliverer's ability to return to Egypt.[24] But it indicates that the change of Pharaoh did not bring a change to Egypt's harsh oppression of Israel, implying that the new Pharaoh continued his predecessor's tyrannical policies and placing the reader squarely in the present of the story world as it continues in the vein of the past.[25]

Yet these verses do report two more very important changes. One is that Israel cried out to God in distress from the agony inflicted upon them by the Egyptians.[26] The description of their appeal to God heavily emphasizes the wretchedness of their situation and the fact that it was due to the slavery imposed on them by their oppressors, implicitly drawing attention to the Egyptians' injustice and guilt in the matter: 'The sons of Israel groaned because of the slave labour. And they cried out, and their cry for help went up to God because of the slave labour' (2.23b).

The second additional change in the situation arises directly from the first: 'Therefore God heard their groaning, and God remembered his covenant with Abraham, with Isaac, and with Jacob. God saw the sons of Israel, and

---

21.   Ibid., 21.

22.   Fretheim, *Exodus*, 42, which see for further detail; capitalization and emphasis removed. Fretheim also details how 'Moses' action anticipates/foreshadows God's action' (42–43; capitalization and emphasis removed).

23.   Cf. e.g., Durham, *Exodus*, 24–26; Stuart, *Exodus*, 102; Childs, *Exodus*, 32–33; G. W. Coats, *Exodus 1–18* (FOTL, 2A; Grand Rapids: Eerdmans, 1999), 33–34.

24.   Cf. Durham, *Exodus*, 25; Stuart, ibid.

25.   Cf. D. M. Gunn, 'The "Hardening of Pharaoh's Heart": Plot, Character and Theology in Exodus 1–14', in D. J. A. Clines, D. M. Gunn and A. J. Hauser (eds), *Art and Meaning: Rhetoric in Biblical Literature* (JSOTSup, 19; Sheffield: JSOT, 1982), 72–96 (74); Meadors, *Idolatry*, 27.

26.   So most scholars. Brueggemann, 'Exodus', 706, asserts that the Israelites' cry was not directed to God, but the language is frequently used of laments to God (Fretheim, *Exodus*, 47), the text explicitly says that their cry for help (who else were they asking for help?) went up to God, and Deut. 26.7 states that they cried to the Lord.

God took concerned notice' (2.24-25).[27] The prayers of Israel moved God to attend to their cursed situation of suffering under Egyptian bondage and maltreatment. When he did so, 'God remembered his covenant', which 'is idiomatic for covenant *application* rather than *recollection*', carrying the meaning that 'God decided to honour the terms of his covenant at this time'.[28] So the action God is about to take on behalf of Israel is depicted as a fulfilment of the Abrahamic covenant as dictated by its terms.

One of the foundational promises of the covenant was that of land, a promise that we have seen to imply the deliverance of Israel from Egypt, since God promised them the land of Canaan. We have also seen that God promised specifically to rescue Israel from the very land in which they would be enslaved and to judge the nation of their enslavers (Gen. 15.13-16; 46.3-5), which has turned out to be Egypt. The promise to punish Israel's oppressors is simply an application of a more fundamental covenant promise made to Abraham in Gen. 12.3: 'I will bless those who bless you, and the one who curses you I will curse'.[29] Thus, all that the narrative is about to report concerning God's intervention to rescue Israel from slavery and punish their oppressors results from Pharaoh's/Egypt's oppression of God's covenant people Israel on the one hand, and his faithfulness to his covenant promises to Israel on the other hand. Accordingly, 'This little "postscript" prepares us to expect that God will now take action'.[30]

The significance of this pivotal[31] section can hardly be overestimated for understanding the following narrative as it identifies the impetus for the actions God is about to take in response to the miserable and oppressive situation of Israel described by Exodus 1–2. As H. L. Ellison states, these verses are 'actually the turning point in the story'.[32] Moreover, as Peter Enns observes, they answer a question that 'is crucial for understanding' the book of Exodus, revealing that God would respond to Israel's cry because of his covenant with her.[33] Similarly, Durham notes that, 'Although this postscript

---

27.   It very well could be that 'God took concerned notice' is a scribal corruption, and should read 'he revealed himself to them', as supported by the LXX (so e.g., Stuart, *Exodus*, 104), though most scholars opt to stay with the MT as we have. Articulating the exact nuance of the MT's verb here (וַיֵּדַע) is difficult, for which there are several options, including 'took notice' (NASB), 'was concerned about' (NIV), 'knew' (ESV), 'understood' (NET) and 'acknowledged' (NKJV). In light of the covenantal context, it is tempting to take ידע in its covenantal sense, meaning that God covenantally acknowledged, viz., that he acknowledged Israel as his covenant partner.

28.   Ibid., 103, who also rightly points out that the text refers to 'an ongoing covenant fully applicable to the generations that followed Abraham', as indicated by mention of its renewal to Isaac and Jacob.

29.   Cf. Meadors, *Idolatry*, 17, 36; D. G. Coover Cox, 'The Hardening of Pharaoh's Heart in its Literary and Cultural Contexts', *Bsac* 163 (July–Sept. 2006) 292–311 (294).

30.   Stuart, *Exodus*, 102. Cf. similarly e.g., Houtman, *Exodus*, 1.322–23; Fretheim, *Exodus*, 49; Childs, *Exodus*, 32–33.

31.   Recall that it functions as a literary hinge. See e.g., Brueggemann, 'Exodus', 705, and cf. the references in the previous note.

32.   H. L. Ellison, *Exodus* (DSB; Philadephia: Westminster, 1982), 13.

33.   Enns, *Exodus*, 84.

must certainly interrupt the sequential narrative flow of the story of the book of Exodus, it does so with a telling emphasis upon what that story is all about'.[34] In fact, the interruption to the sequential flow of the narrative posed by 2.23-25 makes the verses even more prominent, underscoring their importance. Introducing the following narrative of God's salvation of Israel and judgment of Egypt and her Pharaoh, they provide the lens through which it is to be understood.

Thus, this passage establishes God's salvation of Israel and judgment of Egypt, including the hardening of Pharaoh's heart that is so prominent throughout the narrative, as (1) conditional on Pharaoh's sin against Israel and Israel's appeal for help, and (2) an expression of God's faithfulness to his covenant promises to Israel. The conditional nature of the divine hardening of Pharaoh's heart is of paramount importance for considering Paul's use of the theme in Romans 9, since one of the main questions generated by the historical debate concerning this aspect of Paul's argument is whether God's judgment of Pharaoh is conditional or unconditional,[35] and some scholars have attempted to argue that Exodus presents it as unconditional with a view toward supporting the contention that Paul argues for unconditional election.[36] The bearing of 2.23-25 on the question has escaped the notice of most interpreters, probably because they have failed to pay attention to the whole and proper context of the hardening theme (Exodus 1–15).[37] Indeed, it is hard to read the passage contextually in any other way than as providing the provocation for God's action on behalf of Israel and hardening judgment against Pharaoh.[38] In fact, the conditional nature of God's action in response

34.   Durham, *Exodus*, 26.
35.   See G. K. Beale, 'An Exegetical and Theological Consideration of the Hardening of Pharaoh's Heart in Exdous 4–14 and Romans 9', *TJ* 5 NS (1984) 129–54 (130).
36.   For example, Beale, 'Hardening'; Piper, *Justification*, 159–81.
37.   For example, Piper, *Justification*, 159–71, limits his attention to Exod. 4–14; Beale, 'Hardening', implicitly acknowledges that Exod. 1–15 is the proper context of the hardening theme (130), but then only gives detailed attention to 3.18ff.; and despite the inclusion of Exod. 1–15 in the title, Kellenberger, *Verstockung*, gives very little attention to Exod. 1–2. Cf. P. Gilbert, 'Libre arbitre et déterminisme: Une réflexion sur la figure de Pharaon', *Theoforum* 32 (2001) 5–21 (5 n. 3), who notes that Exod. 1–3 is important for the interpretation of chs 4–14. See further C. D. Isbell, 'Exodus 1–2 in the Context of Exodus 1–14: Story Lines and Key Words', in Clines, Gunn and Hauser (eds), *Art and Meaning*, 37–61.
38.   Indeed, Neh. 9.9-10 explicitly states that God acted against Pharaoh and Egypt because he knew they had acted arrogantly against his people. Even if one were to approach the text of Exodus with the presupposition of exhaustive divine determinism, it would still need to be admitted that the text portrays God as responding to Egypt's oppression of Israel and her cry for help, which therefore serve as conditions for the divine action. In my opinion, the attempt to read texts such as these deterministically would only show up the inadequacy of determinism to account for Scripture's frequent reference to conditions, for it essentially renders any difference between conditional and unconditional action meaningless, especially if raised to nullify the theological significance of conditions. One could argue that since God foretold of Israel's slavery while making his covenant with Abraham, then Egypt's enslavement of Israel should be understood as part of the covenant terms or promises (so Stuart, *Exodus*, 116) and therefore necessarily caused by God. But notice to Abraham that his descendants would be enslaved in a foreign land does not have the character of a

to the report of 2.23-25 is so pronounced that it has led Walter Brueggemann to overstate the text's implications: 'this sequence of events challenges all talk about divine priority and sovereign initiative. The Exodus is not initiated by either the power or the mercy of God. God is the second actor in the drama of liberation. It is Israel's self-assertion that begins the process ... God is a crucial agent in the story of liberation, but is second and not first'.[39] Fretheim, on the other hand, while bold, manages to avoid overstatement while doing justice to the text's far-reaching implications:

> This text signals a change in the portrayal of ... God. The change in Egyptian kings must not be separated from this. The narrative ties these changes together; the one provides the occasion for speaking of the other. Theologically, changes in the world affect the way in which God can be spoken of in relationship to that world. Even more, changes in the world can affect the way in which God is active in that world ... Thus the death of the king in Egypt provides possibilities or opportunities for God that were not available heretofore ... God has a new 'point of view' with respect to the situation. The context has changed among both Egyptians and Israelites such that God's creational intentions for the world can now take a new turn. God can move forward with respect to the divine purposes in new ways.[40]

6.4. *The Commission of Moses, Part 1 (Exodus 3.1–4.20)*

As we have just seen, 2.23-25 suggests that God is about to take action on behalf of his people. Chapter 3 now begins to tell of the action that God took. It begins with God revealing himself to Moses in the burning bush (3.2ff.). He identifies himself as the God of Abraham, Isaac and Jacob, establishing that this is the same God as the God of Genesis and the covenant promises to Abraham and his seed (3.6)[41] just as do the opening verses of the book and 2.23-25, all of which evoke God's commitment to fulfil his covenant promises. Accordingly, YHWH goes on to indicate his intention to deliver his people:

> And YHWH said, 'I have certainly seen the affliction of my people who are in Egypt, and I have heard their cry because of his slave-drivers, for I know his sufferings. Therefore I have come down to deliver him from the hand of the Egyptians to bring him up from that land to a good and spacious land, to a land flowing with milk and honey, to the place of the Canaanites and the Hittites and the Amorites and the Perizzites and the Hivites and the Jebusites. So now, behold, the cry of the sons of Israel has come to me, and I have also seen the oppression with which the Egyptians

stipulation or a promise (with friends like that, who needs enemies?). It is better understood as the necessary background for understanding the covenant promises that God would rescue Israel from slavery, judge their oppressors and bring the people to the Promised Land. For more on the possibility that Egypt's oppression of Israel is to be attributed to YHWH from the start, see further my response to Beale's invocation of Ps. 105.25 toward this end in section 6.7 below.

39.   Brueggemann, 'Exodus', 707.
40.   Fretheim, *Exodus*, 47, 49.
41.   Cf. Houtman, *Exodus*, 1.350; Stuart, *Exodus*, 116.

are oppressing them. So now, go in order that I may send you to Pharaoh. And bring out my people, the sons of Israel, from Egypt'. (3.7-10)

Just like 2.23-25, these verses reveal YHWH's concern for Israel and stress that YHWH is taking action on behalf of Israel in response to their suffering of unjust oppression at the hands of the Egyptians and their cry arising from it. Just as YHWH's self-identification as the God of Abraham, Isaac and Jacob (3.6), the double reference to Israel as his people (3.7, 10) and the reference to them as 'the sons of Israel' call to mind God's covenant with them,[42] evoking again that the action YHWH is beginning to undertake is in fulfilment of his covenant with this people. All of this underscores the conditional nature of YHWH's judging and saving actions in the narrative that follows, a feature that is further underscored by YHWH's inclusion of Moses in his plan to judge Egypt and liberate Israel in such a way that YHWH's own plan is partially contingent on Moses' cooperation, allowing Moses to resist the divine will and leading YHWH to make the effort to persuade Moses to do as he asks and even to modify his plan in response to Moses' input (3.11–4.17).

We have noted (1) the pivotal role of 2.23-25 in providing the lens through which the main exodus narrative is to be understood and (2) that 3.7-10 is very similar to 2.23-25. Hence, it is not surprising to find Fretheim drawing attention to the great importance of 3.7-10 even as he takes note of its similarity to 2.24-25: 'Verses 7-10 are similar to 2:24-25 but constitute an important advance in the narrative. While 2:24-25 is the narrator's report concerning what God is doing, 3:7-10 is the direct speech of God. This, the first word of God in Exodus, is *programmatic*; it both sets all that follows into motion and reveals the kind of God it is who acts in the narrative to follow'.[43] By repeating the essence of 2.23-25 in YHWH's own words as he begins to take the action adumbrated by those earlier verses, the text confirms and strengthens its emphasis on the conditional nature of YHWH's actions in judging Egypt and saving Israel, and the character of those actions as an expression of his covenant faithfulness.[44] Repetition of the emphasis thrusts it upon the reader again as the necessary background for understanding the following narrative.

Moses questions his own worthiness to be God's emissary to Pharaoh, which meets with encouragement from YHWH in the form of a promise that the divine presence would be with him (3.11-12). At Moses' request, God reveals his name to Moses so that he can identify him to the people of Israel, followed by instructions as to what he should say to them about this new movement of God for their liberation (3.13-17). Yet again the same themes we have witnessed in 2.23-25 and 3.7-10 are repeated. God instructs

42. Cf. Fretheim, *Exodus*, 59. Gunn, 'Hardening', 82, notes the covenantal language of God's response to Israel's oppression.

43. Fretheim, ibid.; emphasis original.

44. Gunn, 'Hardening', 82, stresses fulfilment of covenant obligation as YHWH's motivation for taking action.

Moses to identify him to the sons of Israel as YHWH, the God of Abraham, Isaac and Jacob, implicitly invoking, as before, the covenant relationship and YHWH's commitment to fulfil his covenant promises (3.15). The next verse repeats the same self-identification for Moses to communicate to the elders of Israel, stressing the same themes still more as YHWH also directs Moses to tell the elders, 'I have indeed attended to you and what was done to you in Egypt. So I said, "I will bring you up out of the affliction of Egypt to the land [of Cannan] ..."' (3.16-17). YHWH then informs Moses that Israel's leaders would heed his message, and he instructs him concerning what they should do: 'Go, you and the elders of Israel, to the king of Egypt and say to him, "YHWH, the God of the Hebrews, has met with us. So now, please let us go a journey of three days in the wilderness in order that we may sacrifice to YHWH our God"' (3.18b). We should note that the request is to be presented in the name of YHWH, which raises it from a mere desire for a vacation, or even for freedom, to God's claim upon Israel and his demand laid upon Egypt and her Pharaoh.

This request probably implies 'full and permanent departure from Egypt' in accordance with ancient Near Eastern custom of making requests that literally state less than they mean.[45] Thus, while it was undoubtedly to be expected that Pharaoh would deny even a more modest request for the nation to take leave of their slave labour to go on a three-day trip,[46] his denial is even more expected in this case. Stuart explains: 'What they were asking for was the very sort of thing that could create the situation his predecessor feared, namely, an Israelite movement of separate national identity, disassociating itself from Egypt and heading out into Asiatic reaches where the Israelites might join with anti-Egyptian forces and become effective enemies of Pharaoh and his people' (cf. 1.10).[47] Of course, granting the request would also result in the loss of a huge slave labour force, a benefit of inestimable value.

45.   Stuart, *Exodus*, 124–25 (quotation from 124); Houtman, *Exodus*, 1.376–77; R. A. Cole, *Exodus: An Introduction and Commentary* (TOTC, 2; Leicester; Downer's Grove: IVP, 1973), 71–72. On other views of the request, see Cole and esp. Houtman, who notes some who see the request as deceptive, but that interpreters typically see a sincere request that, if granted, eventually would have led to a request for complete freedom.

46.   This is true despite the fact that 'the Egyptians did give their laborers vacations of a week or two, sometimes for explicitly religious holidays' (W. H. C. Propp, *Exodus 1–18: A New Translation with Introduction and Commentary* (AB, 2; New York: Doubleday, 1999), 207), since the oppressive slavery of the Israelites as depicted in Exodus is of a different sort than other forced labourers (Egypt had enacted a policy of systematic infanticide against Israel (1.15-22), many seem to have been slaves in Egyptian households (3.22)), and they were asking for leave for the entire exceedingly numerous nation, a much different thing than a few or even dozens of individual workers asking for time off. Given the situation as reported in Exodus, readers could not be expected to think that the Pharaoh would even be open to granting the nation a short vacation for fear that Israel would never return and even join in war against Egypt (see Stuart's comments below).

47.   Stuart, *Exodus*, 125. The military risk would hold true whether Israel was merely asking for time off or for permanent release. Both would allow Israel the opportunity to go and do as they willed, though permanent release would pose an even greater risk.

Therefore, it is not surprising that God then says, 'But I know that the king of Egypt will not let you go unless by a strong hand' (3.19). Indeed, the addition of the personal pronoun אֲנִי ('I') to the verb, which includes person in its form, appears to highlight YHWH's foreknowledge in this case as an obvious fact.[48] The statement stands in adversative relationship to the direction to request release, as most translations indicate.[49] Despite the request that will be made to Pharaoh, God knows that he will deny it; and despite this knowledge, God insists that Moses and the elders of Israel make it.

There is some question about how to take the phrase וְלֹא בְּיָד חֲזָקָה ('unless by a strong hand'), for the words we have translated as 'unless' (וְלֹא) are more literally 'and not', which means that 3.19 could be understood in an almost completely different way, viz. 'But I know that the king of Egypt will not let you go, not even by a strong hand'. It would express that God knew that Pharaoh would not be able to be compelled to let Israel go. In favour of this alternative understanding is the fact that 'unless' is an unusual meaning of וְלֹא. However, וְלֹא can essentially mean 'unless'[50] and context is determinative for meaning. Here the context virtually demands taking it this way.

Exodus 3.20 explicitly indicates that God would compel Pharaoh to let Israel go: 'So I will stretch out my hand and strike Egypt with all my wonders which I will do in its midst; and after that he will let you go'. Some who take 3.19 as indicating that Pharaoh would not yield to compulsion suggest that

---

48.   See Houtman, *Exodus*, 1.377, who draws out the sense of the construction by translating, 'Of course I know '; Durham, *Exodus*, 35, translates, 'Now I know very well'; cf. B. Jacob, *The Second Book of the Bible: Exodus* (trans. W. Jacob; Hoboken: KTAV, 1992), 80; P. Joüon and T. Muraoka, *A Grammar of Biblical Hebrew* (SB 14/1–14/2; 2 vols; repr. with corrections, Rome: Editrice Pontifico Istituto Biblico, (1991) 1993), § 146a.3. On Pharaoh's refusal as something obviously to be expected, see further J. L. Mackay, *Exodus* (Fearn, Ross-shire: Mentor, 2001), 82; Bruckner, *Exodus*, 73; G. Ashby, *Go Out and Meet with God: A Commentary on the Book of Exodus* (ITC; Grand Rapids: Eerdmans, 1998), 26–27.

49.   The Hebrew conjunction וְ most naturally reads as contrastive here, carrying the meaning 'but'. However, see Durham, ibid.

50.   As in 1 Sam. 20.2; cf. 2 Sam. 13.26; 2 Kgs 5.17. See *HALOT*, s.v. לֹא, § 11.d–12 (cf. § 8); Propp, *Exodus*, 207; W. A. Ford, *God, Pharaoh and Moses: Explaining the Lord's Actions in the Exodus Plagues Narrative* (PBM; Milton Keynes: Paternoster, 2006), 86 n. 8. Stuart, *Exodus*, 126 n. 57, strangely restricts focus to וְלֹא בְּ, which never means 'unless' in any of its 20 occurrences, as if the collocation were a discrete expression. However, it is not וְלֹא together with בְּ that means 'unless', but וְלֹא itself, which occurs close to 1,600 times in the Hebrew Bible. Admittedly, it rarely means 'unless' or the like. But the fact that it can carry this meaning opens up the possibility in this passage, and the question must therefore be decided by context. 4QExod[b] reads כִּי אִם (Propp, 186), a more usual way of expressing 'unless'. But the MT most likely represents the original reading, since וְלֹא is the more difficult reading and כִּי אִם can be explained as a scribal clarification. It is difficult to know if the LXX's ἐὰν μή ('unless') followed a Hebrew *Vorlage* represented by 4QExod[b], or if that is its translation of וְלֹא. The Samaritan Pentateuch's הלוא ('will it not be') is probably too difficult to be original, though not nonsensical as Propp suggests. It supports the same basic understanding of the text as 4QExod[b], the LXX and the typical understanding of MT's וְלֹא, which we are advocating.

the text presupposes a distinction between human compulsion, represented by the mighty hand referred to in 3.19, and the divine compulsion spoken of in 3.20.[51] But there is no indication that this is the case, and the narrative explicitly identifies YHWH's mighty acts against Pharaoh as the 'strong hand' that will compel him to let Israel go (6.1; 13.9, 14, 16; cf. 7.4-5; 9.3, 15; 32.11; Deut. 4.34; 5.15; 6.21; 7.8; 9.26; 26.8; Jer. 32.21; Dan. 9.15, and the various references in Exodus to Moses' hand as the instrument of God's power against Egypt). Therefore, we agree with most translations and interpreters that in 3.19 God predicts that Pharaoh will not let the people go *unless* compelled to do so.[52]

That compulsion is identified by 3.20: the wonders (נִפְלְאֹתַי) God would inflict on Egypt, which undoubtedly refer to the signs and plagues of judgment that he would unleash in response to Pharaoh's stubborn refusal to let God's people go. Together, 3.19 and 3.20 reveal that God's affliction of Egypt will be conditional on Pharaoh's defiance of the divine will and demand since God's intention in the matter is predicated on his foreknowledge of Pharaoh's refusal to heed his demand for Israel's release, as suggested by the *waw*-consecutive grammatical construction that begins 3.20 (וְשָׁלַחְתִּי; 'So I shall stretch out').[53] Though some interpreters believe that God's prediction concerning the need to compel Pharaoh by force to let Israel go hints at the hardening theme introduced in 4.21 and that becomes so prominent in the narrative,[54] nothing is said about that here. As just indicated, the theme is *introduced* in 4.21. It is more accurate to say that 3.19-20 'foreshadows the entire plague narrative and deliverance'.[55] But these verses do explicitly prepare the reader for Pharaoh's denial of God's demand for his people's release and the divine response conditioned upon that refusal along with the will from which it would come. Continuing a stress on God's rousing to action against Egypt and for Israel in response to Egypt's unjust oppression of his people and in faithfulness to his covenant promises, 3.19-20 prepares the reader to view the hardening (and its prediction in 4.21) that God will inflict on Pharaoh's heart as similarly conditional on Pharaoh's (at least initial) refusal to let Israel go, not to mention his prior hostility and mistreatment of the nation.

---

51.   So Stuart, *Exodus*, 125–26; Durham, *Exodus*, 40.

52.   See Houtman, *Exodus*, 1.377–79, for a summary and evaluation of various views of 3.19, including ones not mentioned here, and from which he concludes that the view argued for here is 'the most obvious' (378).

53.   It could be argued that only chronological sequence is envisioned, but it would be very difficult to maintain that there is no logical connection here between Pharaoh's refusal to let Israel go (3.19) and God's subsequent judgment against Egypt (3.20). Hence, most translations indicate logical consequence with the use of 'so' to translate וְ at the beginning of 3.20. This is the most natural reading.

54.   So Stuart, *Exodus*, 126; Beale, 'Hardening', 133. Against this, see Kellenberger, *Verstockung*, 95.

55.   Enns, *Exodus*, 108, speaking specifically of the phrase 'mighty hand'; cf. Durham, *Exodus*, 40.

Excursus 6.1: Initial Thoughts on Relating Exodus 3.19-20 to 4.21

Whether the hardening of Pharaoh's heart is meant to be viewed as partly conditional on his initial refusal remains to be seen from examination of the unfolding narrative, particularly 4.21–7.13. Be that as it may, the prediction of 3.19-20 together with the previous narrative's stress on the conditional nature of God's action against Egypt would predispose the reader to take it this way. Greg Beale essentially argues that God's foreknowledge of Pharaoh's refusal in 3.18-20 is due to his intention to harden Pharaoh's heart and cause him to refuse the divine demand to let Israel go.[56] But this is unlikely because of a fact we noted earlier, that the prospect of the Pharaoh's refusal would have been an obvious expectation and foregone conclusion for anybody and did not need the supernatural knowledge of God to perceive nor the supernatural hardening of God to effect (see further the end of section 6.5.b below). Beale's view is rendered even less likely when we take account of the purpose of the hardening, viz. to embolden Pharaoh to persist in his own already established will to keep Israel under Egyptian oppression against the force of God's mighty wonders wrought before and against him, enabling YHWH to demonstrate his power and sovereignty as well as to enact protracted and fitting judgment against Pharaoh, Egypt and her gods. Without signs displaying God's divine power, there would be no need to embolden Pharaoh's will. Lyle Eslinger's conclusion provides a good illustration of how fundamentally at odds with the text this line of thinking is: 'With this glimpse into the divine character's intention and motivation for hardening the heart of Pharaoh, the narrator has discarded the possibility of telling a tale of real triumphs over the Egyptian king. After this, any conflict or victory can only be seen as a sham'.[57]

Surprisingly, Beale appeals to what he calls general agreement that יָדַע ('to know') 'revolves around the nuance "to be actively-experientially involved in a relationship"', and appears to suggest that its use in 3.19 therefore means that God knowing that Pharaoh will do something is equivalent to him causing Pharaoh to do it necessarily.[58] But this verges on and may even cross into the root fallacy. The word can be used to express 'a multitude of shades of knowledge gained by the senses',[59] as can be seen in any Hebrew lexicon. Indeed, according to R. Bultmann, 'the element of mere information can, of course, be emphasized (Ps. 94:11; 139:1)'.[60]

Upon inspection, the passages Beale cites for support do not lend any credence to his position. Jeremiah 16.21, Ezek. 25.14 and Ps. 106.8 all refer to God causing others to know his judgment or power rather than God's knowledge causing something. And the texts he cites of the use of יָדַע to refer

---

56.   Beale, 'Hardening', 133, 135–36; cf. similarly, Eslinger, 'Freedom', 56.

57.   Eslinger, 'Freedom', 57.

58.   Beale, 'Hardening', 136 n. 37.

59.   P. R. Gilchrist, 'יָדַע', *TWOT*, 1.366–67 (366).

60.   R. Bultmann, 'γινώσκω, κτλ'., *TDNT*, 1.689–719 (697; treating the OT usage of יָדַע).

essentially to election of some sort merely show one of the many possible meanings the term can carry, but not in a text like Exod. 3.19. None of those contexts is comparable to 3.19, which combines יָדַע with כִּי to indicate the content of knowledge – 'to know that' (such knowledge can be more than merely cognitive, but in no case does the knowledge itself establish what is known).[61] The exodus narrative's own repeated emphasis on people knowing that God is the Lord is a good example of this usage, as in 7.17: 'Thus says the LORD, "By this you shall know that I am the LORD: behold, I will strike the water that is in the Nile with the staff that is in my hand, and it will be turned to blood"' ((NASB); see also 6.7; 8.6, 18; 9.14, 29; 10.2, 7; 16.6, 12; 18.11; 21.36; 29.46; 31.13; 34.29). Genesis 22.19 gives an illuminating and indisputable example with God as the subject: 'He said, "Do not stretch out your hand against the lad, and do nothing to him; for now I know that you fear God, since you have not withheld your son, your only son, from Me"' (NASB).

From a more conceptual point of view, Charles Isbell asserts, 'It is widely recognized that for YWHW to **speak** a thing is tantamount to his **creation** of that very thing, for in the biblical idiom, anything spoken by YHWH must inevitably come to pass'.[62] The claim for widespread recognition is questionable; but in any case, the more essential claim plainly runs counter to the biblical evidence. Surely the Bible represents God as *able* to speak things into existence and to make them inevitably come to pass if he so chooses (I believe this *is* widely recognized). But it just as surely shows that he can speak things that he allows to happen or not, depending on the free actions of human beings. YHWH's spoken commands generally fall into this category (e.g., 'You shall have no other gods before Me'; Exod. 20.3). More explicitly, passages such as Jer. 18.5-11 directly contradict Isbell's claim.

* * *

While not unconditional, the exercise of God's sovereign and irresistible power will grant his people favour with the Egyptians when that same power compels Pharaoh to let them go, with the result that the Egyptians will grant the Israelites' requests for silver, gold and clothing, making for a just plundering of the Egyptians (3.21-22). It is possible that this granting of favour is to be thought of as a direct, supernatural control of the will of the Egyptians by God, but it is more likely that it is to be regarded as a result of the great power he would unleash against them, moving them to such fear that they would readily agree to almost any request in hurrying the Israelites out of their land (cf. 11.1-3; 12.33-36). In either case, he takes a different tack with Moses in commissioning him to go to Pharaoh to liberate Israel from Egypt and its slavery.

61.   Cf. R. B. Chisholm Jr, 'Divine Hardening in the Old Testament', *Bsac* 153 (Oct.–Dec. 1996) 410–34 (416–17 n. 20).

62.   C. D. Isbell, *The Function of Exodus Motifs in Biblical Narratives: Theological Didactic Drama* (SBEC, 52; Lewiston: Mellen, 1992), 30; emphasis original.

As we noted earlier, God allows Moses to resist his will to go to Pharaoh as God's emissary (3.10–4.17). In response to Moses' concern that the people might not heed him, God attempts to persuade Moses to do as he asks and provides him with three different signs to convince the Israelites that YHWH had indeed appeared to him, in case they are reluctant to take Moses' word for it (4.1-9). The intention was not that all the signs were necessarily to be performed; but each successive sign provided a more impressive display of divine power *in case* the former sign failed to convince,[63] further indication of YHWH's contingent activity in his dealings with humanity.[64] But this still does not convince Moses to consent to YHWH's assignment. He pleads that he is not eloquent enough for the task, but YHWH rebukes him with the fact of his sovereign power over such human phenomena as sight, hearing and speech, followed by a renewed command to go along with the promise to aid Moses' speech (4.10-12). But Moses remains unconvinced. He simply asks that YHWH send somebody else (4.13), which incites YHWH's anger (14a), yet moves him to modify his plan by appointing Moses' brother Aaron to be Moses' spokesman in order to procure the latter's cooperation (14b-17).

6.5. *The Commission of Moses, Part 2 (Exodus 4.21-23)*

After all of YHWH's efforts to persuade Moses and the eventual compromise he offered, Moses finally consents to go as he has been asked (4.18-20). Exodus 4.21 finally brings us to the introduction of the theme of the hardening of Pharaoh's heart:

> YHWH said to Moses, 'When you go back to Egypt pay attention to all the wonders which I have placed in your hand so that you perform them before Pharaoh. But I myself will strengthen his heart and he will not let the people go. Then you will say to Pharaoh, "Thus says YHWH: 'Israel is my son, my firstborn. I said to you, "Let my son go so that he may serve me". But you have refused to let him go. Behold, I will kill your son, your firstborn'."' (4.21-23)

YHWH commands Moses to make sure that he performs the miracles YHWH had enabled him to do (4.21a). But along with the performance of

---

63. On the escalation of impressiveness in each successive miraculous sign, see Stuart, *Exodus*, 130–31.

64. On this contingency as portrayed by Exod. 4.1-17, see further Fretheim's comments (*Exodus*, 67–75) on these verses, though he misreads this as presenting God's foreknowledge as not absolute. For a different and less convincing perspective, which sees no freedom of choice for Moses, see Brueggemann, 'Exodus', 719–20. On the story as a whole, Gunn, 'Hardening', 84–89, presents a sort of mediating position that views Moses as mostly controlled by YHWH, practically a puppet for most of the story, but allowed a measure of freedom, yielding the risk of insecurity for YHWH, creating external pressure on him and circumscribing his actions. But he misses the mark by going to both extremes, at first overplaying YHWH's causation in relation to Moses and failing to observe the dynamic interplay between the two, and then overplaying the freedom given to Moses as if it could put the almighty sovereign God portrayed in Exodus at risk or force his actions.

these miracles, which would normally force compliance by their application of divine power and pressure, YHWH will strengthen/harden Pharaoh's will, which was already set against letting Israel go (1.10; cf. 2.23-25), to persist in its resolve in the face of the miracles. This would bring about the intended result that Pharaoh would continue to refuse YHWH's demand to let Israel go, which would eventually culminate in YHWH slaying Pharaoh's own firstborn son. In order to apprehend further the meaning of 4.21-23, we will now assess its terminology for strengthening/hardening the heart along with similar language throughout Exodus 4–14.

6.6. *The Vocabulary of Hardening*

As is well known, Exodus 4–14 uses three different roots for hardening: חזק, כבד and קשה. Before discussing their meanings, we will list their occurrences along with Hebrew verbal stems and conjugations, equivalents from the LXX, and translation of enough context to show the person, number, subject and object of the verb:[65]

Exodus 4.21:   חזק   piel imperfect; σκληρυνῶ
YHWH said to Moses, 'When you go back to Egypt, pay attention to all the wonders which I have placed in your hand so that you perform them before Pharaoh. But <u>I myself will strengthen his heart</u> and he will not let the people go.
Exodus 7.3:   קשה   hiphil imperfect; σκληρυνῶ
But <u>I myself will harden Pharaoh's heart</u>, and so I will multiply my signs and wonders in the land of Egypt.
Exodus 7.13:   חזק   qal converted imperfect; κατίσχυσεν
Yet <u>Pharaoh's heart was strong</u>, and he did not listen to them, as YHWH had said.
Exodus 7.14:   כָּבֵד   masculine singular adjective;[66] βεβάρηται
Then YHWH said to Moses, '<u>Pharaoh's heart is heavy</u>; he refuses to let the people go'.
Exodus 7.22:   חזק   qal converted imperfect; ἐσκληρύνθη
But the magicians of Egypt did the same by their secret arts, and so <u>Pharaoh's heart grew strong</u>, and he did not listen to them, as YHWH had said.

---

65. I have also underlined the most relevant part of the translated text. This listing of the distribution of Exodus 4–14's hardening statements combines information from Meadors, *Idolatry*, 19–20, and Piper, *Justification*, 159–60, following the former for the basic structure of the presentation, and supplementing with additional information from the latter. Translations are mine. Meadors apparently missed the hardening statement of 13.15, though he may have omitted it because it does not explicitly speak of Pharaoh's heart. For a detailed chart of many aspects of the exodus narrative related to its hardening theme, see Bailey, *Exodus*, 114–15; cf. similar charts in Enns, *Exodus*, 194; N. M. Sarna, *Exploring Exodus: The Heritage of Biblical Israel* (New York: Schocken, 1986), 76.
66. Piper, ibid., incorrectly labels this as a verb in the perfect when it is actually an adjective.

Exodus 8.11 (15):[67] כבד hiphil infinitive absolute; ἐβαρύνθη

But when Pharaoh saw that there was relief, <u>he made his heart heavy</u>, and he did not listen to them, as YHWH had said.

Exodus 8.15 (19): חזק qal converted imperfect; ἐσκληρύνθη

Then the magicians said to Pharaoh, 'It is the finger of God'. But <u>Pharaoh's heart was strong</u>, and he did not listen to them, as YHWH had said.

Exodus 8.28 (32): כבד hiphil converted imperfect; ἐβάρυνεν

Then <u>Pharaoh made his heart heavy</u> this time also, and he did not let the people go.

Exodus 9.7: כבד qal converted imperfect; ἐβαρύνθη

And Pharaoh sent, and behold, not even one of the cattle of Israel had died. But <u>Pharaoh's heart was heavy</u>, and he did not let the people go.

Exodus 9.12: חזק piel converted imperfect; ἐσκλήρυνεν

But <u>YHWH strengthened Pharaoh's heart</u>, and he did not listen to them, as YHWH had said to Moses.

Exodus 9.34: כבד hiphil converted imperfect; ἐβάρυνεν

But when Pharaoh saw that the rain and the hail and the thunder ceased, he sinned again <u>and made his heart heavy</u>, he and his servants.

Exodus 9.35: חזק qal converted imperfect; ἐσκληρύνθη

<u>So Pharaoh's heart was strong</u>, and therefore he did not let the sons of Israel go, as YHWH had said by the hand of Moses.

Exodus 10.1: כבד hiphil perfect; ἐσκλήρυνα

Then YHWH said to Moses, 'Go to Pharaoh, for <u>I myself have made his heart heavy, and the heart of his servants</u> for the purpose of my putting these signs of mine in his midst'.

Exodus 10.20: חזק piel converted imperfect; ἐσκλήρυνεν

<u>But YHWH strengthened Pharaoh's heart</u>, and he did not let the sons of Israel go.

Exodus 10.27: חזק piel converted imperfect; ἐσκλήρυνεν

<u>But YHWH strengthened Pharaoh's heart</u>, and he was not willing to let them go.

Exodus 11.10: חזק piel converted imperfect; ἐσκλήρυνεν

So Moses and Aaron did all these wonders before Pharaoh, <u>but YHWH strengthened Pharaoh's heart</u>, and he did not let the sons of Israel go from his land.

Exodus 13.15: קשה hiphil perfect; ἐσκλήρυνεν

It came about that when <u>Pharaoh was stubborn about letting us go</u>, YHWH killed every firstborn in the land of Egypt, from the firstborn of man even unto the firstborn of beast.

Exodus 14.4: חזק piel[68] converted perfect; σκληρυνῶ

<u>And so I will strengthen Pharaoh's heart</u>, and he will chase after them, and I will get glory through Pharaoh and all his army, and the Egyptians will know that I am YHWH.

---

67.   When different, English versification is given in parentheses or brackets throughout this investigation unless otherwise noted.

68.   Piper, *Justification*, 160, incorrectly identifies this as a hiphil.

Exodus 14.8:   חזק   piel converted imperfect; ἐσκλήρυνεν
Thus YHWH strengthened the heart of Pharaoh, King of Egypt, and so he
chased after the sons of Israel while they were going out boldly.
Exodus 14.17:   חזק   piel participle; σκληρυνῶ
And I, behold, will strengthen the heart of the Egyptians so that they will
go in after them and I will thus get glory through Pharaoh and through all
his army, through his chariots and through his horsemen.

Scholars disagree over whether the three words used for hardening are
wholly synonymous in the exodus narrative,[69] or whether they bear some
difference in meaning, even if slight.[70] According to Meadors, most studies
find the terms to have slightly different connotations from one another.[71]
Our research corroborates this view, as the following discussion will
show.

6.6.a. Heart (לֵב)

Before examining the three main words used for hardening, it will be
helpful to look at the meaning of the Hebrew word for 'heart' (לֵב), which
is used in combination with each of them. We are not merely interested
in what it means to harden, but more specifically, what does it mean to
harden the *heart*?[72] It is widely recognized that the Hebrew term for heart,

69.   So Cole, *Exodus*, 77; R. L. Harris, *TWOT*, 1.276; A. E. Steinmann, 'Hardness of
Heart', *DOTP*, 381–83 (382); Stuart, *Exodus*, 146–49; Bruckner, *Exodus*, 73; J. E. Currid,
'Why Did God Harden Pharaoh's Heart'?, *BRev* 9 (1993) 46–51 (48); Piper, *Justification*,
161.
70.   So G. Bush, *Notes, Critical and Practical on the Book of Exodus* (2 vols in 1;
Boston: Henry A. Young & Co., 1870), 1.65 (Bush sees a marked difference between the
terms); R. T. Forster and V. P. Marston, *God's Strategy in Human History* (Eugene, OR: Wipf
and Stock, 2nd edn, 2000), 64–65, 267–71; Beale, 'Hardening', 147–48; Ashby, *Exodus*, 40;
Mackay, *Exodus*, 131; Kellenberger, *Verstockung*, 45–47; Meadors, *Idolatry*, 20–21.
71.   Meadors, *Idolatry*, 20. I would concur, but point out that the consensus is not
strong, and that many take the 'wholly synonymous' view. However, there does seem to be
a strong consensus that the terms are at least largely synonymous, even if they bear some
difference in connotation. So Kellenberger, *Verstockung*, 32, is still correct to say that most
view the terms as 'mehr oder weniger Synonymität'.
72.   There is one instance of a hardening statement that does not reference the heart
– 13.15 – but its meaning is functionally equivalent to the rest of the hardening statements;
contra Isbell, *Function*, 34–35, who thinks that the verb's combination with an infinitive
conveys a different idea, though he does not take into account grammatical considerations
that suggest that the statement of 13.15 is basically equivalent to the other hardening
statements in Exodus 4–14. According to M. Zipor, 'קשה', *TDOT*, 13.189–95 (193),
13.15 is an example of the hiphil of קשה used without an object, and such use 'is generally
considered an elliptical construction, with the obj. "neck", "heart", "or [sic] "spirit" to be
supplied'. But Zipor also mentions the possibility that the hiphil may be used intransitively,
which seems to be the most likely sense, especially in light of the intransitive and stative
senses of the qal and the unlikelihood that the construct infinitive is to be taken as the
object of the verb in this instance. Both of these possibilities make the construction basically

which corresponds almost completely with the Egyptian word for heart,[73] 'functions in all dimensions of human existence and is used as a term for all the aspects of a person: vital, affective, noetic, and voluntative',[74] with 'a dominant metaphorical use in reference to the center of human psychical and spiritual life, to the entire inner life of a person'.[75] Its metaphorical range of meaning includes inclination, determination/courage, will, reason, mind, conscience, strength and the inner self as the seat of emotion.[76] But as Heinz-Joseph Fabry points out, Old Testament anthropology viewed individuals as composite in their make-up.[77] Thus, Beale may give the best basic definition of לֵב as 'that faculty which combines into a psychical unity the volitional, intellectual, emotional and spiritual aspects of a person'.[78] He goes on to judge that, 'Among these the volitional, decision-making aspects should be viewed as primary but always influenced by the thoughts and emotions, all of which impinge on the spiritual'.[79]

Be that as it may generally, the volitional and decision-making aspects are certainly primary in the hardening of Pharaoh's heart, yielding the primary sense of 'will' and/or 'mind/reason' for 'heart'. For the text clearly has to do with Pharaoh's will with respect to YHWH's demand that he let Israel go and his decision regarding this matter, resulting in common reference to obstinacy, obduracy, stubbornness and the like in discussion of the hardening of Pharaoh's heart among commentators. It is difficult to say whether one of these aspects, the will (volitional) or the mind (reason/decision-making), is more fundamental than the other, because the two are so intertwined.[80] The will directs the decision of the mind and the judgments of the mind influence the will. Both are typically in view in the hardening statements of Exodus, and one may be more fundamental in any given statement. But generally, reference to the will is probably most fundamental as that which directs Pharaoh's decision to refuse Israel's release. The 'will' seems to go best with the specific vocabulary of hardening, especially the most fundamental word used of the phenomenon in the text – חזק (see 6.5.b below). It is more natural to speak of the will being strengthened/hardened than the mind/reason.

The Egyptian background of the exodus story throws further light upon the function of Pharaoh's heart specifically and the significance of YHWH

---

equivalent to the other hardening statements. See further note 111 below.

73. N. Shupak, *Where Can Wisdom Be Found?: The Sage's Language in the Bible and in Ancient Egyptian Literature* (OBO, 130; Fribourg/Göttingen: University Press/Vandenhoeck & Ruprecht, 1993), 299 (cited by Meadors, *Idolatry*, 14); Beale, 'Hardening', 132–33.

74. H.-J. Fabry, 'לֵב', *TDOT*, 7.399–437 (412).

75. A. Luc, 'לֵב', *NIDOTTE*, 2.749–54 (749).

76. See the entry on לֵב in *HALOT*. For a full discussion of the complete range of meaning, see Fabry, 'לֵב'.

77. Fabry, 'לֵב', 412–13.

78. Beale, 'Hardening', 132.

79. Ibid., who notes that Eichrodt, Johnson and Jacob have reached similar conclusions.

80. Cf. Fabry, 'לֵב', 423.

hardening it so as to exercise substantial control over it. '[T]he king of Egypt's heart was held to be the locus for control of cosmic order'.[81] It was Pharaoh's role and responsibility to uphold the cosmic order. By exercising control over Pharaoh's heart, YHWH showed that the religion of Egypt was false along with her king's claims to deity and supreme sovereignty, and that he himself was the true God and the true sovereign.

One further piece of Egyptian background related to the heart to consider at this point is that 'Egyptians prized the ability to appear strong, firm, resolute, and unmoved by events', describing 'it as being "hard of heart"'.[82] Ironically, the very quality prized by Pharaoh and the Egyptians turns out to be their undoing, functioning as something of a judgment on their basic convictions. By hardening Pharaoh's heart, YHWH showed up Pharaoh and the idolatrous system he represented for what it was – vastly inferior to YHWH, powerless before the sovereign might of the one true God. As Dorian Coover Cox describes it, 'when the Lord hardened Pharaoh's heart, Pharaoh lost control. He could not maintain the appearance of being unflappable or of controlling the elements vital to Egypt, and the truth about his sinful character came out. By both the Lord's standards and Pharaoh's own, Pharaoh was inadequate'.[83]

6.6.b. *To Be Strong/Firm/Bold (חזק)*

As can be seen from the listing of hardening statements above, חזק is the most prominent and fundamental word used to describe the hardening of Pharaoh's heart. Its basic meaning is 'to be/become strong', 'from which all

---

81. Coover Cox, 'Hardening', 307. See also Beale, 'Hardening', 149; B. A. Strawn, 'Pharaoh', *DOTP*, 631–36 (635); Currid, 'Harden', 51; idem, *Ancient Egypt and the Old Testament* (Grand Rapids: Baker, 1997), 118–20; J. H. Sailhamer, *The Pentateuch as Narrative: A Biblical-Theological Commentary* (Library of Biblical Interpretation; Grand Rapids: Zondervan, 1992), 252. Meadors, *Idolatry*, 25 n. 25, objects to Beale's articulation of this point because the text he cites does not refer to Pharaoh. But Beale's point is that, since the Pharaoh was viewed as the divine incarnation of the gods Re and Horus, whom the cited text represents as exercising 'absolute control over everything by means of their *hearts*', then the heart of the living Pharaoh should also be understood as possessing the same power.

82. Coover Cox, 'Hardening', 306, following Shupak. Kellenberger, *Verstockung*, 44, finds the basis of Shupak's case unsatisfactory as presented in N. Shupak, 'ḤZQ, KBD, QŠH LĒB: The Hardening of Pharaoh's Heart in Exodus 4:1–15:21 – Seen Negatively in the Bible but Favorably in Egyptian Sources', in G. N. Knoppers and A. Hirsch (eds), *Egypt, Israel and the Mediterranean Worlds: Studies in Honor of Donald B. Redford* (Probleme der Ägyptologie, 20; Leiden: Brill, 2004), 389–403, but he does not say why.

83. Coover Cox, 'Hardening', 307. This effectively harmonizes the narrator's polemical use of both the positive Egyptian language of hardness of heart and the negative Egyptian concept of heaviness of heart (see the treatment of כבד in section 6.5.c below). Shupak, ibid., generalizes too much in her characterization of the Egyptian terminology as positive and the Hebrew as negative. Indeed, she herself acknowledges that the Egyptian terminology and some of the Hebrew can be used either positively or negatively (394–96).

other meanings that are found can be derived'.[84] Robert Wilson has provided a helpful description of the term's basic range of meaning and its application to the heart/mind:

> The basic meaning of חָזַק[85] is 'to be firm or strong' (Judg 7:11; 2 Sam 2:7; Ezek 30:21), and the verb also has the extended meaning 'to be courageous' (Deut 31:6, 7, 23; Josh 1:6, 7, 9, 18; 10:25; 23:6; 2 Sam 10:12; 13:28; 1 Kgs 2:2). Therefore, the firm heart or mind is one that is steadfast, unswerving in its purpose, unchanging, and courageous (Pss 27:14; 31:25 [24]; Josh 11:20). However, if the course of action being pursued by a firm-hearted and persistent person is one that ought to be changed, then the person's persistence is seen in a negative light and can be called 'stubbornness' (Ezek 2:3-4; 3:7-9; Jer 5:3). Thus, the description 'firmhearted' can be either positive or negative, depending on the point of view of the person using the description.[86]

In light of this data, Coover Cox judiciously concludes, 'The phrases "to strengthen his resolve" or "to become firmly determined" convey the thought'.[87] However, Wilson too quickly combines the notion of courage with the element of resoluteness, appearing to assume that since חָזַק can mean 'to be strong-willed' and 'to be courageous', that it therefore carries both meanings when applied to the heart. But the sense of strong will/determination must be considered primary, and any notion of courage/boldness must be indicated by the context, for the latter implies the former but the former does not necessarily imply the latter, though it can be the cause of the latter when present. Nevertheless, Wilson's assumption proves true in the case of Pharaoh, for the context of the exodus narrative does indeed indicate that Pharaoh's strength of will had to do with persisting in its course against the overwhelmingly fearsome opposition of divine power brought to bear in the miraculous signs and devastating plagues doled out by YHWH.[88] Exodus 14.17 makes the sense of boldness particularly clear, as it speaks of YHWH strengthening the heart of the Egyptians to chase after Israel into the sea that YHWH would part,[89] a reference in which the idea of stubbornness has receded into the background.

Exodus 4.21's introduction of the hardening theme tightly connects the wonders Moses was to perform with the hardening of Pharaoh's heart. The Hebrew construction of 4.21 marks the verse's hardening statement

84.   F. Hesse, 'חָזַק', *TDOT*, 4.301–08 (301).
85.   I have replaced Wilson's transliteration with the Hebrew.
86.   R. R. Wilson, 'The Hardening of Pharaoh's Heart', *CBQ* 41 (1979) 18–36 (23).
87.   Coover Cox, 'Hardening', 306. Presumably, the former phrase refers to the use of the (factitive) piel (to strengthen/make strong) and the latter phrase refers to the use of the (stative) qal (to be strong).
88.   Others who see the giving of strength/courage to Pharaoh as part of the hardening of his heart include: Bush, *Exodus*, 65; Forster/Marston, *Strategy*, 63–69, 264–70 (who also cite G. A. Chadwick); Propp, *Exodus*, 217; Bailey, *Exodus*, 113–14; Gilbert, 'Libre arbitre', 16, 21; Coover Cox, ibid.; Morison, *Exposition*, 144–47; cf. Bruckner, *Exodus*, 73. Hesse, 'חָזַק', 308, and Piper, *Justification*, 161, deny the nuance.
89.   Cf. Chadwick (cited by Forster/Marston, *Strategy*, 265).

as a disjunctive clause that is almost certainly to be taken as contrastive,[90] indicating action YHWH will take that will work against what would normally result from the wonders he would perform. As Beale describes the logic, 'In 4:21 two functions are in view: (1) Moses' sign-performing function would supposedly influence Pharaoh to release Israel; (2) Yahweh's hardening function was to influence Pharaoh negatively toward refusal, thus reversing any positive effect the signs might have had'.[91] Consequently, hardening is to be construed as conditional on signs and חזק is best taken to mean 'to be or become strong/bold'.

Excursus 6.2: The Relationship between Signs and Hardening

Beale strains to try and drive a substantial separation between signs and hardening.[92] Chisholm rightly complains of Beale's 'overly atomistic syntactical approach' in trying to dismiss the grammatically tight connection between 4.21a and 4.21b based on the fluidity of the conjunction ן that connects them.[93] It is the entire *waw* + subject (pronoun) + verb construction that grammatically indicates that hardening (4.21b) is conditional on signs (4.21a).[94]

Perhaps even more problematic is that Beale also employs an overly atomistic *thematic* approach in arguing that hardening is even more closely related to the refusal of request for release so that hardening may take place without connection to signs but in connection with request alone. For the text explicitly connects signs and hardening while Beale has to *infer* refusal of request from the text. He is right to do so, but this only goes to show how fundamental the signs are to the situational matrix described in 4.21. The signs, hardening, and refusal are to be taken together as integral elements of the same whole. Indeed, Beale admits that 'the 4:21 hardening is integrally related to the performance of signs'.[95] He goes on to show that it is logically and theoretically possible for there to be hardening without signs, but this is practically irrelevant. The question is not whether it is *possible* for there to be hardening without signs on a theoretical level, as if the question is to be considered in a vacuum, but what the text indicates about hardening and its relationship to signs. On that score, Beale fails to reckon with the primary logical role of hardening as he himself identifies it – to embolden Pharaoh to refuse letting Israel go in the face of YHWH's mighty signs/wonders, which would normally compel Pharaoh's cooperation apart from YHWH's hardening of his heart. To put it simply, signs necessitate hardening (for there to be refusal) in the context of the exodus narrative,

---

90.   Cf. Chisholm, 'Hardening', 416. On disjunctive clauses and the options for the sense of the conjunction ן in them, see T. O. Lambdin, *Introduction to Biblical Hebrew* (New York: Charles Scribner's Sons, 1971), § 132 (cf. § 197b).

91.   Beale, 'Hardening', 135 n. 35.

92.   Beale, 'Hardening', 134–36.

93.   Chisholm, 'Hardening', 416 n. 20.

94.   Ibid.

95.   Beale, 'Hardening', 135.

and hardening is unnecessary without signs in that context. So the context-specific psychology of hardening actually works against Beale's argument.

Beale also cites Exod. 7.2-4, 14.4, 8, 17; Deut. 2.30 and Josh. 11.20 in support of there being request without signs, but with hardening. However, prior to Exodus 7 the significance of signs and their connection to hardening had already been stated and the signs begin being displayed before the other exodus texts Beale mentions (4.21 is a general statement about signs, hardening and Pharaohnic refusal, encompassing the whole process, and does not tie these elements together in such a way as to stipulate that a new act of hardening must accompany each sign).[96] As for hardening texts outside of Exodus, they appear in different contexts so that it cannot be assumed that their specific features apply to the Exodus context (this accords with the point that it is logically possible for hardening to take place without signs, but that the important question is what relationship between the two the context in Exodus establishes). Indeed, hardening does not prolong signs and judgment in those passages as they do in the Exodus context, but actually serves to bring swift destruction. Nevertheless, and quite significantly, Deut. 2.30 and Josh. 11.20 both have a contextual equivalent to the signs of the exodus narrative – the paralyzing fear of Israel produced by YHWH in fulfilment of his promise to afflict Israel's enemies in such a manner (Exod. 23.27; Deut. 2.25; Josh. 2.9-11; 5.1; 9.9-10, 24; 10.1-2). Furthermore, the very signs given in the Exodus context are identified as producing great fear in the nations Israel would encounter (Exod. 15.14-16; Josh. 2.9-11; 9.9-10, 24) so that the signs of the exodus also required hardening for Israel's enemies to stand against them.

***

Piper objects forcefully to the idea of strength being present in חזק in this context.[97] He acknowledges that the verb often carries this meaning, but argues that the usage before us refers rather to hardening and that, 'The idea of strengthening has fallen aside'.[98] He produces evidence that חזק can mean 'harden' (Jer. 5.3; Ezek. 2.4; 3.7-9). However, Piper's argument rests on the unwarranted assumption that there is a substantial difference between strengthening and hardening. Yet, a moment's reflection will reveal that the two mean largely the same thing. A strong will and a hard will both refer to a resolute and inflexible will. Recall Wilson's point that a strong heart can be viewed positively as persistent or negatively as stubborn (or hard if one prefers), depending on the viewpoint of the person providing the description.

Even the evidence that Piper adduces turns out to support the notion of strengthening or emboldening when looked at more closely. He cites Jer. 5.3's use of חזק in a metaphorical comparison to rock as requiring the meaning hardness over against that of strength. But strength is one of the

96. See further note 173 below.
97. Piper, *Justification*, 161.
98. Ibid.

chief Old Testament metaphorical significations of rock,[99] only reinforcing the congruence of strength and hardness.[100] Moreover, the notion of strength of will that boldly persists in its course against pressure that would normally induce capitulation is surely present in some if not all of these contexts cited by Piper. In the case of Israel in Jer. 5.3, there is bold resoluteness in spite of YHWH's chastising judgments: 'You have smitten them, but they did not weaken; You have consumed them, but they refused to take correction. They have made their faces harder than rock; they have refused to repent' (NASB).[101] In the case of the prophet Ezekiel, he was not to fear, but with hard (חֲזָקִים) face and hard (חָזָק) forehead continue preaching to rebellious Israel in spite of the persecution they would inflict upon him (Ezek. 2.6-7; 3.7-9).[102]

In his argument against the idea of strengthening, Piper fails to discuss the most important text outside of Exodus bearing on the question – Josh. 11.20.[103] Continuing a report of Joshua's conquest of the Promised Land, Josh. 11.18-20 reads,

> Joshua waged war with all these kings [identified in vv. 16-17] many days. There was not a city which made peace with the sons of Israel except the Hivites, the inhabitants of Gibeon; they took the whole [lot of them] in battle. For it was from YHWH to strengthen [לְחַזֵּק] their heart to meet Israel in battle in order to devote them to complete destruction, that they would not receive mercy, but in order that he might annihilate them, as YHWH commanded Moses.

The reference to strengthening/hardening of heart here involves strength of determination and boldness, as it has in view engaging Israel in battle. This is best understood in light of the paralyzing fear of Israel that Joshua reports had fallen on the people of the land (Josh. 2.9-11; 5.1; 9.9-10, 24; 10.1-2), which was a fulfilment of YHWH's promise to afflict Israel's enemies in such a manner (Exod. 23.27; Deut. 2.25).[104] YHWH had decreed destruction

99. See H. Haag, 'סלע', *TDOT*, 10.270–77 (276–77); J. E. Hartley, 'צור', *TWOT*, 2.762, and cf. R. D. Patterson, 'סלע', *TWOT*, 2.627, who observes that these two words for rock are 'often used interchangeably' (similarly Haag, 276).
100. The congruence is strengthened still more if the NASB is right to construe חָלוּ in Jer. 5.3 as from חלה and meaning 'weaken', resulting in the linking of hardening with the negative corollary of 'not weakening'.
101. Italics and some capitalization removed.
102. While the very immediate context of Ezek. 2.4; 3.7-9 (2.1–3.15) does not explicitly mention the past judgment that Israel had ignored in its rebellion nor the future judgment that Ezekiel would warn of in the preaching he was being commissioned to deliver, this is probably implied by the standard expectation of judgment for rebellion against the Lord established in the covenant, the known history of Israel, the nature of prophecy in Israel and Ezekiel's Spirit-inspired anger (3.14), and certainly confirmed very quickly by the section that immediately follows (3.16ff.). Therefore, the reference to Israel's strong/hard heart (חִזְקֵי־לֵב) in 2.4 probably carries at least a hint of boldness in it too, making the idea present in all the contexts cited by Piper.
103. Most important because it is the only text outside Exodus that applies the verb to the heart and because the conquest narrative is a sort of extension of the exodus narrative.
104. See further Excursus 6.2 above.

for the Canaanites because of their great wickedness and the great spiritual danger they posed to his people. Normally, they would surely fight against an invasion of their land. But they had been struck by supernatural fear so intense that they were likely to surrender to Israel and beg for mercy, or perhaps abandon the land or some other strategy that would preserve their lives despite YHWH's judicial intention to wipe them out. By giving them the courage to follow their natural inclination to fight Israel in spite of their great fear, YHWH ensured that they would fight, removing the temptation for Israel to disobey his command to destroy them by having mercy on them (Deut. 7.1-3, 16)[105] and the possibility of them escaping God's judgment in any other way. In the words of Richard Hess, 'the hearts of the Canaanites, sunk with fear, need to be hardened so that their inclination can become a firm resolve to fight the Israelites'.[106]

The facts that חזק frequently means 'to strengthen/encourage' in military contexts[107] and that the clash between YHWH and Pharaoh has the character of a military conflict[108] further strengthen the likelihood that a similar meaning obtains in the hardening of Pharaoh's heart. Support for this meaning is increased even further by the use of חזק in some connection with לֵב (heart) elsewhere. In Isa. 35.4, חזק implicitly refers to לֵב with the main idea of courage ('Say to those with fearful heart, "Be strong [חִזְקוּ]; do not fear"'). In Ezek. 13.22, those who discourage the heart of the righteous also encourage (לְחַזֵּק) the hands of the wicked. In Ezek. 22.14, a heart that endures is parallel to hands that are strong (תֶּחֱזַקְנָה). Lastly, in Ps. 27.14 and 31.25, the command to be strong/courageous (חֲזַק) is essentially equivalent to strengthening the heart or taking courage in the heart (וְיַאֲמֵץ לִבֶּךָ / לְבַבְכֶם), apparently referring to determination to wait for YHWH in the face of opposition from enemies in Ps. 27.14. On the other hand, fear is sometimes associated with soft (רכך)

---

105. See T. C. Butler, *Joshua* (WBC, 7; Dallas: Word, 1983), 130; R. S. Hess, *Joshua: An Introduction and Commentary* (TOTC, 6; Downer's Grove: IVP, 1996), 218.

106. Hess, ibid. Contra Beale, 'Hardening', 131, who seems to misconstrue the passage to say that YHWH gave the Canaanites the (initial) desire to fight as if they would not normally desire to resist invaders of their land. חזק refers to a strengthening of a will already present rather than creation of a will not yet in existence.

107. Gilbert, 'Libre arbitre', 16; cf. Wilson, 'Hardening', 33. Shupak's ('Hardening', 393–94 n. 10) criticism of Wilson on this point is off target, as if he claims that the collocation of חזק and לֵב is typical holy war language. But his claim is actually that חזק is frequently used in holy war contexts. I would add that the use of חזק with לֵב is rare outside of the exodus narrative, as Shupak acknowledges (394). Therefore, in a holy war context – as Shupak acknowledges the exodus context to be – it would seem natural to take חזק in its normal sense when then combined with לֵב in that context, especially since the idea of encouragement goes naturally with the Hebrew concept of the heart. See further the assessment of other usage of חזק in some connection with לֵב below, and note that Shupak (394 n. 13) agrees that חזק לֵב sometimes means 'to gain strength', 'to take courage'.

108. See Wilson, 'Hardening', 33–34; Isbell, 'Exodus 1-2', 45–46; Gilbert, 'Libre arbitre', 13–14, 16; Shupak, 'Hardening', 394; Durham, *Exodus*, 121. This is not necessarily to claim that 'the notion of "hardening the heart" is of military origin' (Fabry, 'לֵב', 428; speaking against the suggestion), but to recognize that its military and prophetic-judgment usages can overlap.

hearts in the Old Testament (Isa. 7.4; Jer. 51.46; 2 Kgs 22.19; 2 Chron. 34.27).[109]

Another piece of data that supports a strengthening sense for חזק in relation to Pharaoh's heart is the fact that only YHWH is said to harden Pharaoh's heart when חזק is used; that is, YHWH is the only subject of the verb חזק when used in the piel stem. In the hardening statements, חזק is only used in the piel and the qal. The qal usage is stative and intransitive, describing the state of being or growing strong, while the piel usage is factitive, expressing the bringing about of the state of being strong.[110] Pharaoh is never said to strengthen (חזק) himself or his own heart. But he is said to make his own heart heavy/stubborn (hiphil of כבד; 8.11 (15), 28 (32); 9.34) and to make himself hard/stubborn (hiphil of קשה; 13.15).[111] This is striking given the fact that חזק is used much more frequently than the other two verbs –12 times as compared with six times for כבד and only two times for קשה. These usage patterns support a strengthening sense in חזק, because even though the verb can be used of one taking courage in other contexts, amounting to strengthening one's own heart, the extraordinary power unleashed by YHWH in the mighty wonders of the plagues and exodus practically prohibited Pharaoh from stirring up courage in his own heart. Though he could make himself stubborn and harden his resolve, YHWH had to strengthen his heart so that he could do so. This points toward the context-specific semantic relationship between the three verbs. But we will leave discussion of that until after we look at the meanings of כבד and קשה. For now, it is time to articulate our conclusions about the meaning of חזק with respect to the hardening of Pharaoh's heart.

The qal of חזק means 'to be/become strong'. Applied to the heart of Pharaoh and other Egyptians, it refers to a strong will, one that is resolute, inflexible and bold to persist in its course against great pressure, which would

---

109. Coover-Cox, 'Hardening', 300 n. 16. See also A. P. Brown, II, 'Does God Harden People's Hearts'?, *God's Revivalist and Bible Advocate* 121.3 (April 2009), 14, on 2 Chron. 13.7, where the soft heart is not strong (note the usage of חזק) and so does not have the nerve to do as it wishes against those of stronger resolve.

110. Chisholm, 'Hardening', 415 n. 18, rightly criticizes Beale's ('Hardening', 134) classification of the piel of חזק in 4.21b as intensive-iterative to be 'linguistically unsound' in view of the intransitive nature of the qal. Scholars have come to reject the older view of 'the Piel as primarily and basically intensive' (B. T. Arnold and J. H. Choi, *A Guide to Biblical Hebrew Syntax* (New York: CUP, 2003), 42). For a clear, concise explanation of contemporary scholarly understanding of the piel vis-à-vis factitive, intensive and iterative nuances, see Arnold and Choi, 42–45.

111. The usage in 13.15 is most likely an internal (or intransitive) hiphil, representing Pharaoh as acting on himself, or possibly the object 'heart' has been elided as Zipor, 'קשה', 193, says is generally assumed. On internal hiphils, see B. K. Waltke and M. O'Connor, *An Introduction to Biblical Hebrew Syntax* (Winona Lake: Eisenbrauns, 1990), 439–41. Even if 13.15 is judged not to be an instance of Pharaoh hardening himself, this would not take much away from the point being made, since קשה is only used twice in Exodus 1–15. Moreover, it would make 13.15 to differ so sharply from the hardening statements that it could be excluded from classification among them, as Isbell would have it. See further note 72 above.

normally cause the will to yield.[112] This may be called boldness, but also stubbornness. The piel of חזק means 'to strengthen, make strong, embolden'. Applied to the heart of Pharaoh and other Egyptians, it refers to emboldening the will to act according to its inclination against extraordinary pressure that would otherwise compel the will to yield, resulting in a firm and unyielding resolve that may be called stubbornness. In the exodus narrative, YHWH alone has the power to embolden Pharaoh's will in the face of YHWH's overwhelming power expressed in mighty miracles.

The notion of strengthening implies an already established will that is given the necessary boldness to persist in its desired course. This is strongly supported by our exegesis so far, which has observed that it was entirely to be expected that Pharaoh would not be willing to let Israel go.[113] As John Mackay comments, in predicting Pharaoh's refusal in 3.19 YHWH points

> to a feature of the king's character, indeed of the whole political and religious system of which he was the embodiment. They would stubbornly refuse to let the Israelites go. It was not just that they were determined not to lose a valuable economic resource. Yielding to the religious claims embodied in the Israelites' request would undermine the whole religious and social philosophy on which Egypt had been founded. Only force – overwhelming external compulsion – would lead Pharaoh to act in the way the Lord required.[114]

The strengthening of an already established will in the case of Pharaoh is also supported by the fact that his refusal is identified as sin in 9.34 (cf. 9.27; 10.16-17) despite YHWH's *virtual* control of his resistance. It can be called sin because YHWH is merely strengthening Pharaoh to do what he already wants to do and would surely do if not opposed by overwhelming force. As G. A. Chadwick observed, 'to harden Pharaoh's heart was to inspire him, not with wickedness, but with nerve', and 'it was against prudence, not penitence, that he was hardened',[115] with no 'infusion of evil passion, but the animation

---

112.   Beale, 'Hardening', 131, is not far off with his definitions of 'having power to accomplish a function' and 'strength to continue to perform a function' (this latter quotation is not a direct quote, but adapting his wording for definition), though use of the word 'function' could give the mistaken impression that the word has to do with an assigned role or task. The word is less specific with respect to the role of intention behind the possession or giving of strength, and the word 'action' should be substituted for 'function' in Beale's definition to arrive at a more accurate articulation. In personal communication, T. D. Alexander has informed me that he is replacing the term 'hardening' with 'strengthening' in his forthcoming commentary on Exodus in the Apollos OT series.

113.   See 6.5 above including the excursus in that section.

114.   Mackay, *Exodus*, 82. However, I would add that the concern for economic loss is not to be underestimated; 'money makes the world go round', as they say. Ashby, *Exodus*, 26–27, also puts the matter in perspective: 'what semidivine autocrat would listen to an outlawed demagogue who demanded the release of the state work force'? We might as well ask how nineteenth-century America's confederation of southern states would have responded to a representative of its slaves, who had escaped to the North, demanding that they all be released (or even given a three-day vacation in the North!).

115.   Cited by Forster/Marston, *Strategy*, 264–65. Cf. Coover Cox, 'Hardening', 311.

of a resolute courage, and the overclouding of a natural discernment'.[116] In the words of Forster and Marston concerning God hardening Pharaoh, 'This is not, of course, about moral repentance, but of a foolhardy courage to defy a powerful God'.[117]

6.6.c. *To Be Heavy/Stubborn (כבד)*

The earlier listing of hardening statements shows that כבד is the next most prominent word used to describe the hardening of Pharaoh's heart. Its basic meaning is 'to be heavy', from which its other meanings can be derived, such as 'to burden' (i.e., 'to be heavy upon'), to be dull/unresponsive (i.e., 'to be weighed down, and thus hindered, in functioning'), and 'to be honoured' (i.e., 'to be weighty in honour or importance or wealth').[118] As Beale has incisively observed, 'In its most concrete usage it refers to a *quantitative* heaviness (of wealth, animals, people, etc.) but it can also indicate a *qualitative* weightiness, referring to an intensification of the quality of actions or attitudes'.[119] More commonly, scholars have observed that when כבד is used of a part of the body, it (typically) indicates that the body part is not functioning properly.[120] The underlying thought seems obvious – when significant weight is added to a functioning organ of some sort, proper functioning becomes difficult if not impossible.[121]

This last observation is often taken in a misleading direction by characterizing the language basically to indicate unresponsiveness. But that is not quite accurate.[122] Unresponsiveness might result from the malfunction caused by heaviness, but the more basic sense has to do with malfunction. For example, the description of Moses' mouth and tongue as heavy does not mean that these organs are unresponsive or that Moses is dumb, but that they do not work well; that is, Moses does not speak well, easily or eloquently (4.10). Similarly, the heavy eyes of Isa. 6.9-10 are to see but not understand; they do function on some level, but not correctly. Whether a case can be made

116. Forster/Marston, *Strategy*, 267.
117. Ibid., 64.
118. Cf. C. Dohmen and P. Stenmans, 'כָּבֵד', *TDOT*, 7.13–22; *HALOT*, s.v. כבד; C. J. Collins, 'כבד', *TDOTTE*, 2.577–87 (577). I would argue that 'unresponsive' is not the most accurate description for the sense of malfunction that כבד can bear; see below.
119. Beale, 'Hardening', 131.
120. Stenmans, 'כָּבֵד', 7.18; Wilson, 'Hardening', 22; Meadors, *Idolatry*, 21; Coover Cox, 'Hardening', 304–05. Application to the hand(s) is an exception.
121. Rightly, Coover Cox, 'Hardening', 305 n. 35. Contra Piper, *Justification*, 160–61 (cf. Collins, 'כבד', 578), who seems to think that the figure directly means unresponsiveness/ deadness. But this does not fit the figure as appropriately as the view taken above; see further below. Any sense of unresponsiveness that does pop up in the usage would more likely derive from the notion of malfunction caused by heaviness.
122. To be fair, the language of unresponsiveness could bear the meaning of 'not responding positively', and so be accurate. But it is not the most natural use of the language, and can be misleading. It appears solidly inaccurate when linked to descriptions such as 'insensible' and 'deadened', as in Piper, *Justification*, 160.

for unresponsiveness as the main sense at times, this does not work in the case of Pharaoh's heart. For Pharaoh *does* respond. He responds negatively, refusing YHWH's demand for Israel's release.

Thus, Wilson's characterization of the heavy heart as 'referring to an organ of perception that is no longer receiving outside stimuli' is not well stated.[123] It is not that Pharaoh's heart fails to receive outside stimuli, but that, insofar as it is an organ of perception, it does not properly process external stimuli that it receives. Even so, while perception is undoubtedly part of the heart's role in Hebrew thought, the heart is, as we concluded earlier, to be construed primarily as an organ of volition and reason in the exodus narrative (see section 6.5.a above). Heaviness intensifies the heart/will,[124] making it difficult if not impossible to move. (This is similar to strengthening the will as designated by חזק, minus the sense of courage.) It also causes the reasoning process of the mind to malfunction so that it has great if not insuperable difficulty in making wise choices, choices that are the most beneficial to the subject.[125] Hence, while 'the heart' (לֵב) still most fundamentally refers to 'the will' in the hardening statements that use כבד (see the discussion of the meaning of 'heart' in 6.5.a above), it is this verb that most strongly brings out the sense of 'mind/reason' among the hardening statements.

In combination with לֵב (heart), כבד may also bring out a special nuance of thought rooted in the Egyptian background of the text. According to John Currid, it is well known that 'a good deal of the Exodus story is illuminated by its authentic Egyptian setting. The author clearly understood the Egyptian world, and especially Egyptian religion, from the inside, for the story is nothing so much as a contest between the powers of Yahweh and the powers of the Egyptian pantheon, including the Pharaoh himself'.[126] Currid explains,

> In ancient Egyptian sacred texts, the heart (*ib*) represents the essence of the person ... After someone died, the heart was weighed in the balance of truth to determine the kind of afterlife the deceased would receive. The heart of the deceased, on one side of the scale, was balanced on the other with a feather. If the heart outweighed the feather, the deceased was in trouble ... The condition of one's heart thus determined whether or not one entered the afterlife. If a person's heart was heavy-laden with misdeeds, the person would, in effect, be annihilated; if the heart was filled with integrity, truth and good acts, the person would earn an escort to heavenly bliss ... When Yahweh made

123. Wilson, 'Hardening', 22; cf. 26. However, Wilson does initially state that heavy organs 'no longer receive external stimuli *in the normal way*' (emphasis added). Thus qualified, this way of putting it is passable, though not ideal. The more basic sense of the figure seems to be malfunction. Applied to an organ of perception, that would mean it does not receive external stimuli properly. But it is questionable whether the heart should be classified primarily as an organ of perception, at least in Exod. 1–15. See below.

124. Recall Beale's definition cited earlier in this section.

125. Cf. Coover Cox, 'Hardening', 305; Forster/Marston, *Strategy*, 64; Chadwick (cited by Forster/Marston, 264–65, 267); Gunn, 'Hardening', 76–77.

126. Currid, 'Harden', 47. Cf. Meadors, *Idolatry*, ch. 3, esp. p. 18. But see Shupak, 'Hardening', 389 n.1. At the least, it seems that some Egyptian colouring to the narrative is widely recognized, no matter what its source(s).

Pharaoh's heart heavy, this should be understood against the Egyptian background of the story. The God of the Hebrews was serving as the judge of Pharaoh. Yahweh weighed the heart of the Egyptian king and then proclaimed the result for all to see. Pharaoh was simply judged to be a sinner and worthy of condemnation. This is striking in contrast to the Egyptian belief in Pharaoh's perfection ... When the biblical text tells us that Yahweh hardened Pharaoh's heart, this is a polemic against the prevailing thought of Pharaoh's pure and untainted character.[127]

Additionally, when Exodus tells us that Pharaoh made his own heart heavy, it is portraying him to be acting as a sinner and showing himself to be worthy of condemnation. Secondly, references that do not identify an agent of כבד draw attention to the sinful state of Pharaoh's heart and YHWH's

127   Currid, 'Harden', 48–51. Cf. Stuart, *Exodus*, 149–50; Coover Cox, 'Hardening', 305–06. Meadors, *Idolatry*, 24–25 (following Shupak), finds this purported background to be provocative but speculative because he finds that (note my critical responses in parentheses) (1) there is no reference to the afterlife in Exodus' hardening passages (but such a reference seems unnecessary since uncovered cultural background often remains unstated in a text precisely because it was well known to the original context, and the afterlife is not necessarily the focus of Exodus' use of the material); (2) there is no explicit indication of polemic concerning the heart in Exodus (but (a) again, important background often remains unstated, giving rise to the label 'background'; (b) Meadors acknowledges an explicit and prominent polemic against Egyptian polytheism, and this background fits perfectly into that; (c) indeed, the hardening of Pharaoh's heart is just as prominent a theme in the text as polemic against polytheism, and the two seem to be intertwined in light of Pharaoh's divine status in Egyptian belief; (d) Exodus does tie Pharaoh's heavy heart to his sinfulness (9.34; cf. 9.27; 10.16)); and (3) the Egyptian *Book of the Dead*, from which this Egyptian background is drawn, was not a part of popular Egyptian culture due to its expense (nevertheless, it seems very likely that *The Book of the Dead* reflects Egyptian theology pervading the culture, and that possession of it was not the only means by which such religious thought was spread; Shupak, 'Hardening', 402 n. 32, admits that 'Egyptian beliefs and practices concerning death and posthumous life were apparently known in the Israelite sphere'; moreover, Coover Cox, 306 n. 40, points out that it was not necessary for early readers to know much about Egyptian beliefs to apply the purported background 'since the ideas that sin is heavy (Isa. 1:4; 24:20) and that the Lord weighs hearts (Prov. 21:2; cf. 16:2) appear elsewhere in the Bible). Steinmann, 'Hardness', 382, questions this background based on the following points (my critical responses follow again in parentheses): (1) 'it is only stated once in Exodus that God made Pharaoh's heart heavy' (but (a) God's agency and Pharaoh's agency in 'making heavy' are fundamentally related, God's action judging Pharaoh as a sinner and Pharaoh's action showing himself worthy of that judgment; (b) the rough synonymy of the terms for hardening nullifies this point as does the likelihood that YHWH is to be understood as the agent on some level in occurrences of כבד without an agent explicitly identified, and even stands behind Pharaoh's own self-hardening to some degree); (2) this is not the only term for hardening the heart in Exodus (but it is possible that different terms bring out different nuances); (3) 'heaviness of other body parts is also a sign of spiritual deficiencies' (but this background specifically has to do with heaviness of *heart*, and there is no reason that sinfulness and condemnation cannot be signalled by this terminology along with spiritual deficiency; indeed, such a confluence is quite natural). Finally, Kellenberger, *Verstockung*, 44, approvingly registers Shupak's observation that the cited Egyptian material does not mention heaviness of heart. But the idea of heaviness is intrinsically related to the notion of weighing so that its invocation in a context of Israelite polemic against Egyptian polytheism/idolatry and its tie to sin would render its significance readily discernible.

judgment of it as worthy of condemnation. Finally, this nuance is part of Exodus' polemic against Egyptian religion. YHWH's hardening activity reveals his supremacy and sovereignty over Pharaoh, who was regarded as divine in Egyptian thought.[128] Similarly, by taking over the role thought to belong to the Egyptian gods in the judgment of the heart, YHWH usurped any supposed authority they were thought to possess and demonstrated his unrivalled supremacy and sovereignty over them.

6.6.d. *To Harden/Make Stubborn* (קשה)

קשה is only used twice in the hardening statements of the exodus narrative (Exod. 7.3; 13.15). The word's basic meaning is, 'to be hard, difficult',[129] and appears 'with a wide range of meanings, mostly figurative: difficult, rough, severe, cruel, obdurate, obstinate'.[130] In the two occurrences under consideration, it refers to stubbornness, as the word does when used of 'the heart' elsewhere (Ps. 95.8; Prov. 28.14; Ezek. 3.7).[131] More specifically, utilizing the hiphil, these two occurrences mean 'to make stubborn, obstinate'. The word 'almost always has negative connotations'.[132]

Although used only twice in the hardening statements, קשה occupies a strategic place in the narrative at 7.3. For the verse summarizes the hardening of Pharaoh's heart, referring 'to [the] whole process [of hardening] and not to any specific instance',[133] and repeating the initial notice of the hardening theme given in 4.21 before the actual hardening commences. By summarizing all of the remaining hardening notices with קשה, the narrator 'encourages the reader to interpret all of them negatively'.[134] More than that, he encourages the reader to take YHWH as the agent of all the remaining hardening notices that do not explicitly specify an agent, as he also did in 4.21.

6.6.e. *Concluding Synthesis of the Terms for Hardening*

The three main terms for hardening are roughly synonymous, all indicating stubbornness – 'to be or make stubborn'. However, each verb carries its own distinctive nuance. חזק is the most prominent and fundamental word used.

---

128. For a concise description of modern scholarship on the Pharaoh's divine status, see Strawn, 'Pharaoh', 632–33. It seems clear that at the very least, the Pharaoh was considered semi-divine.
129. See *HALOT*, s.v. קשה; Zipor, 'קשה', 189.
130. Zipor, 'קשה', 190.
131. Ibid., 192–93. Such usage may derive from the notion that the heart/will is difficult for another to move. For more reflection on the development of this usage with a slightly different conclusion, see Beale, 'Hardening', 132. On the special usage in 13.15 lacking a direct object, see notes 72 and 111 above.
132. Wilson, 'Hardening', 31.
133. Forster/Marston, *Strategy*, 64, 267; cf. Wilson, ibid.
134. Wilson, ibid.

It introduces the hardening theme (4.21), thereby encouraging the reader to understand the rest of the hardening statements as expressions of its action.[135] This impression is confirmed by the fact that חזק is used much more frequently than the other two words, 12 times as compared with six times for כבד and only two times for קשה.

חזק emphasizes the courage/boldness to persist in a desired course against fearsome opposition and the resulting strength of will that amounts to stubbornness. In accord with חזק's fundamental role, it is this boldness that similarly gives rise to the stubbornness indicated by the other two verbs. כבד emphasizes malfunction in the reasoning and willing process that such boldness can engender and the immovability of the will that results. It also draws attention to Pharaoh's sinfulness in his treatment of the Israelites and his attitude toward the God of Israel on the one hand, and YHWH's verdict of Pharaoh's attitude and actions as worthy of condemnation on the other hand. All three verbs refer to a fixed/firm/unbending/stubborn will, חזק in terms of strength and boldness, כבד in terms of heaviness with a view toward immovability, and קשה in terms of difficulty with respect to moving of the will.

The specific use of the vocabulary of hardening in Exodus portrays Pharaoh with a will already fixed upon keeping Israel under Egyptian bondage and oppression before any hardening activity on the part of YHWH. God's hardening activity emboldened Pharaoh's will to persist in its already chosen course despite the immense pressure applied by the miraculous signs and wonders of God, resulting in the stubbornness indicated by all three words used for hardening. Hence, this stubbornness remains rooted in Pharaoh's own previously formed, immoral will.

There are a number of reasons for this hardening, some that we have already noted and others still to be identified as we examine the rest of Exodus 1–15. At this point, we will restrict our comments to the purpose of the hardening as it inherently emerges from the language of hardening itself. From that standpoint, it emerges as a fitting judgment for an unjust tyrant, giving him his own fierce will as its own punishment[136] and showing the total supremacy of YHWH over the supposedly divine Pharaoh and the gods of Egypt.

---

135. Contra Currid, 'Harden', 48, who appears to take כבד as the primary term because of the special meaning it appears to bear against the Egyptian background. But special nuance emerging from relevant background does not seem to be enough justification for taking one of the terms in question as fundamental, and חזק also gains colouring from Egyptian background. It is actual usage that should be determinative; see below.

136. Cf. the Lord's judgment upon Israel for complaining about not having meat in Numbers 11; his granting the sinful request of Israel to have a king in 1 Samuel 8; the fitting irony of hardening judgment that makes idolaters like idols (see Meadors, *Idolatry*; G. K. Beale, 'Isaiah VI 9-13: A Retributive Taunt against Idolatry', *VT* 41/3 (1991) 257–78; idem, *We Become What We Worship: A Biblical Theology of Idolatry* (Downer's Grove: IVP, 2008)); God's judicial handing over of humanity to their own sinful will in Rom. 1.18-32, etc. Gunn, 'Hardening', 94 n. 29, speaks of the hardening as conveying 'a measure of poetic justice'.

6.7. *Israel as YHWH's Firstborn Son*

Having instructed Moses to make sure he performs all the wonders put in his power, it would seem that YHWH tells Moses of his intention to harden Pharaoh in order to keep Moses, who was already resistant to the Lord's commission (4.1-17), from becoming discouraged at Pharaoh's persistent refusal to let Israel go despite the mighty miracles that Moses would perform.[137] YHWH's warning about the obstinacy Moses would encounter leads into instruction about the message he was to deliver to Pharaoh concerning the climactic plague of death to the firstborn of Egypt just before it was to be inflicted: 'Then you will say to Pharaoh, "Thus says YHWH: 'Israel is my son, my firstborn. I said to you, "Let my son go so that he may serve me." But you have refused to let him go. Behold, I will kill your son, your firstborn'"' (4.22-23).

The reference to Israel as God's firstborn son indicates that Israel is corporately in covenant relationship with YHWH, that the nation belongs to God as his people and enjoys a familial relationship with him in which he is committed to bestow love, care, protection, discipline and blessing, and his people are committed to act as a faithful 'son', responding to their divine father with love, trust, obedience and worship.[138] The notion of being firstborn added to that of sonship indicates a special position of favour for Israel before God in line with ancient Near Eastern values of special privilege and inheritance for the firstborn son,[139] who would even come to represent the father of the family as he grew to maturity.[140] Thus, Pharaoh's enslavement and oppression of Israel was an attack on YHWH's covenant relationship with his people,[141] a denial of his covenantal rights, and action perpetrated against him as well as Israel since the two were united in a familial bond (established by covenant). The conflict between YHWH and Pharaoh was, among other things, over mastery of Israel, as evidenced by YHWH's demand that Pharaoh let Israel *serve* (עבד) him.[142] This special status of Israel as YHWH's firstborn son determined the final plague upon Egypt, which brought death to all its firstborn, including Pharaoh's own firstborn son and intended successor.

---

137. So e.g., Beale, 'Hardening', 133–34; cf. Bush, *Exodus*, 64; Mackay, *Exodus*, 95.

138. See Abasciano, *Romans 9.1-9*, 122. Israel's sonship is another way of referring to her elect status.

139. On firstborn status, see ch. 2.1 and 2.3 above and the literature cited there. In relation to Exod. 4.22-23 specifically, see further Stuart, *Exodus*, 146.

140. Stuart, ibid.

141. Cf. Meadors, *Idolatry*, 17, 27.

142. See Isbell, 'Exodus 1–2', 45; Gunn, 'Hardening', 80–81, 88. Remember that עבד is often used in the OT of covenantal service/subjection; see note 20 in ch. 2 above.

6.8. *The Time Scope of Hardening in Exodus 4.21-23*

Exodus 4.21-23 indicate that (1) hardening of Pharaoh's heart would be generally contingent on Moses' performance of the wonders YHWH had enabled him to do (see Excursus 6.2 above and just prior to it), and (2) Moses is to warn Pharaoh of the plague of the firstborn after his refusal of YHWH's demand but before the plague would fall. Then the first report (rather than prediction) of actual hardening explicitly indicates fulfilment of the prediction of hardening and Pharaohnic refusal ('as YHWH had said'; 7.13). Therefore, the time scope of 4.21-23 covers from the performance of the first wonder before Pharaoh (7.8ff.) and the associated hardening (7.13) through to Moses' final encounter with Pharaoh (11.8) and the accompanying summary statement from the narrator (11.10). In sum, the time period of 4.21-23 is covered by 7.8–11.10.[143]

But the most common view of the time frame of 4.21-23 places the beginning of YHWH's hardening activity much later, with the sixth plague (9.12), because that is the first time the text explicitly reports YHWH as the agent of hardening that has occurred.[144] Prior to 9.12, either Pharaoh is identified as the agent of hardening or no agent is explicitly identified, which has led many scholars to conclude that all such references are instances of Pharaoh hardening himself.[145] However, proponents of this view usually miss the hardening/refusal fulfilment phrase punctuating the narrative (כַּאֲשֶׁר דִּבֶּר יְהוָה – 'as YHWH had said'), following upon the first miraculous sign given to Pharaoh (the serpent sign; 7.8-13) before any of the plagues fell, and repeated three more times before the sixth plague.[146]

143. Cf. Chisholm, 'Hardening', 417.

144. For a list of representatives of this view, see B. P. Irwin, 'Yahweh's Suspension of Free Will in the Old Testament: Divine Immorality or Sign-Act'?, *TynBul* 54.2 (2003) 55–62 (56–57 n. 6), whose substantial list could easily be expanded, as with e.g., Fretheim, *Exodus*, 98; Steinmann, 'Hardness', 383. Gunn, 'Hardening', 74–76, finds the point at which YHWH begins hardening Pharaoh to be ambiguous, though he seems to think YHWH's agency implicit starting with the serpent sign (7.13) until stated explicitly with the sixth plague (9.12).

145. See e.g., Sarna, *Exodus*, 64; W. C. Kaiser, 'Exodus', in F. E. Gaebelein (ed.), *The Expositor's Bible Commentary*, II (Grand Rapids: Zondervan, 1990), 285–498 (331). Isbell, *Function*, 27, who opposes this view, notes its frequency among commentators.

146. The phrase occurs in 7.13, 22; 8.11(15), 15 (19); 9.12, 35. For detailed treatment of the phrase, see Beale, 'Hardening', 140–41, who along with Piper, *Justification*, 163–68, stresses the phrase as critical for fixing the timing of hardening (cf. Isbell, *Function*, 30–33). Coover Cox, 'Hardening', 308–09 n. 51, argues that the fulfilment phrase should be limited to the clause that immediately precedes it, which in five of its six occurrences is, 'and he did not listen to them' (וְלֹא שָׁמַע אֲלֵהֶם), and in its final occurrence, 'and he did not let the sons of Israel go' (וְלֹא שִׁלַּח אֶת־בְּנֵי יִשְׂרָאֵל) which would exclude from its purview the statement of hardness/hardening that occurs immediately prior. While she makes a reasonable case, it is not ultimately convincing. For it is most natural to apply the fulfilment phrase to anything YHWH previously said that later appears in collocation with the fulfilment phrase. It is not a matter of a formal rule that states generically to which clauses the fulfilment phrase refers, but linking what YHWH previously said to that which occurs in collocation with the fulfilment phrase. Coover Cox's discussion of various occurrences of the phrase bears

On the other hand, Beale argues vigorously that the hardening commences at 5.1 and that 4.21-23 encompasses 'from the time that Moses returns to Egypt until he performs the first nine plague signs'.[147] But Chisholm has largely refuted Beale's case,[148] and we have countered some of his points in Excurses 6.1 and 6.2 above. Therefore, we will mostly restrict our comments to additional observations that add to the refutation of the position he represents.

Beale advances five reasons for his view: First, he argues that hardening is not conditional on signs, as evidenced by the fact that hardening could be present even if signs are absent (see Excursus 6.2 above for response).[149] Second, he argues that it cannot 'be shown that Moses did *not* perform a sign [for Pharaoh prior to his initial refusal] ... since it is a characteristic of the plague narrative to assume certain events, without stating their occurrence'.[150] But such implications must be clear from the context, unlike what Beale is suggesting for 5.2. (Indeed, we shall see that the evidence points in the opposite direction from Beale's position.) For example, Beale cites 4.21 as an example of such ellipsis, 'where the "request" [for Israel's release] is assumed and not stated'.[151] But there are solid contextual reasons that imply the request, such as prior instructions to Moses to request release and mention of Pharaoh's refusal in 4.23. Surely the burden of proof rests with the one who would insist that signs were presented to Pharaoh prior to

out this point, since in Deut. 11.25 the phrase does not apply to the immediately preceding clause, but to an earlier clause, and in Deut. 31.3 the phrase refers to multiple clauses. Repetition of the phrase in the same immediate context is therefore a stylistic choice of an author that does not indicate the phrase is limited in other contexts. Nevertheless, one could argue that since YHWH's hardening predictions specified himself as the agent of hardening and Pharaoh is sometimes identified as agent, the fulfilment phrase should only be applied to hardening statements in which YHWH's agency is explicitly stated; see the detailed argument of Ford, *Explaining*, 94–99. But this seems overly restrictive. Still, T. D. Alexander remains unconvinced that the fulfilment phrase necessarily refers to hardening and thinks it could refer to Pharaoh's refusal alone, leaving hardening as commencing in 9.12; see his forthcoming Exodus commentary in the Apollos OT series.

147. Beale, 'Hardening', 134–36. See similarly though less rigorously, Piper, *Justification*, 162–63; Isbell, *Function*, 27–37; R. E. Clements, *Exodus* (CBC; Cambridge: CUP, 1972), 30.

148. See Chisholm, 'Hardening', 416–17 n. 20.

149. Beale, 'Hardening', 135.

150. Ibid., 135–36.

151. Ibid., 136 n. 36. Beale also cites plague narratives that he takes as not involving Moses as the divine intermediary for effecting the plagues, arguing, 'If 4:21 were taken to mean that God would never effect a sign unless it were through the instrumentality of Moses, then these three narratives could never have occurred (8.13-19, 20-28; 9.6-7)'. But these narratives imply Moses' intermediary role. The first involves Aaron as Moses' intermediary. The other two involve Moses as YHWH's messenger to Pharaoh, prophetic proclamation which may be regarded as partially instrumental to YHWH effecting the plagues. But even if one sees no intermediary role for Moses in these passages, his role does not have the same tight logical and psychological connection to the effecting of the plagues that the signs do to hardening; see Excursus 6.2 above. Moreover, YHWH is always in view as the one doing the miracles even if Moses typically serves an intermediary role.

5.1 that were not mentioned. As Chisholm notes, reading between the lines in the way Beale does here 'is unwarranted and makes one's argument appear tendentious'.[152]

Third, Beale asserts that 'the divine omnipotence necessary for a proper effecting of the *Heilsgeschichteplan* of Exodus is incongruous with a "by chance" refusal of Pharaoh, since this refusal was already an integral part of the plan' (see Excursus 6.1 above for response).[153] Fourth, Beale contends that Moses blaming YHWH for the harm perpetrated by Pharaoh against Israel in response to the initial request that Pharaoh let Israel go (5.22-23) suggests that his refusal was a result of YHWH's hardening as announced in 4.21.[154] But this is an unlikely reading of the text, for as we have seen, the hardening is conditional on the performance of signs. Moreover, in 5.22-23 Moses equates YHWH's doing of harm to Israel with YHWH sending Moses to request release from Pharaoh yet not delivering his people. Sending Moses to demand Israel's release led to Pharaoh's oppressive reaction recorded in 5.4-19, and it was for this reason, compounded by YHWH's inaction despite Pharaoh's oppression and YHWH's promise of deliverance, that Moses blamed YHWH for the intensification of Egyptian oppression.[155] In response to Moses' complaint, YHWH indicates that he would now begin the promised process of deliverance (6.1).

Furthermore, even apart from the preceding points, it is gratuitous to suggest that the predicted hardening is at work here, because the designated effect of the hardening was to be that Pharaoh would not let Israel go, not that he would intensify their oppression. No hardening statement in the entirety of the exodus narrative encompassed by 4.21-23 is connected with an intensification of oppressive action against Israel. That was simply not the intention or the effect of the hardening. Rather, it emboldened Pharaoh to resist YHWH's demand for the release of Israel despite YHWH's awesome divine power displayed in signs and plagues against Pharaoh and Egypt.

Fifth, Beale alleges that Ps. 105.25 asserts that YHWH directly caused the harsh actions of the Pharaohs during the whole course of Israel's Egyptian

---

152. Chisholm, 'Hardening', 416 n. 20.

153. Beale, 'Hardening', 136.

154. Ibid. See similarly Piper, *Justification*, 162. Piper ignores the connection of signs to hardening in arguing for this point.

155. Cf. Ford, *Explaining*, 87–88. Cf. also the immediately preceding verse (5.21): as a result of the same Pharaohnic response to Moses' demand for release, the Israelite foremen blame Moses and Aaron for making them stink in the sight of Pharaoh and his servants, and putting a sword in the Egyptians' hand to kill them. The foremen blame Moses, and then Moses blames God. Or cf. Joshua's statement that Achan brought trouble upon Israel (Josh. 7.25). It is not that Achan himself attacked Israel or that he had some sort of control over God, but that his action led the Lord to oppose Israel in judgment. In neither of these cases is the party (Moses and Aaron or Achan) who provoked the party that actually inflicts harm coercing or irresistibly controlling the latter. But since their actions provoke a harmful reaction, they are blamed by those who suffered as a result. Cf. the people of Judah having 'done evil to themselves' because their sin provoked God to wrath against them (Isa. 3.9) and similar passages (e.g., Jer. 2.17, 19; 4.18).

bondage.[156] But Exodus does not give so much as a hint that YHWH was *directly* causing Pharaoh's oppression of Israel at the beginning, and it is telling that Beale must appeal to a text outside of Exodus to make this point. Indeed, this is a questionable interpretation of Ps. 105.25, which refers to the events of Exodus 1–2, and primarily to 1.8-14.[157] As Chisholm observes, 'Psalm 105.23-27 seems to be in chronological order. Verse 23 refers to Exodus 1.1-5, verse 24 relates to Exodus 1.6-7, verse 25 refers to Exodus 1.8-14 primarily, but perhaps also encompasses the rest of chapter 1 and all of chapter 2, verse 26 refers to Exodus 3–4, and verse 27 relates to Exodus 7'.[158]

Attention to the context of Ps. 105.25 suggests that the verse actually refers to the blessing of God upon the Israelites as that which 'turned' the heart of the Egyptians to hatred of his people, not an act of direct divine causation upon their heart: 'He [YHWH] made his people very fruitful, and he made him more numerous than his enemies. He turned their heart to hating his people, to dealing craftily with his servants' (Ps. 105.24-25). The psalm makes the point that God's blessing of fruitfulness upon his people – in fulfilment of his covenant promise according to the broader context (105.8-11) – provoked the Egyptians to oppress Israel. Thus it could be said that 'he turned their heart to hating his people', for it was his action of blessing his people that the Egyptians responded to with oppression of that people.[159] This is exactly what Exod. 1.7-14 describes. But this is a far cry from implying direct divine causation of the Egyptians' heart or actions toward Israel.[160] Rather, in both

156. Cf. Piper, *Justification*, 170 n. 23.
157. See Chisholm, 'Hardening', 414 n. 17. On the ground that Ps. 105.25 specifically refers to Exodus 1, Chisholm, 417 n. 20, criticizes Beale for trying to apply it to Exodus 5. Chisholm's response to Beale regarding Ps. 105.25 is the weakest part of his otherwise compelling critique of Beale. He may have caught Beale in a slight inaccuracy, who seems to take Ps. 105.25 as speaking directly of the whole course of Israel's bondage in Egypt when its direct focus is actually Exod. 1.8-14, or possibly as much as chs 1–2. But Beale's point is that Pharaoh's actions in Exodus 5 were the fruition of the attitude directly engendered in him by YHWH. It could easily be clarified to say that this attitude was first formed in the events of 1.8-14. Chisholm also errs when he says that, 'Even if Psalm 105 25 [sic] includes the actions of the Egyptians described in chapter 5, it refers specifically to Egyptian hostility to Israel (5 6-18 [sic]), not necessarily to Pharaoh's refusal to recognize Yahweh's authority', for part of Egypt's hostile intentions toward the Israelites was that they not be allowed to leave (1.10). Nonetheless, I regard Chisholm's study to be the best overall treatment of the hardening of Pharaoh's heart.
158. Ibid.; Chisholm's footnotes lack full stops for some reason, and I have added them in as appropriate in this quotation.
159. Cf. F. Delitzsch, *Psalms* (trans. J. Martin; Commentary on the Old Testament, 5; 3 vols in 1; repr., Grand Rapids: Eerdmans, 1973), 3.145.
160. Eslinger, 'Freedom', 53, gratuitously assumes that God's action meeting with this response in the Egyptians indicates him to have engineered their response, but this is contrary to the normal expectation for response to the actions of others or situations that people encounter. Eslinger thinks that God's foreknowledge of the Egyptians' oppressive action combined with his power to do as he pleases with the Egyptians confirms his assumption. But that is a non sequitur. Knowing how someone will respond to one's action and having the power to stop it, yet allowing that person's choice of response, does not amount to

Psalm 105 and Exodus 1 the text indicates the result of YHWH blessing his people vis-à-vis the response the Egyptians gave to it.

Thus, YHWH's hardening activity is to be construed as beginning in connection with the first miraculous sign presented to Pharaoh, indicated by 7.13. It is too striking to be mere coincidence that 4.21 links hardening so tightly with the performance of miraculous signs and that the first notice of the fulfilment of 4.21's hardening occurs precisely in immediate subsequence to the performance of the first miraculous sign presented to Pharaoh. Moreover, the further development of the narrative confirms this reading.

For first, *after* Pharaoh refuses Moses' first demand for Israel's release and harshly increased the oppressive burden upon the Israelites (ch. 5), '*Then* YHWH said to Moses, "*Now* [עַתָּה] you will see what I will do to Pharaoh, for by a strong hand he will let them go and by a strong hand he will drive them out from his land"' (6.1; emphasis mine). YHWH's use of 'now' (עַתָּה) implies a change in YHWH's actions, and surely hardening Pharaoh's heart is part of what he would 'do to Pharaoh'. Admittedly, the focus of the statement concerning what YHWH would do is the powerful compulsion he would bring against Pharaoh to force him to let Israel go. But the hardening is critical to bringing forth the full operation of YHWH's strong hand, for it enables Pharaoh to deny Israel's release despite the display of YHWH's incomparable power so as to bring forth greater plagues of divine power against Pharaoh. The terminology of the 'strong hand' (יָד חֲזָקָה) bolsters this reading by using the adjective 'strong' (חָזָק) to describe YHWH's action against Pharaoh, which is cognate to the verb 'to be strong' (חָזַק) used in 4.21 for the hardening of Pharaoh's heart. Hence, 6.1 gives the strong impression that YHWH's miraculous works and hardening against Pharaoh are about to begin, in contrast to what has happened so far.

Second and relatedly, as YHWH speaks further to Moses in 6.2-13, the text repeats much of what was said prior to 4.21-23, much of which emphasizes the conditional nature of YHWH's actions against Pharaoh, such as their character as a response to harsh Egyptian oppression of Israel in fulfilment of YHWH's covenant obligations to his people. Exodus 6.28ff. then picks up the narrative from 6.13 after an intervening genealogy (6.14-27), recapitulating some of the earlier narrative and expanding its description of what YHWH told Moses (6.1ff.) after his complaint about YHWH's inaction (5.22-23), and thus *after* his initial encounter with Moses.[161] From

---

engineering the response. Should God not have blessed his people and not fulfilled his covenant promises because he knew the Egyptians would respond with oppression? One could argue that he should have stopped them from responding that way, but that raises a different issue, the question of what God's purpose(s) might be in allowing the Egyptians to act as they chose, a matter that cannot be said to itself imply that God engineered the actions of the Egyptians.

161. On the recapitulative and summarizing nature of 6.28ff., see esp. Houtman, *Exodus*, 1.522–23. Durham, *Exodus*, 88, thinks 7.6 refers to Moses' and Aaron's actions in 5.1-5, but most interpreters rightly regard 7.6 as a general reference to Moses' and Aaron's obedience over the course of the rest of the conflict with Pharaoh, as suggested by the telescoping reference in 7.4-5 to the resolution of the conflict in the accomplished

what he had communicated earlier, YHWH draws together the basic events that are to come: the demand Moses and Aaron were again to put to Pharaoh for Israel's release, YHWH's intent to harden Pharaoh, infliction of the plagues, Pharaoh's refusal and the exodus (7.2-5). It is as if the text repeats so much of what was said in preparation for the course of deliverance, and YHWH now repeats his instructions to Moses and the plan for the course of deliverance – including the hardening – because the predicted course is about to commence in full now that Pharaoh has refused YHWH's initial demand for Israel's release. The fact that the report of the occurrence of signs and hardening predicted in 4.21-23 has been absent from the narrative since then, but that these begin to appear only after 6.28–7.7's recapitulating instruction and prediction with respect to the entire predicted course of events, supports taking 6.28–7.7 as preparatory to the actual commencement of the events predicted by 4.21-23.

6.9. *Beginning the Mission (Exodus 4.24–7.7)*[162]

After YHWH met with Moses and commissioned him, climaxing in 4.21-23, Moses' brother Aaron went to meet with Moses in the wilderness at YHWH's command (4.27). Together they went to Egypt and gathered the elders of Israel (4.28-29). Aaron related what YHWH had said to Moses and performed the signs YHWH instructed them to perform before the people, successfully convincing them that YHWH had appeared to Moses – who was therefore to be regarded as his representative – and that YHWH knew about their affliction and was concerned so as to take action in their behalf, moving them to worship (4.30-31).

So Moses and Aaron went to Pharaoh and demanded Israel's release in YHWH's name. 'But Pharaoh said, "Who is YHWH that I should listen to his voice to let Israel go? I do not know YHWH. And indeed, I will not let Israel go"' (5.2). Moses and Aaron then reworded their request, providing a little more explanation (5.3), to which Pharaoh responded with rebuke and harsh intensification of oppression upon Israel by requiring more work than they could accomplish (5.4-19). Pharaoh's reply in 5.2 'is not a profession of ignorance but a refusal to grant recognition' to YHWH as holding any authority.[163] His question mockingly challenges YHWH's status and authority, and his statement declares that he does not in fact recognize YHWH's authority and that he will therefore not

deliverance; see e.g., Houtman, 1.491–92; Stuart, *Exodus*, 182; Beale, 'Hardening', 138–39; Bush, *Exodus*, 90.

162. See section 6.7 above for important additional treatment of Exod. 5.1–7.7.

163. Irwin, 'Suspension', 58; cf. Enns, *Exodus*, 153; Bailey, *Exodus*, 102; Brueggemann, 'Exodus', 726; Mackay, *Exodus*, 105; Houtman, *Exodus*, 1.462; Chisholm, 'Hardening', 417 n. 21. Coover Cox, 'Hardening', 302–03, emphasizes that 'Exodus, in fact, casts Pharaoh in the role of a vassal rebelling against his sovereign'. On the other hand, T. D. Alexander has suggested to me in personal communication that Pharaoh is rather presented as a rival king, since Pharaoh has not accepted YHWH's rule.

heed his demand. This response seals Pharaoh's fate by confirming his self-determined oppressive claim on YHWH's people, placing him in direct conflict with YHWH over lordship of Israel and the fulfilment of YHWH's covenant promises to her.[164] His question, 'Who is YHWH'? and his denial of knowing YHWH (5.2) introduce an important motif of the following narrative, which reveals that one of YHWH's main purposes in judging Pharaoh with hardening and plague is that Egypt and her Pharaoh would know that he is YHWH.

Exodus 5.1-2 occupies an important place in the narrative. The verses 'introduce a conflict that is ... the pivotal didactic instrument of the entire sequence, 5:1–6:1, 7:8–12:36',[165] a 'conflict that drives the subsequent chapters'.[166] Moreover, according to Brueggemann, 5.1-2 'sets the conflict in its sharpest, most comprehensive and uncompromising form'.[167] Enns even suggests that 'nowhere is Pharaoh's hardness of heart demonstrated more clearly'.[168] Given the importance of 5.1-2 in recalling the attitude of Pharaoh toward Israel and introducing his attitude towards YHWH, portrayed as oppressive, cruel, defiant and unyielding, it is noteworthy that this programmatic response and pronounced hard-heartedness occur before YHWH hardens Pharaoh's heart. It strengthens the conditional nature of YHWH's actions toward Pharaoh. Not only does he bring hardening judgment and plague upon Pharaoh for his prior oppression of his covenant people, but he also does so in response to Pharaoh's freely chosen refusal to stop the oppression and free his victims after being confronted by divine command, not to mention Pharaoh's intensifying of oppression and his rebellion against YHWH's sovereignty. Thus, Pharaoh is shown to be a terrible villain fully deserving of the judgment YHWH intends to inflict on him.[169]

We have already seen that after the first encounter with Pharaoh (5.1-19) YHWH tells Moses that he would now begin the promised judgment against

164. Cf. section 6.6 above; Meadors, *Idolatry*, 17–36, passim; Kaiser, 'Exodus', 336; Gunn, 'Hardening', 80–81, 83, 88; Isbell, 'Exodus 1–2', 45, 50, and the references in the previous note.

165. Durham, *Exodus*, 64. To clarify, even though the conflict has been introduced by way of prediction, 5.1-2ff. now introduces it by way of reporting its initial actual engagement.

166. Enns, *Exodus*, 153.

167. Brueggemann, 'Exodus', 726.

168. Enns, *Exodus*, 153.

169. Cf. Isbell, *Function*, 22–23, who, despite his opinion that Pharaoh is not a free moral agent in the story, points out that the narrator of Exodus sees no need to defend YHWH's morality in his treatment of Pharaoh, but addresses whether YHWH can defeat Pharaoh and celebrates his victory over him. This is noteworthy for implying that Pharaoh, the oppressor and enslaver of Israel, is seen as the villainous enemy of Israel and her God from the start, worthy of severe punishment. This is also how the original audience of Exodus would see him. To put it simply, Pharaoh's genuine guilt and moral liability are assumed by the warp and woof of the text with no thought of YHWH making Pharaoh sinful or guilty. Cf. B. J. Oropeza, 'Paul and Theodicy: Intertextual Thoughts on God's Justice and Faithfulness to Israel in Romans 9–11', *NTS* 53 (2007), 57–80 (64–65).

Pharaoh (which entails the hardening) and deliverance from his oppressive rule (6.1; see the end of section 6.7 above). We have further seen that in 6.2-13 and 6.28–7.5 YHWH therefore repeats much of what has already been said in the previous narrative in preparation for the commencement of his plan, including the persistent note of conditionality to YHWH's actions against Pharaoh already encountered in 2.23-25; 3.6-10, 19-20. It remains for us to take note of some other important specifics in 6.1–7.7.

In 6.6, YHWH states that he will redeem Israel from Egyptian bondage 'with great judgments'. This is an obvious reference to the signs/plagues YHWH would bring upon Pharaoh/Egypt. This redemption by means of the signs/plagues would lead to YHWH taking Israel as his people anew and to their coming to know that YHWH is their God and liberator (6.7).[170] In light of the fact that one of the purposes of the hardening is to facilitate the performance of YHWH's signs before Pharaoh (10.1), 6.6-7 implies that hardening serves as a means to the (renewed) election of God's people and their knowledge/acknowledgment of him as their covenant God.

In 7.2-5, when YHWH repeats his instructions to Moses before Moses heads back to Pharaoh, he says:

> You yourself shall speak all that I command you, and Aaron your brother shall speak to Pharaoh in order that he will let the sons of Israel go from his land. But I myself will harden Pharaoh's heart, and even though I will multiply my signs and wonders in the land of Egypt, Pharaoh will not listen to you. Then I will place my hand on Egypt and bring out my troops, my people, the sons of Israel, from the land of Egypt with great judgments. And then the Egyptians will know that I myself am YHWH when I stretch out my hand against Egypt and bring out the sons of Israel from their midst.

These verses contain the same basic scenario as 4.21-23: Moses and Aaron would demand Israel's release (implied in 4.21-23), but YHWH would harden Pharaoh's heart, leading him to refuse YHWH's demand despite the performance of multiple signs and wonders of divine might.[171] Just as the

---

170. Israel was already God's people by virtue of the Abrahamic covenant, but YHWH would confirm their covenantal election at Sinai and progress it to its next stage of fulfilment in the Sinaitic/Mosaic covenant. Most scholars take 6.7's reference to Israel's election to point forward to the Sinaitic covenant as we do. But because Israel is already God's people in Egypt, Fretheim, *Exodus*, 93, understands 6.7 to speak of God taking Israel out from Egypt (cf. Deut. 4.20, 34; 30.4; Ezek. 36.24; 37.21).

171. There are several main options for understanding the grammatical relationship between 7.3a (hardening) and 7.3b (signs). Beale, 'Hardening', 137 n. 40, argues for a view rarely taken – that the *waw* connecting the two clauses denotes purpose, citing the NASB translation. However, he indicates that the NASB might intend to mark a result clause – a second option – and this is far more likely, for purpose does not seem to be a use of *waw* in the type of construction present in 7.3 (non-converted, non-telic imperfect followed by *waw* consecutive with the perfect). Houtman, *Exodus*, 1.527, takes 7.3b as a final clause, but the only grammar he cites only allows for a *secondary* idea of purpose in this type of construction; see GKC, § 112m, p; 165a. No major translation I am aware of uses an unambiguous purpose clause except for the NLT, which is one of the freer major translations, and the NASB is the only possibility for an ambiguous one. A third and common option

hardening was presented as conditional on the performance of signs in 4.21, so 7.3 presents the hardening as conditional on request.[172] Thus together 4.21-23 and 7.2-4 depict the hardening as generally conditional upon request and signs,[173] which goes along with its aim to offset the compelling power of the signs to bring about submission to the request, resulting in a denial of the request instead.

Hardening is depicted with the Hebrew word קשׁה in 7.3, which we have seen refers to stubbornness in terms of difficulty with respect to moving the will. The idea is not that the stubborn person cannot move his own will, but that others cannot move his will.[174] In this context, it means that Pharaoh's will is too difficult for Moses, Aaron and the signs and wonders of YHWH to move to the point of granting the request for Israel's release (until the time

is to construe a simple future in sequence (so KJV, NJB, NRSV), but this leaves the logical relationship between the clauses unclear when the fourth and final option matches a natural logical connection that has already been established by the parallel passage of 4.21 – taking 7.3b to be in adversative relationship with the clause that follows it (7.4a) as reflected in our translation above ('and even though I will multiply my signs ... Pharaoh will not listen to you'). This is possibly the most common understanding in contemporary scholarship, rightly adopted by the NIV, ESV, NET, NAB and RSV. It is preferable to the resultative option, which has a more indirect though reasonable logic to it that coheres with an element of the narrative, viz. that the hardening makes for more signs because the refusal it fosters provokes more signs/plagues (see e.g., 10.1). See further note 173 below. Ultimately, there is little difference between the purposive and resultative options, and the simple future option would tend to imply purpose and result in context. If any of these other options are adopted, 7.2-4 should still be understood as assuming and building on 4.21-23, which has already established the hardening as conditional on signs. Before the performance of any signs, hardening would be unnecessary. But once the signs begin to be displayed, hardening gives Pharaoh the boldness necessary to do as he would want to do without the opposition of overwhelming divine power. In this way the hardening brings about refusal in response to request and despite signs. But because the hardening brings about refusal, it leads to more signs as further judgments and ostensible inducements to heed YHWH's demand for Israel's release. Exodus 7.3 would thus highlight this particular role of hardening to multiply the signs.

172.	The hardening statement of 7.3 is the same sort of contrastive disjunctive clause as occurs in 4.21; see section 6.5.b above.

173.	That the text is speaking only generally rather than indicating a tight order of events that must be repeated exactly in the same order over the course of Israel's liberation is suggested by the telescoped presentations in both 4.21-23 and 7.1-5 that read on the surface as if there would be only one run through the cycle of request, signs, hardening and refusal before YHWH would bring the final deadly plague that would secure Israel's release. Cf. Excursus 6.2 above. This renders irrelevant Beale's ('Hardening', 137 n. 40) observation that Pharaoh is often not given an opportunity to respond to the announcement of the next plague before it begins. It is not as if a new request must be made before each plague or that Pharaoh did not have the formal opportunity to relent at any time during the process. In other words, surely the demand for release is to be considered a standing demand as YHWH pummels Egypt with plague after plague for defiance of the demand and punctuates the process with renewed communication of it.

174.	Contra ibid., who thinks that the person with the hard heart finds it too difficult to accede to a request. But this does not make much sense in conjunction with the essential meaning of stubbornness, which typically refers to a person's firmness of resolve in his own will. A stubborn person might grant a request that accords with his already fixed will. But his will is immovable *by others* to anything other than it already is.

that YHWH decides to overpower Pharaoh's will). We have already seen that one of YHWH's main purposes in judging Pharaoh with hardening and plague is that Israel would know YHWH to be their God and saviour (6.6-7). Now we are told for the first time that another purpose YHWH has is that Egypt and her Pharaoh would know that he is YHWH, that is, that they would recognize his sovereignty and supreme divine status (7.5).

6.10. *The First Sign and the Beginning of the Hardening (7.8-13)*

This section serves as an introduction to the rest of the signs/plagues to follow.[175] It reports the initial engagement of the battle between YHWH and Pharaoh as rival gods.[176] As Enns observes, 'This one brief incident embodies the main elements of the ten plagues that follow: God shows his power and Pharaoh resists the obvious conclusion that he is no match for the God of Israel. He should concede victory to Yahweh. But he does not, which will yield disastrous consequences'.[177]

Having prepared Moses for further resistance from Pharaoh with the knowledge of the intended hardening, YHWH instructs him to have Aaron perform the first miraculous sign when Pharaoh would demand one (7.8-9). So 'Aaron threw his staff before Pharaoh and before his servants, and it became a serpent' (7.10b).[178] This act is filled with symbolic meaning.[179] Pharaoh's crown bore the image of a serpent on it, representing Pharaoh's divinity, divine power and all-encompassing sovereignty invested in him by the gods of Egypt, and it was thought to hold great magic that gave Pharaoh magical abilities.[180] By casting the staff before Pharaoh and turning it into Pharaoh's own emblem, Moses and Aaron challenged Pharaoh, his sovereignty, his allegedly divine power and the gods of Egypt that supposedly stood behind him.[181]

But Pharaoh summoned the wise men and magicians of Egypt, and the magicians, who would have been priests representative of the Egyptian gods,[182] also turned their staffs into serpents by their secret arts (7.11-12a). The mention of 'secret arts' (לְהָטִים), which may suggest trickery, most likely refers to the magicians' knowledge of snake charming, which could put a serpent into a state of catalepsy that made it rigid and appear as a staff, and then rouse the serpent to an active state at the charmer's provocation.[183]

175. Durham, *Exodus*, 90; Stuart, *Exodus*, 286; Enns, *Exodus*, 196.
176. Enns, ibid.
177. Ibid.
178. Some scholars argue that the Hebrew word translated 'serpent' (תַּנִּין) more likely refers to a crocodile here, but Currid, *Egypt*, 86–87, shows this to be unlikely.
179. See ibid., 83–95, for a full discussion.
180. Ibid., 89–93.
181. Cf. ibid., 92–94; Mackay, *Exodus*, 139.
182. Mackay, *Exodus*, 138–39.
183. See ibid.; K. A. Kitchen, 'Magic and Sorcery: Egyptian and Assyro-Babylonian', *NBD*[2], 724–26 (725); cf. Stuart, *Exodus*, 195; Currid, *Egypt*, 94–95, who rightly reminds us that it is not *certain* that this is in view here. For a strong objection to the snake charming

But whatever the nature of the miracle they performed, the text is clear that YHWH's power was greater,[184] for 'Aaron's staff swallowed up their staffs' (7.12b), presumably referring to Aaron's staff, changed into a serpent, swallowing the serpents presented by the Egyptian magicians. The significance is palpable. While the Egyptian magicians tried to imitate YHWH's miracle to show Egypt's king and power impervious to any threat from these Hebrew slaves and their God, YHWH's power proved too great, overwhelming the magic of Egypt as it swallowed up the very symbol of Pharaoh's divinity, sovereignty and divine power.

Thus, Pharaoh should have acknowledged YHWH's superiority and submitted to his demand. 'But Pharaoh's heart was strong, and he did not listen to them, as YHWH had said' (7.13). Here we encounter the first occurrence of actual hardening, though it is most likely that the Hebrew qal stative perfect verb[185] used for hardening is intransitive and indicates the state of Pharaoh's heart that led to his refusal of Moses' and Aaron's request for Israel's release despite this miraculous sign rather than indicating the transitive action of Pharaoh's heart being strengthened ('was strengthened') or even intransitively entering into a strong state ('became strong').[186] The aspect of the perfect verb seems to be one of effected state (i.e., resultative)[187] since the strength of will (heart) referred to here is undoubtedly the result of YHWH's hardening activity, as indicated by the fulfilment phrase, 'as YHWH had said' (see further section 6.7 above), referring back to the two

---

view, see Enns, *Exodus*, 198. For a description of approaches to the question of the nature of the magicians' miracle, see Houtman, *Exodus*, 1.535.

184. Currid, ibid.

185. More precisely, it is a converted imperfect, which carries the meaning of the perfect.

186. Cf. Beale, 'Hardening', 139 (especially), who argues convincingly for the intransitive; J. P. Hyatt, *Exodus* (NCB; London: Marshall Morgan and Scott, 1971), 104; Steinmann, 'Hardness', 382; Stenmans, 'כָּבֵד', 7.21. However, most translations seem to opt for either the transitive sense or an ingressive intransitive sense.

187. Although Beale, ibid., is right to conclude this (despite incorrectly presenting aoristic vs perfective action as the only two possibilities of the meaning of the perfect in 7.13; the stative with the perfect can simply denote a past state without implicit reference to an action that brought about that state (cf. Joüon/Muraoka, *Hebrew*, § 112b; as Waltke/O'Connor, *Hebrew*, § 30.5.3.b, note, statives in past time can be constative)), he tries to squeeze more out of the Hebrew perfect in 7.13 than the evidence can bear when he argues that 'the verb refers to Pharoah's heart already being in a hardened condition *before* the signs of this narrative were performed before him' (emphasis original). Despite the resultative use of the perfect here, the text does not give any indication of the exact timing of the hardening that produced the hardened state in relation to the serpent sign, whether it took place long before, just before, concurrently or even after the sign but before Pharaoh's refusal of YHWH's demand. Even if it did place it before the serpent sign as Beale asserts, there would still be no tension with the position that hardening is presented as conditional on signs in 4.21 since the conditionality is not one that requires temporal priority, but is one of logical and psychological import. It is not that the signs directly produce the hardening, but that the signs give rise to the need for hardening to give Pharaoh the courage to defy YHWH despite the powerful signs. Thus, hardening is integrally connected to signs and presented as taking place in general conjunction with them.

previous announcements of hardening and consequent Pharaohnic-refusal-despite-signs in 4.21 and 7.3-4.[188] YHWH's plan for Israel's deliverance is beginning to unfold as he foretold, and as Enns observes, 'this passage summarizes the battle between Yahweh and Pharaoh that follows. It gives us a snapshot of the drama to unfold and of the final victory that will be won'.[189]

6.11. *The First Plague Narrative (Exodus 7.14-25)*

After the serpent-sign incident, 'Then YHWH said to Moses, "Pharaoh's heart is heavy; he refuses to let the people go"' (7.14), after which he proceeded to commission Moses to confront Pharaoh again and carry out the plague that was to fall as a result of Pharaoh's refusal (7.15-19). The root כבד appears for the first time with respect to Pharaoh's hardening in 7.14, in this instance as the adjective כָּבֵד, which refers to the 'heavy' (i.e., strong, immovable) state of Pharaoh's heart/will, presumably due to the same divine cause of the state of heart referred to in 7.13.[190] This strength of will is what led to Pharaoh's refusal of YHWH's demand despite the display of YHWH's divine power and superiority. As we have already seen, this is not because YHWH's hardening activity made Pharaoh desire to refuse Israel's release, but because it gave Pharaoh the boldness to do as he already wanted to do in the face of superior power.

YHWH's remark to Moses about the heaviness of Pharaoh's heart would further prepare Moses for the continued obstinacy he would face from Pharaoh. Literally, it adds stress to the theme of the hardening of Pharaoh's heart, and thus, to YHWH's role in funding Pharaoh's stubbornness and to his own sovereignty.[191] Moreover, as the hardening facilitates YHWH's plan to inflict protracted justice and judgment on Pharaoh and Egypt, this repetition highlights the burgeoning fulfilment of his plan. Repeated again towards the

---

188. With respect to hardening, 7.13 most strongly invokes 4.21, since it uses the same Hebrew word for harden, חזק, whereas 7.3 uses קשה. However, 7.13 shares the same phraseology for refusal with 7.4, 'not listening', whereas 4.21 speaks of 'not letting go'. Be that as it may, the terminology used in these passages is roughly synonymous, and so 7.13 looks back to both 4.21 and 7.3-4. As for the nature of the hardening mentioned in 7.13, judging from the later narrative it may be that the hardening was accomplished through YHWH's choice of a miracle that the Egyptian magician's could imitate on some level, allowing for some hope that their power could rival his (cf. 7.22; 8.11(15); 9.34; 14.4). But at 7.13, the text is silent as to the means of hardening.

189. Enns, *Exodus*, 196.

190. Cf. Beale, 'Hardening', 141–42.

191. Cf. Stuart, *Exodus*, 196. Beale, 'Hardening', 142 (see esp. n. 58), overreaches in his attempt to argue against contingency of hardening on signs from 7.14. Puzzlingly, he states, 'here the hardening is mentioned before the performance of any signs'. But this is plainly false. These verses immediately *follow* the performance of the first sign (7.8-13) as does the placement of YHWH's statements in narrative time. It is true that the hardening here is mentioned before the performance of any *more* signs. But that would seem to be irrelevant. See further, Excursus 6.2 and note 173 above.

end of this first plague narrative (7.23), these themes receive even greater emphasis.[192]

Moses and Aaron performed the sign-plague of turning the water of the Nile into blood (7.19-21). 'But the magicians of Egypt did the same by their secret arts, and so Pharaoh's heart grew strong, and he did not listen to them, as YHWH had said' (7.22). The hardening statement uses the same Hebrew wording as in 7.13 – the qal stative perfect of חזק. There we concluded that the verb is intransitive with a focus on the effected state of Pharaoh's heart. But in this context, following immediately with a *waw* consecutive upon reference to the Egyptian magicians reproducing the miracle, it probably emphasizes the growth of Pharaoh's heart in its resolve. Contextually, this would amount to entering into a new, greater state of strength of will due to the appearance of the magicians matching YHWH's miracle in some measure.

Nevertheless, Pharaoh should have recognized YHWH's sovereignty and superiority in this miracle, for even though the magicians were able to duplicate the miracle on some level,[193] their efforts paled in comparison to YHWH's mighty act in scope and devastating effect. Moreover, Egyptians considered the Nile to be a god and Pharaoh to be the divine keeper of cosmic order.[194] For YHWH to take control over the Nile and to harm it in this way showed his sovereign supremacy over Pharaoh and the gods of Egypt.[195] So 7.23 expresses some surprised indignation that Pharaoh 'did not take even this [miracle] to heart' despite the fact that the increased strength of Pharaoh's will is a fulfilment of YHWH's stated intention of strengthening his heart as indicated by the fulfilment phrase of 7.22 (cf. 4.21; 7.3).[196] Apparently YHWH's choice of a miracle that Egypt's magicians could imitate on some level, paltry as it may have been, prompted Pharaoh to take courage to do as he wished, viz. to keep Israel enslaved, standing firm against the demand for her release. Yet YHWH had declared that Pharaoh would know his identity as YHWH, that is, his divine identity and supreme sovereignty, by this miracle of turning the water of the Nile into blood (7.17). It would seem that through this plague Pharaoh did learn that YHWH was the true, supreme God, but

192. Cf. Stuart, ibid.

193. Again, their use of 'secret arts' probably connotes trickery.

194. See Coover Cox, 'Hardening', 303, 307; Currid, 'Harden', 47–48; Stuart, *Exodus*, 131–32, 197 (on just the Nile as a god); cf. Sailhamer, *Pentateuch*, 252–53, though he does not think that the author intended a specific polemic against Egyptian theology.

195. All the plagues seem to carry this implication of supremacy over Pharaoh and the other gods of Egypt given (a) their destructiveness to the created order, (b) the Egyptians believed their gods to be personified in nature (Currid, ibid), (c) Pharaoh's divine status and role as protector of the cosmic order. Due to our special focus, we will not point out this specific theme of the text in each plague.

196. 7.23's surprised indignation fits with the hardening theme because, as we have seen, YHWH emboldens Pharaoh's will to act as he already desired to act of his own accord. Moreover, YHWH's hardening action here does not appear as direct and irresistible, but as the presentation of his power in such a way that Pharaoh could take courage to do as he wished despite the clear revelation of his supremacy.

that YHWH's hardening action of choosing a miracle that could be copied in some fashion gave him the boldness to stand against YHWH anyway.[197]

6.12. *The Second Plague Narrative (Exodus 7.26 (8.1)–8.11 (15))*

After giving Pharaoh seven days, YHWH sent Moses to him again with a demand for Israel's release and the threat of the next plague that would fall *if* Pharaoh would refuse this renewed demand (7.25-29 (8.4)). As Fretheim and Chisholm argue, the conditional language implies that Pharaoh can choose to let the people go or not.[198] It would seem that the hardening does not irresistibly determine Pharaoh's response,[199] since it is most natural to assume that the hardening of 7.22-23 is still in effect, helping to explain Pharaoh's implied negative response to YHWH's ultimatum.[200] Chisholm

197. One could well take the imperfect tense of 7.17's declaration as obligative, e.g., 'you should know' (as do Houtman, *Exodus*, 2.37, and seemingly Durham, *Exodus*, 93), or perhaps more likely as potential ('you will [be able to] know'), indicating that the plague provided what was necessary for Pharaoh to be able to know YHWH's true identity. But the language is similar to other predictions that someone will know YHWH's identity using the simple future, and it is not incompatible with Pharaoh's knowledge of YHWH's true identity that he would nevertheless refuse to submit to it, especially given his hardened condition.

198. Fretheim, *Exodus*, 99; Chisholm, 'Hardening', 420 (following Fretheim).

199. Rightly, Fretheim, ibid. But Chisholm, ibid., seems to assume that the hardening is predetermining. It could be that Pharaoh had no choice, but that being offered a choice when he in fact had no choice was part of his just punishment for brutal oppression of Israel (cf. Pharaoh requiring Israel to do work they could not possibly complete and the consequent beating of the Israelite foremen when Israel failed to deliver their impossible quota). But this is not as likely since it is never made clear to Pharaoh that he did not really have a choice, which would be necessary for it to function as a punishment. See note 204 below for how the hardening can allow for genuine choice.

200. Chisholm, ibid., n. 31, thinks Pharaoh is acting apart from the influence of divine hardening here and makes a good case for the view that the effect of the hardening tended to wear off from one plague cycle to the next. But there is never any mention of hardening wearing off or being withdrawn. Moreover, his reasoning rests substantially on the questionable assumption that the hardening is irresistibly predetermining of Pharaoh's actions; see note 199 above and 204 below. Chisholm further supports his view by pointing to the broader narrative feature of repeated hardening as evidenced in 9.12. But it seems more natural to understand that the effect of prior hardening remained, but was not enough to ensure Pharaoh's obstinacy at times due to added divine pressure (e.g., in the case of 7.26 (8.1)–8.1 (8.5), the threat of another plague following on the previous two signs; in the case of 9.12, the plague of boils), necessitating further hardening for Pharaoh to resist the awesome divine power pressing upon him. Even so, it could not be said that Pharaoh's heart was still strong/hard/heavy in the terminology of the exodus narrative at the times at which Pharaoh needed additional hardening. But this does not mean that its effects are completely gone. Chisholm argues that hardening should not be viewed like a switch that is turned on and left on. But his view makes hardening like a switch that gets turned on and off. I would suggest that the language of hardening offers a better analogy, that of strength or weight of will. While one act of hardening might result in a certain strength of will, the appropriate amount of further divine pressure can overcome that. But further hardening can then strengthen the will enough to withstand the additional

has largely captured the flow of the narrative at this point:

> Apparently Pharaoh could have avoided this plague, if he had let the people go. Though the text does not record the delivery of the message or Pharaoh's response, one can assume that Pharaoh rejected the warning, for the Lord instructed Moses to bring the plague on the land (v. 5). The omission has a rhetorical function, as if the narrator were saying, 'I won't even bother reporting the actual delivery of the message and Pharaoh's response. You know he didn't listen' ... His obstinance prompts two rounds of judgment, facilitated by divine hardening.[201]

But while Pharaoh's resolve was strong enough to resist the threat of the second plague, it was not strong enough to resist the actual infliction of the plague. Pharaoh agreed to let Israel go when afflicted with the plague of frogs (8.4 (8)). It took additional hardening to embolden Pharaoh to renege on his promise to free Israel. This came by way of withdrawal of the plague (added to continuing effects of previous hardening): 'But when Pharaoh saw that there was relief [from the plague of frogs], he made his heart heavy, and he did not listen to them, as YHWH had said' (8.11 (15)).

This is the first explicit statement in the narrative of Pharaoh hardening his own heart. The verb is the hiphil of כבד, referring to Pharaoh making his own will 'heavy' (i.e., immovable), digging in his heels so to speak. 'This is the verb form employed when Pharaoh hardened his heart after relenting (as in 8:32 and 9:34)'.[202] Although Pharaoh is identified as the agent of hardening in this case, the fulfilment phrase, 'as YHWH had said', signals that this hardening and refusal are fulfilments of YHWH's intention to strengthen Pharaoh's will so as to bring about his refusal. It is probably not that Pharaoh hardening his own heart is merely another way of describing YHWH hardening his heart,[203] but that YHWH's emboldening of Pharaoh's will naturally brought Pharaoh to fix his own will unyieldingly on what he already most wanted to do – defy YHWH's demand for Israel's release – but because of the plagues would not dare to do without this divine enablement.[204] Thus, it can be said

---

pressure. If Chisholm is right to assume that hardening is irresistibly predetermining of Pharaoh's actions when its effects are present, then his construal is the most likely.

201. Chisholm, 'Hardening', 420.

202. Ibid., 421.

203. Contra Piper, *Justification*, 163, who also cites Schmidt and Nygren.

204. This understanding is supported by Beale's ('Hardening', 143) own point that the text presents Pharaoh as performing the hardening and so making a genuine choice rather than his hardened refusals being mechanistic mock actions. However, Beale's own view of Pharaoh's refusals as irresistibly determined by God is inconsistent with this point. For genuine choice denotes selecting between possible alternatives, and irresistible predetermination allows only one course of action and therefore no choice. It does appear that Pharaoh is allowed some measure of genuine choice because YHWH essentially frees him from fear of acting as he desired. Some interpreters view Pharaoh as having no choice when under YHWH's hardening, making him little more than a puppet (e.g., Chisholm, 'Hardening', 421; Gunn, 'Hardening', 79–80; Isbell, *Function*, 28–29; Irwin, 'Suspension', 59). But ironically, it would seem that YHWH's strengthening of Pharaoh's heart increased his freedom of choice in the situation, for it took away the literally *overpowering* effect the plagues would otherwise have of forcing Pharaoh to grant Israel's release, enabling

both that YHWH hardened Pharaoh's heart and that Pharaoh hardened his own heart, for YHWH's emboldening action (in essence, taking away his fear of YHWH's power) led to Pharaoh hardening his own will.

6.13. *The Third Plague Narrative (Exodus 8.12 (16)-15(19))*

After Pharaoh went back on his word (to release Israel) upon seeing that the plague of frogs was lifted, YHWH commanded that Moses and Aaron perform the next plague (of gnats). This time the magicians were unable to duplicate the miracle at all. 'Then the magicians said to Pharaoh, "It is the finger of God." But Pharaoh's heart was strong, and he did not listen to them, as YHWH had said' (8.15 (19)). By attributing the plague to the finger of God, the magicians let Pharaoh know that the miracle was genuinely divine. Apart from the divine hardening, one would expect Pharaoh to capitulate quite readily now that even his magicians acknowledge YHWH's divine power. The statement of hardening is the same as in 7.13, utilizing the Hebrew qal intransitive stative perfect of the verb חזק.[205] Again the perfect stative is most likely resultative, indicating the state resulting from previous hardening – in this case most likely the hardening mentioned in 8.11 (15) from the previous plague (see our treatment of the nature of this hardening above). Once again the hardening is attributed to YHWH by the fulfilment phrase, 'as YHWH had said'. YHWH is beginning to make Pharaoh look outright foolish.[206]

6.14. *The Fourth Plague Narrative (Exodus 8.16 (20)-28(32))*

In response to Pharaoh's renewed refusal, YHWH commands Moses to confront him again (8.16 (20)-19(23)). Just as with the second plague, YHWH gave Pharaoh an ultimatum and a choice to avoid the next plague by yielding to YHWH's demand.[207] This message to Pharaoh introduces a new element into the narrative that will feature in several later plagues (numbers five, seven, nine and ten) – YHWH's concern to make a distinction between Israel and Egypt, protecting his people from the plague of judgment that would fall on their enemies (8.18-19).[208] Here YHWH identifies the purpose

---

Pharaoh to choose as he desired. Nevertheless, because of the stubborn will Pharaoh already autonomously had toward Israel's situation, YHWH could practically control his reaction by emboldening him. Even if one disagrees with this approach, removing Pharaoh's freedom in this situation is compatible with the Pentateuch's portrayal of YHWH's character as righteous, for as we have seen, the text presents hardening as a just judgment against Pharaoh for his autonomous wicked treatment of Israel.

205. See above on 7.13. The same form was also used previously in 7.22, but there we found that the perfect carries an ingressive nuance.

206. Cf. Gunn, 'Hardening', 76.

207. See Chisholm, 'Hardening', 421–22. See also discussion of the second plague narrative above for the pertinent exegetical and theological implications.

208. Stuart, *Exodus*, 212.

of making the distinction to be that Pharaoh would know YHWH is 'in the midst of the land' (8.18), that is, that YHWH was present in Egypt as the divine sovereign with total power over the land Pharaoh and the gods of Egypt were supposed to control.

YHWH's enacting of the plague of flies implies that Pharaoh defied YHWH again.[209] And again, just as with the second plague, the fourth plague elicits Pharaoh's concession to YHWH's demand, suggesting that even though the effect of previous hardening likely remained, it was not enough to ensure Pharaoh's obstinacy given added divine pressure in the form of this plague, so that Pharaoh's heart can no longer be considered strong or hard in the terminology of the exodus narrative. After Pharaoh's concession and before departing from him, Moses warned him not to 'act falsely again' by going back on his word (as he did after the second plague was halted; 8.25 (29)).[210] But after YHWH removed the plague, 'Then Pharaoh made his heart heavy this time also, and he did not let the people go' (8.28 (32)).

The phrase 'this time also' (גַּם בַּפַּעַם הַזֹּאת) looks back to Pharaoh's hardening of his own will after withdrawal of the second plague (8.11 (15)). There we saw that YHWH's emboldening action enabled Pharaoh to set his will firmly in opposition to YHWH. But now, as Chisholm has observed, 'In contrast to the earlier incidents no mention is made in the record of this plague of Yahweh's involvement in the hardening. The statement "as the Lord had said" is conspicuous by its absence'.[211] The effect is not to indicate that YHWH's hardening work played no role in Pharaoh's self-hardening,[212] but to stress Pharaoh's responsibility for his treacherous choice and willfulness.[213] As with the second plague, removal of the fourth plague added to the remaining effects of previous hardening appears to have emboldened Pharaoh to do what he wanted to do, but dared not do while experiencing the plague.

6.15. The Fifth Plague Narrative (Exodus 9.1-7)

209. Chisholm, 'Hardening', 421–22.

210. There is no need to suppose that Pharaoh was lying *when* he agreed to let Israel go. Going back on his word after the fact also qualifies as acting falsely. This is more in line with the pivotal role of hardening and the fact that Pharaoh hardened his heart after seeing removal of the plague. If he planned not to honour his word from the start, and only agreed to liberate Israel as a strategy to end the plague, then his heart would already be hard, and returning to refusal could not fairly be characterized as him hardening his heart (as Beale, 'Hardening', 143–44, notes, the hardening statement here functions as a perfect definite past, presenting a distinct act of hardening).

211. Ibid., 422.

212. Pace ibid., 422–23. Mentioning good literary reasons for understanding YHWH as involved despite absence of the fulfilment phrase, Chisholm is more compelling in favour of the view he ends up rejecting than is Beale, 'Hardening', 144, who advocates the view, though he does not refer to the absence of the fulfilment phrase.

213. See our treatment of the second plague narrative above for explanation of how YHWH's hardening allows for Pharaoh's genuine choice/freedom and responsibility.

After Pharaoh broke his word again, YHWH sent Moses to him yet again to demand Israel's release and to threaten him with another plague *if* he would continue to refuse to let them go (9.1-5). As with past ultimatums (7.26 (8.1)-29 (8.4); 8.16 (20)-19 (23)), YHWH's giving Pharaoh a choice suggests that Pharaoh could genuinely choose to let Israel go and avoid the threatened plague.[214] But Pharaoh chose to refuse YHWH again, as implied by the fact that YHWH went ahead with the plague of death by pestilence to Egypt's cattle (9.6).[215] 'And Pharaoh sent, and behold, not even one of the cattle of Israel had died. But Pharaoh's heart was heavy, and he did not let the people go' (9.7). The statement of hardening employs the qal stative converted imperfect of כבד, which probably carries a resultative nuance as in earlier uses of the perfective qal stative with חזק (7.13, 22; 8.15 (19)), describing the state of Pharaoh's heart as heavy as the result of previous hardening.[216] The most recent hardening mentioned, which uses the same verb (though a different form), is most likely in view – Pharaoh's self-hardening in 8.28 (32), which was apparently in effect in Pharaoh's initial response to YHWH's ultimatum before the plague of pestilence fell. Connection to Pharaoh's recent self-hardening and omission of any reference to divine hardening again fixes attention on Pharaoh's own guilt and responsibility for his stubborn defiance of God and refusal to release God's people from oppressive slavery.

6.16. *The Sixth Plague Narrative (Exodus 9.8-12)*

This time YHWH does not give Pharaoh a specific opportunity to escape the next plague. He simply commands Moses and Aaron to perform the plague, bringing boils on the Egyptians and their animals (9.8-11). YHWH's superior power expressed in this plague gains greater prominence not only from the increased intensity of the plague, but also from the fact that even the Egyptian magicians are struck by the plague so that they could not stand before Moses (9.11). There can be no question of who is supreme. The priests representative of Egypt's gods and wielders of Egypt's divine power were defeated before YHWH's representative. 'But YHWH strengthened Pharaoh's heart, and he did not listen to them, as YHWH had said to Moses' (9.12).

This is the first time that YHWH is explicitly identified as the agent of hardening since he first predicted he would strengthen Pharaoh's heart in 4.21. From here on out the narrative stresses YHWH's role in hardening even more strongly than it has so far. The reappearance of the fulfilment phrase, 'as YHWH had said', bolsters this stress here all the more. This particular expression of hardening (piel of חזק) highlights YHWH's action in emboldening Pharaoh to act as he wanted despite the display of YHWH's unparalleled power and the unstoppable suffering he was inflicting on Egypt.

214. Chisholm, 'Hardening', 422.
215. Ibid.
216. Cf. Beale, 'Hardening', 144.

6.17. *The Seventh Plague Narrative (Exodus 9.13-35)*

In response to Pharaoh's continued resistance, YHWH sends Moses to him again with the demand to let God's people go (9.13), backed by the threat that YHWH would unleash all his plagues (9.14a). The purpose of these plagues was that Pharaoh would know that there is no one like YHWH in all the earth (9.14b). Exodus 9.15-16 then ground YHWH's threat to unleash all of his plagues and his purpose of showing his incomparability by declaring that YHWH could have destroyed Egypt all along and by revealing YHWH's purpose in tempering his own hand of judgment: 'for now I could have stretched forth my hand and struck you and your people with pestilence, and you would have been obliterated from the earth.[217] But indeed, because of this I have caused you to stand, in order to show you my power and to proclaim my name in all the earth'. YHWH's threat to unleash all of his plagues (9.14a) and his incomparability (9.14b) are bolstered by the fact that he could have unleashed total destruction at any time heretofore, but has withheld it for his own purposes (9.15-16). The plagues are completely at his discretion to inflict at any time; he has graciously allowed Pharaoh to live thus far, and the purposes he mentions for withholding absolute destruction have been substantially fulfilled. Together 9.14-16 provide reason for Pharaoh to let Israel go (i.e., 9.14-16 ground 9.13c). In short, they are a statement of YHWH's incomparable power and sovereignty. Exodus 9.17 further supports the injunction to let Israel go by drawing attention to Pharaoh's continued rebellion, the stance he is being called upon to abandon.

Paul quotes Exod. 9.16 in Rom. 9.17, and therefore it merits closer attention. 'I have caused you to stand' (הֶעֱמַדְתִּיךָ) could mean that YHWH created Pharaoh or that he established Pharaoh in his position. But standing in adversarial relationship to 9.15's declaration that YHWH could have obliterated Pharaoh and his people, it most likely refers to YHWH allowing Pharaoh to remain alive, as most interpreters recognize.[218] YHWH identifies

---

217. The verbs in 9.15 would normally be understood in the simple past tense, but most translations and interpreters rightly favour the past with the potential perfect or the conditional perfect here because of the context. Durham, *Exodus*, 127, rejects this consensus, arguing for a simple present-future sense. Others opt for an obligative nuance, but the strong adversative that begins 9.16 (אוּלָם) weighs against this (Enns, *Exodus*, 221 n. 64). Houtman, *Exodus*, 2.86–87, reviews several options for the use of the perfect in 9.15, and concludes that the potential perfect is the most plausible.

218. Durham, *Exodus*, 128, asserts that 'kept stubborn' is part of the meaning, but this seems unlikely for a statement made to Pharaoh, who knew nothing of YHWH's hardening. It could be that the statement is meant to evoke a secondary association for the reader. Piper, *Justification*, 167, asserts that there is no other usage of the hiphil of עָמַד in the OT in the sense of 'preserve alive' and argues that the word should be understood with a more common use of this form to refer to YHWH's raising up of Pharaoh in his position. But the basis of Piper's argument is contradicted by *HALOT*, s.v. עָמַד, hif. § 3; cf. BDB, s.v. עָמַד, hiph. § 2; H. Ringgren, 'עָמַד', *TDOT*, 11.178–87 (185). The meaning of 'preserve, maintain' links naturally to the use of the qal's meaning, 'to remain, endure' (cf. *HALOT*, qal § 3c; BDB, qal § 3b–d; Ringgren, 184–85). Indeed, even if Piper's premise were granted, it seems too restrictive to require other instances of preservation of *life* with עָמַד when the

two related purposes for having allowed Pharaoh to remain alive: (1) to show Pharaoh his power, and (2) to proclaim YHWH's name in all the earth. The first purpose ties into what the narrative has already made clear is a fundamental purpose of YHWH – that Pharaoh and the Egyptians would know/acknowledge his sovereignty and supreme divine status, or to put it more succinctly, that they would bow to him.[219] Showing Pharaoh YHWH's power in an extended display facilitated by YHWH allowing Pharaoh's continued existence serves as the means to Pharaoh coming to know YHWH's identity and to acknowledge his supreme sovereignty. It also serves as the means to the second purpose mentioned in 9.16, the proclamation of YHWH's name in all the earth.

The proclamation of YHWH's name is equivalent to making known his sovereignty and supreme divine status. By prominently displaying his almighty power, laying Egypt waste, and publicly humiliating Pharaoh, Egypt and the gods of Egypt, YHWH would make his supreme divinity and sovereignty known in all the earth. This second purpose is essentially the extension of the first beyond Pharaoh and Egypt to the whole earth by means of the same first mentioned purpose. This universal purpose includes within it another major purpose of YHWH in the exodus, mentioned earlier in 6.7, that Israel too would know YHWH. Thus YHWH would ultimately seek to bring all people to fear and submit to him.[220] These purposes all coalesce to advance YHWH's climactic covenant purpose of bringing blessing to the whole world through the seed of Abraham (Gen. 12.3; 22.18; 26.4; 28.14), contributing to Exodus' continuation and development of the story begun in Genesis.

While 9.14-16 are logically subordinate to the call to submit to YHWH's sovereignty by letting Israel go to serve him, they play a prominent and distinctive role in the total exodus narrative, introducing new material in providing 'an explanation of the number of mighty acts (Childs, 158), ... "an apology for all of the plagues" (Hyatt, 118), ... [and] an announcement of a terrible intensification of the force and effect of the mighty acts leading up to the last of them affecting the Egyptians, the death of their first-born and the deliverance at the sea (cf. Cassuto, 115–16)'.[221] YHWH does something else that is unprecedented with this plague, one which develops 9.16's universal

---

verb itself could indicate preservation generally, with the specific nature of the preservation connoted by the context. This is undoubtedly the case with the LXX's choice of διατηρέω. Moreover, while Piper's construal of the logic of the text is intelligible on his view, it is less direct and more difficult to fit with the contrast to YHWH's declaration that he could have obliterated Pharaoh and his people.

219. Summing up the idea as 'bowing' was suggested to me by Enns, *Exodus*, 221.

220. On the universality of YHWH's purpose in 9.16, cf. Stuart, *Exodus*, 232, who regards 9.14-16 as 'something of a *proto-evangelium*'; Bruckner, *Exodus*, 89–90, who perhaps states the matter most boldly (see quote below); Mackay, *Exodus*, 171; Keil, *Pentatecuh*, 1.490; Fretheim, *Exodus*, 124–25.

221. Durham, *Exodus*, 127. Although Durham treats these as alternative understandings, they are best seen as complementary. Stuart, *Exodus*, 231, views the latter two as jointly operative and notes the novelty of the content of 9.14-16.

concern – he offers a genuine choice to avoid its consequences despite the actual infliction of the plague (of hail) by trusting his word and following his instructions (9.18-19). According to James Bruckner, 'Yahweh's actions in carefully providing shelter for anyone who feared (or trusted) the word of the Lord demonstrates *the second purpose* of the plague. God's goal was that all would come to fear and trust the Lord (14:31)'.[222] Indeed, some of the Egyptians had come to fear and trust YHWH, for some of them heeded his word and escaped the consequences of the plague whereas others disregarded his word and suffered dearly (9.20-26). Within the exodus narrative, the universalistic edge of this theme reaches its practical pinnacle when a large group of Gentiles (i.e., non-Israelites) joins Israel and participates in the mighty redemption of the exodus wrought by YHWH (12.38). The text, aimed at God's covenant people Israel, implicitly calls the reader to trust in YHWH and his word so as to be saved from his wrath.

Exodus 9.27 reports another unprecedented occurrence in the story – after the plague of hail fell and wreaked destruction upon Egypt but left Israel's area of the land (Goshen) untouched, Pharaoh confessed his and his people's wrongdoing and YHWH's righteousness: 'Then Pharaoh sent and called for Moses and Aaron, and said to them, "I have acted wrongly this time. YHWH is the righteous one, and I and my people are the guilty ones."' Pharaoh then asked Moses and Aaron to supplicate YHWH to put a stop to the plague with the promise that he would let Israel go (9.28). As many commentators point out, Pharaoh's confession does not likely indicate that he is truly repentant, turning to YHWH in contrite reverence.[223] Moses points out as much in his response to Pharaoh when he says, 'But as for you and your servants, I know that you do not yet fear YHWH God' (9.30), with the fear of YHWH indicating 'an attitude of reverent submission to the authority of God'.[224] Yet neither does this mean that Pharaoh was being duplicitous about his confession and promise in 9.27-28, intending all the while to break his word once the plague ceased. That would not cohere with the characterization of Pharaoh going back on his word as a result of Pharaoh hardening his heart, signalling a marked change of will/intention (see note 200 above). Rather, YHWH has forced Pharaoh to admit the truth about the tyrant's behaviour and to agree to let Israel go.

However, Pharaoh's true heart is revealed when YHWH withdraws the plague: 'But when Pharaoh saw that the rain and the hail and the thunder ceased, he sinned again and made his heart heavy, he and his servants. So

---

222. Bruckner, *Exodus*, 90; bold removed; remaining emphasis original.

223. See e.g., Stuart, *Exodus*, 237–38; Durham, *Exodus*, 129; Childs, *Exodus*, 158–59.

224. Mackay, *Exodus*, 177. See Stuart, *Exodus*, 238, on this; cf. U. Cassuto, *A Commentary on the Book of Exodus* (trans. I. Abrahams; Jerusalem: Magnes Press, 1967), 121. Some commentators try to draw a distinction between moral wickedness and legal guilt in Pharaoh's confession of wrongdoing (e.g., Bruckner, *Exodus*, 91), but that seems like a distinction without a difference here. In this instance, as is often the case, moral guilt and legal guilt overlap; it is hard to imagine how Pharaoh's admission of guilt in this circumstance of oppression and broken word could lack moral import.

Pharaoh's heart was strong, and therefore he did not let the sons of Israel go, as YHWH had said by the hand of Moses' (9.34-35). YHWH's withdrawal of plague once again incites Pharaoh to intensify his own will, who is followed by his servants. The fact that the narrator describes Pharaoh's self-hardening as sin heightens the narrative's stress on Pharaoh's responsibility for his stubbornness and suggests that YHWH does not irresistibly cause his actions. But, as just mentioned, they are rather incited by YHWH's withdrawal of the plague.[225] Hence, the strength of will resulting from Pharaoh's self-hardening is once again attributed to YHWH via the fulfilment phrase in 9.35.

This seventh plague narrative is a particularly important one in the overall story scheme, standing out as the longest plague account yet and introducing a number of new elements. The most important of these appears in the very words Paul quotes from 9.16 in Rom. 9.17, which specify YHWH's purposes for allowing Pharaoh to remain alive in his resistance to YHWH, which is tantamount to prolonging the assault on Egypt. Since the divine hardening enabled Pharaoh to choose to continue resisting YHWH, and continued resistance brought additional plague, Exod. 9.16 therefore also implicitly explains YHWH's purposes for hardening Pharaoh's heart.

6.18. *The Eighth Plague Narrative (Exodus 10.1-20)*

After Pharaoh sinned again by hardening his heart and refusing to let Israel go as he had promised, 'Then YHWH said to Moses, "Go to Pharaoh, for I myself have made his heart heavy, and the heart of his servants, for the purpose of my putting these signs of mine in his midst and in order that you may tell in the ears of your son and your grandson that I dealt severely with Egypt and [about] my signs that I put among them, in order that you may know that I am YHWH"' (10.1-2). Now YHWH actually cites his strengthening of Pharaoh's will as the reason for Moses to go to him with the same demand for Israel's release, and this for the purposes of multiplying his signs in Egypt and Israel's consequent recounting to future generations of his devastating defeat of her great enemy, all of which has the more ultimate purpose that Israel (represented here by Moses) would know YHWH (i.e., acknowledge his sovereignty and supreme divine status) – what Stuart aptly calls 'an evangelistic purpose'.[226] This is the first time that the text explicitly states a point that has been implicit for some time in the narrative – that multiplying signs was a purpose of hardening Pharaoh's heart.[227] The general underlying logic is that hardening leads to refusal of the request for release,

---

225. Exodus 9.27's verb for acting wrongly is the same verb used for sinning in 9.34 (חטא). In Pharaoh's mouth (9.27), the word is best understood in reference to wrongdoing without YHWH-centric religious overtones. But used in the narrator's theocentric perspective, the word refers to sin, transgression of the will of God, which humans are bound to obey from God as Creator and supreme sovereign of all. ·

226. Stuart, *Exodus*, 243.

227. Unless 7.3 expresses the idea, which is doubtful; see note 171 above.

and refusal leads to signs/plagues, which in turn show forth YHWH's divine power and supremacy with a view toward bringing Israel (as well as Egypt and the nations for that matter; cf. 9.16) to know YHWH. This serves as a reason for Moses to go back to Pharaoh in order to continue the process and more fully achieve YHWH's purposes.

The reference to YHWH having made Pharaoh's heart heavy in 10.1 looks back especially to Pharaoh's own self-hardening provoked by YHWH's withdrawal of the last plague (9.34-35).[228] The heart of Pharaoh and that of his servants was now bold enough to put up enough further resistance to another command from the all powerful YHWH so as to warrant another blow of plague and judgment. Moses relays YHWH's castigation of Pharaoh's arrogance in resisting him and again brings an ultimatum to Pharaoh to let Israel go or suffer a devastating plague, this time of locusts (10.3-6). Interestingly, even though Pharaoh's servants' hearts were strong along with his, they urge him to compromise with Moses and allow the men (הָאֲנָשִׁים; rather than the people [הָעָם] as Moses has consistently stated) to go to worship YHWH, asking him the humiliating and even accusatory question, 'Do you not yet know that Egypt is ruined'? (10.7). But the hardness of their hearts is shown precisely in their counsel to offer a compromise to Moses rather than a full capitulation to YHWH's demand.[229] They still do not take YHWH as seriously as they should, failing

---

228. Cf. Chisholm, 'Hardening', 424. Beale, 'Hardening', 146, follows Hesse in the very unlikely suggestion that the perfect of 10.1 is to be construed as prophetic, referring to YHWH's determination of later hardening and events in this section. His attempt to cut 10.1 off from the immediately preceding 9.34-35 because it starts a new literary section is unpersuasive; while the narrative surely utilizes literary sections, these are not rigidly cut off from one another, but generally build on one another. Moreover, his claim that 9.34-35 seem to summarize the hardening predictions of the various sections is baseless. Quite to the contrary, these verses are tied tightly to the seventh plague narrative ('when Pharaoh saw ... he sinned again and made his heart heavy') and function as other concluding hardening statements do in other sections. That they might look back to earlier sections in some way or other confirms that the sections are not rigidly cut off from one another, but does not provide enough of a basis to conclude that these verses specifically sum up previous hardening predictions. Finally, even if the sections were rigidly cut off from one another, there is no reason to think that a hardening statement in the perfect beginning a section would refer unusually to the future rather than more naturally to a new, accomplished act of hardening in preparation for what is to come. I am unaware of anyone who has followed Beale's position. Another possibility is that 10.1 could summarize all of the previous hardening – supported by the reference to 'these signs of mine' – without reference to Pharaoh's present state. But if it summarizes all previous hardening, that includes the very recent hardening of 9.34-35, which would most naturally be assumed to remain in effect. Following immediately on 9.34-35, it is most likely that 10.1's reference to hardening at least and especially refers to the hardening mentioned in these former verses.

229. Remember that we concluded that YHWH's demand was known to be for full and total release of Israel from the first. Chisholm, 'Hardening', 424–25, thinks that the servants are no longer under the effects of hardening in 10.7. But this does not fit as well with the text. YHWH sent Moses with the message of the eighth plague partly because he had made the heart of Pharaoh's servants heavy with a view toward bringing further plagues against Egypt (10.1). There is no intervening material since that hardening to suggest a withdrawal

to offer him unqualified submission as the supreme divine sovereign.

This reading receives confirmation as Pharaoh appears to take the servants' advice, offering Moses a compromise of taking only the men to worship YHWH (10.8-11), a compromise that would ensure the men's return and therefore Israel's continuance as slaves to the Egyptians. But the compromise was unacceptable to YHWH, and so he unleashed the plague of locusts, which broke Pharaoh's hard-heartedness and brought him to confess his sin again and to beg Moses to supplicate YHWH to stop the plague, implying that he would now release Israel on YHWH's terms (10.12-17). YHWH did withdraw the plague (10.19), 'But YHWH strengthened Pharaoh's heart, and he did not let the sons of Israel go' (10.20). Once again YHWH emboldened Pharaoh to do what he really wanted to do despite YHWH's undeniable and absolute superiority, to Pharaoh's and his people's detriment.

6.19. *The Ninth Plague Narrative (Exodus 10.21-29)*

That detriment came with YHWH's response to Pharaoh's renewed refusal to let Israel go, given without any further overture toward Pharaoh: the plague of darkness (10.21-23). Pharaoh, still retaining some strength of will in the face of this new plague, offered Moses another compromise, but he would have none of it (10.24-26). Faced with Moses' refusal to compromise, it would seem that Pharaoh was about to capitulate again as at other times, 'But YHWH strengthened Pharaoh's heart, and he was not willing to let them go' (10.27). Indeed, Pharaoh threatened Moses' life if he ever saw Pharaoh's face again (10.28).

6.20. *Introduction to the Culminating Events (Exodus 11.1–10)*

YHWH announced to Moses that he would bring one more plague, after which Pharaoh would finally release Israel (11.1).[230] After 11.2 records YHWH's instruction to have the people ask their neighbours for valuables,

---

of the hardening from them. If the approach offered above is rejected, then the servants' capitulating action would suggest something for which we have already found evidence in the broader narrative – that hardening does not remove genuine choice and so is not irresistibly determining.

230.   There is some question of whether 11.1-3 should be taken as retrospective and its opening verb as pluperfect in meaning (so NIV; Stuart, *Exodus*, 262; Enns, *Exodus*, 245), which would make for a smoother connection between the previous section ending at 10.29 and 11.4ff. But this is not the most natural reading with the consecutive verbal construction beginning at 11.1, which suggests that YHWH spoke the content of 11.1b-2 to Moses during his encounter with Pharaoh, continuing on from 10.29. Despite some awkwardness, it is better to let the more natural reading of the grammar lead us in the order of events than to allow a smoother flow to lead us to adopt a rather unlikely (though not impossible; see Waltke/O'Connor, *Hebrew*, § 33.3.2) view of the grammar. For fuller discussion and references, see Houtman, *Exodus*, 2.129–30, who argues against reading a pluperfect.

11.3 reports that 'YHWH gave the people favour in the eyes of the Egyptians', which further testifies to YHWH's awesome divine power. Moses announced to Pharaoh the final, climactic plague that would come – the death of all the firstborn of Egypt – highlighting the rigid distinction YHWH would make between his people and her enemies (11.4-7) and boldly boasting that Pharaoh's servants would bow before Moses and beg him and his people to leave Egypt, which would in fact be followed by their departure (11.8). Interestingly, Moses then 'went out from Pharaoh in burning anger' (11.8d). Moses' intense anger with Pharaoh adds some support to the view that the divine hardening of his heart (1) has to do with strengthening his already autonomously established will, and (2) does not remove his choice in the situation or necessitate his actions. For Moses knew YHWH had hardened Pharaoh's heart. But Moses' anger at Pharaoh would not make much sense if he knew that Pharaoh could not act in any other way.

This, of course, does not mean that the divine hardening would not result in Pharaoh's refusal to let Israel go as YHWH said it would, only that the text does not present YHWH as irresistibly causing Pharaoh's will or actions. Indeed, after Moses left Pharaoh's presence, 'Then YHWH said to Moses, "Pharaoh will not listen to you in order that my wonders will be multiplied in the land of Egypt"' (11.9).[231] The purpose referred to here is the same as YHWH's purpose in strengthening Pharaoh to be able to defy Moses' demand, mentioned in 10.1. Since YHWH's hardening activity will purposely bring Pharaoh to refuse Israel's release, which will in turn bring YHWH to add to the wonders he has performed,[232] YHWH could say that the (divine) purpose for Pharaoh's refusal was to multiply his wonders.

Exodus 11.10, which interrupts the narrative flow with a disjunctive clause,[233] then summarizes what has taken place to this point: 'So Moses and Aaron did all these wonders before Pharaoh, but YHWH strengthened Pharaoh's heart, and he did not let the sons of Israel go from his land'. The vocabulary of this verse recalls the two predictions of Pharaoh's hardening given before its commencement (4.21; 7.3-4), forming an inclusio with the predictions and indicating their fulfilment.[234] This summary repeats the

---

231. It could be that 11.9 reports what YHWH had said (reading וַיֹּאמֶר as a pluperfect) to Moses earlier (so e.g., NIV; Stuart, *Exodus*, 268), but this is not the most natural reading with the consecutive verbal construction that begins at 11.9 (cf. note 230 above), and the context does not demand that 11.9 be retrospective. Against the retrospective interpretation, see Houtman, *Exodus*, 2.135, who questions whether the pluperfect is even possible here (but see our previous note). It probably refers to Pharaoh's continuing refusal up until the final plague forces him to let Israel go; but see Houtman, 2.135–36, who understands a present rather than future reference. In any event, 11.10's reference to 'all these wonders' appears to exclude the final plague since the verse states that Pharaoh did not let Israel go despite all the wonders.

232. Notice that Pharaoh's actions can rightly be characterized as bringing about YHWH's response, but there is no hint that they do so irresistibly. So it is with YHWH's actions bringing about Pharaoh's response to his wonders.

233. Cf. Chisholm, 'Hardening', 425.

234. On the connection to 4.21 and 7.3-4, see Beale, 'Hardening' 146, and esp. Piper, *Justification*, 169–70; cf. Chisholm, 'Hardening', 425, who misses the connection to 4.21,

psychological and logical relationship between the wonders and hardening, showing hardening to be conditional on wonders, the former made necessary by the latter to provide the boldness for Pharaoh to defy YHWH. By identifying YHWH as the agent of hardening, the synopsis statement underscores YHWH as the primary agent of hardening throughout the narrative.[235] Appropriately, 11.10 uses the dominant word for hardening from the narrative – חזק – confirming the fundamental essence of YHWH's hardening activity as a strengthening of Pharaoh's will to do as he already wanted to do.

6.21. *The Culminating Events (Exodus 12.1–15.21)*

Exodus 12.1-27d record YHWH's instructions to Moses and Aaron for Israel regarding preparation for and conduct during the imminent plague of death to the firstborn of Egypt as well as instructions for regular, future commemoration of the redemption it would win for Israel that day. After receiving this instruction, the people responded with worship and obedience (12.27e-28). Exodus 12.12 deserves note for its statement that the death plague will be an execution of judgment against all the gods of Egypt. By bringing such lethal catastrophe to every part of Egypt except for those he designated as under his protection, YHWH humiliated all the gods of Egypt and demonstrated his absolute superiority over them, who were unable to protect their people and realms, as well as his absolute sovereignty over life and death.[236] The final statement in 12.12 of God's identity – 'I am YHWH' – echoes previous statements that YHWH would bring all to know his supreme divine power and sovereignty through his mighty acts against Egypt (6.7; 7.5; 7.17; 10.2; cf. 8.6 (10); 8.18 (22); 9.14-16, 29; 11.7).

YHWH inflicted the tenth plague, killing all the firstborn of Egypt (12.29), which overcame Pharaoh's strength of will (i.e., his hard-heartedness) so that he finally capitulated to YHWH's demand fully and released Israel (12.30-32). Israel asked the Egyptians for valuables as YHWH had commanded and received them as YHWH had predicted due to his granting of favour to Israel in the eyes of the Egyptians (12.35-36; 11.2-3; cf. 3.21-22), which most likely amounts to the Egyptians' willingness to give to Israel as a result of the incredible fear YHWH effected in them through the plagues (cf. 12.33). This demonstrates YHWH's immense power even more. Exodus 12.36 refers to Israel's enrichment as a plundering of the Egyptians, contributing to the portrayal of the conflict between YHWH and Egypt as represented in her

which seems even stronger than the connection to 7.3-4.

235. Cf. Beale, ibid.; Piper, ibid. This accords with our exegesis so far, without the implication that Pharaoh's hardening of his own heart is merely another way of describing YHWH's hardening of Pharaoh's heart. Rather, we have found that YHWH's hardening is primary because it funded Pharaoh's self-hardening.

236. For a full discussion of the thought of 12.12, see Stuart, *Exodus*, 278–82. Cf. Houtman, *Exodus*, 184.

Pharaoh as a holy war (cf. 3.22) as does the reference in 12.51 to YHWH bringing Israel out of Egypt 'by their troops' (cf. 6.26; 7.4; 12.17; 12.41). Exodus 12.38's note that a mixed multitude joined Israel when they left Egypt hints at the fulfilment of YHWH's universalistic purposes in hardening Pharaoh's heart and bringing mighty plagues upon Egypt – that the whole world would acknowledge YHWH's supreme divinity, power and sovereignty (cf. 9.16).

After YHWH brought Israel out of Egypt, he instructed Moses that all firstborn should be devoted to him, and Moses instructed the people about this as well as about commemorating the exodus with the Feast of Unleavened Bread (13.1-16). Part of this instruction was to pass on the story of the exodus to the next generation. It is in that part of the instruction that we encounter the next hardening reference: 'It came about that when Pharaoh was stubborn about letting us go, YHWH killed every firstborn in the land of Egypt ...' (13.15). This reference is notable for excluding mention of Pharaoh's heart. But this hiphil of קשה is most likely an internal hiphil, which represents Pharaoh as acting on himself, specifically here, making himself difficult (for others to move in his will), that is, stubborn.[237] The verse catches up the general course of Pharaoh's refusal to release Israel up until the final plague with its reference to Pharaoh's self-imposed stubbornness, which suggests his freedom of will throughout and highlights his responsibility for his actions despite YHWH's role in making him stubborn.

We catch a further glimpse of God's interaction with human will in his choice of a longer route than necessary for Israel's journey out of Egypt based on concern that the Israelites might change their minds when faced with war and return to Egypt (13.17-18). Clearly the text presents God as dealing with his people in a contingent way and without predetermining their will, which accords with our assessment of YHWH's interaction with Pharaoh in Exodus 1–15.[238] The notice that Moses took Joseph's bones with him (13.19) underscores that Exodus is a continuation of the story of Genesis and that God is working to fulfil the covenant promises to Abraham in these events.

YHWH told Moses to turn back to a specific location in order to embolden and lure Pharaoh to chase after the Israelites to his doom (14.1-4) based on the reasoning that Israel's movement and location would lead Pharaoh to think that Israel was confused and trapped (14.3), and so probably forsaken by YHWH, and therefore vulnerable to being captured by Pharaoh's army.[239] Hence, after explaining this plan, YHWH said, 'And so I will strengthen Pharaoh's heart, and he will chase after them, and I will get glory through Pharaoh and all his army, and the Egyptians will know that I am YHWH' (14.4). The appearance of Israel's vulnerability would embolden Pharaoh to chase after them and so serve as the means by which YHWH would strengthen Pharaoh's heart to pursue Israel. He would gain glory through

237. See notes 72 and 111 above.
238. For reflection on God's providential interaction with human will from 13.17-22, see Fretheim, *Exodus*, 150–51.
239. See Stuart, *Exodus*, 330, for explanation of the logic behind such thinking.

Pharaoh and his army by defeating them, showing again his supremacy over them and their gods with unmistakable clarity. Therefore, 'the Egyptians will know that I am YHWH' (14.4d), the same purpose and result we have seen to be operative throughout the hardening and plagues.

'When it was reported to the king of Egypt that the people had fled, the heart of Pharaoh and his servants was turned against the people' (14.5a-b), leading them to regret letting Israel go and to chase after them (14.5c-9). The change of heart mentioned in 14.5 doubtless refers to the result of the divine hardening that was promised in 14.4 and accomplished through Israel's apparent vulnerability.[240] Israel's apparent vulnerability emboldened Pharaoh to do what he already wanted to do – chase after Israel and re-enslave them – but was afraid, and so unwilling, to do because of the incomparable power YHWH had unleashed on Egypt in the plagues, which had culminated in the death of the firstborn of the land.[241] By way of summary, 14.8 states, 'Thus YHWH strengthened the heart of Pharaoh, King of Egypt, and so he chased after the sons of Israel while they were going out boldly'. Drawing attention again so quickly to the divine hardening lays great stress upon it. YHWH is once again showing his power and superiority over Pharaoh as he lures him to destruction.

Indeed, as YHWH gave instructions to Moses after the Egyptians drew near to Israel, he promised, 'And I, behold I, will strengthen the heart of the Egyptians so that they will go in after them [Israel] and I will thus get glory through Pharaoh and through all his army, through his chariotry and through his horsemen. Then the Egyptians will know that I am YHWH when I get glory through Pharaoh, through his chariotry, and through his horsemen' (14.17-18). With the supernatural pillar of cloud taking up position in between Israel and the Egyptian army to protect Israel (14.19-20), and with Moses

240. Although 14.5 only mentions that Israel had fled, 14.4's prediction implies that Israel's seemingly vulnerable situation was part of the information relayed to Pharaoh concerning their flight.

241. Beale, 'Hardening', 147 n. 76, asserts that both the context of 14.5 and use of the term וַיֵּהָפֵךְ show that 'this "change of heart" was not a "strengthening of a previously made decision"'. While this is technically true – Pharaoh had not previously decided to chase Israel after letting them go – it misses the concern of the text. It was not a strengthening of a previously made decision, but the strengthening of a previously and presently held desire that Pharaoh had been afraid to follow. The context suggests this, as Pharaoh's autonomous will had always been to retain Israel in slavery and not to release them, and he had to be forced to let them go. As for the term הפך, it is completely consistent with this understanding. Given the element of force that has been at play in Pharaoh's decision and the multiple sometimes-competing desires involved (e.g., to keep Israel enslaved; to let Israel go to avoid being destroyed by YHWH), reference to Pharaoh's change of heart is focused on the change of his will (in the sense of the desire he chose to effect from among multiple desires) concerning letting Israel go. One could even say that Pharaoh's change of heart entails the change in the strength of his desire to have Israel enslaved. Beale also suggests that הפך is another term for hardening, but this is not quite right. It is used here in this one place to describe the hardening (and its effect), but the term itself is neutral. It describes a turn from one state to another, no matter what that turn is, whereas the more formal terms for hardening actually denote an intensification (of will).

miraculously parting the Red Sea for Israel to pass through (14.21-22), the Egyptian army would normally be too frightened to attempt to pursue Israel on the very path that the God of Israel had miraculously made for his people. But the hardening promise of 4.17 makes clear that the Egyptians pursued Israel into the sea (14.23) because YHWH emboldened them to discount the daunting signs of his divine power and aid to Israel, leaving them free to do as they desired, viz. to capture Israel as they were sent to do.

This last hardening reference draws out the sense of hardening/חזק as encouraging/emboldening rather clearly, and the idea of stubbornness seems to have receded very much into the background.[242] It was not until the Egyptians experienced YHWH actually afflicting them in their pursuit of Israel in the sea that they lost their courage and abandoned their intent to capture God's people (14.24-26). Of course, it was too late. Try as they might to escape, YHWH brought the sea in on them, destroying them (14.27-28). Facilitated by the strengthening of the heart of the Egyptians, YHWH's goal of bringing Israel to know him was realized: 'When Israel saw the great hand which YHWH used against the Egyptians, the people feared YHWH, and they believed in YHWH and in Moses his servant' (14.31). Moreover, his goal of making himself known in all the earth was accomplished (at least *in nuce*; 15.14-16). As Piper observes,

> That was God's aim: to so demonstrate his power and glory that his people fear him and trust him always (cf Ps 106:12). But his aim was wider than that: it was also 'that his name be declared in all the earth' (9:16). Hence in the song of Moses [15.1-18; vv. 19-21 continue along similar lines] this achievement is also celebrated [see 15.14-16] ... Thus God's purpose to magnify his name had succeeded far and wide; the demonstration of his glory in Egypt lifted the voices of generations of his own people in praise (Ps 78:12, 13; 105:26-38; 106:9-11; 136:10-15) and the news of it went before them into Canaan (Josh 2:9, 10; 9:9).[243]

6.22. *Concluding Reflections and Summary*

The hardening of Pharaoh's heart has made for one of the most notorious 'problem passages' in all of Scripture, the troublesomeness of which has been exacerbated by Paul's use of the motif in his discussion of election in Romans 9. Our exegesis has provided support for a combination of complementary perspectives that attempt to resolve the difficulty posed by this theme, including the core of the most commonly suggested resolution, that the hardening of Pharaoh's heart was a just punishment for his sin.[244] We have found that Exodus presents God's actions toward Pharaoh as conditional

242. It may be that it has been lost altogether since it was Pharaoh's decision that dictated his army's actions. Their will to go after Israel does not particularly manifest stubbornness on their part but Pharaoh's.

243. Piper, *Justification*, 170-71; emphasis removed; brackets contain my additions.

244. Irwin, 'Suspension', 56-57, has sketched as many as six ways scholars have attempted to resolve the difficulty, listing representatives of each view.

on Pharaoh's unjust oppression of Israel and Israel's prayer for divine deliverance.[245] Relatedly, God's actions were an expression of his faithfulness to his covenant promises to Israel (e.g., to give them their own land; to curse those who curse them).

Moreover, only after he sent Moses and Aaron to confront Pharaoh with the demand for Israel's release, and Pharaoh responded by scorning YHWH and intensifying Egypt's oppression of Israel, did YHWH set about working miraculous signs and plagues against Pharaoh and strengthening his heart against their motivating influence toward submission to the divine demand, adding to the conditionality of the divine hardening. Furthermore, the text most fundamentally depicts the hardening of Pharaoh's heart as a strengthening of his will in the sense of emboldening him to carry out what he already wanted to do of his own free will, despite the fearsome power of God displayed against him and the destructive consequences it would bring upon him, making him stubborn.[246] Moreover, the text frequently appears to present the nature of the divine hardening as indirect and natural – typically, strategic actions that lured Pharaoh to boldness – rather than as a direct, supernatural work in Pharaoh's heart.[247] Thus, Pharaoh's own freely oppressive and rebellious will was made to serve as its own punishment in the execution of ironic and poetic justice.

The hardening had multiple purposes: (1) to bring Pharaoh to refuse YHWH's demand for Israel's release, and therefore (2) to multiply signs/plagues as judgments for Pharaoh's stubborn refusal and continued oppression of Israel, so as to (3) bring about the (renewed) election of God's people and their knowledge/acknowledgment of him as their covenant God, and to (4) glorify YHWH by facilitating the display of his incomparable divine nature, omnipotence and sovereignty (which also shows the impotence of other gods and the folly of idolatry) for the further goal of (5) bringing Israel, Pharaoh, Egypt and the whole earth to acknowledge YHWH's supreme divinity and sovereignty. The final and ultimate purposes of the hardening (numbers 3–5 above) relate to the passage that Paul quotes from the exodus account – Exod. 9.16 – as well as the main point of the entire narrative. The main point of Exodus 1–15 is that YHWH is the supreme, omnipotent God and sovereign who is to be trusted and obeyed above all others, a point that would encourage the original audience of Exodus to reject idolatry and be loyal to YHWH

---

245. Beale's ('Hardening', 149–50) claim that 'it is never stated in Exod 4-14 that Yahweh hardens Pharaoh in judgment because of any prior reason or condition residing in him' is incredible in light of our exegesis. It betrays a grave insensitivity to the demands of narrative interpretation.

246. Even Pharaoh's self-hardening was made possible by YHWH emboldening him.

247. The text's presentation of the hardening is complex, frequently portraying it as indirect and natural in the sense that it is provoked by some action of YHWH not directly connected to Pharaoh's heart, such as the choice of miracles the Egyptian magicians could imitate to some degree or the withdrawal of plague (7.22; 8.11 (15); 9.34; cf. 14.2-4). At other times, YHWH does seem to directly and supernaturally infuse boldness into the heart of Pharaoh (or his servants or army) such as during the plague of boils (9.12) or when Pharaoh's army chased Israel into the sea (14.17, 23).

and his covenant with Israel. Together with 9.14-15, 9.16 contributes to a statement of YHWH's incomparable power and sovereignty, communicating the main thrust of the whole exodus narrative. It further reveals the larger purposes for the divine hardening and all of YHWH's actions towards the deliverance of his people, that his supreme divinity and sovereignty would be made known to Pharaoh and all the earth.

Chapter 7

INTERPRETIVE TRADITIONS SURROUNDING
EXODUS 33.19B AND 9.16

Having provided an exegesis of Exod. 33.19b in my previous study, and one
of Exod. 9.16 in the preceding chapter of the present study, it is now time
to turn to ancient interpretive traditions surrounding these passages. We will
consider the material related to each passage in the order Paul quotes them.

7.1. *Interpretive Traditions Surrounding Exodus 33.19b*

There does not appear to be much use of Exod. 33.19b in extant literature
prior to or contemporaneous with Paul. This might be because the verse
provides a summary statement of the meaning of the divine name that is given
an extended explication in 34.6-7, which is echoed many times in the Bible
and in ancient Jewish literature, and became a central text in biblical and
Jewish tradition.[1] So it is not surprising that Exod. 33.19 gets short shrift.
The attention it does receive comes from rabbinic literature, which is less
certain in identifying traditions that Paul might have known.[2]

The use of Exodus 33.19 by the Midrashim conforms to its two main
elements as we identified them in our exegesis of the verse – God's great
mercy and his sovereign freedom to bestow it as he sees fit, with some greater
stress on his mercy. So *Exod. R.* 2.1 cites Exod. 33.19b as an expression of
God being gracious and full of compassion. Similarly, *Exod. R.* 45.2 cites
Exod. 33.19b as an affirmation of God's graciousness and willingness to
answer prayer for the purpose of encouraging supplication. In *Exod. R.* 45.6,
God's goodness passing by is equated with showing forth God's attribute
of dispensing goodness and his attribute of punishment. Linked to Exod.
33.19b, it would seem that this conclusion proceeds from both the element
of grace and mercy and the element of sovereign freedom. This midrash goes
on to highlight God's precious rewards to the righteous/obedient, who receive
reward for their good deeds. But God is also said to have a pile of treasure for
disbursing to those who do not have good deeds to their credit, but to whom

---

1.   See Kugel, *Traditions*, 721–27, who provides a collection of texts; cf. Dunn,
Romans, 552.
2.   For caveats about our usage of rabbinic material, see note 44 in ch. 4 above.

God desires to be gracious. Here the midrash brings out Exod. 33.19b's stress on both divine freedom and divine graciousness.

One tradition took Moses' request to know the ways of the Lord (Exod. 33.13) to be a request to know about God's ordination of good and evil in the world, understood in terms of happiness and suffering with respect to the just vs the unjust.[3] God reveals that he rewards the just for their deeds, but also blesses those who are not deserving, 'for I am gracious to those who may lay no claim to My graciousness, and I am bountiful to those also who are not deserving of My bounty',[4] an echo of Exod. 33.19b. This left Moses with no answer as to the basis of God's decision to bless evil doers when he decides to do so.[5] But another tradition concerning Moses' request to know God's ways illustrates the inscrutable ways of the Lord by describing how what might look to the human eye like a wicked man prospering by wronging an innocent man actually brought justice to both men, a fact God knew full well.[6] Yet another tradition probes this issue more deeply with God's answer to Moses' question about what law God uses to govern the blessing vs misfortune of men given that both the just and the wicked can experience happiness or misfortune. God refuses to reveal all the principles he applies to governing the world, but he does reveal that, 'When I see human beings who have no claim to expectations from Me either for their own deeds or for those of their fathers, but who pray to Me and implore Me, then do I grant their prayers and give them what they require for subsistence'.[7]

Finally, some of the targums contain a striking addition in their translation of Exod. 33.19b that clashes violently with the tenor of Paul's argument in Romans 9: 'and I will have pity on whoever is worthy of pity, and I will have mercy on whoever is worthy of mercy'.[8] For the tradition of these targums, God bestows mercy on those who deserve it. But for Paul, God bestows mercy by faith to those who do not deserve it. These targums underplay the notion of divine freedom while Paul's view is much closer to what we saw in some of the midrashim, especially the tradition that views God's mercy as found through appeal to him (cf. Rom 10.8-13).

By way of summary, rabbinic use of Exod 33.19b brings out God's great mercy and his sovereign freedom to bestow it as he sees fit, with some greater stress on his mercy. But it also views God's benevolence as due to those who perform good deeds, and at times even sees grace and mercy as dispensed on the basis of merit. Exod. 33.19b arises in connection with theodicy and is also used as a motivation for prayer.

3.   Ginzberg, *Legends*, 3.134.
4.   Ibid., 3.135.
5.   Ibid.
6.   Ibid., 136.
7.   Ibid.
8.   *Targum Neofiti*; all translations from *Targum Neofiti* in this investigation come from M. McNamara and R. Hayward, *Targum Neofiti 1: Exodus* (TAB, 2; Collegeville, MN: Liturgical Press, 1994); italics removed here. Ps.-Jonathan's translation is similar.

7.2. Interpretive Traditions Surrounding Exodus 9.16

The final step in our investigation of Paul's use of the Old Testament in Rom. 9.14-18, before moving to an exegesis of this text, is to survey the relevant interpretive traditions surrounding Exod. 9.16.

7.2.a. *Jubilees*

The second-century-BCE book of *Jubilees* does not quote Exod. 9.16 or even allude to it. But it does present the purpose of Moses' mission to Egypt as including infliction of vengeance on the Egyptians for their heinous oppression of Israel (*Jub.* 48.3), and it depicts the execution of the plagues accordingly: 'And everything happened according to your [Moses'] word, ten great and cruel judgments came on the land of Egypt so that you might execute vengeance upon it for Israel. And the Lord did everything on account of Israel and according to his covenant which he made with Abraham that he would take vengeance upon them just as they had made them serve by force' (48.7-8). *Jubilees* 48.14, which speaks of the climactic destruction visited upon the Egyptians in the Red Sea, also indicates that throwing the Egyptians to their death in the middle of the sea was vengeance for the Egyptians throwing Hebrew infants into the sea. Verse 17 then goes on to intertwine this theme of just punishment with the hardening of the Egyptians' hearts (citing a portion of the hardening statement of Exod. 14.8): 'And he [Mastema] hardened their hearts and strengthened them. And it was conceived of by the Lord our God that he might smite the Egyptians and throw them into the midst of the sea'.

Thus, the hardening of the Egyptians' hearts is depicted as facilitating just divine punishment for their sin against Israel, making the hardening itself part of the just punishment they deserved.[9] Although the text does not specifically mention the role of hardening throughout the plagues, the data we do have suggests that the author of *Jubilees* viewed it as 'a means for having the Egyptians continue to hold out until they had been fully punished for their earlier crimes'.[10] This punishment of Egypt is, moreover, depicted as a fulfilment of God's covenant promises,[11] a point we found emphasized by Exodus itself.

Interestingly, 48.17 links the idea of hardening and strengthening. This could reflect an understanding of Exodus in line with our exegesis, that hardening is most basically to be understood as strengthening/emboldening and the notion of stubbornness arises from this strengthening. This receives some confirmation from the fact that this section of *Jubliees* posits Mastema

---

9.   Cf. Kugel, *Traditions*, 549–50. Kugel probably errs in presenting this theme as inherently restricting the role of hardening to a means of prolonging punishment in the plagues. These types of texts seem open to allowing other, complementary roles for the hardening, including the other main traditional interpretation he highlights, viz. making Pharaoh undiscerning (548–49).

10.   Ibid., 550.

11.   Cf. ibid.

(i.e., Satan) as the agent of hardening. This would presumably be an attempt to distance God from the hardening to some degree,[12] even though it is part of his plan.[13] In any case, Mastema becoming 'strong' is linked to his drawing the Egyptians to pursue Israel after they left Egypt (48.12). In the biblical text, it is the divine hardening that moves Pharaoh to chase after Israel. So *Jubilees* appears to soften the notion of hardening beyond depiction of it as a just judgment by attributing it directly to Satan. And it appears to understand hardening as strengthening, or perhaps as a result of strengthening or as its cause. This shows that some of the emphases we struck in our exegesis of Exodus 1–15 were also perceived by ancient interpreters, and could well have been perceived by Paul.

7.2.b. *Ezekiel the Tragedian, Exagōgē*

The second-century-BCE work of Ezekiel the Tragedian, *Exagōgē*, recounts the story of Exodus 1–15 with various embellishments in accordance with the genre of Greek tragic drama in which he wrote.[14] In his telling of the exodus story, Ezekiel writes, 'And swarms of flies shall come and sore afflict the men of Egypt; then another plague shall come, and they shall die whose hearts are hardened' (*Exagōgē*, 138–40). Here Ezekiel mentions the plagues of flies and sores (138), and then another plague, which would bring death to people with hard hearts (139–40). This latter plague probably refers to the plague of hail (141–43), which was the first plague to take human life.[15]

12.   Cf. M. Segal, *The Book of Jubilees: Rewritten Bible, Redaction, Ideology and Theology* (JSJSup, 117; Leiden: Brill, 2007), 216–17.

13.   The vast majority of Ethiopic manuscripts read 48.17b so that God is the agent of hardening rather than the deviser of it. But we have followed B. C. Charles, *The Book of Jubilees or the Little Genesis* (London: Adam and Charles Black, 1902), Wintermute, 'Jubilees', and Kugel, *Traditions*, 586, who read the verbal stem x-l-y ('to devise') contained in mss 12, 20 and 25 rather than the verbal stem x-y-l ('to make strong/stubborn'). This makes much better sense of the text given that 17a attributes the hardening to Mastema (Segal, *Jubilees*, 218–22, who follows the majority text, believes that 17a and b contradict one another, and devotes significant attention to explaining why the text might contradict itself so blatantly and immediately), and it is easy to see how the original reading could be contained in so few mss given the ease with which metathesis could occur with such similar stems and the fact that the use of x-y-l in 17a could alternatively suggest an instance of dittography helped along by the similarity between the stems. I wish to thank Michael Segal for helping me understand the text critical issue here in personal correspondence; he bears no responsibility for my text critical decision, which differs from his.

14.   For a brief introduction to Ezekiel the Tragedian, see R. G. Robertson, 'Ezekiel the Tragedian: A New Translation and Introduction', *OTP*, 2.803–19 (803–07). Citations of this work have been taken from Robertson's translation.

15.   Kugel, *Traditions*, 561–62, thinks Ezekiel refers to the plague of livestock, but he acknowledges that this creates a problem with no convincing solution yet offered, since Ezekiel actually refers to people rather than livestock dying. It makes better sense to identify the plague as that of hail, though this is not without difficulty either, making for a strong focus on the plague (139–43) and demanding that Ezekiel omits the plague of livestock. But this seems less difficult since Ezekiel's presentation of the plagues does not follow the biblical text strictly and other

In the text of Exodus, those who believed the word of the Lord and acted accordingly escaped the consequences of the plague while those who disregarded God's warning suffered. This suggests that Ezekiel saw some sort of relationship between hardheartedness and unbelief, whether he equated them or took one to bring about the other. In any event, hardheartedness (and unbelief) brought death in the plague to which Ezekiel refers, for 'they shall die whose hearts are hardened' (140). This seems to reflect Exodus' emphasis on the great guilt of Pharaoh and the Egyptians and their responsibility for their own hardheartedness. The final plague would 'bring down the wanton pride of men' (148). God's role in the hardening is not mentioned.

Further insight into Ezekiel's understanding of the hardening is given in 149–51: 'Yet Pharaoh shan't be moved by what I say until his firstborn child lies as a corpse; then, moved with fear, he'll send the people forth'. This is another ancient exegetical tradition that appears to agree with our understanding of the hardening as an emboldening of Pharaoh in the face of terrifying divine plagues. Ezekiel does not say why Pharaoh would remain unmoved. But it is obvious in the exodus narrative that divine hardening is the reason. Ezekiel sees that as strengthening Pharaoh against fear that would otherwise move him to yield to the Lord.[16]

7.2.c. *Sirach*

The second-century-BCE book of *Sirach*, written in the tradition of Jewish wisdom literature, contains a couple of verses that bear on the thought of Exod. 9.16 as well as the theme of the hardening of Pharaoh's heart (*Sir.* 16.15-16). The verses are probably a later addition to the text.[17] But even if they are not original, they undoubtedly represent an ancient view of divine hardening. They conclude a section that 'describes how God punishes without fail the wicked for their sins'.[18] In their context, the verses present Pharaoh as an example of yet another prominent sinner who received his due from divine justice. *Sirach* 16.12-14 stresses the certainty of God's justice: 'Great as his mercy is his punishment; he judges people, each according to his deeds. A criminal does not escape with his plunder ... Whoever does good has his reward, which each receives according to his deeds'.[19]

---

ancient recitations of the plagues omit some of them, e.g., Josephus and Artapanus (mentioned by Robertson, 'Ezekiel', 812 n. m2, though he notes they are less complete than Ezekiel).

16.   The debate about whether we are to read the verb πείθω or πάσχω in 148 does not affect this analysis. Whether Pharaoh was not convinced or did not suffer the first nine plagues, he was not taken by fear to actually let Israel go until God took his son's life. Kugel, *Traditions*, 561, understands *Exagōgē* 149–50 with πάσχω to be an example of hardening referring to the fostering of ignorance.

17.   This seems to be the scholarly consensus. See e.g., P. W. Skehan and A. A. Di Lella, *The Wisdom of Ben Sira* (AB, 39; New York: Doubleday, 1987), 270.

18.   Ibid., 273. Interestingly, Skehan/Di Lella identify the theme of the broader section in which 16.15-16 appears (15.11–16.23) as 'Free Will and Responsibility'.

19.   Skehan's (ibid., 268) translation.

Verses 15-16 then proclaim Pharaoh's just deserts: 'The Lord hardened Pharaoh to not know him, so that his acts were made known under heaven; his mercy is evident to every creature, and he apportioned his light and the darkness to Adam' (my translation). Appearing in the context of *Siarch* 16, it is clear that the text sees the hardening of Pharaoh's heart as a conditional judgment upon Pharaoh for his sin, who thus 'receives according to his deeds' (16.14). Hardening is seen as preventing Pharaoh from knowing the Lord, which could be taken as an issue of mere cognition, but most likely has the fuller notion of the biblical text in mind, viz. acknowledging and submitting to the Lord's sovereignty.

Interestingly, the effect of the divine hardening identified by the text seems to correspond to the one identified by Exod. 9.16 – to make God/his acts known 'under heaven'/'in all the earth'.[20] This confirms the importance of Exod. 9.16 for the theme of hardening in the exodus narrative. The context has been concerned to hold up God's mercy on the one hand – which in 16.11 especially has to do with God forgiving sin in response to human repentance – and his justice and judgment on the other. It appears that this reference to the hardening of Pharaoh serves as a prime example of God pouring out deserved wrath set within the scheme of God as a God of both mercy and wrath/justice recalled in 16.16. While v. 16 is somewhat obscure, I propose that the context suggests that we understand it as follows: '[H]is mercy is evident to every creature' highlights the merciful aspect of God's character, perhaps conveying that God's hardening of Pharaoh was an act of mercy to the world by making him known, giving the world the opportunity to turn to him. The reference to the apportioning of light and darkness then refers to the whole scheme of God doling out mercy in the form of light/knowledge of God on the one hand and judgment in the form of darkness, exemplified by hardening, on the other hand.

7.2.d. *3 Maccabees*

The first-century-BCE book of *3 Maccabees* records a prayer offered by the high priest Simon in response to the impending desecration of the temple of Jerusalem by Ptolemy IV Philopator, who insisted on profanely entering the sanctuary, an act reserved only for the Jewish high priest once a year. Simon appeals to God to oppose Philopator's wickedness, making mention of God's commitment to justly condemn 'those who have done anything in insolence and arrogance' (2.3; NRSV), going on to cite past examples of divine destruction of men for their wicked deeds in the following verses. *3 Maccabees* 2.6 mentions the case of Pharaoh: 'You, having tested with various and many punishments the brazen [θρασύν] Pharaoh, who enslaved your holy people Israel, made known your power upon those to whom you made known your great might'.

This text seems to take Pharaoh's hardheartedness as boldness, using an adjective cognate to the verb that Symmachus uses for the emboldening

20.   Cf. ibid., 275.

(hardening) of Pharaoh's heart in Exod. 4.21. The theme of testing Pharaoh's heart through the plagues strengthens this assessment, since it is unlikely that the author of *3 Maccabees* would understand God to be testing Pharaoh by irresistibly causing wicked stubbornness in him. Invocation of the concept of testing here implies that the plagues would show up what was really in Pharaoh's heart. Moreover, the context makes it clear that God's actions against Pharaoh were just penalty for his wickedness, not something he had implanted in Pharaoh. Hardening/emboldening would amount to bringing out more clearly what was already there. Interestingly, N. Clayton Croy states that the chief argument of Simon's prayer up to 2.8 'has been God's sovereignty over all nations, indeed, over all the earth'.[21] Paul has similar concern in Romans 9.

7.2.e. *Wisdom of Solomon*

J. L. Kugel suggests that *Wisd.* 16.15-16 (c. first century BCE or CE) understands hardening as God keeping Pharaoh in a state of ignorance: 'To escape from your hand is impossible; for the ungodly [Egyptians], refusing to know you, were flogged by the strength of your arm ...' (NRSV).[22] But the text does not explicitly mention hardening, and the ignorance mentioned here is chosen/self-imposed, probably referring to acknowledgment as in the biblical text rather than cognitive knowledge.[23] Still, given the author's interaction with the exodus narrative, he must have had some view of the hardening that is so prominent in it. *Wisdom of Solomon* 19.4 supports Kugel's conclusion: 'For the fate they deserved drew them on to this end [destruction in the sea], and made them forget what had happened [the plagues, especially the death of their firstborn], in order that they might fill up the punishment that their torments still lacked'. The biblical text attributes the Egyptians' decision to pursue Israel to hardening while *Wisd.* 19.4 attributes it to their just fate,[24] making them forget God's devastating judgment recently levelled against

---

21.   N. C. Croy, *3 Maccabees* (SCS; Leiden: Brill, 2006), 53.

22.   Kugel, *Traditions*, 549. Quotations of *Wisdom of Solomon* in this investigation are from the NRSV unless otherwise noted.

23.   Intriguingly, S. Cheon, *The Exodus Story in the Wisdom of Solomon: A Study in Biblical Interpretation* (JSPSup, 23; Sheffield: SAP, 1997), 60–61, observes that Pseudo-Solomon shares with Exodus the idea that God wanted to bring Pharaoh and the Egyptian people to knowledge of him through the plagues, citing Exod. 9.14 and tying in Exod. 9.16 for comparison. Similarly, J. M. G. Barclay, 'Unnerving Grace: Approaching Romans 9–11 from the Wisdom of Solomon', in Wilk and Wagner (eds), *Explorations*, 91–109 (106 n. 28), observes that, 'In Wisdom the preservation of Pharaoh and the Egyptians (their punishment "little by little") is to enable them to change and repent (Wis 11:15-12:2)'.

24.   Cheon, *Wisdom*, 93 n. 61, notes that Pseudo-Solomon's use of 'fate' is not predestinarian, but, quoting Gregg, 'the inevitable sequence of cause and effect'. Cf. P. Enns, *Exodus Retold: Ancient Exegesis of the Departure from Egypt in Wis 10:15-21 and 19:1-9* (HSMM, 57; Atlanta: Scholars Press, 1997), 108–09.

them,[25] bringing them to make 'another foolish decision' (19.3). All of this approaches the same realm as understanding the hardening as emboldening – action God takes that enables Pharaoh to overcome any fear of reprisal for carrying out his immoral will. Indeed, it is hard to know if the reference to 'forgetting' is to be taken literally or, as I would think more likely, simply as a way of indicating boldness (i.e., they did not literally forget the death of their firstborn, but became so bold as to put it out of their mind or act as if they did not remember it).[26] On the other hand, God could have emboldened Pharaoh through imposed ignorance. But if so, the text's view of the hardening would stress cognition rather than boldness, and might derive from the sense of hardening as organ malfunction.

Two more considerations support this general type of reading (i.e., imposed ignorance or emboldening) of *Wisdom of Solomon*. First, the author strongly emphasizes the Egyptians' free will, God's justice, God's love for all, and God's desire to see the wicked come to repentance (see e.g., 11.23-26; 12.1-21 (note particularly 12.8a, 10a, 15-16, 20b); 13.8-9; 15.14; 16.1, 9; 17.4-5; 19.1-5). It would seem that any view of the hardening held by the author of *Wisdom of Solomon* would cohere with Pharaoh's will remaining free. One intriguing reference to God's justice in punishing the Egyptians interweaves the theme with his foreknowledge: 'But the ungodly [Egyptians] were assailed to the end by pitiless anger, for God knew in advance even their future actions' (19.1), wicked action detailed in the following verses. Second, the book takes the view that God uses the sins of the wicked to punish them (11.16; 12.23), a principle that coheres with the ideas of the divine hardening of the Egyptians consisting either of an enforced ignorance upon those who insist on remaining ignorant of God or of an emboldening of the will to act despite fearsome opposition.

7.2.f. *Pseudo-Philo/Liber Antiquitatum Biblicarum*

The first-century-CE book *Liber Antiquitatum Biblicarum* (*LAB*) does not mention the hardening of the Egyptians' heart until referring to the hardening that brought the Egyptians to pursue Israel on their departure from Egypt, though it alludes to earlier hardenings by indicating that 'the heart of the Egyptians was hardened once more' (10.2; italics removed). This reference does not give any particular insight into Pseudo-Philo's conception of divine hardening in the exodus narrative, but 10.6 does (at least in the case of the Egyptians' rush into the sea): 'And Israel passed through the middle of the sea on dry ground. And the Egyptians saw this and continued following

---

25.   Cheon, *Wisdom*, 95, notes that, 'This interpretation is unique to Pseudo-Solomon'. Enns, *Retold*, 107–12, emphasizes the just measure for measure aspect of the divine punishment envisioned by Pseudo-Solomon.

26.   Cheon, ibid., n. 69, observes that 'Wis. 14.26 indicates that "forgetfulness of favors" was one of the vices ascribed to idolaters'.

them. And God hardened their perception, and they did not know that they were entering the sea'. Pseudo-Philo understood hardening here as imposing ignorance on the Egyptians as to the danger they faced (from God). It is reasonable (though not certain) to suppose that he would take the same view of divine hardening in the rest of the exodus narrative. With respect to the plagues, such a view would take God to block the Egyptians' perception of the danger in the plagues. This again would place such a view in some proximity to the idea of emboldening, though it remains distinct. It would appear that Pseudo-Philo's view of hardening took its lead from the meaning of כבד, which highlights organ malfunction.

7.2.g. *Josephus*

The first-century author Josephus tells the story of Israel's bondage in and exodus from Egypt in book two of his work *The Antiquities of the Jews*. According to Josephus, the plagues inflicted upon Egypt serve as a warning to mankind, 'Not to do anything that may displease God, lest he be provoked to wrath, and avenge their iniquities upon them' (*Ant.* 2.293).[27] He mistakenly reports that Pharaoh agreed to let Israel go in response to the first plague, which turned the water of the Nile to blood (295). But his report about how this played out helps reveal an implicit emphasis on Pharaoh's free will and guilt in all of this already hinted at in Josephus' view that the plagues serve as warnings: 'but when the plague ceased, he [Pharaoh] changed his mind again, and would not suffer them to go. But when God saw that he was ungrateful, and upon the ceasing of this calamity would not grow wiser, he sent another plague upon the Egyptians: – An innumerable multitude of frogs ...' (295–96).

Josephus reports that Pharaoh capitulated because of the plague of frogs as well, but again reversed his decision when the plague was removed (298–99). While not referring to hardening, his description is in line with ancient understanding of hardening as some sort of imposed ignorance: 'But as soon as Pharaoh saw the land freed from the plague, he forgot the cause of it, and retained the Hebrews; and, as though he had a mind to try the nature of more such judgments, he would not yet suffer Moses and his people to depart, having granted that liberty rather out of fear than out of any good considerations' (299). However, it seems most likely that Josephus speaks of Pharaoh wilfully forgetting, or at least leaving the cause of the plague disregarded, possible meanings of the word he uses (ἐπιλήθω),[28] since relief of the plague occasions his 'forgetfulness'. Followed by Josephus' observation that Pharaoh assented to let Israel go out of fear rather than good considerations, the notion of boldness does seem to be in view. It seems fair

27. Translations of Josephus are from W. Whiston (trans.), *The Works of Josephus: New Updated Edition Complete and Unabridged in One Volume* (Peabody, MA: Hendrickson, 1987).
28. See LSJ, s.v. ἐπιλήθω, 2.

to say that Josephus understood relief from the plague to have emboldened Pharaoh to disregard the cause of the plagues Egypt had suffered. 'Accordingly God punished his falseness with another plague ...' (300).

Josephus continues his retelling with similar observations and emphases for other plagues. In reflecting on why Pharaoh would act this way, while one might think he would at least mention divine hardening, Josephus makes no mention of it and thrusts responsibility entirely upon Pharaoh: 'One would think the forementioned calamities might have been sufficient for one that was only foolish, without wickedness, to make him wise, and to make him sensible what was for his advantage. But Pharaoh, led not so much by his folly as by his wickedness, even when he saw the cause of his miseries, he still contested with God, and willfully deserted the cause of virtue' (307). For Josephus, Pharaoh acted freely in defying God and was terribly wicked and guilty in doing so. We would expect any notion of divine hardening he might have held to cohere with this viewpoint.

7.2.h. *Testament of Solomon*

The *Testament of Solomon* 25.3-5 (c. first to third century CE) attributes the hardening of Pharaoh and his servants to a demon (named Abezethibou):

> I [Abezethibou] was present at the time when Moses appeared before Pharaoh, king of Egypt, hardening his heart ... I am the adversary of Moses in (performing) wonders and signs ... During the time of the Exodus of the sons of Israel, I gave Pharaoh pangs of anxiety and hardened the heart of him, as well as of his subordinates. I caused them to pursue closely after the sons of Israel, and Pharaoh followed with (me) and (so did) all the Egyptians.[29]

The report that a demon was responsible for the hardening of Pharaoh's heart is intriguing, but is not developed. Presumably the notion is introduced partly to distance God from sin and evil. But one wonders how the author reconciled this with Exodus' direct statements of divine hardening. Without any explanation, we are left to speculate that he thought the biblical text to speak generally in light of God's sovereignty,[30] while he gave the more complete truth of the matter. The demon even takes on a role that goes a little beyond the hardening, giving Pharaoh pangs of anxiety that presumably made him regret letting Israel go in the first place. One wonders if the author would then view the hardening (using the same word as Paul (Rom. 9.18): σκληρύνω) as an emboldening, with the demon first making Pharaoh regret letting Israel go and then emboldening him to chase after Israel despite all the plagues Egypt suffered.

---

29.   Translations from *Testament of Solomon* are from D. C. Duling, 'Testament of Solomon: A New Translation and Introduction', *OTP*, 1.935–87.

30.   That is, for his own purposes God allowed the demon to harden Pharaoh though he did not cause the demon to do so, or less likely, God simply used the demon as a secondary cause, making the demon harden Pharaoh.

7.2.i. Rabbinic Literature[31]

The most prevalent theme found in the rabbinic literature surrounding Exod. 9.16 and the related topic of the hardening of Pharaoh's heart is that Pharaoh deserved everything he got from the Lord. The hardening and the plagues were just punishment for Pharaoh's wickedness.[32] It is common to mention Pharaoh's wickedness even when just retribution is not the specific concern of the text.[33] At other times Pharaoh is portrayed as foolish (*Exod. R.* 9.8) or perverse (*Exod. R.* 10.6) or stubborn (*Exod. R.* 9.8). Emphasis on Pharaoh's wickedness was one of the purposes for which the rabbis cited Exod. 9.16.[34] They commonly noted that Pharaoh was hardened only after he failed to repent (*Exod. R.* 7.3; 9.12; 10.1; 11.6; 13.3). Thus, the hardening was seen as Pharaoh's own fault.[35] He actually hardened his own heart,[36] and indeed, intentionally did so with the first five plagues until God punished him with being unable to repent even if he came to want to do so.[37] It was his own anger that made him stubborn (*Exod R.* 9.8).

Earlier, we mentioned Kugel's characterization of hardening in some ancient traditions as an imposed ignorance (see 7.2.b, e above). He cites *Exod. R.* 15.10 as an example, which asserts that Pharaoh did not feel the plagues that the Egyptians experienced until he was impacted personally in the plague of hail, when he admitted his wickedness and the Lord's righteousness.[38] But it is not clear that this indicates ignorance. It could simply indicate that Pharaoh was not moved by the plagues until he was personally affected, that is, it took personal impact to 'reach' him. *Exodus Rabbah* 15.10 does, however, emphasize God's justice in his dispensing of the plagues. Pharaoh is said to have confessed God's righteousness because the plagues affected only Egypt.

Some rabbinic texts mention God's foreknowledge in such a way that implies human freedom. Treating Exod. 3.19, *Exod. R.* 3.9 mentions that 'God foresaw that the wicked Pharaoh would only make the people's burdens heavier from the time Moses would undertake his mission, and in order not to deceive Moses, he told him that Pharaoh would do this ... to prevent

---

31.   For caveats about our usage of rabbinic material, see again note 44 in ch. 4 above. For convenient collections of rabbinic material related to the exodus narrative, see *Exod. R.* 1.1–23.15; Ginzberg, *Legends*, 2.245–3.36.

32.   See *Exod. R.* 5.7; 7.3; 9.12; 11.6; 13.1; Ginzberg, *Legends*, 2.341–47, 353; 3.23–25, 30–31.

33.   See *Exod. R.* 3.9; 10.6; 12.1, 7; Ginzberg, *Legends*, 2.334.

34.   See *Exod. R.* 12.1; Ginzberg, *Legends*, 2.334, 355. The tradition mentioned in Ginzberg, 2.234, makes the declaration of Exod. 9.16 a response to Pharaoh's denial of knowing YHWH in Exod. 5.2, an understandable move since the latter effectively captures the essence of Pharaoh's attitiude while the former summarizes YHWH's purposes and rationale for his response to Pharaoh.

35.   Ginzberg, *Legends*, 2.352.

36.   Ibid., 2.353.

37.   Ibid., 2.355.

38.   Kugel, *Traditions*, 561.

Moses from reproaching God; yet despite this, he did utter reproaches against God'.[39] In our exegesis, we saw that there is some question about what the refrain in the exodus narrative, 'as the Lord said', refers to, whether only the prediction of Pharaoh's refusal to let Israel go or also to YHWH's prediction of hardening his heart. And *Exod. R.* 10.6 ties Exod. 3.19 directly to Pharaoh's refusal. With respect to Israel, God affirmed that he knew the sin they would commit in the future, exciting his wrath. 'Nevertheless, though I know all the perverseness of their hearts, wherein they will rebel against Me in the desert, I will redeem them now, for I accord unto man the treatment he merits for his present actions, not what he will deserve in the future'.[40]

At the same time, Israel's time of affliction, presumably speaking of their slavery and oppression in Egypt, is said to have been appointed by God.[41] But this would seem to refer to the length of time God would allow their affliction as opposed to his bringing it about. Still, another tradition holds that the increase in Israel's oppression occasioned by an audience with Pharaoh for Moses and Aaron was part of God's plan,[42] though it is unclear exactly what this means, whether it is to be understood deterministically or permissively or something in between. The final possibility seems most likely.[43]

A few other traditions about the exodus might give further insight into rabbinic conception of divine hardening. One tradition relates that God left just one Egyptian idol uninjured and 'caused wild beasts to obstruct the road to the wilderness' to trick the Egyptians into thinking 'that this idol was possessed of exceeding might, which it exercised to prevent the Israelites from journeying on',[44] presumably to embolden the Egyptians to pursue Israel despite the devastation inflicted upon them by God. Another tradition relates that Pharaoh was told 'that the Israelites had resolved not to return to Egypt' and the resultant reasoning that then turned the heart of the Egyptians against Israel after their departure from the land, viz. that Egyptians could bear suffering the plagues and being forced to let Israel go, but the addition of Israel's permanent departure with the Egyptians' riches was more than they were willing to endure.[45] A third tradition relates that God got the Egyptians into the sea by causing fiery steeds to swim on the sea and so lure the Egyptians' horses into the sea after them.[46] None of these three traditions actually mention hardening, but they overlap with hardening in describing why the Egyptians pursued Israel, which the biblical text attributes to hardening. They suggest (especially the first two) that any notion of hardening lying behind these traditions conceived of hardening as

---

39.   Cf. Ginzberg, *Legends*, 2.320.

40.   Ibid., 317.

41.   Ibid.

42.   Ginzberg, *Legends*, 2.336.

43.   Cf. e.g., ibid., 341, where the tradition speaks of God having the original intention of speaking only to Moses, but changed his plan, including Aaron in his address and the performance of miracles.

44.   Ginzberg, *Legends*, 3.10–11.

45.   Ibid., 3.11.

46.   Ibid., 3.26.

an emboldening accomplished by strategic divine actions rather than direct supernatural work upon Pharaoh's heart.[47]

7.2.j. *Summary*

Interpretive traditions surrounding Exod. 9.16 and the hardening of Pharaoh's heart emphasized Pharaoh's wickedness, viewing the hardening of his heart and the plagues as just punishment for his (and his people's) severe oppression of God's people Israel, a fulfilment of God's covenant promises. The nature of hardening was often seen as strengthening/emboldening and sometimes as imposed ignorance. Issues of God's sovereignty, theodicy and divine foreknowledge arose around God's treatment of Pharaoh. Some ancient interpreters attempted to distance God from the hardening by attributing it to Satan or a demon. Others pointed out that Pharaoh hardened himself first, and that God only hardened him after Pharaoh persisted in obstinate rebellion at length.[48]

---

47. The targums differ slightly from Exodus and Romans, but with no significance for our purposes.

48. Though this is from rabbinic tradition, the dating of which is uncertain. For a summary of interpretive traditions surrounding Exod. 33.19b, see the end of section 7.1 above.

Chapter 8

IS THERE UNRIGHTEOUSNESS WITH GOD? ROMANS 9.14-18

Now that we have examined the two quotations Paul puts forward in
Rom. 9.14-18 in their original contexts and surveyed ancient interpretive
traditions surrounding them, we will proceed in this chapter to compare the
forms of Paul's quotations with their Old Testament wording and to provide
an exegesis of Rom. 9.14-18 informed by our research of its intertextual
background. Our exegesis of the first of Paul's Old Testament quotations
in this section (Exod. 33.19b cited in Rom. 9.15) has been set forth in our
previous study of Rom. 9.1-9 (see note 2 in ch. 1 above), and the reader is
urged to look there for the exegetical basis of any claims made about Exod.
33.19b and its context in this chapter. We will now conduct the textual
comparisons in the order Paul quotes his intertexts and then move on to an
exegesis of Rom. 9.14-18.

8.1. *Textual Comparison of Romans 9.15 and Exodus 33.19b*

A textual comparison of Rom. 9.15 and Exod. 33.19 reveals that Rom. 9.15
reproduces Exod. 33.19 LXX exactly in a direct formal quotation.[1] The
LXX translation of Exod. 33.19 is itself a close translation of the Hebrew,
mirroring the LXX's translation of Exodus 32–34 generally, which closely
follows the Hebrew text represented by the MT.[2]

---

1.   Curiously, Jewett, *Romans*, 582 n. 137, states that there is a minor spelling
discrepancy between Paul and the LXX, claiming that the LXX has οἰκτειρμήσω/οἰκτείρω
where Paul has οἰκτιρήσω/οἰκτίρω. But the LXX text is identical to Paul's. Only a few late
manuscripts read οικτιρησω (426, DialTA, and 84). The reading Paul follows is almost
certainly original. Ει and ι are easily confused (cf. BDF § 23), and it is not surprising that
some manuscripts would differ in this way. It is actually surprising that there are not more
manuscripts with the minority reading, which is strong evidence for the standard reading.
2.   See Abasciano, *Romans 9.1-9*, 73. The LXX differs from the MT in one minor
respect: its use of the present tense for the MT's future tense in the case of ἐλεῶ (for אָחֹן) and
οἰκτίρω (for אֲרַחֵם).

Rom. 9.15   τῷ Μωϋσεῖ γὰρ λέγει Ἐλεήσω ὃν ἂν ἐλεῶ καὶ οἰκτιρήσω
                   ὃν ἂν οἰκτίρω
Exod. 33.19b LXX   ἐλεήσω ὃν ἂν ἐλεῶ καὶ οἰκτιρήσω ὃν ἂν οἰκτίρω
Exod. 33.19b MT   וְחַנֹּתִי אֶת־אֲשֶׁר אָחֹן וְרִחַמְתִּי אֶת־אֲשֶׁר אֲרַחֵם

8.2. *Textual Comparison of Romans 9.17 and Exodus 9.16*

We now turn to a textual comparison of Rom. 9.17 and Exod. 9.16. The following underline codes have been used to classify the relationship between the texts of the New Testament, LXX and the MT:

Single Underline: NT and LXX differ
Dotted Underline: NT and LXX share the same word but differ
                     in form
Double Underline: NT and LXX agree against MT
Squiggle Underline: LXX agrees with MT against NT

Rom 9.17   Εἰς αὐτὸ τοῦτο ἐξήγειρά σε ὅπως ἐνδείξωμαι ἐν σοὶ τὴν δύναμίν
           μου καὶ ὅπως διαγγελῇ τὸ ὄνομά μου ἐν πάσῃ τῇ γῇ

Exod. 9.16 LXX   καὶ ἕνεκεν τούτου διετηρήθης ἵνα ἐνδείξωμαι ἐν σοὶ τὴν ἰσχύν
                 μου καὶ ὅπως διαγγελῇ τὸ ὄνομά μου ἐν πάσῃ τῇ γῇ

Exod. 9.16 MT   וְאוּלָם בַּעֲבוּר זֹאת הֶעֱמַדְתִּיךָ בַּעֲבוּר הַרְאֹתְךָ אֶת־כֹּחִי
                 וּלְמַעַן סַפֵּר שְׁמִי בְּכָל־הָאָרֶץ

Paul and the LXX largely agree with the MT, though they differ some from one another. The LXX preserves the וֹ ('and') of the Hebrew with καί, which Paul omits, an insignificant omission that adapts the quotation to the syntax of its new context.[3] Both Paul and the LXX lack anything that represents the MT's adversative אוּלָם ('but'), another inconsequential omission, at least in the Pauline context.

Paul's εἰς αὐτὸ τοῦτο ('for this very purpose') and the LXX's ἕνεκεν τούτου ('for this reason') both accurately render the Hebrew בַּעֲבוּר זֹאת, indicating purpose or reason. According to Cranfield, Paul's rendering is closer to the

---

3.   Cf. ch. 5.2 above and note 6 in that section. Piper, *Justification*, 166, errs when he says that the LXX substitutes καί for אוּלָם. Rather, it retains καί and omits אוּלָם. Piper, 165, also probably errs in taking the verbs of 9.15 LXX as futures. J. W. Wevers, *Notes on the Greek Text of Exodus* (SBLSCS, 30; Atlanta: Scholars Press, 1990), 131, is more likely correct in stating, 'The verbs are aorist subjunctives and must be translated as potentials and contrary to fact', which matches the Hebrew construction. Piper, 166, then attributes too much significance to the omission of the adversative at the beginning of 9.16. Καί can be used adversatively (BDAG, s.v. 1bη), and it could be that the LXX is simply less clear in its marking of the adversative relationship (Wevers, ibid) or chose to leave it implicit because of its obviousness.

Hebrew and 'brings out more emphatically the idea of purpose'.[4] The fact that there is no variation in either the LXX or Pauline textual traditions strongly suggests that Paul's wording is his own,[5] which finds further support in the fact that the LXX wording does not occur anywhere in Paul while Paul does use εἰς αὐτὸ τοῦτο elsewhere (Rom. 13.6; 2 Cor. 5.5; Eph. 6.22; Col. 4.8).[6] This further suggests that Paul provided his own translation from Hebrew, though it could be that he altered the LXX to draw out his understanding of the text more forcefully, quoted it loosely from memory (i.e., intended only to reproduce the sense of the quotation rather than the exact words), or quoted it inaccurately due to a slip of memory. The fact that Paul's differences in this quotation from the LXX tend to be closer to the Hebrew (see below) supports the view that he made use of Hebrew in his citation.

Excursus 8.1: The Issue of Paul's Use of Hebrew in His Use of the Old Testament

The opinion that Paul sometimes made use of Hebrew in his use of the Old Testament has been common in the history of scholarship.[7] While still probably the most common view,[8] there has been a trend in some recent

---

4.   Cranfield, *Romans*, 485–86; so also Seifrid, 'Romans', 643; Sanday/Headlam, *Romans*, 256; cf. Moo, *Romans*, 595 n. 42. Stanley, *Paul*, 107 (cf. Piper, ibid), claims that Paul's wording is more clearly anticipatory than the LXX's and suggests that this is the most likely motive for alteration if Paul consciously altered the LXX. But εἰς αὐτὸ τοῦτο does not seem to be any more obviously anticipatory than ἕνεκεν τούτου; it is used anaphorically in two of its other four Pauline uses. The phrase can refer backward or forward, and the new, epistolary context here makes it clear that the phrase is kataphoric.

5.   Stanley, *Paul*, 106–07.

6.   Cf. ibid., 107, who strangely finds the significance of this datum unclear.

7.   Ibid., 12, notes that the position 'has found countless adherents over the centuries'.

8.   See e.g. (those who indicate that they think Paul relied on Hebrew in Rom 9.17 specifically have been marked with an asterisk), S.-L. Shum, *Paul's Use of Isaiah in Romans: A Comparative Study of Paul's Letter to the Romans and the Sybilline and Qumran Sectarian Texts* (WUNT, 2.156; Tübingen: Mohr Siebeck, 2002), 175–76, who also mentions that this is the view of most scholars; D. C. Mohrmann, 'Semantic Collisions at the Intertextual Crossroads: A Diachronic and Synchronic Study of Romans 9:30–10:13' (unpublished PhD thesis; University of Durham, 2001), 130, 161 (cautiously); T. M. Lim, *Holy Scripture in the Qumran Commentaries and Pauline Letters* (Oxford: OUP, 1997), 161–64 (Wagner's (*Heralds*, 7–8 nn. 29–30) implied criticism of Lim for allegedly taking 'it for granted that Paul could read Hebrew and Aramaic' seems unfair; Lim shows awareness of potential objection to his view and cites support for it as matching 'the cultural linguistic situation of Jews in first-century Palestine' (Lim, 162)); E. E. Ellis,* *Paul's Use of the Old Testament* (Grand Rapids: Baker, 1957), 14 nn. 5–6, 19–20; Bruce,* *Romans*, 194; Michel* (cited by Moo, *Romans*, 594); Hübner,* *Schriftgebrauch*, 40; Siegert,* *Argumentation*, 129; C. A. Evans, 'Paul and the Hermeneutics of "True Prophecy": A Study of Rom 9–11', *Bib* 65 (1984), 560–570 (563–65; seemingly); A. Maillot, 'Essai sur les citations vétérotestamentaires continues dans Romains 9 à 11, ou comment se servir de la Torah pour montrer que le "Christ est la fin de la Torah"', *ETR* 57 (1982), 55–73 (72); Piper,* *Justification*, 78, 166; R. Badenas, *Christ the*

works on Paul's use of the Old Testament to argue that, in cases where his citations agree with the Hebrew against the LXX, Paul made use of Greek texts, now lost, that had been revised toward Hebrew exemplars.[9] Stanley lays out the reasoning against Paul's use of Hebrew:

> (1) Paul often follows the wording of the Septuagint where the latter diverges sharply from the Masoretic Hebrew text; (2) Paul fails to correct his text from the Hebrew in certain places where it would actually have aided his argument to do so; and (3) only a handful of Paul's deviations actually bring the wording of the Septuagint closer to a known Hebrew text, and all of these can be explained equally well by other means.[10]

The first and third points do not count for much since, 'It would be natural for those writing in Greek to have recourse to Scripture in that language'.[11] This is similar to the way scholars and educated preachers sometimes quote modern translations of the Bible even when they think that the translation varies from the original. Moreover, with respect to the third point, it is questionable whether all of Paul's quotations that are closer to the Hebrew 'can be explained equally well by other means'. This may be true theoretically, that

---

End of the Law: Romans 10.4 in Pauline Perspective (JSNTSup, 10; Sheffield: JSOT, 1985), 92; B. D. Chilton, 'Romans 9–11 as Scriptural Interpretation and Dialogue with Judaism', *Ex Auditu* 4 (1988), 27–37 (35 n. 9); D. M. Smith, 'The Pauline Literature', in D. A. Carson and H. G. M. Williamson (eds), *It is Written: Scripture Citing Scripture: Essays in Honour of Barnabas Lindars* (Cambridge: CUP, 1988), 265–291 (273); Dunn,* *Romans*, 563; M. Silva, 'Old Testament in Paul', *DPL*, 630–42 (632); cf. L. J. Greenspoon, 'Old Testament Versions, Ancient', *DNTB*, 752–55 (753–54); T. W. Berkley, *From a Broken Covenant to Circumcision of the Heart: Pauline Intertextual Exegesis in Romans 2:17-29* (SBLDS, 175; Atlanta: SBL, 2000), 61. See further, note 12 below.

9.   See Stanley, *Paul*, 6, 41–48; R. B. Hays, *Echoes of Scripture in the Letters of Paul* (New Haven & London: Yale University Press, 1989), x–xi; Wagner, *Heralds*, 16–17 n. 60, 344–45. Indeed, S. J. Hafemann, *Paul, Moses, and the History of Israel: The Letter/Spirit Contrast and the Argument from Scripture in 2 Corinthians 3* (Peabody, MA: Hendrickson, 1995), 191 n. 7, now refers to this as the consensus view. But this is overstated, as the previous note demonstrates. This trend seems to go back especially to the groundbreaking study of D.-A. Koch, *Die Schrift als Zeuge des Evangeliums: Untersuchungen zur Verwendung und zum Verständnis der Schrift bei Paulus* (BHT, 69; Tübingen: Mohr Siebeck, 1986).

10.   Stanley, *Paul*, 12.

11.   Greenspoon, 'Versions', 753. Moreover, it also seems that the number of Pauline Hebraizing deviations may be more than sometimes thought. A. B. Du Toit, 'A Tale of Two Cities: "Tarsus or Jerusalem" Revisited', *NTS* 46 (2000), 375–402 (399 n. 12), has identified only four or five instances in which Stanley thinks Paul's deviations come closer to the Hebrew (Rom. 9.17(?), 33; 10.15; 12.19; 1 Cor. 15.54). But in his comprehensive list of OT citations in Paul, Silva, 'Old Testament', 631, lists six instances in the undisputed Pauline epistles (Rom. 1.17; 11.4; 11.35; 12.19; 1 Cor. 3.19; Gal. 3.11), only one of which overlaps with Stanley's list (Rom. 12.19). Hinting further at there potentially being more passages in which Paul's citation is closer to the Hebrew in some respect is the fact that Silva's classification of verbal agreements/disagreements by verse (rather than verse elements) is necessarily general, having to classify verses in an overall sense. For example, he classifies the different verses Stanley lists as not agreeing with the LXX or the MT. See later in the present excursus for discussion of Stanley's second point.

is, other means are possible and therefore able to explain the form of Paul's quotation equally well. But it is another question of what is the most likely explanation and what degree of supporting evidence each possibility has.

I am skeptical of the current trend – but not consensus – to favour on principle a conjectural assumption of a manuscript for which there is no evidence in a specific instance in light of the fact that (a) it is most likely that Paul knew Hebrew and the Hebrew Bible, as most scholars believe,[12] (b) the New Testament evidence favours this possibility,[13] and (c) it is the

---

12.   In addition to the references in note 8 above, see M. Hengel with R. Deines, *The Pre-Christian Paul* (Philadelphia: TPI, 1991), 18–62, esp. 25, 34–35, 37–38, 55; J. Murphy-O'Connor, *Paul: A Critical Life* (Oxford: OUP, 1996), 36–37, 47–48; W. D. Davies, 'Paul from the Jewish Point of View', in W. Horbury, W. D. Davies and J. Sturdy (eds), *Cambridge History of Judaism III: The Early Roman Period* (Cambridge: CUP, 1999), 678–730 (687); W. R. Stegner, 'Jew, Paul the', *DPL*, 503–11 (504–05); B. H. Young, *Paul The Jewish Theologian: A Pharisee among Christians, Jews, and Gentiles* (Peabody: Hendrickson, 1997), 15–16, 44 (cited by Shum, 'Romans', 176 n. 15). According to Du Toit, 'Tale', 390, 'very few researchers would disagree that removing Jerusalem totally from the pre-Christian Paul's biography would overrate the tendentiousness of Acts to the extreme'. U. Schnelle, *Apostle Paul: His Life and Theology* (trans. M. E. Boring; Grand Rapids: Baker Academic, 2005), 68–69, is one of the few scholars to go so far as to think the matter of Paul's education in Jerusalem substantially uncertain. There would seem to be some inconsistency in readily accepting Acts' testimony that Paul was from Tarsus (Acts 9.11; 21.39; 22.3; cf. 9.30; 11.25) while easily dismissing its testimony that he was educated in Judaism under Gamaliel in Jerusalem (22.3; 26.4) and could speak Aramaic (21.40; 22.2; cf. 26.14), all the more so when, as Hengel and Deines, 21, observe, Luke's and Paul's statements bearing on Paul's background 'are very close together in content'. If Paul studied (as a Pharisee) with Gamaliel as Acts claims, then he surely knew Hebrew and studied the Hebrew Bible. Even Du Toit, 'Tale', who thinks Paul did not make use of Hebrew in his OT quotations but utilized 'a "Hebraizing" LXX revision' (398–99; quote from 399; but Du Toit relies completely on the work of Koch and Stanley), accepts that Paul studied under Gamaliel (385–86), a point with which R. F. Hock, 'Paul and Greco-Roman Education', in J. P. Sampley (ed.), *Paul in the Greco-Roman World* (Harrisburg: TPI, 2003), 198–227 (218), agrees. Schnelle, ibid., downplays the lack of evidence for Pharisaic education outside of Jerusalem and does not really grapple with Hengel's (*Paul*, 28–34) argument that it was impossible to observe the Torah strictly outside of Israel. Schnelle's observations that Paul never mentions Jerusalem when he talks about his past life as a Pharisee and that Jerusalem does not play a significant role in his thought do not count for much. Paul neglects to mention many things that are nonetheless true, and it is presumptuous to suppose that we know what he should have chosen to highlight in his comments about his past. Moreover, there is no reason to think that having been educated in Jerusalem should have somehow made Jerusalem important in his overall thought. Finally, Schnelle's implication that if Paul was trained by Gamaliel, then we should expect him to think exactly like his teacher and to display the same temperament, strikes me as both gratuitous and unrealistic. Many students differ with their teachers and display very different temperaments from them.

13.   For discussion of the most relevant texts (such as Acts 7.58; 8.3; 9.1-2, 11, 13-14, 21, 30; 11.25; 21.39-40; 22.2-3; 23.6-9; 26.4-11, 14; 2 Cor. 11.22; Gal. 1.13-14 ; Phil. 3.5-6), see e.g. the references in the previous note, esp. Hengel and Deines, and also Du Toit, whose understanding of Paul's background as including Pharisaic training by Gamaliel in Jerusalem should imply extensive knowledge of the Hebrew Bible for Paul despite Du Toit's opinion, following Koch and Stanley, that Paul did not make use of Hebrew in his OT quotations.

simplest hypothesis to account for varying quotation patterns, since it allows more room for variety due to Paul's individual judgment. As W. D. Davies has stated, 'We can assume that Paul as a Pharisee studied the Scriptures in Hebrew. That he respected and generally cited the Septuagint in his epistles does not gainsay this. From as early as the middle of the second century BCE, the Septuagint was used as a matter of course in Palestine itself by people who knew Hebrew'.[14] Thus it is very likely that Paul knew the Scriptures in Hebrew.

On the other hand, there were Greek manuscripts that had been revised toward Hebrew.[15] And Ross Wagner has made good cases that Paul made use of Greek revisions of LXX Isaiah toward a Hebrew exemplar in Rom 9.33 (Isa. 8.14/28.16) and Rom. 10.15 (Isa. 52.7).[16] Yet it should be noted that the likelihood in the former case is that both Paul and the author of 1 Peter, who quotes the same Isaiah passages as Paul in 1 Pet. 2.6, 8, made use of a Christian anthology of Scripture passages which used an LXX text revised toward the Hebrew and was used as testimony to Jesus as the Messiah,[17] making Rom. 9.33 a special case that does not necessarily give us a glimpse of the type of Greek manuscript Paul normally used. Nevertheless, in the case of Rom. 9.33, there is still an aspect of the quotation that is both closer to the Hebrew[18] and unique to Paul, which must be accounted for: Paul uses οὐ καταισχυνθήσεται where the LXX and 1 Pet. 2.6 have οὐ μὴ καταισχυνθῇ for the Hebrew לֹא יָחִישׁ.

Paul and the Hebrew have only one negative and the future tense whereas the LXX and 1 Pet. 2.6 have a double negative with the subjunctive. Both Greek readings render the Hebrew adequately, but the LXX is more emphatic and Paul is formally closer to the Hebrew. The 'use of a form of καταισχύνω is a significant agreement between Paul and LXX, particularly in light of the difficulty of the Hebrew idiom and the quite divergent translations found in the versions'.[19] But since it appears that both Paul and 1 Peter used a common source that revised the LXX toward the Hebrew, but the form of καταισχύνω Paul uses is unique to him and closer to the Hebrew, it would seem that Paul is responsible for this change to his *Vorlage*. It is quite possible that he simply changed the form of the word in his Greek *Vorlage* based on the Greek alone,

14.   Davies, 'Paul', 687.
15.   See e.g., Stanley, *Paul*, 14–15.
16.   Wagner, *Heralds*, 126–36, 170–74 (cf. 344–45).
17.   See e.g., J. R. Michaels, *1 Peter* (WBC, 49. Waco, Texas: Word, 1988), 94; Dunn, *Romans*, 584; Ellis, *Paul's Use*, 89, following Dodd. Shum, *Romans*, who lays out five options for accounting for the relationship between Rom. 9.33 and 1 Pet. 2.6, 8 (214), calls the view that Paul used a pre-Pauline Christian tradition the consensus (216), though he argues contrariwise, i.e., that Paul is responsible for the text form he uses and that 1 Peter depends on Paul to some extent; see his full discussion on 212–16. If Shum is right, then Rom. 9.33 would actually support Paul's use of Hebrew in his use of the OT. Against 1 Peter drawing these quotations from Romans, see Wagner, *Heralds*, 134–35, including n. 51.
18.   Slightly closer according to Wagner, *Heralds*, 129, though there is more similarity than he observes.
19.   Ibid.

but there is no obvious reason why he would do so. Hence, Koch thinks the change is merely stylistic, perhaps due to Paul's tendency to avoid using οὐ μή (which occurs only four times in Paul outside of quotations) and a desire to remove the emphasis of the double negative.[20] But as Stanley reasons,

> Koch's appeal to Pauline usage is weakened by the observation that Paul allows the same construction to stand in a quotation from Ps 32.1 in Rom 4.8 ... and seems to have done the same in his quotation from Gen 21.10 in Gal 4.30. Moreover, there is nothing to indicate that Paul had any reason to tone down the emphatic nature of the LXX wording in Rom 9:33, as the present form surely does.[21]

Stanley's own opinion is that Paul's pre-Pauline Christian source is the most likely background.[22] But this does not explain Paul's unique reading, unless his source text actually contained it and 1 Peter altered that source to match the LXX. However, this seems unlikely. The common source is based on the LXX even though it revises toward Hebrew. It seems unlikely that the author of 1 Peter would revise his source away from the Hebrew when there is no obvious reason for him to do so, one of the marks of his source was revision toward Hebrew no matter how uneven, he let other revisions toward Hebrew stand in the quotation, and conformity toward Hebrew is the more natural orientation over against revision away from it (i.e., it is more natural that someone might want to revise toward the original than it is that someone would revise with a purpose of specifically moving away from the original).

Wagner has suggested that Paul chose the future tense over the aorist subjunctive because 'the sense of expectation attached to the future tense may have better suited Paul's eschatological framework'.[23] But οὐ μή + the subjunctive refers to the future[24] and Paul uses the construction in eschatological statements in three of his four other uses of it (Rom. 4.8; 1 Thes. 4.15; 5.3).[25] Thus, eschatological concern does not offer a good reason for Paul to have altered his source text. It does appear that Paul is the source of this unique reading that is closer to the Hebrew than either the LXX or Paul's main source. However, the change seems too small to be motivated by a desire simply to conform more closely to the Hebrew. But given the likelihood that Paul knew the Hebrew text, the most plausible reconstruction is that this knowledge influenced his own articulation of the Old Testament text even as he made use of the Christian source tradition/text common to him and 1 Peter. Rom. 9.33 actually stands as evidence that Paul's knowledge of the Hebrew text impacted his citation of the Old Testament.

---

20.   Koch, *Schrift*, 115; cf. Stanley's (*Paul*, 125) perception of Koch's argument.
21.   Stanley, ibid.
22.   Ibid.
23.   Wagner, *Heralds*, 129 n. 31; cf. Jewett, *Romans*, 614.
24.   BDAG, s.v. μή, 4; Zerwick, *Greek*, § 444.
25.   Jewett, *Romans*, 316, surprisingly mistakes λογίσηται in Rom. 4.8 for a future when it is in fact an aorist subjunctive.

As for Isa. 52.7 in Rom. 10.15, it does seem that Paul used a manuscript that revised the LXX toward a proto-masoretic Hebrew text.[26] But this does not give strong support for assuming that whenever Paul's Old Testament quotations are closer to the Hebrew than to the LXX that he used a Hebraizing revision of the latter. For in this case there is solid *evidence* in the textual tradition that this has taken place. But when there is no evidence for such a manuscript, it is much simpler – despite the incompleteness of our textual evidence – to assume that Paul followed the Hebrew since he almost certainly knew Hebrew and the Hebrew Bible.

Stanley's second point of three against Paul making use of Hebrew in his Old Testament citations remains to be considered (we have already discussed points one and three), namely that 'Paul fails to correct his text from the Hebrew in certain places where it would actually have aided his argument to do so'.[27] The point is too subjective to provide much support for Stanley's position. It runs the risk of presumptuousness to claim to know how Paul should have argued or what he would regard as most important to say or to emphasize. For example, Stanley cites 1 Cor. 2.16 as what one would assume he intends as a clear example of this point when he invokes it to deny that Paul used Hebrew in quoting Exod. 9.16.[28] Stanley does not explain this citation, but presumably he refers to Paul following the LXX's νοῦν for the Hebrew רוח when πνεῦμα would be a closer rendering and fit nicely with Paul's emphasis on the Spirit in 1 Corinthians 2.

However, it is quite reasonable to think that Paul wanted to connect the important themes of wisdom and knowledge of God in 1 Corinthians to the Spirit via reference to the concept of the mind here. More specifically, Paul appears to indicate that the Holy Spirit offers true wisdom and knowledge of God to those in whom he dwells, believers in Christ.[29] As Silva observes, 'As it turns out, 1 Corinthians 2 focuses on the Spirit ... as the one who makes it possible for us to know God ... (see especially 1 Cor 2:11)'.[30] Therefore, 1 Cor. 2.16 does not support the contention that Paul had no knowledge of the Hebrew text. Rather, in light of Stanley's appeal to it, it serves as an example of how such claims about what translation would best fit Paul's argument run the risk of being subjective and unreliable.

There are five main theoretically possible explanations for when Paul disagrees with the Hebrew against the LXX in his Old Testament quotations: (1) Paul provided his own translation from Hebrew, whether directly or by way of the Hebrew text's influence upon him; (2) he altered the LXX without reference to Hebrew to draw out his understanding of the text more forcefully, coming closer to the Hebrew unintentionally; (3) he used a

---

26. See Wagner, *Heralds*, 170–74; Stanley, *Paul*, 134–41.
27. Stanley, *Paul*, 12.
28. Ibid, 107.
29. Cf. Silva, 'Old Testament', 633–34; G. D. Fee, *The First Epistle to the Corinthians* (NICNT; Grand Rapids: Eerdmans, 1987), 119–20; D. E. Garland, *1 Corinthians* (BECNT; Grand Rapids: Baker Academic, 2003), 101–02.
30. Silva, 'Old Testament', 633.

Greek text revised toward the Hebrew; (4) he quoted the LXX loosely from memory (i.e., intended only to reproduce the sense of the quotation rather than the exact words), coming closer to the Hebrew unintentionally; (5) he quoted inaccurately due to a slip of memory, coming closer to the Hebrew unintentionally. Each instance of quotation in Paul's writings must be analysed on a case-by-case basis on the evidence available for the particular case in question. Given the likelihood that Paul knew Hebrew and the Hebrew Bible, (1) is to be preferred over (3) when there is no evidence for a lost Greek manuscript revised toward a Hebrew exemplar. While there almost certainly were Old Testament Greek manuscripts revised toward Hebrew that are no longer extant, it is dubious to assume Paul used one when there is no evidence that he did since he likely knew the Hebrew text.

***

Paul's ἐξήγειρά σε is another portion of his quotation that is closer to the Hebrew (הֶעֱמַדְתִּיךָ) than is the LXX (διετηρήθης),[31] at least in formal equivalency, most likely Paul's own translation from the Hebrew. 'To raise up' (ἐξεγείρω) is obviously closer to 'cause to stand' (hiph. of עמד) than is 'to keep' (διατηρέω). Moreover, Paul's wording preserves the active voice and direct object of the Hebrew text whereas the LXX uses the passive voice and eliminates the direct object.[32] Compared to the passive verb of the LXX, Paul's active ἐξήγειρά σε accentuates God's initiative and sovereignty in his dealings with Pharaoh.[33] Yet the LXX more *explicitly* captures the contextual, dynamic sense of the Hebrew, which we saw to be that YHWH had allowed Pharaoh to continue living.[34] But this is probably also the sense of Paul's use of ἐξεγείρω.[35] Paul's only other use of the verb – in fact, its only other use in the New Testament – refers to raising to life/resurrection (Rom. 6.14). Moreover, he almost always uses the cognate verb ἐγείρω in the same sense, including nine of ten usages in Romans (4.24, 25; 6.4, 9; 7.4; 8.11 (x2), 34; 10.9).[36] The idea is that

31.   So e.g., ibid.; Seifrid, 'Romans', 643; Michel (cited by Moo, *Romans*, 594); Ellis, *Paul's Use*, 14 nn. 5–6; Piper, *Justification*, 166; Schreiner, *Romans*, 509.

32.   An active form with the direct object (διετήρησα σε) does appear in the LXX minuscules 135, 85[mg], 343, 344[mg], and the Ethiopic and Arabic versions (Stanley, *Paul*, 108 n. 71).

33.   Cf. Moo, *Romans*, 594–95; Seifrid, 'Romans', 643; Cranfield, *Romans*, 486–87; Dunn, *Romans*, 563. But most if not all of these commentators probably have their conclusion about the meaning of the verb in view too, perhaps even most prominently.

34.   Cf. Wevers, *Exodus*, 131–32, who regards διετηρήθης to be 'a clear rendering' of the MT. Stanley's (*Paul*, 108 n. 71) claim that διατηρεῖσθαι is an inappropriate translation of עמד is puzzling even with its lack of use elsewhere to translate the Hebrew verb.

35.   So J. Goodwin, *An Exposition of the Ninth Chapter of the Epistle to the Romans* (London, c. 1652), 192; Hofmann (cited by Godet, *Romans*, 353); Morison, *Exposition*, 127, in his original position, later changed; Bruce, *Romans*, 194; Wright, 'Romans', 639; W. Hendriksen, *Exposition of Paul's Epistle to the Romans* (NTC; Grand Rapids: Baker Book House, 1980–81), 325.

36.   Only two out of 41 occurrences in Paul bear a different meaning: Rom 13.11 and Phil. 1.17. Eph. 5.14 roughly bears this meaning with respect to spiritual life, using ἐγείρω

sparing Pharaoh's life – especially when he deserved death and God had been unleashing destruction upon Egypt – was tantamount to giving him life. As G. Bush said, 'a person may be said to be "raised up" who is preserved alive when in danger of dying'.[37] The same sort of logic can be seen in 3 Macc. 7.6, which equates the granting of clemency/sparing of life with the granting of life (literally, 'giving them to live' (τὸ ζῆν αὐτοῖς χαρισάμενοι)). Similarly, Heb. 11.19, which uses ἐγείρω of resurrection from death to life, regards the sparing of Isaac's life as a sort of resurrection.[38]

But this is not the only possible meaning of ἐξεγείρω in 9.17. Writing in 1888, James Morison noted that the meaning of the verb here had 'been much and vehemently debated by doctrinal commentators'.[39] There are five main positions: (1) to spare/allow to remain alive;[40] (2) to create;[41] (3) to rouse/incite to opposition/hardness;[42] (4) to elevate to kingship/authority/ higher role or status;[43] (5) to cause to appear (in prominence) on the stage

to refer to waking as a spiritual resurrection. As for the four NT non-Pauline epistolary occurrences of ἐγείρω, those in Heb. 11.19 and 1 Pet. 1.21 bear the same sense of giving life in resurrection, Rev. 11.1 bears a different sense and Jas 5.15 is notable for the sense of raising from sickness to restored life/health. Usage in the Gospels and Acts is more varied. In literature prior to Paul, ἐγείρω translates the hiphil of עמד in LXX Dan. 8.18; 1 Esd. 5.43; 8.78 (these first three references of a literal/physical raising up); Sir. 10.4 (of raising to authority; Wagner, *Heralds*, 55 n. 36).

37. Bush, *Exodus*, 116, who after citing Jas 5.15 also states, 'It was in this sense of being spared from imminent destruction that Pharaoh was raised up'; emphasis removed.

38. From a different line of evidence, Rom. 9.22, which contains similar wording and develops the thought of 9.17, speaks of God bearing the vessels of his wrath with great patience, providing a sort of parallel to the raising up of Pharaoh in 9.17. Cf. Wagner, *Heralds*, 55, who fails to note the support this gives to reading ἐξεγείρω in 9.17 as suggested above.

39. Morison, *Exposition*, 127; emphasis removed. For fuller than usual discussion of the options, in addition to Morison, 126–30, see Godet, *Romans*, 353–54; Sanday/Headlam, *Romans*, 255–56.

40. As opposed to the view advocated above, some take this in the direction of a restoring to health/life from sickness as envisioned in Jas 5.15, but specifically referring in Rom. 9.17 to Pharaoh being raised from the sickness inflicted by the plague of boils; so Gifford (cited by Sanday/Headlam, ibid.); possibly Bush, *Exodus*, 116. But Godet, ibid., is surely correct that this is too difficult for assuming something the text does not state. Not surprisingly, the view has few supporters, so much so that some detailed commentators do not even mention the view, e.g., Cranfield, *Romans*, 486; Moo, *Romans*, 494–95.

41. A. Oepke, 'ἐξεγείρω', *TDNT*, 2.338; Dunn, *Romans*, 554 (though curiously he refers readers to Sanday/Headlam for the view, who expressly reject it, and the Scripture references he provides do not support this meaning; see note 46 below); cf. BDAG, s.v. ἐξεγείρω, 4 (as a possibility).

42. Beale, 'Hardening', 151, following M. Stuart. This meaning is predicated on the more general LXX meaning of 'to rouse to action' (see Beale, n. 92, for Scripture references), the specific action being specified by context. It weighs against this view that it is the Exodus context that must provide specification, for if it is granted that Paul's meaning relies on the Exodus context, then there is good reason to opt for number 1 instead, a meaning more in accord with that of Exod. 9.16 in both the Hebrew and the LXX.

43. Theodoret; Bengel; both cited by Morison, *Exposition*, 127; BDAG, s.v. ἐξεγείρω, 5 (as a possibility). This is not a normal meaning of ἐξεγείρω except insofar as it overlaps with

of history/appoint to a special role.[44] Number 5 commands 'a fairly large consensus'.[45] But it, along with the rest of the options except for number 1, is predicated on general LXX usage of ἐξεγείρω.[46]

Yet Paul's own usage of the word and the context and background of his discourse in Rom. 9.17, which presents a quotation of Exod. 9.16, should determine our judgment of his meaning here, supporting a meaning of 'to spare/allow to remain alive'. It is telling that Sanday and Headlam argue against this meaning with the point that it would require reference to be made to the original context of Exodus.[47] For as we have seen very clearly in our study of Romans 9 so far (in the present volume and its predecessor), Paul's Old Testament quotations function as pointers to their original contexts. Paul's quotation of Exod. 9.16 in Rom 9.17 is no exception. In fact, it is an especially clear example in which Paul assumes knowledge of the original context of his quotation on the part of his audience (see our treatment of 9.18 below).

There are two purpose clauses that follow the first verb (Paul's ἐξήγειρά ('I raised')) in Exod. 9.16. The Hebrew text uses a different word that indicates purpose for each purpose clause (בַּעֲבוּר and לְמַעַן respectively), followed by the LXX, which uses ἵνα for the first purpose clause and ὅπως for the second.[48] Paul, on the other hand, uses ὅπως for both purpose clauses, increasing the

number 5, and Godet, *Romans*, 353, correctly argues that 'so special a qualification as this would require to be expressed more precisely', or, I would add, it would require recourse to the Exodus context, which would supplant this meaning on the same logic as discussed in the previous note.

44.   Cranfield, *Romans*, 486; Moo, *Romans*, 595; Piper, *Justification*, 166–67; Sanday/Headlam, *Romans*, 256. Some interpreters combine more than one of these views, such as Morison, *Exposition*, 127–30, with numbers 2 and 5. There is actually some ambiguity and confusion in scholarly discussion of the meaning of ἐξεγείρω in Rom 9.17. This may be due partly to the nature of the language used by scholars. For example, 'to cause to appear on the stage of history' (number 5) can be construed as involving creation (number 2), and 'elevating to kingship or a higher role' (number 4) sounds very similar to 'appointing to a special role' (number 5). It is sometimes particularly hard to know if advocates of number 5 include number 2 as part of number 5. But it seems that most do not, like prominent advocates of number 5 Sanday/Headlam, who expressly reject number 2. Hendriksen, *Romans*, 325 n. 276, clearly sees the two as the same.

45.   Piper, ibid., who may be consulted for a list of representatives in addition to those mentioned in the previous note.

46.   See e.g. the reasoning of ibid.; Cranfield, *Romans*, 486, both for number 5; Beale, 'Hardening', 151, for number 3. On the other hand, 'to create' (number 2) is not a well-attested meaning in the LXX; Sanday/Headlam, ibid., go so far as to say that the meaning has no support. This is probably overstated slightly. The typical verses cited for support are indeed better taken otherwise, such as rousing to action or appointing to a special or prominent role (Hab. 1.6; Zech. 11.16; cf. similarly Jer. 27.41, which Dunn, *Romans*, 554, appears to cite erroneously as 27.14). But Song 8.5 approaches the meaning and it could also be taken as similar to instances of the verb in the sense of 'to bring about, stir up' (2 Sam. 12.11; 2 Macc. 13.4; Prov. 25.23; Song 2.7; 3.5).

47.   Sanday/Headlam, ibid.

48.   According to Stanley, *Paul*, 108, the respective manuscript traditions are 'nearly unanimous' for both the LXX and Paul; see his note 73 for minor LXX exceptions.

parallelism between the two,[49] and laying slightly greater stress on the notion of purpose since ὅπως is an even clearer marker of purpose than ἵνα.[50] The increased parallelism harmonizes with the addition of ἐν and the conversion of the Hebrew verb's object suffix into an object (σοί) of this Greek preposition (ἐν),[51] found in the first of these two purpose clauses of both the LXX and Paul: 'in order that I might show my power in you' vs the Hebrew text's 'to show you my power'.

The use of ἐν σοί eliminates the Hebrew text's explicit expression of concern for Pharaoh to know God's power, identifying him only as the means through which, or the sphere in which, God's power is displayed.[52] Paul has probably followed the LXX here over against the Hebrew, and this because it fits best with his concern in Romans 9 to argue for God's right to include Gentiles in his covenant people. Paul is especially interested in the effect of God's treatment of Pharaoh bringing the proclamation of his name to the whole world. It is not as if Paul is trying to hide the original text's statement of divine intention to enlighten Pharaoh. As we have mentioned, Paul quotes the Old Testament text as a pointer to its original context. And the original context of both the Hebrew text and the LXX testifies to God's intention that Pharaoh and the Egyptians would come to know his identity as the supreme, sovereign God (e.g., Exod. 7.17; 8.6 (10; Eng./LXX); 9.14; 9.29). But Paul focuses the reader's attention on that which he wants to emphasize from the Old Testament context by the wording of his quotation – the universal ramifications of God's treatment of Pharaoh.

Paul seems to proceed similarly with his use of δύναμίν instead of the LXX's synonymous ἰσχύν for the Hebrew כֹּחַ. It is impossible to know if δύναμίν was Paul's purposeful choice against the LXX or if he followed a variant LXX text, since the LXX textual tradition 'is strongly divided between δύναμίν and ἰσχύν'.[53] But on balance, the former seems more likely

---

49.   Cf. Cranfield, *Romans*, 486. Stanley, ibid., objects to the idea that Paul attempted 'to improve the parallelism' because exchanging ὅπως and ἵνα was common practice and occurs in Paul several times. Whether the notion of improvement is in view is questionable, but it is hard to see how it could be denied that use of the same word in both clauses formally increases the parallelism.

50.   Stanley, ibid., criticizes 'Koch's attempt to discover in this substitution a strengthening of the "final" sense of the clause' based on the fact 'that ἵνα-clauses are actually used more frequently than ὅπως-clauses to express purpose in the New Testament'; Schreiner, *Romans*, 510 n. 13, follows Stanley. But this reasoning is flawed. Frequency of use does not necessarily make for emphasis – indeed, it can make for lesser emphasis. But the issue is clarity. The conjunction ἵνα is more ambiguous in that it can denote other things than purpose, but ὅπως only indicates purpose when used, as here, as a conjunction (see BDAG on both words, and specifically on ἵνα, M. G. Sim, 'A Relevance Theoretic Approach to the Particle ἵνα in Koine Greek' (PhD thesis; University of Edinburgh, 2006)). Nevertheless, the greater stress is very slight.

51.   Cf. Cranfield, ibid.; Sanday/Headlam, *Romans*, 256–57.

52.   Cf. ibid.; Wevers, *Exodus*, 132.

53.   Stanley, *Paul*, 109. Though the textual witnesses may be evenly split, other evidence favours ἰσχύν as the original LXX reading; see Stanley, n. 76; Wevers, ibid. Of course, other standard explanations for Paul's wording remain possible too (see Excursus 8.1 above), but these seem to be the most likely.

because (1) δύναμις is common in Paul while ἰσχύς is rare in Paul, the New Testament and Hellenistic Greek generally, yet common in the LXX;[54] (2) ἰσχύς does not appear in Romans, but δύναμις occurs a number of times, most notably as part of the very theme statement of the epistle (1.16-17),[55] where the notion of the gospel as 'the power [δύναμις] of God for salvation for all who believe, both to the Jew first and the Greek', ties in tightly with part of Paul's purpose in quoting Exod. 9.16 – to highlight God's treatment of Pharaoh as bringing about the proclamation of his name to the whole world and to support Paul's argument for God's right to include Gentiles in his covenant people; and (3) we have already seen that Paul appears to have been the source of other divergences from the LXX in his quotation here of Exod. 9.16.

By way of summary, the form Paul chose for his quotation of Exod 9.16 in Rom. 9.17 highlights God's purpose and sovereignty as well as their expression in seeking the salvation of the world and including Gentiles in the covenant people of God. It is hard to say whether Paul used the LXX as the fundamental basis of his quotation or not. Stanley thinks so.[56] But many scholars observe that Paul's quotation differs from the LXX,[57] Mark Seifrid even concluding that Paul's 'citation of Exod. 9:16 appears to be basically independent of the LXX'.[58] Indeed, as Dunn says, Paul's quotation 'is significantly different from the LXX, and it is difficult to think that just these divergences can be explained solely by a variant text with which Paul was familiar'.[59] Moreover, some of Paul's differences from the LXX are of such a minor nature as to give the impression of fresh translation, or at least of a lack of fundamental/general reliance. Yet there is also substantial agreement with the LXX in ways one might not expect if Paul made no use of it, particularly its addition of ἐν σοί.[60] It seems like it would be going too far to say that Paul's quotation of Exod. 9.16 relies fundamentally on the LXX. But he clearly made some use of it. Perhaps it would be best to say that Paul was aware of both the Hebrew and the LXX, and that he made use of both in providing his quotation of Exod. 9.16 in a way that would

54.   See Cranfield, *Romans*, 486; Stanley, ibid., who notes that ἰσχύς never occurs in Paul's undisputed letters 'versus nearly [exactly by my count] three dozen instances of δύναμις'. In his disputed epistles, it occurs only three times (Eph. 1.19; 6.10; 2 Thes. 1.9; Cranfield, n. 5) vs 13 instances of δύναμις, making a total of three instances of ἰσχύς vs 49 instances of δύναμις in the traditional Pauline corpus.

55.   Cf. Cranfield, *Romans*, 487; these verses are typically recognized as the theme of the letter (Dunn, *Romans*, 38). Δύναμις occurs in 1.16 as well as 1.4, 20; 8.38; 15.13, 19 (x2).

56.   Stanley, *Paul*, 106–09 (esp. 107).

57.   For example, Cranfield, *Romans*, 485–86; Moo, *Romans*, 594; Dunn, *Romans*, 563; Silva, 'Old Testament', 631.

58.   Seifrid, 'Romans', 643; cf. Dunn, ibid.

59.   Dunn, ibid.

60.   See Stanley, *Paul*, 107. Stanley also points to 'its rendering of the active סַפֵּר by the passive διαγγελῆ', though it is easy to imagine Paul arriving at that adjustment on his own because of the infinitival Hebrew construction and the proclamation of God's power being entrusted to intermediaries such as Paul in his own first-century context.

best apply his understanding of the passage to his context and make his point most effectively.

8.3. *Intertextual Exegesis of Romans 9.14-18*

It is important to keep the context of Paul's argument in mind as we approach Rom. 9.14-18. Paul has just been defending his claim that only those who believe in Christ are rightful heirs of his covenant promises (9.8) – and its grievous corollary, the rejection of unbelieving ethnic Israel from the covenant she enjoyed – by defending God's right to name his people based on faith rather than works/ancestry (6-13). Most immediately, he has done so by arguing that God retains the right to choose who his people are according to his own good pleasure (for any or no reason whatsoever) because the election of his people depended wholly on his sovereign will from the beginning through his election of Jacob, the covenant head, and therefore remained subject to the dictates of his own will (10-13). But this raises further question of whether God has acted justly toward Israel.

So Paul now addresses the objection that God's choice of his people without regard to works or ancestry makes him unrighteous. This part of his argument thus targets and supports a potentially objectionable aspect of the way God carries out his purpose for election (a purpose to save the world) – that he now chooses his people without regard for works or ancestry. This method of fulfilling his saving purpose serves as the foundation for the real, practical thrust of concern in the objections to his gospel Paul has been considering in Romans 9 – that God's election of the Church and rejection of unbelieving ethnic Israel violates his covenant promises to Israel. Hence, Paul's argument in 9.14-18 supports his argument in 9.10-13, which our exegesis has found supports 9.8, the clearest and most focused expression of Paul's point in support of 9.6b, which in turn supports 9.6a, the main point of Romans 9–11.[61] It all aims to demonstrate God's faithfulness to his promises to Israel. Most technically, the objection of 9.14 arises out of the main point of 9.10-13, contained in the purpose statement of 9.11c-12b, which maintains that God's purpose to save the world is to be fulfilled not on the basis of works, but on the basis of God's call, which he issues according to his own good pleasure.[62] However, the objection of 9.14 arises most immediately out of the stark, concise expression of this principle recorded in 9.13, Paul's quotation of Mal. 1.2-3: 'Jacob I loved, but Esau I hated'.[63]

---

61.   Hence, Moo, *Romans*, 589, calls 9.14-18 (along with 9.19-23) 'a detour from the main road of Paul's argument'.

62.   It should be remembered that in Romans God's good pleasure is to issue his call on the basis of faith in Christ rather than works or ancestry, and that is what evoked the objections Paul addresses in Rom. 9–11.

63.   Cf. Jewett, *Romans*, 581, though he thinks that the question of 9.14 is 'provoked by the harsh arbitrariness of the quotation from Malachi'.

8.3.a. Is There Unrighteousness with God? (Romans 9.14)

8.3.a.1. A Rhetorical Question
With the questions at the beginning of 9.14, Paul returns to use of the diatribe, which he has used earlier in the epistle (e.g., 3.1-9, 31; 6.1-3, 15-16; 7.7, 13):[64] 'What, therefore, shall we say? Is there unrighteousness with God'? (14a-b).[65] According to K. P. Donfried, it is now well recognized that, 'The so-called diatribe is not a literary genre but rather a series of rhetorical devices'.[66] It was in fact a method of instruction marked by a dialogical format that often used question and answer to accomplish its educational intent, whether through rhetorical questions or use of an imaginary interlocutor to pose questions/ objections, all answered by the teacher.[67] Use of the diatribe implies nothing about whether its content addresses a purely theoretical issue or a concrete historical situation.[68] Nor does it necessarily imply a polemical intention when it raises and addresses objections.[69] Rather, it implies a pedagogical purpose, which could apply to any number of disparate situations.

This weighs against the suggestion that some specific opponent lies behind this question,[70] for the suggestion tends to be inferred from the sheer fact of an objection being raised. As Cranfield observes, it is a 'needless complication'.[71]

64.   See Moo, *Romans*, 589–91; Schreiner, *Romans*, 505; Jewett, ibid.; Byrne, *Romans*, 296; Fitzmyer, *Romans*, 566; D. F. Watson, 'Diatribe', *DPL*, 213–14 (214). Dunn, *Romans*, 537 (cf. 551, 555), and Seifrid, 'Romans', 644, appear to think the diatribe does not resume until 9.19.

65.   Some commentators suggest that Paul's unusual wording of the latter question seeks to avoid irreverently characterizing God as unrighteous in his nature (so e.g., Jewett, ibid.; Morris, *Romans*, 359 n. 65). But this is unlikely since Paul uses the adjective ἄδικος of God in the parallel question of 3.5.

66.   K. P. Donfried (ed.), *The Romans Debate* (Peabody: Hendrickson, rev. edn, 1991), lxx; cf. idem, 'False Presuppositions in the Study of Romans', in Donfried (ed.), *Debate*, 102–25 (112–19); Watson, 'Diatribe', 213; S. E. Porter, 'Diatribe', *DNTB*, 296–98 (297).

67.   On the diatribe, see concisely, Watson, 'Diatribe'; Porter, 'Diatribe'. The standard, extensive study is S. K. Stowers, *The Diatribe and Paul's Letter to the Romans* (SBLDS, 57; Chico, CA: Scholars Press, 1981).

68.   Cf. Watson, 'Diatribe', 214.

69.   Cf. ibid.

70.   For the view, see Godet, *Romans*, 351–52, and more recently, Piper, *Justification*, 92–94. Though once a common view, it has few supporters other than Piper in recent scholarship. Against it, see e.g. and rightly, Cranfield, *Romans*, 482 (though he frames the view as having to do with an imaginary objector); Jewett, *Romans*, 581; Schreiner, *Romans*, 506; Käsemann, *Romans*, 267; Byrne, *Romans*, 296; L. T. Johnson, *Reading Romans: A Literary and Theological Commentary* (New York: Crossword, 1997), 150.

71.   Cranfield, ibid., n. 2. Piper, *Justification*, 92–94, has taken the viewpoint to a position of gross implausibility by arguing that the term 'unrighteousness' (ἀδικία) carries two different meanings in Paul's question: his opponent's and his own. Yet Paul gives no indication that he is entertaining two different definitions in this one instance of ἀδικία. To be sure, by the use of μή he indicates that the expected answer to the question of whether God is unrighteous is 'no'. But this is a rhetorical question. At the very least, it is Paul's own wording of the question. Piper's approach erroneously treats Paul's argument as if it is over the definition of (un)righteousness when, according to the explicit wording of the text, it is actually about whether God is unrighteous. The most natural reading of Paul posing the

Paul introduces a rhetorical question here to move his argument forward by addressing a natural objection that might arise (especially from the Jewish point of view)[72] in response to his argument. Nevertheless, the question undoubtedly echoes objections Paul encountered as he preached the gospel.[73] Rhetorical questions in argumentative discourse (such as Romans) often reflect typical objections that have arisen in discussion of the topic being addressed. It is hard to imagine that Paul's argument would not reflect objections he had encountered in his gospel ministry even if it is unlikely that it has specific opponents in view or is specifically quoting opponents.

8.3.a.2. *The Significance of Rom. 3.1-8*

There are five other occurrences of the exact phrase τί οὖν ἐροῦμεν ('What, therefore, shall we say'?) in Paul (and the New Testament for that matter), all in Romans (4.1; 6.1; 7.7; 8.31; 9.30). Paul uses τί ἐροῦμεν in one more place, but without οὖν (3.5). As Cranfield observes,

> The closest parallels to the present occurrence are 3.5; 6.1; 7.7, in all of which it is followed by another question and then by μὴ γένοιτο (in 3.5 after a brief parenthesis). In 3.5 and here in 9.14 the form of the following question (μή) expressly indicates that a negative answer is expected ... In these four parallel cases (3.5; 6.1; 7.7, and here) Paul uses this formula at a point where he recognizes that a false conclusion could be drawn, instead of the true one, from what he has just been saying.[74]

Of these parallels, 3.5 is the most significant because (a) it is the only one that is followed by a question expressly expecting a negative answer as in 9.14,[75] and most importantly, (b) addresses a similar subject – whether God is

---

question of whether God is unrighteous and then answering the question in the negative is that he is denying the very charge that has been raised. Few if any scholars follow Piper in this.

72.   For a caveat on speaking about the 'the Jewish point of view', see note 89 below.

73.   Cf. Moo, *Romans*, 590; Schreiner, *Romans*, 506.

74.   Cranfield, *Romans*, 481. Cf. Piper, *Justification*, 91 n. 1. But Piper does not think 3.5 as close a parallel as 6.1 and 7.7, though he does not say why. Perhaps it is because of the omission of οὖν. But that is inconsequential for the parallel, merely making the obviously inferential character of the question explicit. Cranfield's reasoning is more persuasive. See further below.

75.   Ironically (in light of the previous note), a feature of 9.14 Piper, *Justification*, 92, stresses. F. Belli, *Argumentation and Use of Scripture in Romans 9–11* (AnBib, 183; Roma: Gregorian and Biblical Press, 2010), 43, argues that 9.14 alludes to Deut. 32.4. It is an intriguing suggestion because (a) Deut. 32 is prominent in Paul; (b) it has been posited as containing Rom. 9–11 *in nuce* (see Hays, *Echoes*, 163–64); (c) it is prominent in Rom. 9–11 (see esp. Bell, *Provoked*) as Paul quotes Deut. 32.21 explicitly in Rom. 10.21 and alludes to it in 11.11, 14. But the volume of the proposed echo is very low. It does not share any verbal, syntactical or structural similarity to Rom. 9.14 except for the one word ἀδικία. It also lacks support in the history of scholarship, which does not in itself weigh against it as an allusion, but which is practically necessary for the probability of an allusion when there is such low verbal similarity, as in the case of Paul's allusion to Exod. 32.32 in Rom. 9.3. But its strong thematic coherence and its context's recurrence in Paul raises our appraisal of this proposed allusion to 'possible', yet falling short of the higher categories of 'probable' or 'clear'; see

unrighteous.[76] But whereas 3.5 asks whether God is unrighteous for inflicting wrath on the unfaithful if their unfaithfulness highlights God's faithfulness, 9.14 raises the question of whether God is unrighteous for choosing his people without regard to works or ancestry (and thus also excluding others). The specific question of 3.5 will get taken up in 9.19. But these two questions are not unrelated and are in fact practically connected in the context of Rom. 3.5.

Having just argued in Romans 2 that ethnic Jewishness (being a Jew outwardly), having the Law, and circumcision – all wholly intertwined with 'works' in Paul's perspective – do not bring God's approval nor make a person truly part of God's people,[77] Paul then asks in 3.1, 'What, therefore, is the advantage of the Jew, or what is the benefit of circumcision'? Paul's answer? 'Much in every way' (3.2a). He then begins to enumerate Jewish advantages. But he only lists one before turning to address concerns that arise from the conjunction of these two points: (1) Jewish ethnicity and circumcision do not garner God's approval nor bestow membership in God's people, leaving the unfaithful Jew to God's condemnation (ch. 2), and (2) Jewish ethnicity and circumcision still provide advantage (3.1).

The advantage that Paul lists here (that the Jews 'were entrusted with the oracles of God [τὰ λόγια τοῦ θεοῦ]') is significant, standing in parallel to the phrase 'the word of God' (ὁ λόγος τοῦ θεοῦ) in 9.6a, and amounting to a summary description of the catalogue in 9.4-5, which continues the enumeration of Israel's privileges begun in 3.2.[78] The parallel phrases of 3.2 and 9.6a ('the oracles/word of God') refer to the Scriptures of Israel with special reference to the promises of God.[79] But despite the possession of the promises of God recorded in Scripture, some Jews might prove unfaithful to them and therefore end up suffering divine condemnation (3.3a in context), raising the question of whether Jewish unfaithfulness nullifies the faithfulness of God (3.3b). Paul's negative answer includes the point that human unrighteousness serves to display the righteousness of God, which then raises the question of whether God is unrighteous to condemn these who actually showcase his righteousness in this way (3.5).

Abasciano, *Romans 9.1-9*, 22–25, for criteria for identifying allusions and our scale for their level of probability. On the whole, it seems more likely that we have a statement of a basic biblical truth rather than an appeal to a specific text.

76.   Indeed, Rom. 3.1-8 is commonly regarded as a brief discussion that is resumed at length in chapters 9–11. See Abasciano, 'Romans 9:1-9', 84 n. 125, for documentation. Reichert, *Römerbrief*, 177, notes that there is wide-ranging agreement on this connection.

77.   One might object that Paul actually speaks of Gentile obedience to the Law – and thus 'works' – making them part of God's people. But it is highly unlikely that Paul contradicts his doctrine of justification by faith in 2.25-29 in the midst of his argument for it! Most commentators do not think Paul refers to what he considers 'works', and various reasonable interpretations have been offered that support this view. See Schreiner, 'Justification', who surveys the main interpretations of Rom. 2 with respect to justification by works vs faith and argues for what I believe to be the most likely view as well as critiquing the other main views.

78.   See Abasciano, *Romans 9.1-9*, 121, 179.

79.   See ibid., 179.

Thus we see the same basic movement in Romans 2–3 and 9.1-29, a movement from the points that God chooses his people apart from works or ancestry and that many Jews have been rejected by God for their unbelief even though possessing great salvific advantage (9.1-13) to the question of whether God is unjust to condemn those whose unfaithfulness is made to accomplish his will (of glorifying his righteousness; 9.19ff.). Romans 9.14-18 defend the righteousness of God in light of his sovereignty in election. In so doing, like 3.3-4, it shows that God glorifies himself even through human resistance to him (particularly in 9.17), providing a bridge between the ideas of God's sovereignty in election and his righteousness in blaming those who serve his purpose even in their resistance to his will.

The parallel discussion of 3.1-8, evoked by 9.14's echo of 3.5, strengthens what our exegesis of Romans 9 has found up to this point, that Paul has been defending his gospel of justification by faith and all it entails by defending its (and thus God's) faithfulness to God's promises to Israel. For 3.1-8 stands as part of his developing argument in Romans for his gospel and defends God's faithfulness to his promises to Israel. Paul is still defending his gospel of justification by faith at this point in Romans 9. The parallel helps us to understand the nature of the charge Paul considers in the verses before us.

8.3.a.3. *The Meaning of ἀδικία*

As suggested by the parallel to Rom. 3.1-8, 'unrighteousness' in 9.14b most specifically refers to unfaithfulness to the divine promises to Israel.[80] With reference to the meaning of ἀδικία here, Schreiner (who rightly understands 3.1-8 to anticipate chs 9–11) observes that Romans 3 relates God's righteousness to his 'faithfulness' (3.3) and 'truth' (3.7).[81] And as Moo states, 'the word "unrighteousness" comes from a Greek word group that is used in both the OT and in Paul with reference to God's faithfulness to his promises and to his covenant with Israel. Paul may, then, be reflecting a specifically Jewish objection to the effect that God's choosing and rejecting whomever he wants is incompatible with their understanding of his promises to Israel'.[82] However, Moo concludes that the term as used in 9.14 refers to another Pauline use of 'righteousness' language, 'God's faithfulness to his own person and character'.[83] He reasons that the course of Paul's argument suggests this standard, which is revealed in Scripture and creation.[84] But the problem with this is that God's faithfulness to his promises is a more specific expression of his faithfulness to his own person and character, and as the consensus of scholarship recognizes, including Moo himself, Romans 9 (as well as all of chs 9–11) deals specifically with God's faithfulness to

80.   So Dunn *Romans*, 551; Wright (cited by Dunn); Wilckens, *Römer*, 199; Forlines, *Romans*, 264–65; cf. Wright, 'Romans', 638; Schreiner, ibid.; Cranfield, *Romans*, 482; Fitzmyer, *Romans*, 566.

81.   Schreiner, *Romans*, 506.

82.   Moo, *Romans*, 591.

83.   Ibid.

84.   Ibid, 591–92.

his promises to Israel.[85] Indeed, our exegesis so far has found that Paul has been defending this very point since the beginning of his argument in Romans 9. Moo's or similar proposals are not so much incorrect as too general, missing the most precise nuance of 'unrighteousness' intended by Paul in 9.14.[86]

On the other hand, many interpreters take Paul to be speaking of 'unrighteousness' in the sense of 'unfairness' or 'partiality' because of his election of Jacob over Esau, which might be considered arbitrary or unconditional.[87] But in our exegesis of 9.10-13 we have seen that Paul was not particularly describing an arbitrary or unconditional election, but a sovereign one that is 'not by works, but by the one who calls' (9.12a). While commentators who think Paul is suddenly entertaining a general objection of unfairness are right to look to the context for the meaning of the objection, they fail to take specific enough account of the context. Not only does this surface with respect to a failure to integrate the fact that Paul has been directly defending God's faithfulness to his promises to Israel, but it also comes out with respect to the fact that the objection Paul entertains does not arise from God merely choosing one over another, but from God choosing one people over another *apart from works or ancestry*.[88] This is what appears to contradict God's promises to Israel from the Jewish point of view and therefore provokes the charge that God would be unrighteous if he were to act in this way.[89] For Jews would have generally held that Israel

85.   This also weighs against Piper's (*Justification*, 92–96) similar understanding of ἀδικία in 9.14 as contradiction of the truth of who God is. Moo, *Romans*, 592 n. 14, tries to find what he acknowledges as only slight support against the sense of covenant unfaithfulness in the fact that ἀδικία is only used three times of God in the LXX, asserting that we would expect more uses if the word had covenantal connotations. But this does not support Moo's point. It is not a question of how frequently the word is used, but of whether it can refer to covenant unfaithfulness, which it undoubtedly can, and what it means in this specific context. The term is quite general and can refer to all manner of wrongdoing. The fact that it is only used of God three times only decreases the significance of it not being used frequently of divine covenant unfaithfulness. Interestingly, out of the three times it is used of God in the LXX, it is used once in the sense of unfaithfulness in a decidedly covenantal context (Deut. 32.4 where it is contrastively paired with 'faithfulness' (πιστός)), once in the sense of unfairness/partiality (2 Chron. 19.7), and once in the sense of general unrighteousness (Ps. 91.16).

86.   Nevertheless, Moo, *Romans*, 591, is correct to articulate the basic sense of ἀδικία here as acting 'against what is right'. Of course, the question then comes to be about what specific way God has allegedly acted against what is right.

87.   See e.g., Piper, *Justification*, 92–96; Moo, *Romans*, 591; Jewett, *Romans*, 581; L. E. Keck, *Romans* (ANTC; Nashville: Abingdon, 2005), 232–33. This view can be combined with the 'unfaithfulness to God's own character' view just discussed, providing the specific violation against God's character in view just as the breaking of promises can.

88.   A point confirmed by 9.30-33, where Paul sums up the thrust of his argument in 9.6-29 to be that the Gentiles have attained righteousness by faith while the Jews failed to attain righteousness because they pursued it by works rather than faith, echoing the language of 9.12.

89.   It is a generalization to speak of 'the Jewish point of view'. The objection Paul considers could hold great power for Jew and Gentile alike. For Paul presents his gospel

as the covenant people of God, heir to his covenant promises, was made up of those who were ethnically Jewish and kept the Law.[90]

8.3.a.4. *The Logic of the Objection and Paul's Flow of Thought*

To preach that faith in Christ rather than works/ancestry is the basis of covenant membership and heirship would be construed by many Jews as depicting God as unfaithful to his covenant promises by failing to fulfil them to those to whom he promised them – ethnic, Law-keeping Israel. Paul has been addressing this potential charge in various ways since 9.6, calling upon Scripture to make his case. In 9.6-9, he argued that the true Israel, heir to the covenant promises, is not the physical descendants of Abraham ('the children of the flesh'), but is the community of those who believe in Christ ('the children of the promise'). Defending this proposition, in 9.10-13 he addressed the allegation from the perspective of God's purpose in election and the sovereign nature of the divine election of Israel from the beginning. He now raises the potential objection with different wording in the rhetorical question of 9.14b to bring forth more scriptural argumentation against it and to address it from the perspective of God's very nature as well as (again) the nature of Israel's election from the beginning. But before he does so, he denies the charge vehemently: 'Is there unrighteousness with God? Absolutely not! [μὴ γένοιτο]'. The logic of the charge is that any theology that in effect makes God out to be unfaithful or unrighteous, no matter how unintentionally, cannot be true.[91] So after denying

as the fulfilment of God's covenant promises to Israel. Therefore, if Paul's gospel actually entails divine unfaithfulness to the promises, then Paul's gospel is false. But this concern may be characterized as 'Jewish' because it has to do with the righteousness of God's treatment of Israel and would be felt most acutely by Jews as those to whom God's faithfulness is in question. Following Michel and Wilckens, Jewett, *Romans*, 581, observes that the style of Paul's question in 9.14b 'is clearly Jewish, with the expression παρὰ τῷ θεῷ ("before God/ with God") being a Hebraism'.

90.   This is essentially what M. F. Bird, *The Saving Righteousness of God: Studies on Paul, Justification, and the New Perspective* (PBM; Milton Keynes: Paternoster, 2006), 117, has called ethnocentric nomism, which may be defined as 'the view that Jewish identity is the locus of salvation (hence ethnocentric) and that one must perform the law so as to enter the Jewish constituency and be vindicated at the eschaton (hence nomistic)'. In this context, we might adapt this definition to highlight that most Jews would have viewed Jewish identity as the locus of covenant membership and heirship of the promises/salvation, and Law-keeping as necessary for entrance into and/or continuance in the covenant and inheritance of its promises/salvation. We have already seen in our exegesis of 9.1-13 that Paul seems to have been responding to this sort of view; in this volume, see ch. 5.3.d.3.a. above; cf. Rom. 2.12–4.25. See further, Bird, 113–54.

91.   Cf. Morris, *Romans*, 358; Cranfield, *Romans*, 482 n. 2, explanation (i), who articulates the logic of the objection well. Cranfield rejects the explanation as going along with viewing 9.14b as the words of an imaginary opponent. But the same logic can just as easily lie behind Paul's own rhetorical question with respect to the integrity of his argument. Cranfield seems to think Paul is merely clarifying his view without particularly defending it. But it is hard to imagine how that could be given that no Jew or Christian would have assented to the assertion that God is unrighteous. In such a case, clarifying how his view does not mean God is unrighteous would also defend it against the potential objection that it does make God unrighteous. Moreover, our exegesis has found Paul defending his position all along in

the rhetorical accusation unequivocally, Paul sets himself to rebutting it further from Scripture.

8.3.b. *The Sovereign Mercy of God (Romans 9.15/Exodus 33.19b)*

Romans 9.15 provides the ground (as γάρ indicates) for Paul's denial that there is unrighteousness with God for choosing his people without regard for works or ancestry.[92] The ground Paul gives comes in the form of an Old Testament quotation from Exod. 33.19b: 'For he [God] says to Moses, "I will have mercy on whomever I have mercy, and I will have compassion on whomever I have compassion"' (Rom. 9.15). As all Paul's scriptural allusions have been in Romans 9 so far, this quotation is ideal for making the point Paul wants to make. For in its original context, this divine statement is God's answer to Moses' request to see the divine glory, which carried the import of a request that God restore covenantal election and its blessings to rejected Israel, from whom the divine election had been withdrawn due to the people's idolatrous apostasy tied up with reliance on a means of mediating the election-bestowing presence of God other than the Lord had chosen.

In the Exodus context, God had revoked Israel's election because of their idolatrous apostasy with the golden calf. Moses sought to obtain forgiveness for the people, but God refused to forgive the worst apostates among them,[93] purging them from the people (apparently by plague). Yet, Moses' intercession convinced the Lord to grant Israel a permanent existence and restoration of the critical land promise. Nevertheless, he then indicated that, although he would still give Israel the Promised Land, his election-bestowing presence would not go with the people, leaving them separated from YHWH and his covenant. God called them to repent so that he might know what to do with them, signalling that their future was uncertain and that repentance was a condition for any hope of restored covenant relationship with YHWH.

In the section in which Paul's quotation appears (Exod. 33.12-23), Moses

---

Romans 9. As Moo, *Romans*, 591, observes, the question of 9.14b 'embodies an accusation'.

92.   Many have denied that Paul justifies God or grounds his denial of divine unrighteousness here on the assumption that theodicy is an illegitimate human activity which Paul would not have entertained (though this is uncommon among more recent commentators). But such a prejudiced stance is unfit for exegesis. For representatives of the view and a compelling critique, see Piper, *Justification*, 96–98, though we do not share his exact understanding of how the content of 9.15 offers a reasonable ground for 9.14. To Piper's comments we add that, for Paul and those like him, who would accept the Bible as the word of God, assessing God's righteousness would not be a matter of judging him by human standards, but of considering whether his purported actions are consistent with what he himself has revealed in his word of what righteousness is and what his own character is. In this context, the specific issue under consideration is whether Paul's gospel, which claims covenant status/heirship for believers in Christ and denies this for unbelievers apart from works or ancestry, is consistent with God's revealed character of righteousness in the area of truthfulness/faithfulness/promise-keeping.

93.   That is, those most directly involved in the apostasy.

continues to pursue complete restoration to covenantal election and privilege for Israel by seeking restoration of the presence and glory of God to the people. As mentioned above, he finally does so by asking YHWH to see his glory.[94] Therefore, Paul's quotation of Exod. 33.19b in Rom 9.15 is first and foremost to be understood in reference to God's election/rejection of Israel as his covenant people. But the statement of Exod. 33.19b gets expanded in 34.6-7 and applied to God's relationship with his people within the covenant. In a secondary way, then, it can be similarly understood in Paul's quotation. Coming in the midst of the formal establishing of Israel's fundamental election at Sinai, Paul's quotation speaks to the nature of Israel's election from its foundation.

The quotation also speaks to the nature of God himself in relation to humanity.[95] For the statement of Exod. 33.19b is given as a summary interpretation of the name of YHWH referred to in 33.19a, which is also

94.   Seifrid's ('Romans', 641–42) overall approach to the Exodus context – which appeared after my exegesis of the text was published – is terribly misguided. It ignores the broader context (Exodus 32–34) of 33.12-23, so important for an accurate understanding of the text. It misses the obvious covenantal context of the passage and the covenantal meaning of much that is said in it. It assumes too much of an adversarial relationship between God and Moses in their interaction and misjudges Moses' requests as given in an inappropriate, manipulative way. It overplays the relatively meager negative aspects of the divine response to Moses' requests and downplays the substantial divine acquiescence to them. I find myself at odds with his interpretation at almost every step, and would refer the reader to my detailed exegesis of the passage. Some other specific problems to note with his view of the text are that: (1) he asserts that YHWH denies Moses' petition for him to show his ways to Moses when in fact YHWH at first grants the petition partially, and then grants it even more fully, amounting to mostly granting the request; (2) he asserts that YHWH does not allow Moses to know his name when he does in fact allow him to know his name 'YHWH' (confusingly, Seifrid regards the divine name 'YHWH' as not really YHWH's name!) and goes on to explicate that very name summarily and then more fully in response to Moses' requests; (3) he misses the crucial distinction between YHWH's presence going with Moses alone vs going with Israel; (4) he denies that God gives any definition of his name or ways when YHWH does in fact proclaim his name and explains it not only in summary fashion (33.19), but a second time in expanded form (34.6-7) that also states his covenant ways in general, followed by delineation of a number of more specific covenant ways especially relevant to the re-establishment of the covenant (34.10-28) tied up in YHWH's *positive* response to Moses' request to see his glory – the (admittedly limited) theophanic revelation of the divine glory.

95.   I qualify this as concerning God's relation to humanity to avoid the potential misunderstanding that the statement gives an absolute description of God's nature as if his nature requires there to be people to be sovereign over with respect to mercy. T. H. McCall, 'I Believe in Divine Sovereignty', *TJ* 29/2 (2008), 205–26 (217–18), criticizes John Piper on this point vis-à-vis his conclusion about God's nature based on Exod. 33.19b as expressed in Piper, *Justification*, 218–19. While McCall is successful in his critique of Piper's theological project overall (see also T. H. McCall, 'We Believe in God's Sovereign Goodness: A Rejoinder to John Piper', *TJ* 29/2 (Fall 2008), 235–46), Piper ('I Believe in God's Self-Sufficiency: A Response to Thomas McCall', *TJ* 29/2 (Fall 2008), 227–34 (230–31)) successfully qualifies his view of Exod. 33.19b to be, *if* and when relating to the fallen creation, then God's nature is to relate to it in sovereign freedom, though we would disagree with him about the meaning of sovereign freedom.

used in a roughly synonymous way in 33.18-23 to the glory, goodness and presence of YHWH.[96] Each of these terms refers to God's glorious nature with its own distinctive nuance. Hence, not only does the content of Paul's quotation of Exod. 33.19b address the fundamental nature of Israel's election, but it also addresses the nature of God when relating to sinful humanity.[97] We now turn to look at what the quotation tells us about God's nature and his election of Israel.

8.3.b.1. *The Idem per Idem Formula and the Conditional Bestowal of Divine Mercy*

The statement of Rom. 9.15/Exod. 33.19b summarily explicating YHWH's name appears in a tautologous idiom known as the *idem per idem* formula. The idiom typically has a twofold significance.[98] First, it emphasizes the verbal idea by repetition, in this case the idea of bestowing mercy (ἐλεέω). Paul's quotation stresses God's merciful character as emphatically as possible by repeating the formula with a verb of similar meaning (οἰκτίρω).[99] God is above all merciful and compassionate. Paul's quotation of this fervent proclamation of God's merciful character introduces what has been called the keyword of Romans 9–11, the word 'mercy',[100] though Paul has already intimated the concept by nothing less than evocative allusion to the same broad Old Testament context (Exodus 32–34) in the introduction to his argument (Rom. 9.3).[101]

Second, by leaving the action of the verb unqualified, the *idem per idem* formula typically signals the freedom of the subject to perform the action

96.   Contra Seifrid, 'Romans', 642, who does little more than assert that 'the proclamation of God's name' is not 'equivalent to a demonstration of divine glory'. By contrast, see Piper's (*Justification*, 84–88) detailed argument for the glory, goodness and name of YHWH as basically synonymous in Exod. 33.18-23 (followed by Moo, *Romans*, 592; Schreiner, *Romans*, 507; Dunn, *Romans*, 552, 562), though I would differ with him on various particulars as represented by my exegesis of the OT context mentioned earlier.

97.   Schreiner, *Romans*, 506–07, and Piper, *Justification*, 75–89 (cf. 155–56), argue that Paul's quotation should be taken as a general principle expressed to Moses rather than as a context-limited statement to him. But while it is true that the statement articulates a general principle about God's nature, it is important not to ignore its contextualized, salvation-historical expression, which holds implications for the nature of Israel's election. To do so is to ignore part of the statement's basic meaning and so impoverish our understanding of it as well as the full potential available to Paul in his use of it. Showing that the statement is a general principle does not negate its specific use in its context nor cut such usage off from informing the meaning of the statement in its context or in Paul.

98.   The first significance discussed below is probably common to all instances of the idiom. But the second, though typical, is not.

99.   Most scholars are correct to treat the two verbs synonymously here; so e.g., Moo, *Romans*, 592 n. 18. But even if the two verbs are regarded as carrying some difference in meaning here (so Godet, *Romans*, 352), they are still very similar in meaning.

100.   See Cranfield, *Romans*, 448; Dunn, *Romans*, 552; cf. Barrett, *Romans*, 185 (1st edn); L. Gaston, 'Israel's Enemies in Pauline Theology', in L. Gaston, *Paul and the Torah* (Vancouver: University of British Columbia Press, 1987), 80–99 (97).

101.   See Abasciano, *Romans 9.1-9*, 106.

in whatever way he sees fit (within circumstantial limits).[102] This does not in any way imply that the action is unconditional as some would have it.[103] Indeed, when the idiom signals freedom of action elsewhere, it never appears to speak of unconditional action. Rather, in every such instance the context or circumstances suggest that the subject would take factors external to himself into account in deciding how to perform the action.[104] Thus, with respect

102. But the formula does not always signal this. Sometimes it can be used in an opposite manner, when the subject's contemplated action will be irresistibly forced on him (by another/others; Gen. 43.14; Est. 4.16). However, in such cases, the action envisioned as forced upon the subject emerges from the subject's freedom in that the forced action is merely a *possible* result of an action being freely chosen by the subject and with full knowledge of this potential outcome. Sometimes, the idiom only emphasizes the verbal action and is used simply because the speaker does not wish to go into specifics, whether as a matter of economy or for some other reason (Deut. 9.25; Zech. 10.8; 1 Cor. 15.10). It may be that some of the occurrences that signal the subject's freedom overlap with this latter category and do not so much *emphasize* the subject's freedom, as *imply* it. Piper's (*Justification*, 82) treatment of the idiom lacks nuance, treating the idiom as if it always indicates free action, and indeed, emphasizes the subject's freedom. G. S. Ogden, 'Idem per Idem: Its Use and Meaning', *JSOT* 53 (1992), 107–20, argues that the standard view of the idiom as involving freedom is unsubstantiated. But his case is not fully convincing, though it may be that, as suggested above, the formula does not particularly focus on freedom in some cases while still implying it. One good example is Exod. 16.23, since, as Ogden notes (117), it has the same basic syntactical pattern as Exod. 33.19. He thinks that the initial position of the object clause (a feature missing in Exod. 33.19 in any case) draws the syntactical focus of the sentence. But it is hard to see why that would draw greater focus than the striking repetition of the same verb. And even if it did, there is no reason to think it eliminates all significance to the repetition of the verbal idea. In any case, it seems difficult to deny that the verse allows the Israelites a choice as to how much manna of the lot they collected they would either bake or boil, and therefore implies freedom in the action of cooking, even if freedom is not the focus of the statement. Yet this choice would not normally be made unconditionally. Presumably the choice of whether to bake or boil manna, or perhaps a certain amount of each, would be conditioned partly on the character of manna as baked vs its character as boiled, inter alia.

103. Contra Piper, ibid., who seems to take the formula as indicating unconditional action (G. K. Beale, Review of J. Piper, *The Justification of God: An Exegetical and Theological Study of Romans 9:1-23*, *WTJ* 46 (1984), 190–97 (192–93), agrees that Piper argues that the formula indicates unconditionality). This is a fatal flaw in Piper's interpretation of Rom. 9.15, since it is clear that the formula does not itself communicate the idea of unconditional action (see below). Indeed, as pointed out in my previous volume, Beale believes that Piper's chapter on Exod. 33.19 is 'the theological cornerstone for the entire monograph' validating its main thesis (191–92). Hence, his mishandling of the phrase may well undo the foundation of his entire study.

104. Some might be tempted to point to the idiom's occurrence in Exod. 3.14 as an exception, one that is especially important because it is also used of the divine name. Piper, ibid., cites Child's comment: 'The circular *idem per idem* formula of the name [in Exod. 33.19] ... is closely akin to the name in Ex 3:14 – I am who I am – and testifies by its tautology to the freedom of God in making known his self-contained being'. Indeed, Beale thinks that Piper should have explored the possibility that Exod. 33.19cd is literally dependent on 3.14. But the meaning of 3.14's *idem per idem* clause is notoriously difficult to determine, and as Ogden, 'Idem', 111, observes, there is an enormous literature on the question, an endless range of interpretations according to Durham, *Exodus*, 38. Moreover, if one understands the meaning of the phrase to have to do with the freedom of God's self-revelation, as do Childs, Piper and Beale, then there is little reason to think that his act(s) of

to the nature of the action, the most natural way to take the statement of Rom. 9.15/Exod. 33.19b is to affirm that God has mercy on whomever he chooses based upon whatever conditions he establishes.[105] As Durham puts it concerning the statement in Exod. 33.19, YHWH's 'favor and his compassion are given only on his terms'.[106] The context of Exod. 33.19 supports this conclusion.

8.3.b.1.a. *The Context of Exodus 33.19 and the Conditional Bestowal of Divine Mercy*

In Exod. 32.30–33.6, YHWH partly responded to Moses' request for forgiveness for Israel by identifying the grounds on which he would punish (guilt; 32.33) and demanding repentance as a condition for the possibility of mercy/forgiveness/restoration to covenant relationship (33.3-5). As God's response to a renewed request from Moses for merciful restoration of Israel to covenantal election, the declaration of Exod. 33.19b subtly recalls these conditions for God's judgment and mercy.[107] Indeed, when the declaration is explained in greater detail in 34.6-7, it has to do with God bestowing mercy on those who maintain a proper covenant relationship with him and punishing those who do not:

> YHWH, YHWH, a gracious and compassionate God, slow to anger, and abounding in covenant lovingkindness and faithfulness, keeping covenant lovingkindness for

revelation is to be construed as unconditional. It is far more likely that the way God revealed himself would be conditioned partly on those to whom he revealed himself as it clearly is in Exod. 33.20-23, in which God chooses to limit the nature of his revelation to Moses so that he will not die, not to mention other elements of 33.20–34.28 that are tailored to the specific situation of Moses and Israel recorded in the narrative. One would normally expect that God would typically take into account the nature of his audience in deciding on the precise manner and specific content of his self-revelation in any given instance. The same is true for those interpretations that take 3.14 to speak of God's presence with his people or manner of relating to them. On the other hand, if 3.14 refers to God's mere existence, one might argue that the act of God 'being' is unconditional. But this would prove too much, for God's existence is also not free; he necessarily exists. Moreover, 'being' is a unique type of action that is not comparable to many other forms of more proactive, intentional action, including the act of bestowing mercy that appears in Exod. 33.19. In that case, it does not seem that freedom would be indicated by the idiom, but that the verbal action alone is stressed; cf. 1 Cor. 15.10, where Paul cannot mean that his own existence or being is unconditional on anything outside himself. Furthermore, this would highlight 3.14's use of the idiom as exceptional, and so not particularly relevant for 33.19's usage with respect to conditionality. Nonetheless, in principle the formula is compatible with unconditional action though it neither inherently implies it nor ever seems to be used of it.

105.   Ogden, 'Idem', 6, rejects that there is any notion of freedom in the statement, arguing that the *idem per idem* formula here 'functions, as in Ezek. 12.25, to describe the broad or total extent of an action. Thus in the present context [Exod. 33.19], the point being made is that God's mercy and goodness are freely given to all the people. This we can render in translation as "I am/will be gracious to all; I will show mercy to everyone."' Cf. less extremely, Stuart, *Exodus*, 708.

106.   Durham, *Exodus*, 452.

107.   Though the stress remains on God's sovereignty over these conditions.

thousands, forgiving iniquity, rebellion, and sin. But he will certainly not leave [the guilty] unpunished, visiting the iniquity of the fathers on the children, even on the children's children and on the third and on the fourth generation. (Exod. 34.6-7)[108]

This is basically an expansion of the identification of YHWH given in 20.5-6 during the original establishment of the covenant, appropriately expanded here as part of renewing the covenant:[109] 'I, YHWH, am a jealous God, punishing the iniquity of the fathers on the children, on the third and on the fourth generation of those who hate me, but showing covenant lovingkindness to thousands who love me and who keep my commandments'. This seminal passage establishes the textual presupposition that YHWH bestows mercy upon those who love him and generally keep his commandments, but punishes those who hate him and do not maintain a covenant relationship with him.[110] This connects to Paul's concern in Romans 9–11 by providing

108.   This reflects the standard translation and understanding of 34.7. Piper, *Justification*, 85, argues the unlikely view that the infinitive absolute in 34.7 (נַקֵּה) relates to the completion rather than the certainty of absolution; thus: 'but he will not leave completely unpunished'. But certainty is the far more common meaning of the infintive absolute as used in 34.7 (whether termed as an accusative of internal object or as an adverbial complement). Indeed, some grammarians doubt that it can bear a nuance of completion or intensification of the verbal root; but if it can, such instances are rare and usually in postpositive position, unlike the prepositive positioning in Exod. 34.7 (see Waltke/O'Connor, *Hebrew*, § 35.3.1.c, i; Joüon/Muraoka, *Hebrew*, § 123j). More importantly, 32.34 has already shown a concern for the certainty of punishment for the guilty. Moreover, comparison with the parallel statement of Exod. 20.5-6 suggests that certainty is at issue rather than Piper's picture of incomplete forgiveness, since only two alternatives are presented there – love for those who love YHWH vs punishment for those who hate him. Furthermore, the very phrase in question clearly refers to certainty of punishment in Nah. 1.3. On the other hand, the references Piper cites from Bush in favour of the completion nuance can just as easily bear the common asseverative nuance (Jer. 25.29; 30.11; 49.12) or certainly carry a nuance other than completion (Isa. 30.19). Further evidence against Piper's view comes from the fact that the grammar of the text makes a separation between those who find forgiveness because of YHWH's covenant love and faithfulness, and those who are punished. Every verbal clause in the declaration of YHWH's character is participial except for the statement that he will not clear/leave unpunished. The chain of participles is broken by an infinitive absolute followed by the imperfect, which is in turn followed by another participial clause modifying the thought of the imperfect as opposed to the participles preceding it, which speak of YHWH's covenant loyalty and forgiveness. (I am indebted to D. Petter, 'Exodus 34:6-7: The Function and Meaning of the Declaration' (MTh thesis; Gordon-Conwell Theological Seminary, 1997), 53 n. 148, for the observation that there is only one imperfect verb amidst a string of participles in Exod. 34.7.) This argues against Piper's contention that the text speaks of incomplete absolution, since the participles prior to the infinitive absolute speak of those who receive mercy, whereas the infinitive-imperfect construction is unlikely to modify those participles and their subjects, and the participle describing YHWH's punishment also decidedly does not describe those who receive YHWH's covenant mercy. This accords again with Exod. 20.5-6, which pictures two distinct groups (see above).

109.   Cf. Stuart, *Exodus*, 716–17.

110.   It seems wide of the mark to argue, as R. W. L. Moberly, *At the Mountain of God: Story and Theology in Exodus 32–34* (JSOTSup, 22; Sheffield: JSOT, 1983), 88, that because the stipulation of an obedient response stated in Exod. 20.6 is absent from 34.7, 'Yahweh's mercy toward Israel is independent of their responding in the right way', and wider still for

the foundation for God's rejection of unbelieving ethnic Israel as those who had rejected him through their rejection of Christ.

Our exegesis of Romans 9 so far has already shown that Paul regarded unbelieving ethnic Israel to have been rejected from a covenant relationship because of their lack of faith in Christ. He continues to display that conviction in the rest of Romans 9–11 (e.g., 9.30–10.4; 11.13-24). Moreover, we have seen that the essence of Israel's idolatrous apostasy in Exodus 32–34 involved trusting in a means of mediating God's covenant, presence and blessing other than God had ordained.[111] Paul appears to have seen unbelieving ethnic Israel of his day as having done the same basic thing, rejecting the means of covenant heirship God had chosen in the New Covenant, Jesus Christ, and clinging to the way of their own choosing, namely, ancestry and Law-keeping.

In light of Exod. 34.6-7's explication of 33.19, Paul's citation of 33.19 serves to confirm the righteousness of God in choosing his people apart from works or ancestry and cutting unbelieving Jews off from his people. For it shows God's nature to have mercy on those who repent of their sin, maintain covenant relationship with him and who are connected to his righteous and faithful covenant mediator on the one hand, and to reject those who are otherwise. Moreover, it embodies a principle built into the covenant of God with his people. God can hardly be charged with infidelity to his covenant promises for doing just what he said he would do in the covenant.

Thus, the declaration of Exod. 33.19b is best taken as indicating that God bestows grace and mercy on whomever he chooses based upon whatever conditions he chooses. Exodus 34.6-7 explain how the principle of 33.19 gets expressed within the covenant. But 33.19 even more directly addresses the issue of who is accepted as God's covenant people in the first place

Piper, *Justification*, 85–86, to also apply this line of reasoning to the condition of hating YHWH for punishment. There is some sense in these suggestions in that this omission is surely a response to the context of Exodus 32–34 with its themes of sin, judgment and mercy. However, these interpretations fly in the face of the context of Exodus 32–34, as well as the rest of the Scriptures of Israel, where repentance and faith are always necessary for fully experiencing YHWH's grace, and guilt is always necessary for suffering his punishment. Moreover, it is an overly subtle interpretation to think that through this omission the text would attempt to overturn the principle of Exodus 20.5-6. It seems more balanced and makes more sense to take the conditions of 20.5-6 as implicit in 34.6-7, which alludes to the former passage, and understand the omission of the conditions to highlight YHWH's mercy and to reflect the new situation in which Israel has sinned grievously. Cf. the use of Exod. 34.6-7 in Joel 2.12-14, where all reference to judgment is omitted in a call to repentance (see D. E. Gowan, *Theology in Exodus: Biblical Theology in the Form of a Commentary* (Louisville: Westminster/John Knox, 1994), 241). The purpose is not to assert that the Lord will accept the people regardless of their actions, but to emphasize his mercy to induce them to repent! The basic interpretation we are advocating, which understands the text in the context of Exodus and the Pentateuch to mean that YHWH extends mercy and forgiveness to those who have an obedient orientation that repents from sin, but punishes those who have an unrepentant, disobedient orientation, is virtually stated in Exod. 20.5-6 and Deut. 7.9 according to Kugel, *Traditions*, 725–26, and is explicitly adopted by the targums on Exod. 34.7.

111.   Abasciano, *Romans 9.1-9*, 48–49, 101–02.

(albeit against the backdrop of a sinful people that had been ousted from the covenant). For the essence of Moses' request answered by Exod. 33.19b is that God would restore Israel to covenantal election and blessing. The emphasis here is corporate, on the election of God's people rather than on the election of the individual by himself or of certain individuals separately to become part of God's people.[112] In context, God's reply in 33.19b means most directly that God will bestow the grace and mercy of covenantal election and blessing on whatever people he chooses based on whatever conditions he chooses.

8.3.b.1.b. *Answering the Charge of Divine Unrighteousness*

It is easy to see how this answers the charge of unrighteousness to which Paul responds. As we have already observed, his answer concerns the nature of Israel's election from its inception. The charge Paul refutes has to do with the basis of election, viz. that God would be unrighteous to choose his people apart from works or ancestry. In other words, God would be unrighteous to choose his people based on faith in Christ rather than works (i.e., Jewish identity and Law-keeping).

But Paul's quotation points to the fact that when Israel stood stripped of its elect status because of its wickedness and apostasy, and Moses appealed to the Lord for restoration of covenantal election and blessing to the nation under his judgment, God declared that his choice of who he embraces as his people (and any conditions upon which he bases his choice) is entirely up to him. This principle practically serves as a condition for the establishment of the covenant. Indeed, as we have seen, an expanded form of it gets incorporated into the covenant itself while the covenant is being remade. Therefore, God could not possibly be unrighteous for choosing his people based on faith in Christ, the Mediator of the New Covenant. The very foundation of Israel's election included the principle that the conditions for election were subject to the dictates of God's own will.

Moreover, God had essentially disclosed certain conditions for the bestowal of mercy to Israel in again granting her elect, covenantal status: (1) repentance from reliance on any means for mediating the divine covenant and blessing other than the means designated by God, and (2) identification with the means of God's own choosing, his righteous and faithful covenant mediator. Even though, in accordance with the principle of Exod. 33.19b, God has no obligation to keep the same conditions for the election of his covenant people, these are basically the same conditions for the divine election under the New Covenant, with Christ replacing Moses as the covenant mediator in

---

112.   In addition to the exegesis of Exod. 33.19 in my previous volume, see Abasciano, 'Election', 359. T. R. Schreiner, 'Does Romans 9 Teach Individual Election unto Salvation? Some Exegetical and Theological Reflections', *JETS* 36 (1993), 25–40 (34), argues that Paul's use of the singular ὃν indicates that he has specific individuals as objects of the divine mercy in view (cf. similarly Forlines, *Romans*, 267). But the argument does not hold up. The Greek word in the singular can refer to a corporate entity just as it does to the people of God in Rom. 11.2 (!), and the OT background as well as the context of Romans 9 indicate that is the case here. See Abasciano, ibid., for the details.

the eschatological age. Paul's mention of Moses reinforces his point about the sovereignty of God over covenantal election as a vital element of the concept, 'for it is to the mediator of the covenant himself that God reveals his freedom in mercy'.[113]

We have similarly already observed that Paul's citation of Exod. 33.19b in response to the charge of divine unrighteousness also concerns the very nature of God when relating to sinful humanity.[114] This further establishes God's righteousness in choosing his people apart from works or ancestry. For Jews and Christians of Paul's time would have looked to God's character and actions as revealed in Scripture for the standard of righteousness.[115] To show that Scripture reveals that God's character when interacting with sinful humanity is to determine sovereignly the beneficiaries of his mercy including any conditions for choosing them leaves empty the charge that God would be unrighteous to choose his people apart from works or ancestry.

While the sovereign nature of God's mercy flows obviously from the freedom indicated by the *idem per idem* formula of Exod. 33.19b/Rom. 9.15, it is also suggested to some degree by the emphasis on the verbal idea of mercy contained in the statement. For almost by definition, the type of mercy in view here, gracious mercy, mercy that grants forgiveness for wrongdoing in order to adopt a people, can neither be demanded nor earned.[116] Israel stood before God without any claim upon him, guilty and worthy of his wrath for their apostasy. However, this does not address the specific thrust of the objection Paul is addressing, and so is a subsidiary implication of Paul's

113.   Moo, *Romans*, 592, though ironically he thinks the reference to Moses for his role as covenant mediator reinforces the point that God's righteousness is *not* to be understood covenantally here, but according to the standard of God's own character. But this fails to grasp the specific concerns of Paul's argument and the objection he considers, not to mention faltering on a false dichotomy (see 8.3.a.3. above). Nonetheless, Moo is correct to note against Maier and Byrne that, 'It is Moses' role as mediator of the Old Covenant ... and not as exemplar of works ... that accounts for his name being mentioned here' (n. 20). We would add that the thrust of Paul's concern is also not to put Moses forward 'as an example and representative of God's mercy – in contrast to Pharaoh in v 17' (Dunn, *Romans*, 551–52, following Lagrange and Munck) or as one who would most deserve God's mercy or command the most respect from Paul's opponents (Sanday/Headlam, *Romans*, 254). Paul is continuing to argue that God has not been unfaithful to his covenant promises to Israel.

114.   A number of commentators have observed that Paul's quotation addresses the nature of God, e.g., Cranfield, *Romans*, 483; Dunn, *Romans*, 552, 562; Schreiner, 507; Moo, *Romans*, 592 (who also cites Hübner, *Schriftgebrauch*), and above all, Piper, *Justification*. However, there is a serious question over whether God's character of granting mercy is portrayed here as inherently working unconditionally. We have found that this is a highly implausible reading of the evidence in the OT context, and although more reasonable in the NT context, still unlikely there.

115.   That is why showing that Paul's gospel makes God unrighteous would definitively refute Paul's gospel. The charge is tantamount to claiming that God's actions as Paul's gospel presents them are inconsistent with his character and actions as revealed in the Old Testament. Cf. notes 89 and 90 above.

116.   Cf. Murray, *Romans*, 2.26; Barrett, *Romans*, 185; Morris, *Romans*, 359; Schreiner, *Romans*, 507.

citation that adds to the rhetorical force of his response in a supplementary fashion. The statement of Exod.33.19b/Rom 9.15 empathically declares that God is merciful, a God who is inclined to show mercy. But it also declares that he is free to dispense his mercy as he sees fit. A God, both gracious and sovereign, has every right to call his people based on faith rather than works/ ancestry. Indeed, this ties into the very purpose of the sovereign God for election mentioned in 9.11, to bless the world of Jews and Gentiles, requiring that works/ancestry be excluded from the basis for election and the covenant blessing of God it brings.

8.3.b.2. *A Repeated Invocation of the Context of Exodus 32–34*

In our exegesis of Rom. 9.1-5, we saw that Paul alluded to Exod. 32.32 and thereby pointed to its broader context of Exodus 32–34.[117] Moreover, we found that Exodus 32–34 provides important background for Paul's argument in Romans 9–11, influencing many of its details, including major themes. To review some of our findings,

> The similarity in theme and subject matter between the old and new contexts is striking. Both are concerned with the apostasy and hardheartedness of Israel, the resulting divine judgment and loss of election along with all its promises, the ensuing tremendous grief, the faithfulness of God to his covenant word and his great mercy, and the restoration of Israel to election and blessing in a 'new' covenant established primarily with the Covenant Mediator and mediated to the people only through connection with him and the glory of God shining through him. Indeed, it appears that Paul has gone to the scriptural paradigm of the fall and restoration of Israel, Exodus 32–34, to understand and express the present stage of salvation history and the outworking of the eschatological fulfillment of the covenant promises of God ...
>
> Paul has taken upon himself the mediatorial, intercessory, and prophetic aura of Moses in a typologically conditioned response that conceives of his own ministry as the vehicle through which the election-bestowing 'glory of God in the face of Christ' is brought back to Israel in 'the gospel of the glory of Christ, who is the image of God' (2 Cor. 4.4, 6). Paul's grief is a typological fulfillment of Israel's sorrow at their loss of election resulting from their idolatrous apostasy. Even his utilization of the remnant motif later in his argument may be foreshadowed in Exodus 32's remnant motif, the first glimpse of which could be the self-sacrificial prayer contemplated in Rom. 9.3. God's judgment upon Israel in Paul's day is an escalated fulfillment of his merciful judgment upon Israel of old, placing them in the same hardened position as the Gentiles under his wrath yet granting them opportunity for repentance and forgiveness vis-à-vis Christ and the New Covenant as God once again limits his sovereignty in giving Paul, Israel, and the Gentiles pivotal roles in his plan of salvation for the whole world.[118]

117. See Abasciano, *Romans 9.1-9*, ch. 3.

118. Ibid., 143–44. In retrospect, it was not accurate to speak of God limiting his sovereignty. This was an attempt to articulate the biblical text's depiction of God allowing human beings a measure of free will and profound influence on the outworking of his plan of salvation. However, it would be more accurate to speak of this as an expression of God's sovereignty rather than a limitation of it. A. W. Tozer, *The Knowledge of the Holy: The Attributes of God: Their Meaning in the Christian Life* (New York: HarperSanFrancisco, 1961), 110–11, makes this point most eloquently on a general level: 'God sovereignly decreed that man should be free to exercise moral choice, and man from the beginning has

With this second allusion to the context of Exodus 32–34, Paul evokes the same general associations. The fact that he again alludes to the same broad context strengthens its importance as a source for his argument in Romans 9–11.

8.3.c. *The Bestowal of Mercy Is at the Discretion of the Mercy-bestowing God (Rom. 9.16)*

Paul now draws an inference (expressed strongly with ἄρα οὖν)[119] from his quotation of Exod. 33.19b: 'So therefore, [it is] not of the one who wills nor of the one who runs, but of the mercy-bestowing God' (Rom. 9.16). This is Paul's interpretation of Exod. 33.19b, quoted in the previous verse. On both scores (inference and interpretation), the statement of 9.16 draws the logical stress of Paul's support so far for his denial that God is unrighteous.[120] Together, 9.15-16 support 9.14, with 9.16 stating the significance of 9.15.

8.3.c.1. *The Subject and Basic Sense of Romans 9.16*
The sentence of 9.16 lacks both a subject and a basic verb. As noted in our treatment of 9.10, the simplest and most common verb implied by ellipses is a form of εἰμί. That makes excellent sense here in the third person singular (ἐστιν), as represented in the translation offered above, and is to be preferred.[121] As for the subject of the sentence, there have been various suggestions, such as 'salvation', 'God's purpose in election' (9.11), 'the choice', 'mercy', or even 'the matter generally'.[122] Piper claims that 'virtually all commentators agree that *in general* the subject is "God's bestowal of mercy"'.[123] Be that as it may, this does seem to be the most likely subject, for (a) the bestowal of God's mercy is the topic of the immediately preceding verse (9.15), which 9.16 interprets and from which it draws its assertion by way of inference, and (b) the positive stress of 9.16 falls on God, who is described as 'the one who

---

fulfilled that decree by making his choice between good and evil. When he chooses to do evil, he does not thereby countervail the sovereign will of God but fulfills it, inasmuch as the eternal decree decided not which choice the man should make but that he should be free to make it. If in His absolute freedom God has willed to give man limited freedom, who is there to stay His hand or say, "What doest thou?" Man's will is free because God is sovereign. A God less than sovereign could not bestow moral freedom upon His creatures. He would be afraid to do so'.

119.   On ἄρα as strengthened by οὖν, see BDF, § 451. For application to Rom 9.16, see Hübner, *Schriftgebrauch*, 39. Cf. Jewett, *Romans*, 585, on the same construction in 9.18.

120.   Cf. Piper, *Justification*, 157.

121.   Though one might choose a different verb for dynamic clarity based on how one construes the genitives in the verse. It is worth noting that εἰμί is also the least interpretive option, best preserving the inherent ambiguity of the original.

122.   These options were culled from Cranfield, *Romans*, 484; Moo, *Romans*, 593.

123.   Piper, *Justification*, 155; emphasis original. This seems overstated. But Piper appears to take other options as specific expressions of God's mercy, which is probably why he qualifies his statement as general.

bestows mercy' (τοῦ ἐλεῶντος).[124]

The question then arises, what bestowal of mercy is in view? Many interpreters think that Paul speaks of God's mercy in choosing some persons or nations for certain roles in his salvation-historical plan without referring to the eternal destiny of individuals.[125] Others think that Paul is speaking of mercy in the salvation of individuals (as autonomous entities).[126] But the most likely and precise referent of the bestowal of mercy in 9.16 is the corporate election of a people as God's covenant partner, heir to the covenant promises and blessings, which include salvation.[127] For (1) Paul has been speaking about the election of the covenant people of God throughout his argument in Romans 9 and has specifically been defending God's right to elect whomever he wants as his people,[128] and especially (2) as we have seen, Rom. 9.15/ Exod. 33.19 specifically refers to this very bestowal of mercy.

Thus, Paul states that God's bestowal of mercy in the election of his covenant people is 'not of the one who wills nor of the one who runs, but of the mercy-bestowing God' (Rom. 9.16).[129] That is, God's bestowal of mercy in his election of his covenant people comes not from anyone else other than God, who is, after all, the bestower of mercy, no matter what a person might will or do. In other words, God is the source and agent of the bestowal of mercy; so the decision concerning to whom God grants his mercy rests not with the will or effort of man, but with God, as do any stipulations he

---

124. See ibid. Belli, *Argumentation*, 43, considers the possibility (mentioned by H. Hübner, *Vetus Testamaentum in Novo, II, Corpus Paulinum* (Göttingen: Vandenhoeck & Ruprecht, 1997), 154–55) of an allusion in 9.16 to Isa. 49.10 as 'the only place in the LXX where the verb ἐλεέω is used in a participial form to refer to God, as a characteristic of his being', but rightly concludes that an allusion here is unlikely.

125. See e.g., Cottrell, *Romans*, 95–97; Munck, *Christ and Israel*, 44–45; Achtemeier, *Romans*, 163; Forster/Marston, *Strategy*, 60–61; H. L. Ellison, *The Mystery of Israel: An Exposition of Romans 9–11* (Exeter: Paternoster, 3rd edn, rev. and enl., 1976), 49–51. Many commentators who argue that Paul does not have the individual election of people for salvation in mind in Romans 9 in general are hard to figure out on the nature of the mercy (or similar grace) of 9.16. Many seem to write as if salvation or the like is in view in 9.16 (e.g., Morris, *Romans*, 359–60), and it is difficult to see how this coheres with their position that Paul's argument does not concern salvation. Cottrell is notable for consistently and clearly maintaining that the mercy of 9.16 is the mercy of election unto service. Cf. G. Shellrude, 'The Freedom of God in Mercy and Judgment: A Libertarian Reading of Romans 9:6-29', *EvQ* 81.4 (2009), 306–18 (312 n. 11).

126. See e.g., Moo, *Romans*, 593; Schreiner, *Romans*, 508; Piper, *Justification*, 155–58.

127. Moo, ibid., is correct that this appears to be a general principle. Presumably this would apply to any bestowal of God's mercy. But exegetically we must ask with Moo, to what is Paul specifically applying the principle here?

128. See our exegesis of Romans 9 up to this very point in this volume and its predecessor.

129. Although not listed in NA[27], 'a number of MSS. have the more regular ἐλεοῦντος' rather than the more unusual ἐλεῶντος (Cranfield, *Romans*, 484 n. 2). As Jewett, *Romans*, 570, observes, the more difficult reading (ἐλεῶντος) 'is undoubtedly original'. However, the awkward variant in L, εὐδοκοῦντος, is too difficult, with overwhelming manuscript evidence against it. See Cranfield, 485 n. 2, and Jewett, ibid., for speculation on how it arose.

chooses to lay down for the bestowing of his mercy. The bestowal of mercy that is the election of God's covenant people is rightly at the discretion of the mercy-bestowing God. It is subject to the dictates of his own will.

The genitive participial phrases of 9.16 are somewhat ambiguous and are open to more than one interpretation.[130] The most likely options are genitives of source, possession, agency or subject. But these are all rather similar in meaning in this instance, and all of them are likely in view in essence. It must be remembered that ancient writers did not have such labels in mind, but that these categories are simply modern ways of categorizing ancient usage of the genitive. If we have to label Paul's usage here, then genitives of source are probably most fitting.[131] The idea of source captures the heart of the genitival idea in 9.16, giving rise to each nuance present. Paul is stating that the bestowal of mercy comes from God. In this case, that also includes the fact that God is the one who bestows his mercy; he is the subject/agent of the bestowal of his mercy. Hence, the bestowal of mercy may also be said to belong to him. It is his to dispense or not as he sees fit for whatever reasons he deems fitting. There is nothing outside of himself that can constrain him to bestow mercy or choose a particular people.

But contrary to the reading of some interpreters, this neither indicates nor implies that God's bestowal of mercy is unconditional.[132] Indeed, we have seen that the statement of 9.15 partly means that the conditions for God's bestowal of mercy are his prerogative to determine. He may have mercy on whomever he wishes for whatever reason(s) he chooses. As 9.16 now states an inference from 9.15, its wording is completely consonant with this point.[133]

130.   Cf. Piper, *Justification*, 155 n. 4; Dunn, *Romans*, 552.

131.   So Moo, *Romans*, 593 n. 27; D. B. Wallace, *Greek Grammar Beyond the Basics: An Exegetical Syntax of the New Testament* (Grand Rapids: Zondervan, 1996), 110; seemingly most translations with their rendering of 'depend'. A. T. Robertson, *Word Pictures in the New Testament* (Nashville: Broadman Press, 1932–33, 1960), s.v. Rom. 9.16, accessed at http://www.biblestudytools.com/commentaries/robertsons-word-pictures/, states that they might be genitives of quality or source, but I find quality much less likely. Wallace, 109, observes that generally, 'In some ways, the possessive, subjective, and source genitives are similar. In any given instance, if they all make good sense, subjective should be given priority'. All of these do make good sense here, but as noted above and despite his advice, Wallace rightly categorizes the genitives of 9.16 as source. Yet both ideas are present.

132.   Contra e.g., Piper, *Justification*, 153–57; Schreiner, *Romans*, 508; Seifrid, 'Romans', 643.

133.   The point is also supported by the fact that repentance and/or faith are routinely represented as the condition for obtaining divine mercy in Paul and the Bible generally (see e.g., Rom. 1.16-17; 3.1–5.2; 9.30–10.13; 11.20, 22-23; Gal. 3–4; 6.14-16; Prov. 28.13; Isa. 55.1-7; Jer. 18.1-11; Ezek. 18; 33.1-16; Jon. 3.10; 4.2; Mk 1.4; Jn 3.16; Acts 3.19; 16.30-31). Piper, *Justification*, 157, concedes that, 'Faith is indeed a *sine qua non* of salvation'. But he then argues that Rom. 9.16 'necessarily implies that the act of faith is ultimately owing to the prevenient grace of God', an unobjectionable claim by its mere wording (prevenient grace is a prominent element of the theological viewpoint held by the ecumenical consensus of the Christian tradition that is nonetheless at odds with Piper's stance of unconditional election; see T. C. Oden, *The Transforming Power of Grace* (Nashville: Abingdon, 1993)), but by which Piper undoubtedly means a deterministic prevenient grace that irresistibly causes its

It must be acknowledged that 9.16's wording is rather ambiguous in itself.[134] One's interpretation of it will naturally flow from one's interpretation of the verses leading up to it. If one finds unconditional election advanced in 9.6-15, then one will likely find 9.16 to be a summary statement of the point. But if one does not find 9.6-15 to be advancing unconditional election, then one will likely not regard 9.16 to articulate it. Our exegesis of 9.6-15 has concluded that Paul is not teaching unconditional election here. Indeed, 9.15 is determinative for the meaning of 9.16, and our exegesis of 9.15 has found it to be implausible to construe it to imply that the bestowal of God's mercy is unconditional.

Even on the surface, the wording of 9.16 does not lend most naturally to expression of unconditional mercy. The text merely states that the bestowal of mercy does not come from human beings no matter what they will or do,[135] but it comes from God as the one who bestows the mercy. He is its source and agent, not man. On the face of it, this does not so much as hint at excluding the possibility of God partly basing his decision about whom he will show mercy to on something about the potential recipients of his mercy.[136] Specifically, in Paul's concern, it does not exclude the possibility of God bestowing his mercy upon those who believe in Christ because of their faith. It does, on the other hand, exclude the possibility that anyone could *constrain* God to give mercy by any means. He is the one who bestows mercy, the source of this mercy, and the one to whom it belongs to grant as he sees fit. Paul makes this point in order to defend God's right to grant his mercy in the form of covenantal election to those who trust in Jesus rather than to those who trust in their own works or ancestry, as 9.30-32's statement of the upshot of Paul's argument in 9.1-29 suggests.

objects to believe. This of course assumes that 9.16 demands unconditional election. But since the language of 9.16 is in itself perfectly consistent with conditional election, the non-controversial point that faith is a sine qua non of salvation in Paul's thought, previously made clear in Romans itself, offers prima facie evidence in favour of taking 9.16 to speak of a conditional bestowal of mercy.

134.   Cf. Shellrude, 'Freedom', who compellingly and consistently takes language in Rom. 9.6-29 differently than Calvinistic interpreters, who understand the same language as clear Pauline articulations of a Calvinistic viewpoint. The difference in construal is often very slight, but the import for how Paul is applying the statements results in vastly different theological conclusions.

135.   Though this way of stating it lacks nuance and will be qualified later.

136.   We could imagine any number of similar statements that would never be taken in such a way. We could imagine the president of the United States granting a pardon to someone convicted of a crime and various criminals complaining that it is not right for him to pardon someone else yet not themselves, and being told by their lawyers that presidential pardons are not of the one who wills nor of the one who runs nor of the one who has been wrongly convicted nor of the one who is innocent, but of the president who pardons. There would be no implication in such a statement that the president does not take into account the character or actions of the people he considers for pardon – the very opposite would be assumed – but that the pardon comes from him and the determination of who gets pardoned is completely at his discretion. Or we could think of a divine act that is undeniably conditional on faith in Christ in Paul's theology – justification. Even though Paul regarded justification to be by faith, and so conditional on it as the divine response to human faith, I submit that Paul would equally say that justification is not of the one who believes, but of the God who justifies.

8.3.c.2. *Willing and Running*

This is also suggested by the way in which Paul characterizes those from whom the mercy of divine covenantal election does not flow, 'the one who wills' (τοῦ θέλοντος) and 'the one who runs' (τοῦ τρέχοντος). Paul's use of θέλω earlier in the epistle (7.15-21) suggests that the 'willing' of 9.16 specifically refers to desiring to keep the Law of God.[137] Indeed, as Dunn observes, the 'willing' and 'running' of 9.16 'is equivalent to the "willing" and "doing" of 7.15-21'.[138] In 7.15-21, Paul speaks of 'willing' in the sense of human resolve to do the Law, and he speaks of 'doing' in the sense of human performance of the Law.[139] This prior usage prepares the readers/hearers of Romans to understand the similar language of 9.16 in a similar way, particularly coming in a context in which Paul is explicitly arguing that God's election and mercy is neither based on human works nor held captive by them. It especially does so for θέλω, which appears in both contexts. But then, this usage of 'willing' in 9.16 would suggest the possibility of such a meaning for 'running' (τρέχω) in the same verse.[140] At the same time, there is independent evidence for this type of meaning for 'running' in 9.16, which then reinforces our conclusion concerning 'willing'.

According to Piper, 'The explicit allusion to the sport of running in 1 Cor 9:24-26 inclines most commentators to construe the "running" of Rom 9:16 as a similar allusion with the focus being on the exertion required to run'.[141] But several interpreters have turned from this suggestion of a Hellenistic background to favouring a Jewish background for Paul's thought here, one that construes Paul's reference to 'running' as rooted in the Old Testament and Jewish concept of keeping the Law of God.[142] Psalm 119.32 (118.32 LXX) speaks of running the way of God's commandments, a more intense form of the standard biblical concept of walking (which equates to 'conduct oneself') according to God's Law or will (e.g., Exod. 18.20; Deut. 13.4-5; 1 Kgs 9.4; Ps. 86.11 (85.11 LXX); Prov. 28.18; Isa. 33.15; cf. Rom. 8.4; 13.13;

---

137.   Cf. Dunn, *Romans*, 552–53, who highlights 7.15-21, and esp. Jewett, *Romans*, 582–83, who astutely observes that Paul's use of the word there carries a 'legalistic' connotation. Wright, 'Romans', 638, speaks of Israel intending to do what God wants.

138.   Dunn, ibid.

139.   Note the references to the Law in 7.14, 22 forming an inclusio around Paul's discussion of 'willing' and 'doing'.

140.   Cf. Jewett, *Romans*, 583.

141.   Piper, *Justification*, 152. Representatives of this view include V. C. Pfitzner, *Paul and the Agon Motif* (NovTSup, 16; Leiden: Brill, 1967); BDAG, s.v. τρέχω, 2; Cranfield, *Romans*, 485 n. 1; Käsemann, *Romans*, 267; Fitzmyer, *Romans*, 567.

142.   See Piper, *Justification*, 152–53, who follows B. Noack and G. Maier, and summarizes the case well; Munck, *Christ and Israel*, 45 n. 50; Dunn, *Romans*, 553; Moo, *Romans*, 593; Jewett, *Romans*, 583. Cf. Wright, 'Romans', 638, who speaks of Israel expending energy on the task of doing what God wants. J. D. M. Derrett, '"Running" in Paul: the Midrashic Potential of Hab 2,2', *Bib* 66 (1985), 560–67 (566), agrees that the background is Jewish, but thinks it derives from Hab. 2.2 and refers to missionary activity. But few if any have followed him on this in Rom. 9.16; it simply does not fit the specific flow of Paul's thought (cf. Schreiner's (*Romans*, 508) judgment that it is 'surely wrong').

14.15).[143] For Paul, then, 'running' in 9.16 probably suggests a vigorous and wholehearted keeping of the Law and the effort involved in it given (1) the likelihood that θέλω in 9.16 refers to resolve to keep the Law (see above); (2) Paul is most fundamentally a Jewish and biblical thinker;[144] (3) 'The immediate and wider context of Rom 9:16 is marked by a distinctly Jewish concern (cf 9:1-5)' – and I would add, appeal to Scripture – 'and there is no hint (except the one word "run") of an athletic metaphor';[145] (4) 'running the way of the commandments' aligns closely with Rom 9.30-32, which supplies a summary conclusion for 9.1-29 and uses the similar word διώκω to speak of unbelieving ethnic Israel pursuing righteousness by keeping the Law in contrast to Gentiles not pursuing righteousness but attaining it by faith;[146] and (5) Paul has specifically been defending the righteousness of God in choosing his people not by works but by faith, and 9.14-16 specifically grounds Paul's statement in 9.11c-12b that God's purpose for election will be fulfilled 'not by works, but by the one who calls', with 9.16 encapsulating the thrust of these grounding verses.[147]

To expand on this last point, some interpreters regard 9.16 as a sharpened restatement of 9.11-12, with 'not by works, but by the one who calls' of 9.12 precisely paralleling 'not of the one who wills nor of the one who runs, but of the mercy-bestowing God' in 9.16.[148] This is not quite right. The statements are significantly parallel, but not completely. As we have seen, the statement of 9.12 refers to the basis, means and underlying principle of election whereas 9.16 refers to the source, agent and master/owner of election/mercy.[149]

---

143. See Dunn, *Romans*, 315–16, 553.

144. This is not to deny that Paul was impacted by his Greco-Roman milieu or drew from Hellenistic thought to some degree, but to acknowledge what was primary for him. We will actually conclude that both backgrounds are in play; see below.

145. Piper, *Justification*, 152.

146. Cf. ibid.; Munck, *Christ and Israel*, 45 n. 50.

147. Cf. Piper, *Justification*, 153. Piper, 152–53, mentions three other supporting arguments, one of which is mildly supportive (Noack's citation of b. Ber. 28b and b. Pes. 112a, which carry some limitation as rabbinic references codified long after Paul wrote; see O. Bauernfeind, 'τρέχω', *TDNT*, 226–33 (229–31), on the Septuagintal and Qumranic background), and two of which are invalid in my opinion. As for the invalid items, first, I find it methodologically dubious to judge the background of Paul's language on the attempt to translate it back into Hebrew as Maier does, followed by Piper. There is no evidence to suggest that Paul first formulated his epistle in Hebrew or was perhaps 'thinking in Hebrew'. Second, we have already found Maier's claim that Paul was consciously setting himself against a Pharisaic view of free will doubtful (see n. 43 in ch. 5 above). With respect to 9.16, the texts Piper cites from Maier (*Pss. Sol.* 9.4-5; *Sir.* 15.14-15) are not about God's bestowal of mercy or election, nor do they suggest that God's mercy is constrained by human free will. They seem largely irrelevant to 9.16. As Dunn, *Romans*, 553, concludes, an allusion to them is unlikely.

148. So Piper, *Justification*, 153, following Maier; cf. Schreiner, *Romans*, 508.

149. It is worth noting that Paul expresses himself slightly differently in these two verses, using the preposition ἐκ in 9.12, but using only the bare genitive case in 9.16, matching the close but inexact parallel we have perceived. Ἐκ certainly can be used to indicate source or agent, but ἐξ ἔργων has a somewhat established meaning in Paul and Romans, associated with its virtual opposite, ἐκ πίστεως, in both of which ἐκ carries the basic meaning of basis/

Romans 9.16 thus serves as a justification for 9.11-12 by way of supporting 9.14, demonstrating that God has every right to choose his people not by works, but by the condition of his own choosing, namely faith (9.11-12), because he is the source, agent and Lord of the mercy of election.[150] It is a relatively simple point, but the exact one that is needed to counter the objection Paul is answering with respect to the way that God has bestowed his mercy according to Paul. God cannot rightly be called unrighteous in his bestowal of mercy since his mercy is precisely his to bestow as he sees fit, a fact grounded in the very nature of God and the nature of his covenant with Israel as shown by Exod. 33.19 (Rom. 9.15).

Yet even though the parallel between 9.11-12 and 9.16 is not exact, it is very substantial. The call of God in 9.12 is roughly equivalent to the mercy/covenantal election of 9.16.[151] And as Piper argues, the 'willing' and 'running' of 9.16 are an expression of the 'works' of 9.12 'which, according to Rom 9:32, is the way Israel was "pursuing" (i.e., running after) the law'.[152] Technically, this excludes faith from the 'willing' and 'running' Paul mentions in 9.16 since faith and works are mutually exclusive in Romans and Paul generally.[153] But this is not to say that Paul intends to leave room for the idea

means, as testified to by the virtually unanimous translation of ἐκ in these phrases with 'by'. However, I am not basing my comments here merely on the presence or absence of the preposition, but on the exegesis of these texts in context. Nevertheless, it is noteworthy that Paul expresses himself differently in 9.12 vs 9.16, even if slightly, and that this difference corresponds with standard assessments of the precise meaning of his Greek in these two verses.

150.   As Piper himself (*Justification*, 157–58) concedes, who argues for the complete correlation of the not/but statements of 9.12 and 9.16, we would expect Paul here to offer justification for his doctrine of election rather than a mere reassertion of it, since this section of his argument is taken up with offering just such a justification. This supports our interpretation of 9.16 over against approaches like Piper's.

151.   Remember that calling is the appellation of election, the act of designating a group as God's elect people; see Abasciano, *Romans 9.1-9*, 198–208.

152.   Piper, *Justification*, 153.

153.   After successfully arguing that the 'willing' and 'running' of 9.16 are an expression of 'works', ibid., 153–54, is at pains to try to prove that faith is part of such 'works'. But this is implausible in light of Paul's prominent works/faith contrast. Piper *assumes* that faith is a sort of work for Paul without any justification except for mere reference to Gal. 5.7 and 1 Thess. 1.3. But neither of these support his assumption. The 'running' of Gal. 5.7 can hardly be thought to indicate that Paul thought of faith as a work. Rather, faith is what produces the running/work of the Christian life, as Gal. 5.6 indicates along with, ironically, Piper's other reference, 1 Thess. 1.3. (Besides, even if the 'running' of Gal. 5.7 included faith, we would have a different usage of the word in a different context. Paul's works/faith contrast is exceedingly sharp in Galatians and would certainly not allow that faith is a work.) First Thess. 1.3's reference to the Thessalonians' 'work of faith' (τοῦ ἔργου τῆς πίστεως) is highly unlikely to use an epexegetical genitive equating the Thessalonians' work with their faith, but rather, as most commentators seem to take it, a subjective genitive (or a genitive of production or source) indicating that the Thessalonians' faith gave rise to their work, just as the following phrase, 'labour of love' (τοῦ κόπου τῆς ἀγάπης), indicates that their love inspired their labour; so e.g., John Calvin, *Commentary on Philippians, Colossians, and Thessalonians* (http://www.ccel.org/: CCEL, n/d), s.v. Eph. 1.3; E. Best, *The First and Second Epistles to the Thessalonians* (BNTC; Peabody: Hendrickson, 1986), 67–68; C. A.

that the bestowal of God's mercy is of the person who has faith. Since Paul's language refers to the source and agent of mercy, faith could no more make the divine mercy subject to human beings than works could.

Indeed, Paul has already explained earlier in Romans that the problem with works is that the worker would constrain the divine mercy as an obligation, but that with faith, the believer obtains the divine mercy as a free gift granted as a response to faith (3.20–5.2). It is simply that Paul is

---

Wanamaker, *The Epistles to the Thessalonians: A Commentary on the Greek Text* (NIGTC; Grand Rapids: Eerdmans, 1990), 75; G. L. Green, *The Letters to the Thessalonians* (PNTC; Grand Rapids: Eerdmans, 2002), 89; Robertson, *Pictures*, s.v. Eph. 1.3; Wallace, *Grammar*, 106. Piper's further, detailed argument for 9.16 as speaking of unconditional bestowal of divine mercy founders on both fundamental presupposition and its particulars. For the former, Piper assumes that the language of 9.16 is incompatible with God bestowing his mercy on a condition sovereignly determined by himself. But our exegesis has found this to be a false assumption. As for the particulars, Piper's appeals to 9.11-12 and Exod. 33.19 are contradicted by our exegesis of these texts as well as of 9.16, and the reader is directed to the relevant portions of the present volume. Curiously, Piper's final main argument invokes Phil. 2.13 (because of the somewhat similar language of 'willing' (τὸ θέλειν) and 'working' (τὸ ἐνεργεῖν)) as somehow ruling out any condition for the bestowal of God's mercy. But that text does not particularly talk about God's mercy (except insofar as any blessing of God can be considered mercy) and it does not indicate anything about God's bestowal of mercy, or any divine action, being unconditional. Piper seems to be overreaching here, and we conclude that Phil. 2.13 is largely irrelevant to Rom. 9.16 and the question of the conditionality of the mercy it mentions. Piper, 154 n. 3, notes one further reference, cited by Sanday/Headlam as an analogy to 9.16 (though Piper mistakenly refers to 9.6): Jn 1.12-13. This reference actually works against Piper because the regenerating act of God there, performed by God alone, is presented as the divine response to human faith (cf. justification in Paul's thought, which is performed by God alone in response to human faith). John 1.12 indicates that people become children of God by faith. That is, upon believing, God gives them the right to become something that they were not prior to believing – children of God. John 1.13 then clarifies that they become children of God not from human ancestry (that is the significance of 'not of blood, nor of the desire of the flesh [which equates to sexual desire that might lead to procreation], nor of the will of a husband [who was thought to be in charge of sexual/procreative activity]'), but from God, describing their becoming children of God as being born of God. 'Becoming children of God' and 'being born of God' are parallel expressions referring to the same phenomenon (it would be special pleading, and a desperate expedient at that, to argue that becoming God's child and being born of him are distinct in the Johannine context or that the text would allow that a person could be born of God and yet not be his child), so that God's act of regenerating believers, making them his own children, is a response to their faith. The parallel with Rom. 9.16 is significant and quite supportive of our exegesis. Both contexts make the point that elect status (which equates to sonship; cf. Rom. 9.8) is not bestowed by human ancestry, but by God, whose will is to choose as his own those who believe in Christ. Even if one were to deny that reference to θελήματος σαρκός or θελήματος ἀνδρός is to human ancestry specifically and insist that it refers to human willing in general, it would not make the divine action of regeneration any less a response to human faith and hence any less conditional on it. Nor would this be inconsistent with Jn 1.13's attribution of the act of regeneration to God. The text indicates that God is the one who grants the right to become children of God and the one who regenerates. His doing so in response to faith is a matter of his discretion and would not somehow make the human choice to believe the source of regeneration instead of God any more than it makes it the source of justification.

specifically responding here to the charge that God would be unrighteous for choosing his people apart from works. So he fashions his polemic against works being necessary as the basis of the divine calling and mercy for God to be righteous. But the statement of 9.16 carries an implicit greater-to-the-lesser *qal wahomer* logic about it. If works cannot coerce God to bestow mercy, then nothing can, least of all faith, which does nothing that could be thought to earn any blessing from God, but merely receives his mercy as a free gift.

Although we have discerned a Jewish background to Paul's language of 'willing' and 'running', this does not necessarily rule out there being any Hellenistic athletic background.[154] It could be that the Jewish and Hellenistic/athletic usages are both in view and mutually impact one another, making for a sort of amalgamation in which the idea of wholehearted and vigorous keeping of the Law is coloured by the idea of the effort and goal-orientation of running in the arena and vice versa.[155] This actually seems to be typical of Paul's usage (but using the more basic and general Jewish sense of 'wholeheartedly and vigorously conducting oneself' rather than keeping of the Law),[156] and that leads me to think it may be the case here, especially since the *agon* motif seems to be present in 9.30–10.5.[157] In 9.16, the Jewish background appears to be primary, connoting wholehearted and vigorous keeping of the Law, with the Hellenistic background strengthening the idea of strenuous effort and adding the sense of a goal of obtaining the divine mercy by works.

On the other hand, it could be that the reference is more general, simply referring to any human willing, effort or activity whatsoever,[158] perhaps with a special connotation of works (which would be more likely in light of

154.   Cf. D. A. Campbell, *The Deliverance of God: An Apocalyptic Rereading of Justification in Paul* (Grand Rapids: Eerdmans, 2009), 790, 1134 n. 65. However, Campbell's suggestion that the *agon* motif is primary and the OT background merely stylistic is unlikely, greatly underestimating the profundity of Paul's engagement with the OT, which our entire exegesis of Romans 9 so far has amply demonstrated. But the presence of the motif in 9.30–10.5 to which Campbell draws attention strengthens the position that it is also present in 9.16.

155.   On the element of progress toward a goal, see G. Ebel, 'τρέχω', *NIDNTT*, 3.947.

156.   In addition to 9.16, Paul uses τρέχω in 1 Cor. 9.24 (x3), 26; Gal. 2.2 (x2); 5.7; Phil. 2.16; and 2 Thess. 3.1. The athletic metaphor is clear and singular in 1 Cor. 9.24, 26. But it is not so in the other occurrences of interest (Gal. 2.2; 5.7; Phil. 2.16; we exclude consideration of 2 Thess. 3.1 since it has an impersonal subject). Yet, it probably is present in these verses, communicating the sense of labour and progress toward a goal, along with the Jewish metaphor referring to conducting oneself wholeheartedly and vigorously according to a certain way of behaviour. In Gal. 2.2 and Phil. 2.16, the reference is to Paul's carrying out of his (God-appointed) apostolic ministry. In Gal. 5.7, it is to the Galatian believers' spiritual life and progress in it.

157.   See Campbell, *Deliverance*, 790.

158.   So Schreiner, *Romans*, 508. Many commentators speak generally of willing and effort without considering the possibility of a more specific, contextual meaning; see e.g., Morris, *Romans*, 359–60; G. R. Osborne, *Romans* (IVPNTC; Downer's Grove: IVP, 2004), 249.

our discussion).[159] Neither of these readings would conflict with our overall interpretation of 9.16. Practically, the verse does rule out any human willing, effort, or activity from coopting the divine mercy. But those who favour a general meaning do not tend to offer much evidence for it besides the general flow of Paul's argument (if they do not simply take it for granted), which we have found supportive of a more specific meaning. The evidence we have surveyed indicates that in this context Paul most specifically asserts that neither human resolve to keep the Law nor works in actual wholehearted and vigorous keeping of the Law can command God's mercy. He is rightly free to bestow mercy as he sees fit. Therefore, he is not unrighteous for choosing his people by faith in Christ rather than by works or ancestry nor for rejecting from his covenant those who do not believe.

8.3.d. *Paul's Quotation of Exodus 9.16 (Romans 9.17)*

Paul now cites Exod. 9.16 as a further ground for this principle of God's righteousness in sovereign, gracious election: 'For the Scripture says to Pharaoh, "for this very purpose I raised you up, that I might show my power in you and that my name might be proclaimed in all the earth"' (Rom. 9.17).

8.3.d.1. *The Logical Connection of Romans 9.17 to What Precedes*
There is disagreement among interpreters about how to relate this to what precedes. The grounding conjunction γάρ ('for') could relate to 9.14, making 9.17 a second ground (in addition to 9.15-16) for Paul's denial of unrighteousness with God.[160] This is suggested by the structure of 9.14-18, with the γάρ (9.17)/ἄρα οὖν (9.18) of 9.17-18 correlating to the γάρ (9.15)/ ἄρα οὖν (9.16) of 9.15-16, yielding the following flow of thought:

9.14   Main thesis of the paragraph: God is not unrighteous
9.15   Reason 1: Because (γάρ) Scripture citation (Exod. 33.19b)
9.16   Inference indicated by ἄρα οὖν
9.17   Reason 2: Because (γάρ) Scripture citation (Exod. 9.16)
9.18   Inference indicated by ἄρα οὖν[161]

That this is Paul's train of thought is strongly suggested by the way that 'the summary statement (ἄρα οὖν) in 9:18 reaches back to 9:15, 16 for its inference about mercy (18a) and back to 9:17 for its inference about hardening (18b)',

159. So Moo, *Romans*, 593 n. 29. Piper, *Justification*, 151–55, might fit best here, though he is a special case, holding that Paul refers to works, but that all human willing and activity is works.
160. So e.g., Munck, *Christ and Israel*, 45 n. 53; Cranfield, *Romans*, 485; Moo, *Romans*, 594; Schreiner, *Romans*, 508; Morris, *Romans*, 360; Cottrell, *Romans*, 97; Osborne, *Romans*, 248.
161. Cf. the chart in Moo, ibid.

providing two symmetrically balanced principles that together ground Paul's denial of divine unrighteousness.[162]

Alternatively, 9.17 could relate to 9.16, grounding or explaining Paul's assertion that God's bestowal of mercy is at God's discretion rather than man's.[163] This is supported by the fact that one would normally expect γάρ to offer a ground for what immediately precedes it.[164] However, this is not a strict rule, and such an expectation is partially mitigated by the fact that the support the Old Testament quotation in 9.17 would furnish for the principle in 9.16 is somewhat indirect. Moo even argues that, 'vv. 17-18 can hardly be an explanation of God's mercy in v. 16 since the "hardening" that Paul illustrates in v. 17 is, according to v. 18, antithetical to "mercy"'.[165] However, following the citation of Exod. 33.19b as it does, the thought would be that God's sovereignty over his bestowal of mercy is shown by his withholding of mercy from Pharaoh (indeed by his infliction of hardening judgment upon Pharaoh rather than mercy), for sovereignty over the bestowal of mercy entails the ability to either grant mercy or withhold it. This is a natural movement of thought, but not necessarily immediately obvious as Paul's train of thought in this context as evidenced by its lack of transparency to some scholars. Indeed, some who connect 9.17 to 9.16 construe the connection even more indirectly, such as development of the principle of 9.16[166] or proof that it is operative in God's severity as well as his mercy.[167]

Both options are reasonable, and in fact, they are not mutually exclusive. I join Piper in concluding 'from the logical structure of Paul's argument that 9:17 relates to both 9:14 and 16'.[168] However, its relationship to 9.14 appears stronger and more primary.[169] In addition to the structural considerations mentioned above, this also receives support from the way in which 9.17

162   Piper, *Justification*, 171–72. Cf. others who note the strict parallel structure of 9.18, e.g., Moo, *Romans*, 597.

163.   So e.g., Sanday/Headlam, *Romans*, 255; Achtemeier, *Romans*, 162; Dunn, *Romans*, 553; Keck, *Romans*, 233; Seifrid, 'Romans', 643.

164.   As Piper, *Justification*, 158, points out.

165.   Moo, *Romans*, 594.

166.   So Dunn, *Romans*, 553.

167.   So Sanday/Headlam, *Romans*, 255.

168.   Piper, *Justification*, 158–59. Although I agree largely with Piper's overall conclusion, I do not agree with his precise assessment of the text's logic upon which his conclusion is based. He takes 9.15 to support both 9.14 (God's righteousness in election) and 9.16 (God's sovereign freedom in election) distinctly, and so takes 9.17, the negative counterpart to 9.15, to function similarly, supporting 9.14 (God's righteousness in election) on the one hand, and 9.16 and 9.18 (God's sovereign freedom in election) on the other. But the problem is that 9.15-16 *together* support 9.14. Romans 9.16 is an inference from 9.15 that states its significance. Hence, logically we are to read 9.15-16 together in relation to 9.14. The same holds true for 9.17-18 in relation to both 9.14 and 9.16. No matter what view one holds of 9.17's relationship to 9.16, it should be acknowledged that any support the former gives the latter ultimately supports 9.14, since 9.16 supports 9.14, making 9.17's support for 9.16 ultimately to serve the support of 9.14 even if its direct orientation is toward 9.16 alone.

169.   Cf. Moo, *Romans*, 594, who allows for a secondary connection to 9.16, though he downplays it too much.

directly contributes to the justification of God's righteousness in covenantal election, and particularly its corollary, covenantal judgment and rejection – by revealing that God's hardening judgment serves God's purpose for electing in the first place, the salvation of the world (a point to be taken up in more detail below).

8.3.d.2. *Introducing the Quotation*

Paul introduces his quotation by stating that Scripture speaks these words to Pharaoh. By referring to Scripture (ἡ γραφή) as the speaker, Paul buttresses his argument as coming from the authoritative word of God. In 9.15, he introduced the quotation of Exod. 33.19b with God himself as the implicit speaker to similar effect. Depicting the divine word differently, now as the personified word of God, 'enlivens and strengthens Paul's rhetoric with multiple authoritative voices'.[170] The present tense of the verb helps to underscore the relevance of the quotation for the current time of eschatological fulfilment.[171] And identifying Pharaoh as the addressee directs attention more vividly to the quotation's original context and facilitates Paul's use of Pharaoh as a type much as he has used other figures from salvation history as negative types in his argument (i.e., Ishmael (implicitly) and Esau).

8.3.d.3. *Initial Observations about the Meaning and Function of the Quotation*

Whereas 9.15-16 took up the positive side of God's sovereignty in election that was articulated in 9.13b by 'Jacob I loved', 9.17-18 now takes up the negative side that was articulated in 9.13c by 'but Esau I hated'.[172] Just as the former offered a supporting Scripture citation (9.15) for God's righteousness in sovereign election followed by an inference stating the Scripture's significance (9.16), so Paul now gives further scriptural support (9.17) followed by an inference stating the Scripture's significance (9.18b), but this time with special reference to the negative side of God's sovereign election – covenantal rejection and hardening. We have already compared Paul's wording of Exod. 9.16 to the known Old Testament textual traditions available to him and concluded that he worded his quotation in such a way as to highlight God's purpose and sovereignty as well as their expression in seeking the salvation of the world and including Gentiles in the covenant people of God (see section 8.2 above). We will now look more deeply into the semantic content of Paul's quotation.

In its original context, Exod. 9.16 is part of a statement of God's incomparable power and sovereignty in allowing Pharaoh to continue living

---

170. Wagner, *Heralds*, 54 n. 34. The highly unlikely suggestion that Paul used Scripture rather than God as the subject of λέγει to avoid direct address from God to a pagan has rightly not won much support. Against it, see esp. Jewett, *Romans*, 583; Cranfield, *Romans*, 485. For a relatively recent advocate, see Fitzmyer, *Romans*, 567. Seifrid's ('Romans', 643) suggestion that the personification of Scripture itself emphasizes the citation's present relevance is not evident.

171. Cf. Seifrid, ibid.

172. Moo, *Romans*, 593; cf. Piper, *Justification*, 159; Osborne, *Romans*, 249.

despite his arrogant rebellion against the Lord, a statement formally aimed
at bringing Pharaoh to acknowledge YHWH's supremacy and to submit to
the divine will. This is yet another of Paul's appeals to the Old Testament in
Romans 9 that is striking in its aptness for his argument. For Paul is arguing
for God's absolute sovereignty over election (and his righteousness in it) and
also aims to bring his hearers to acknowledge it and submit to the divine
will. More specifically at this point, Paul is, as mentioned above, taking up
the negative side of God's sovereignty in election – judgment and hardening
– for which Pharaoh serves as a good example, who in the Exodus context
'epitomizes the consequence awaiting all human obstacles to the covenant
plan of God' and 'emerges as the archetypal hardened sinner – a classic foil
to the character of faithful obedience Yahweh desires in his people Israel'.[173]
Indeed, as Meadors has concluded, 'God reserved the same curse that he had
inflicted upon Pharaoh for those within Israel who would not maintain the
covenant in faith'.[174]

The aptness of Paul's quotation deepens powerfully with its statement
of the divine purpose for sparing Pharaoh's life up to the time of its
proclamation.[175] Two closely related purposes are mentioned. The first is
that God would show his power in Pharaoh. Ἐν σοί ('in you') is probably a
dative of sphere, characterizing Pharaoh as the sphere in which God displays
his power, implying also that he is the means through which God displays his
power.[176] In other words, God's mighty acts toward Pharaoh would display
God's power, making Pharaoh the theatre, as it were, in which God makes
his power known.

As we have seen, this is a different idea from the LXX than specifically
stated in the Hebrew text's first purpose clause, which speaks of God
showing *Pharaoh* his power rather than showing his power *in* Pharaoh.[177]
The change forges a stronger though still implicit link between God's action
toward Pharaoh and the universal proclamation of God's name referred to in
the quotation's second purpose clause. Thus, Paul appears to have followed
the LXX against the Hebrew in this instance in order to highlight God's
treatment of Pharaoh as that which brings about the proclamation of his
name to the whole world, supporting his argument in Romans 9 for God's
right to include Gentiles in his covenant people and exclude unbelieving Jews,
or to put it another way, God's right to elect his people by faith rather than

173. Meadors, *Idolatry*, 17.
174. Ibid., 36.
175. Earlier we concluded that Paul translated from the Hebrew using ἐξεγείρω in the
sense of 'to spare/allow to remain alive' with stress on God's initiative and sovereignty; see
the detailed discussion in 8.2 above.
176. Alternatively, it could be merely a dative of means without the locative idea, as
Moo, *Romans*, 595 n. 41, takes it. For a usage of ἐν that combines instrumentality and
sphere, see BDAG, s.v. ἐν, 5b. The use of ἐν to denote the object in which something is shown
(BDAG's definition 8) is undoubtedly in view, but this seems to me to be a special case of 5b,
entailed in a dative of sphere.
177. See the full discussion in 8.2 above of this and other issues related to Paul's use of
ἐν σοί in 9.17.

works or ancestry and to reject unbelieving Jews from his covenant people despite their works and ancestry (see below).

But the connection between God's dealings with Pharaoh and the worldwide proclamation of God's name is already clear (though again, implicit) in the Hebrew text. The wording Paul chose for his quotation simply brings this logical connection out more strongly, betraying his universalistic focus, and so focuses his audience's attention on the particular significance of the Old Testament text that he wants to stress. Paul would expect his audience to know the original context's concern for Pharaoh and the Egyptians to come to know God's power, which is still present in the LXX (see 8.2 above). And this may suggest certain secondary meaning-effects for Paul's discourse, which we will explore later. But his emphasis lies with God's purpose to use the exercise of his power vis-à-vis Pharaoh for the accomplishment of the second purpose mentioned in the quotation, the proclamation of God's name in all the earth.

8.3.d.3.a. *God's Power*

There is some question about what Paul means precisely by 'power' (δύναμις) in his quotation. Some interpreters believe he refers specifically to God's saving power.[178] Others think that he refers specifically to God's power as Creator in judgment.[179] Still others think that he refers to both salvation and judgment.[180] And yet others think that he refers to God's power as Creator more generally.[181] I submit that all of these are in view.

Since Paul is quoting Exod. 9.16, we ought to look especially to the Exodus context for his understanding. In Exod. 9.16, God's power refers generally to God's incomparable divine might and sovereignty, which of course is tied up with his identity as Creator. This is most fundamental. But the verse refers to the revelation of this supreme divine power in the acts of judgment upon Pharaoh and his people which also wrought the salvation of God's people from Egyptian slavery and oppression. In the Exodus context, judgment and salvation cannot be separated, but one brings about the other. The two are thoroughly intertwined. This accords with and corroborates our exegesis of Romans 9 so far, which has found Paul arguing that the fulfilment of his covenant promises to Abraham in the covenant inclusion of Gentiles (salvation) requires the rejection of unbelieving ethnic Israel (judgment).[182]

---

178. For example, Cranfield, *Romans*, 487; Dunn, *Romans*, 554. Cottrell, *Romans*, 99, denies a connection to 1.16 and advocates a strictly salvation-historical 'power to deliver his people from Egyptian slavery and oppression'.

179. For example, Käsemann, *Romans*, 268.

180. For example, Schreiner, *Romans*, 509; Moo, *Romans*, 595 n. 43; Osborne, *Romans*, 250.

181. The usual view according to Dunn, *Romans*, 554. See e.g., Michel (cited by Dunn); Seifrid, 'Romans', 644; Jewett, *Romans*, 584.

182. See Abasciano, *Romans 9.1-9*, 169, 192–94, 210, 214. See also further development of this below.

Our approach also receives support from other elements of the context of Romans. The sense of saving power is supported by reference to God's power in raising Christ in 1.4, the power of the Holy Spirit for believers' hope for salvation in 15.13, the power of God in signs and wonders – compare with God's power in signs and wonders in the exodus narrative! – in connection with Paul's preaching of the gospel in 15.19, and above all Paul's use of δύναμις (especially in contrast to LXX Exod. 9.16's use of ἰσχύς) in the prominent theme statement of the epistle to refer to 'the power of God for salvation for all who believe, both to the Jew first and the Greek' (1.16)[183] as well as Paul's concern in Romans 9 for God's sovereignty in *salvific* election and the expression of God's judging power for the purpose of *bestowing mercy* in 9.22-23. The sense of judging power is supported by the theme of the rejection of unbelieving ethnic Israel in Romans 9 (e.g., in the Ishmael and Esau typology we have observed), the inference drawn in 9.18 from 9.17 that God hardens whoever he desires, and the reference to making known (using ἐνδείκνυμι as does 9.17) God's power in wrath in 9.22.[184] Support for the general power of God the Creator as supreme divine power and sovereignty comes from 1.20's reference to God's eternal power (ἀΐδιος αὐτοῦ δύναμις) in conjunction with his divinity (θειότης) and a context highlighting God's identity as Creator, the emphasis in Romans 9 on God's sovereignty, the stress on God's identity as God in contrast to man in 9.20's response to an interlocutor's objection to what Paul says in 9.14-18, and the picture of God as Creator inherent in the potter/clay imagery Paul uses in response to the same objection.

We conclude that in 9.17 Paul refers to God the Creator's supreme divine power and sovereignty generally with special reference to its exercise in judgment and mercy/salvation. In Paul's argument, this has specific application to the exercise of 'the power of God for salvation for all who believe, both to the Jew first and to the Greek' (1.16), which names those who believe in the promise (i.e., children of the promise) as children of God and seed of Abraham (9.6-8) and recipients of the divine elective love (9.13) on the one hand, and on the other hand, the power of God in pouring out the curse of the covenant on unbelieving ethnic Israel (children of the flesh; 9.8), cutting them off from Christ and his people/the seed of Abraham and the covenant promises (9.3-9) and making them objects of the divine hatred that is covenantal rejection (9.13). Our exegesis of 9.1-13 had already concluded that it is this power of God to call/name his people based on faith apart from works or ancestry, and its corollary divine power of judging and rejecting unbelieving ethnic Jews despite works or ancestry, that Paul has been defending in Romans 9 with the more ultimate aim of defending the faithfulness of God to his promises to Israel. This exegesis now receives corroboration from our exegesis of 9.17, which coheres quite well with our exegesis to this point even as it is informed by it.

---

183.   Cranfield, *Romans*, 487, points to uses of δύναμις by Paul in other epistles for further substantiation.

184.   On these last two points, see esp. Schreiner, *Romans*, 509–10.

8.3.d.3.b. *Paul's Rationale for Citing Exodus 9.16*

What Moo insightfully says of 9.17's two purpose clauses together (treating them as one) applies especially to the second one: 'this purpose clause is probably the reason that Paul has cited this particular text since its lack of explicit reference to Pharaoh's "hardening" makes it less suitable than others as a preparation for Paul's conclusion in v. 18'.[185] There are several likely reasons for Paul's choice. First, the reference to God's 'name' (ὄνομά) ties the quotation to Paul's citation of Exod. 33.19 in Rom. 9.15, which is an explicatory, summary declaration of God's name.[186] We have seen that the proclamation of God's name in Exod. 9.16 refers to making known his absolute sovereignty and supreme divine status. It surely includes that here given Paul's regard for the Exodus context (see below). But following so closely upon his citation of Exod. 33.19b, it probably takes on the distinctive nuance of that passage also. According to our exegesis of the passage, God's name in Exodus 33 refers generally to God himself, his presence, nature, glory and goodness. More specifically, it refers to God's character as gracious and merciful and sovereign in his bestowal of mercy. Undoubtedly for Paul, the proclamation of God's name of grace, mercy and sovereignty would involve the proclamation of his sovereign plan for the bestowal of his grace and mercy in Jesus Christ to all who believe, whether Jew or Gentile, 'For there is no distinction between Jew and Greek; for the same Lord is Lord of all, bestowing his riches on all who call on him. For "everyone who calls on the *name* of the Lord will be saved"' (Rom. 10.12-13; ESV; emphasis mine; cf. 1.5; 15.8-9). The tie-in with Exod. 33.19b suggests that God's judgment/hardening of unbelieving ethnic Israel makes possible the proclamation of both his grace/mercy and his sovereign freedom in its bestowal.

Second, Exod. 9.16 plays a distinctive and important role in the exodus narrative that makes it ideal for quotation that points to the verse's broad original context (we will return to this point and elaborate on it later). Third, as Moo puts it, 'Paul wants to make clear that even God's "negative" actions, such as the hardening of Pharaoh, serve a positive purpose (a point Paul will develop further in vv. 22-23)'.[187] But fourth, and most importantly, more than merely showing a positive purpose for God's judgment, the universalistic thrust of this purpose directly supports the righteousness of God in sovereign election expressed in choosing his people by faith rather than works or ancestry, furnishing direct support for 9.14. How so? It shows that the negative side of God's sovereign election – the very thing most acutely raising the charge of divine unrighteousness in the form of unfaithfulness to God's promises to Israel – serves to bring about the fulfilment of the purpose

185. Moo, *Romans*, 595.

186. Cf. Piper, *Justification*, 180. Piper also suggests that Paul chose to cite Exod. 9.16 in order to exploit its purpose clauses again in 9.22. But it is hard to determine the genetic relationship between Rom. 9.17 and 9.22. On balance, it seems more likely that Paul's use of Exod. 9.16 shaped his expression in Rom. 9.22.

187. Moo, *Romans*, 595. From the universalistic thrust of Paul's quotation, Oropeza, 'Theodicy', 65, insightfully emphasizes that this positive purpose is the greater good of bringing God's mercy to Gentiles; cf. his citation of Stowers.

for election itself and therefore the fulfilment of the covenantal promises of God.

We have seen that the purpose of election referred to in 9.11 is the blessing of all the nations of the earth in Abraham and his seed (see 5.3.d.2. in ch. 5 above), which is the climactic promise of the covenant. The declaration of God's name to the world works toward this goal (cf. the logic of 10.14 ('How can they believe in one of whom they have not heard'?) and 10.17 ('faith comes from hearing, and hearing through the word of Christ')), a concern present in the Exodus context itself.[188] This goes back to the challenge to God's faithfulness that lies at the back of Paul's entire argument in Romans 9–11 as well as to the fundamental nature of election meant to serve the fulfilment of God's covenant promises. Paul's citation suggests that it cannot legitimately be maintained that God is unrighteous (in the sense of failing to keep his covenant promises to Israel) to reject unbelieving Jews despite their works and ancestry when the very purpose of election is to include the Gentiles in Israel's covenant and its blessings, and God's rejection of unbelieving Jews leads to the accomplishment of this goal. Indeed, Paul will later explain in chapter 11 that the hardening and rejection of Israel leads to the salvation of the Gentiles.

Interpreters have missed the depth and precise directness of 9.17's support for 9.14 in its universalistic thrust. It does not merely add a good purpose resulting from the negative side of God's sovereign election that softens the blow of it or the like. Rather, it cites a purpose that works toward the accomplishment of the very heart of election and the fulfilment of God's covenant promises. But just how does the hardening and rejection of unbelieving ethnic Israel work toward the blessing of the Gentiles? With that question before us, we now turn to examine 9.18, which will involve us in continued reflection on Paul's quotation of Exod. 9.16.

8.3.e. *Romans 9.18 in Intertextual Perspective*

Using the same inferential construction as Rom. 9.16 (ἄρα οὖν), Paul now draws a strongly expressed inference from his quotation of Exod. 9.16 in light of all that he has said in this paragraph (9.14-18): 'So therefore, he has mercy on whom he desires, and he hardens whom he desires' (Rom.

---

188. The proclamation of God's name to the nations, of course, does not equate to salvation for the nations. Indeed, in the Exodus context not even acknowledgment of God's supreme divinity and sovereignty equated to salvation. But such acknowledgment was the basic, necessary and monumental step towards salvation, which called for the added element of trust in YHWH as the supreme God and sovereign. But Exod. 9.16 itself issues forth into concern for even the Egyptians to come to fear and trust YHWH and his word with a view toward avoiding his wrath (see 9.18-19).

9.18).[189] The first part of this statement (9.18a)[190] articulates Paul's inference from 9.15-16, summing up the thrust of those verses and supporting 9.14. The second part (9.18b) articulates Paul's inference specifically from his Old Testament quotation in 9.17 (just as 9.16 stated Paul's inference from his Old Testament quotation in 9.15), summing up the thrust of that verse and also supporting 9.14. Here in 9.18b we have Paul's interpretation of Exod. 9.16 as it bears on his argument: God hardens whom he desires.

8.3.e.1. *Pointing to the Original Context of Exodus 9.16*

But we might ask how Paul draws this conclusion from Exod. 9.16 when the verse does not specifically mention anything about hardening. The answer can only be that Paul interpreted the quotation with respect to its broad original context, in which divine hardening is extraordinarily prominent, and that by his quotation he points his audience to that same broad original context, assuming their familiarity with it and their ability to follow his argument which relies on it. Indeed, this is confirmed by the fact that virtually all commentators find it necessary to refer to the original context of Paul's quotation in order to explain his line of thought in Rom. 9.17-18.

Moreover, Paul shows an impressive grasp of the original context of his quotation. For as we saw, Exod. 9.16 captures the main thrust of the entire exodus narrative. In that context it contributes to a statement of God's incomparable power and sovereignty, forming part of the main point of Exodus 1–15 that YHWH is the supreme, omnipotent God and sovereign who is to be trusted and obeyed above all others, a point intended to encourage the original audience of Exodus to reject idolatry and be loyal to YHWH and his covenant with Israel. Paul repeats it partly to encourage his own audience in the time of eschatological fulfilment to reject the idolatry of trusting in a means of mediating God's covenant, presence and blessing other than God

---

189. The contention of A. A. Di Lella, 'Tobit 4,19 and Romans 9,18: An Intertextual Study', *Bib* 90 (2009), 260–63, that Paul took his wording of 9.18, specifically his use of ὃν θέλει, from G[II] ms 319 of Tobit is unlikely. Even if his reconstruction of the text of Tobit is correct (in any case, the text that serves as the basis for most translations still has some of the same wording), the thematic link he claims does not really seem to be there. He asserts that the text refers to the doctrine of Israel's election, and indeed stresses it, when, at best, it assumes it and has a different focus than Rom. 9. Moreover, while the phrasing is very similar, it is not even exact; if we accept Di Lella's reconstruction, Tob. 4.19 includes ἂν whereas Rom. 9.18 lacks it, which would be a strange omission if Paul were taking the wording from Tobit. In any case, while the exact wording ὃν θέλει might not be used elsewhere in the NT, the basic wording does appear elsewhere to the same effect of indicating free choice (e.g., Mt. 20.15; 27.15; Mk 3.13; Jn 5.21; Rom. 7.15, 19). Moreover, it is only a matter of two words and it is easy to see how it would be used in this way. So it may be that there is simply a use of common language here for expression of a broadly similar phenomenon. However, the language of 9.18 is most likely based on the *idem per idem* formula from Paul's quotation of Exod. 33.19b in Rom. 9.15 and its use of ὃν. While it also uses ἂν, it is not a matter of Paul borrowing a phrase from Exod. 33.19b, but naturally wording his present discourse in conformity to his immediately preceding discourse.

190. ὁ θεός is added by D *pc* ar m vg[ms] Ambst, but is to be rejected as a clarifying and expansive longer reading.

had ordained for the present eschatological age, Jesus Christ, and to be loyal to God and his covenant with Israel in its eschatological expression of the New Covenant in Christ.

We also saw that in its original context Exod. 9.16 reveals the larger purposes for the divine hardening of Pharaoh and all of YHWH's actions towards the deliverance of his people, namely, that his supreme divinity and sovereignty would be made known to Pharaoh and all the earth. Indeed, we saw that the purposes of the divine hardening of Pharaoh were tied into God's ultimate, worldwide covenantal purpose to bless the world. At the same time, the broad context of Exod. 9.16 implies that the hardening of Pharaoh would serve as a means to the renewed election of God's people and their knowledge/acknowledgment of him as their covenant God (see, e.g., our exegesis of Exod. 6.6-7). But of course, within the storyline of Genesis and Exodus these two divine intentions (God's covenantal purpose to bless the world and his election of his people) are inextricably linked. God's election of Israel serves as the foundation and prerequisite to the blessing of the nations. This is also Paul's view, in which God would seek to bless the nations by incorporating them into the people of God by faith in Christ (3.21–4.25; Gal. 3.7-18 (note especially 7-9)). The negative side of this is that any Israelites (to use Paul's term from 9.4) who would not place their faith in Christ would be rejected from the covenant under its fatal curse despite their works and ancestry (9.3; 9.30–10.4; 11.7, 17-24). Hence, Paul's need to address what was the most compelling objection to his gospel, which purported to be the fulfilment of God's promises to Israel, viz. that those to whom the promises were ostensibly made were not enjoying their fulfilment and had in fact rejected Paul's message, a problem exacerbated by the fact that Gentiles, to whom the promises were never made, were enjoying their fulfilment with acceptance of Paul's message.

Exodus 9.16 therefore made an excellent choice from the exodus narrative for Paul to quote concerning hardening as the negative side of God's sovereign election vis-à-vis his ultimate covenant and elective purposes, which he was eager to take up because of the pressing objection to the gospel he devotes Romans 9–11 to answering.[191] For God's treatment of Pharaoh in the Exodus context relates precisely to these matters (among others). Most scholars are therefore correct to take Paul as applying the principle of hardening he has inferred from the exodus narrative to unbelieving ethnic Israel of his own day,[192] for (1) his whole argument to this point has been dealing with God's faithfulness to his promises to Israel given unbelieving ethnic Israel's rejected status; (2) he has been employing salvation-historical figures from the scriptural passages he has been invoking as types of rejected Israel throughout his argument (apostate Israel, Ishmael (implicitly), and Esau; see our exegesis

---

191. Indeed, he began to answer it in chapter 3, but left the matter in order to lay out his gospel more fully before taking up the objection more fully in chs 9–11.

192. So e.g., Moo, *Romans*, 595 n. 44 (who cites Barth, Cranfield, Byrne, and Räisänen); Schreiner, *Romans*, 511; Dunn, *Romans*, 564; Barrett, *Romans*, 187; Piper, *Justification*, 176–81; Jewett, *Romans*, 586.

of 9.1-13), with the current leg of his argument arising partly from his Esau/ Israel typology; and (3) he explicitly addresses the hardening of Israel in Romans 11, which is part of the same unified argument covered by Romans 9–11.[193] Indeed, in 9.17-18 Paul sets forth Pharaoh as a type of unbelieving ethnic Israel.

Paul's quotation of Exod. 9.16 suggests that just as God hardened Pharaoh for the purposes of (a) choosing his people in a new covenant developing and fulfilling the Abrahamic covenant, (b) making his power and name known in all the earth, and (c) fulfilling his climactic covenant purpose of blessing the world, so he has hardened unbelieving ethnic Israel in the time of eschatological fulfilment to accomplish the same purposes. Paul's stress obviously falls on the universal revelation of God's power and name since this is the purpose he states explicitly. But in the original Exodus context to which Paul clearly points, these purposes are thoroughly intertwined, with the other two being dependent on this one that Paul brings out most forcefully. It was the exercise of God's power facilitated by the hardening of Pharaoh's heart that served as the means to the redemption and subsequent renewed election of Israel as his people as well as the revelation of his supreme divinity and sovereignty in all the earth necessary for the blessing of the world. But how does the hardening of Israel in Paul's day lead to the revelation of God's power and name in all the earth, and how does that in turn lead to the New Covenant election of God's people and the blessing of the world? To answer these questions, we must first address the basic exegetical question of what Paul means by hardening.

8.3.e.2. *The Meaning and Means of Hardening*

Paul uses the verb σκληρύνω for the hardening of Pharaoh, which the LXX uses as its main term for the concept in the exodus narrative, reflecting its use to translate the main verb for hardening used in the Hebrew text, חזק ('to strengthen/harden').[194] In light of Paul's appeal to Exodus, the exodus narrative's usage is most determinative for his meaning here. The basic meaning of σκληρύνω in the exodus narrative mirrors the basic meaning of the Hebrew terms used for hardening there, 'to make stubborn, unyielding, obstinate', which is also the basic meaning of the term in the New Testament generally, though it is only used five other times (Acts 19.9; Heb. 3.8, 13, 15; 4.7), and the most common meaning in the rest of the LXX. It also carries an added nuance of strength ('to make strong') in the Exodus context, where it gets applied to the heart/will and applies to the strengthening of

---

193. As Moo, *Romans*, 596–97, notes, 'while the Greek word is a different one, most scholars recognize that Paul's references to Israel's "hardening" in Rom. 11:7 and 25 are parallel to the hardening here'.

194. The LXX uses σκληρύνω for hardening even more than the Hebrew text uses חזק, 14 times as opposed to 12, which is accounted for by its use of σκληρύνω to translate the two instances of the Hebrew word קשה in the exodus narrative (7.3; 13.15) as well as one of the occurrences of כבד (10.1), while opting to use κατισχύω to translate חזק one time (7.13).

an already freely formed will.[195] When set against the Almighty God, the idea of stubbornness becomes tinged with the sense of boldness.[196] Paul here conceives of God as making ethnic Israel of his day unyielding to the claims of the gospel message. Just as God made Pharaoh stubbornly resistant to his call for Israel's release partly as a judgment for his sin, so he had made ethnic Israel in the time of the New Covenant stubbornly resistant to the call of the apostolic gospel in judgment for their sin.[197]

But what is involved in God making ethnic Israel stubborn? As we have found repeatedly in Romans 9, the Old Testament background to which Paul points is suggestive for understanding his argument. It is especially so for Paul's conception of hardening in 9.18 since it is certain that he has derived it from the broad original context of his quotation. Our exegesis of Exod. 9.16 and its context revealed that God typically strengthened Pharaoh's already self-established will to resist him in an indirect and natural manner rather than in a direct, supernatural work in Pharaoh's heart. That is, the divine hardening of Pharaoh's heart frequently took the form of some external action of God that provoked Pharaoh to obstinacy rather than some sort of direct, supernatural infusion of stubbornness into Pharaoh's heart or direct divine control of his will or withdrawal of assisting divine grace. I would suggest that the hardening of Israel with which Paul's argument has to do is of

195.   See our treatment of the Hebrew terms in ch. 6.5. above. It might be objected that while the Hebrew term חזק can certainly mean 'to strengthen', it is questionable whether the Greek term σκληρύνω can. But 'strength' is a natural connotation of 'hardness', and can even be seen as part of its meaning in the literal usage of the word in some occurrences (see e.g., Arist., *Part. an.*, 1.1; 2.8-9; 3.1; 4.7, 9; 9.7; Theophrastus, *Lap.* 42–43; idem, *Caus. pl.*, 5.4.1). Moreover, words derive their meaning from context, and the context of the exodus narrative suggests a strengthening of Pharaoh's will as laid out in our exegesis of the passage. Furthermore, the natural connotation of 'strength' seems to be the most obvious root of the LXX's usage of the term for severity/harshness, amounting to a strong/intense action, as e.g., when 'the hand of the sons of Israel went, going and hardening [which equates to increasing in strength/intensity] against Jabin King of Canaan, until they utterly destroyed Jabin King of Canaan' (Judg. 4.24); cf. Gen. 49.7; 2 Sam. 19.44; 2 Chron. 10.4; 1 Macc. 2.30. Since the word itself can suggest strength, the Exodus context suggests this nuance, and the word translates a Hebrew word that most basically means 'to strengthen' and carries this meaning in the exodus narrative, it is likely that Paul's use here carries this sense too. The use of κατισχύω in Exod. 7.13 throws an interesting twist into the mix. On the one hand, it could be argued that since this word more clearly has to do with strength, then the LXX translator should have used it when he wanted to indicate strength as involved in hardening. But since σκληρύνω is fit for indicating strength, and 7.13 is the lone use of κατισχύω with no obvious reason for its use over against σκληρύνω, it rather suggests that the LXX translator uses σκληρύνω and κατισχύω synonymously, supporting the idea of strength in the LXX's use of σκληρύνω in the exodus narrative. Be this as it may, a connotation of strengthening is not essential to our interpretation of Paul, which works perfectly well with the meaning of 'stubborn/unyielding' alone.

196.   Though this nuance is far more pronounced in the Exodus context than in the Romans context.

197.   On the early church's view of contemporary Israel as sinful and liable to God's judgment, see e.g., S. H. Travis, 'Judgment', *DJG*, 408–11 (409, 411); Abasciano, *Romans 9.1-9*, 102–04.

the same character, though of course, with different divine action provoking to obstinacy fitted to those involved and their specific context.

Specifically, drawing on our exegesis of Romans 9 so far as well as the context of Romans 9–11, I would suggest that Paul's conception of the way that God made ethnic Israel of Paul's day resistant to the gospel has to do with the very objection to the gospel that Paul is now addressing, that God would be unrighteous to choose his people by faith in Christ rather than by works or ancestry. What Paul regarded as having provoked the vast majority of ethnic Israel to stubbornly resist God's overtures in the gospel is God's sovereign act of making elect status conditional on faith in Christ apart from works or ancestry.[198] As Paul says in his concluding summary to the argument of Romans 9, Israel did not obtain righteousness[199] – which includes elect status – 'because [they pursued it] not by faith, but as by works. They stumbled over the stone of stumbling, just as it is written, "Behold, I lay in Zion a stone of stumbling and a rock of offence, and the one who believes in him will not be put to shame"' (9.32b-33). The language used here indicates Israel's taking offence at Christ, the stumbling stone, an offence that leads to rejection of Christ and is tied up with Israel's pursuit by works of the Law and righteousness.[200] Indeed, concerning the ethnic Israel of Paul's day 10.3-4 goes on to tell us that, 'seeking to establish their own [righteousness], they did not submit to the righteousness of God. For Christ is the end of the Law for righteousness to everyone who believes'. In context, this reveals that Paul believed his fellow Jews rejected God's call to believe in Christ for righteousness because they insisted on seeking to establish their own righteousness in the Law.

All of this accords with the picture Acts paints of Jewish response to Paul's gospel ministry. According to Acts, Paul was controversial among even

---

198. This is not to say that this is the only factor in Paul's estimation, but that it is the one especially in view in Romans 9–11. Certainly Paul regarded Christ's crucifixion as a major factor in Jewish rejection of the gospel (1 Cor. 1.22-23). Moreover, it is important to note that my description of the hardening in Rom. 9.18 does not speak to whether there are other types of divine hardening of human beings in Scripture, such as a more direct, deterministic type or another indirect type consisting of the withdrawal of divine grace needed to submit to the divine will. There may be other types of hardening in Scripture or even in Paul, but I am describing the specific kind of hardening Paul has in view in 9.18. Cf. Piper, *Justification*, 178 n. 31, who distinguishes between a reversible hardness (citing Eph. 4.18 and 2 Cor. 3.14) and a decisive hardening he believes to be in view in 9.18.

199. Romans 9.31 more specifically says that Israel did not attain the Law of righteousness, but not attaining the Law of righteousness implies not attaining the righteousness connected to it. Moreover, the contrasting parallel with Gentiles obtaining righteousness in 9.30 pushes concern for Israel's failure to obtain righteousness to the forefront along with the Law in 9.31-32. Interpreters regularly speak of these verses as indicating Israel's failure to obtain righteousness.

200. See the lexicons (e.g., BDAG) on προσκόπτω and σκάνδαλον. Evans, 'Paul', treats identification of the stumbling stone as Christ (565 n. 19) and as the concept of righteousness by faith (566) as the same. In his judgment, 'According to Paul's argument it is the concept that righteousness may be obtained through faith, as opposed to works, that has caused his fellow Jews to stumble (vv. 30-32)' (566). Cf. also Oropeza, 'Theodicy', 66, who suggests that the occasion of Israel's hardening 'has to do with relying on works for righteousness'.

Christian Jews,[201] who were zealous for the Law and had heard false reports about Paul that he taught Jews to forsake the Law (Acts 21.20-21; cf. the slanderous charges against Paul of antinomianism he refers to in Rom. 3.8). We get a glimpse of non-Christian Jewish opposition to Paul and his gospel in Acts' report of the charges of Asian Jews who seized him in the Temple, and the aftermath that ensued:

> 'Men, Israelites, help! This is the man who teaches all everywhere against the people, and *the Law*, and this place; and what is more, he has even brought *Gentiles* ['Ελληνας] into the Temple and has defiled this holy place'[202] ... Then all the city was provoked, and the people rushed together, and taking hold of Paul they dragged him out of the temple, and immediately the doors were shut. While they were seeking to kill him, a report came up to the commander of the [Roman][203] cohort that all Jerusalem was in confusion. (Acts 21.28, 30-31)

When Paul was allowed to address the violent crowd, they listened to him speak about Jesus as Lord, indeed as a supernatural figure, presumably known to them as having been crucified but believed by Christians to have risen from the dead (21.40–22.20). But as soon as he mentioned mission to the Gentiles, 'they raised their voices and said, "Away with such a fellow from the earth, for he should not be allowed to live!"' (22.22; NASB). What seems to have especially roused resistance in them to Paul's ministry is anything so much as even hinting at disparagement of the Law or Jewish ancestry. As Paul himself said in 1 Thess. 2.14-16, he believed the Jews 'both killed the Lord Jesus and the prophets, and drove us out. They are not pleasing to God, but hostile to all men, hindering us from speaking to the Gentiles so that they may be saved; with the result that they always fill up the measure of their sins. But wrath has come upon them to the utmost' (NASB).[204]

This construal of Paul's view of the hardening in Romans 9 receives confirmation from, on the one hand, the illumination and greater cogency it brings to the prominent theme developed in chapter 11 of the hardening/transgression/rejection/disobedience of Israel bringing about the salvation of the Gentiles (11.11-12, 15, 19-20, 30-31), and on the other hand, the strengthening of the connection between the concept of hardening in Romans 9 and 11 it yields. For in the typical understanding of this theme, it is not at all clear why ethnic Israel's transgression and rejection by God means the salvation of the Gentiles. Most commentators think the theme has to do with Paul's practice of turning to the Gentiles with the gospel in response to Jewish

---

201. Paul's wrangling with Judaizers in his ministry is evidence enough of that.

202. Tranlsation and emphasis mine here. The rest of the quotation that follows is from the NASB

203. I have replaced the NASB's italics with brackets for showing wording added to the original text for clarity.

204. Hence, given Pharaoh's oppression of Israel in the OT context, Munck's (*Christ and Israel*, 47–55) view that Paul conceives of Pharaoh as a type of Israel as persecutor of the Church is intriguing. Nonetheless, it is ultimately unconvincing because Paul shows no concern for this theme in his argument and it does not bear on any of his concerns in Rom. 9–11.

rejection of it (Acts 11.19-21; 13.44-48; 18.4-7; 19.8-10; 28.23-29).[205] But there is no particular reason why Jewish rejection of the gospel should be thought necessary for turning to the Gentiles. If the Jews received the gospel, then Christian evangelists could still have gone to the Gentiles.[206]

The view that Jewish rejection of the gospel was necessary for Gentile salvation because it was the apocalyptic plan of God faces a similar problem.[207] It does not provide any inherently necessary reason for Jewish rejection of the gospel to bring about Gentile salvation. God could have simply planned it differently and there is no particularly natural connection between the two as there is, for example, between the preaching of the gospel and people believing it. But making covenant membership and inheritance of the covenant promises contingent on faith in Christ apart from works or ancestry does provide a compelling rationale for the connection between Jewish resistance to the gospel and Gentile salvation, one for which there is strong evidence in the context of Romans 9–11, and that beyond the substantial evidence we have already mentioned.

First, there is the extended discussion of faith and the gospel in Romans 10 following upon material to which we have already drawn attention (9.31–10.4), Paul's explanation of ethnic Israel failing to obtain righteousness because they pursued it by works rather than faith – attempting to establish their own righteousness – and were offended at Christ, who 'is the end of the Law for righteousness to everyone who believes' (10.4). Paul continues his argument in the verses that follow by contrasting the righteousness based on the Law with the righteousness based on faith. Second, Paul explains the statement of the principle of 'Jewish rejection for the purpose of Gentile salvation' in 11.19-20 with the assertion that unbelieving Jews were cut off from the people of God because of their unbelief whereas believing Gentiles were incorporated into the people of God because of their faith. This implies that membership in the elect people of God being based on faith is what facilitates fulfilment of the purpose of incorporating Gentiles into the chosen people. And it furnishes a natural and intrinsic connection between the cutting off of unbelieving Jews and incorporation of believing Gentiles. That this principle of faith is the primary condition by which God determines the membership of the elect people of God is shown by the fact that Paul goes on

205.   Jewett, *Romans*, 674 n. 70, notes that this is the typical explanation.

206.   Cranfield's (*Romans*, 556) view, following Barth, 'that it was the Jews' rejection of Jesus Himself and their delivering Him to the Gentiles (cf. Mk 10.33; 15.1) which led to His death and so to the redemption of the world (of both Gentiles and Jews)' makes more sense, but it does not fit the context as well as our proposal; cf. Jewett's (ibid.) criticism, though his denial of Christological focus is curious given the broad context, esp. of ch. 10. It also does not fit the context of Jewish rejection of the Pauline/apostolic gospel of Christ (i.e., the gospel that includes Christ's death and resurrection) nor the characterization of Israel's transgression as presently still taking place (e.g., 11.31). It could be that this view could be combined with the one being advocated here, taking the distinct elements as part of a continuum of factors that are organically connected. But if so, the factor we are advocating is the one most in view in Romans 9–11.

207.   Advocated by Jewett, *Romans*, 674.

to explain that Gentiles who forsake faith will be cut off from God's people and Jews who come to faith will be grafted in (11.20d-24).

Third, in 11.5-6 Paul indicates that a remnant of ethnic Israel had been chosen by grace and that 'if [it is] by grace, [then it is] no longer on the basis of works; for otherwise, grace is no longer grace'. But it must be remembered that in 4.16-17 Paul presented faith as making heirship of the promises/elect status according to grace. He grounds grace in faith so that for heirship or sonship or justification or election (and so on) to be by grace is for them also to be by faith, and indeed, by grace because they are by faith.[208] Speaking of election by grace here is another way of speaking about election by faith, a point that is supported by Paul's sharp contrast of grace vs works in the style of his prominent faith vs works language in the epistle, not least in chs 9–11.[209] This then connects to the hardening mentioned in the next verse: 'What then? What Israel is seeking, this he did not obtain [cf. 9.31 in which Israel did not obtain the righteousness it pursued because they pursued it by works!], but the elect obtained [it] [cf. 9.30 in which Gentiles attained righteousness by faith] and the rest were hardened [cf. 9.32-33 in which Israel's pursuit of righteousness by works is interpreted as them taking offence at Christ]' (11.7). Jews who believed were therefore chosen by grace, but the rest were offended at Christ 'the end of the Law for righteousness to everyone who believes' and in this way hardened or made obstinate to the gospel of God's grace in Christ through faith apart from works or ancestry.

Fourth, returning to the context of Romans 9, our exegesis of 9.6-9 found that Paul saw the election of Isaac and the concomitant rejection of Ishmael as a type of the events of salvation-history that have dawned in the age of inaugurated covenantal fulfilment.[210] Ishmael is a type of ethnic Israel excluded from the covenant in order that the Abrahamic covenantal promise could be fulfilled whereas Isaac is a type of the Church, those who believe in Christ and are members of the New Covenant, heirs to the eschatological Abrahamic covenantal promises, and indeed, who are already enjoying their inaugurated fulfilment. Just as Ishmael, Abraham's physical descendant, had to be cut off from the covenant for its promise to be fulfilled, so Israel qua *ethnic* Israel had to be cut off from the covenant for its promise of bringing blessing to the Gentiles in Abraham to be fulfilled. Ethnicity and the Law intertwined with it had to be dropped as a basis for covenant membership so that the Gentiles could be included in the covenant by faith, a principle that also allows for Jews to remain in the covenant as long as they believe, making for fulfilment of God's covenant purpose to bless the world of both Jews and Gentiles.

We then found that in 9.10-13 Paul explains that the sovereign election of Jacob over Esau for covenant headship apart from works or ancestry maintained God's sovereignty over the basis of membership in the elect

---

208. See also ch. 5.3.d.3.b. above. Cf. Rom 5.2, which indicates that grace is accessed by faith.

209. Cf. our treatment of Paul's 'works' language in 9.12 in ch. 5.3.d.3.a. above.

210. See our exegesis of Rom. 9.6-9 in Abasciano, *Romans 9.1-9*, 177–215.

people and therefore enabled him to fulfil his purpose in election to bless the world by making faith the condition for covenant membership.[211] We have now found that Paul is further defending the righteousness of this principle in 9.14-18, which adds support to the suggestion that hardening is tied up with this principle of election by faith apart from works or ancestry so offensive to Paul's kinsmen according to the flesh. The fact that Paul began to discuss the same basic issue in Romans 3 (with hints of its live controversial nature in his own ministry; see 3.8) only to return to a fuller treatment of it in chs 9–11 shows how important the issue was in assessing the validity of Paul's gospel and gives still further support to our view of hardening in 9.18.

We conclude that the divine hardening of ethnic Israel mentioned in 9.18 refers to God making ethnic Israel unyielding to the claims of the gospel message by making covenant membership (i.e., elect status) conditional on faith in Christ apart from works or ancestry. But this does not make the divine hardening purely accidental as an unintended consequence of God's means of fulfilling his covenant promises. Just as the hardening of Pharaoh was a judgment on Pharaoh's sin and rebellion against God,[212] so Paul's use of Pharaoh as a type of unbelieving ethnic Israel intimates that God's choice of faith as the exclusive basis of covenant membership was meant *partly* to bring judgment upon Israel for the very ethnocentrism, pride and self-reliance that would lead them to seek to establish their own righteousness (10.3), take offence at Christ (9.32-33), 'the end of the Law for righteousness' (10.4), and become resistant to accepting the gospel of salvation by faith. As Paul argued earlier, faith precludes boasting whereas works permits and fosters it (3.27-30; 4.2ff.; cf. 2.17-24; 3.19-20; 1 Cor. 1.18-31; 4.7; Phil. 3.1-11; Eph. 2.8-9). Just as God made Pharaoh's own freely rebellious will to serve as its own punishment in the execution of ironic and poetic justice, so Paul's typology would suggest that God was now making ethnic Israel's own freely formed zeal for establishing their own righteousness by the Law to serve as its own judgment.

The view of hardening we have set forth finds further confirmation from our findings concerning Paul's handling of the concept in 2 Cor. 3.12-18 as it is drawn from Exodus 32–34, to which Paul alludes in Rom. 9.3 and from which he quotes in Rom. 9.15.[213] Paul's focus in the Corinthians context is on the self-hardening, sinful character and guilt of Israel; but insofar as it bears on the divine hardening of Israel, his discussion in 2 Corinthians 3 suggests a judicial divine hardening that is neither absolute nor inherently final nor totally prohibitive of anyone from turning to the Lord in faith. The case is similar in Rom. 1.23-32, where Paul uses the language of Psalm 106's interpretation of the golden calf episode to describe idolatry that receives the divine punishment of a type of hardening, the giving over of people to their sin so that their own sin becomes its own punishment.[214] At the same

211. See our exegesis of Rom. 9.10-13 in ch. 5 above.
212. We will address objections to this claim later in this chapter.
213. See Abasciano, *Romans 9.1-9*, 110–112 (cf. 103–04).
214. See ibid., 103–04.

time, our findings relative to Rom. 9.18 help to explain how those who are hardened can still turn to the Lord in faith since divine hardening is not a matter of divine deterministic control of the human will, but divine action that provokes a free response of obstinacy. Indeed, our exegesis of Exodus 1–15 discovered that the divine hardening actually increased Pharaoh's freedom of choice.

8.3.e.2.a. *Hardening and the Final Destiny of Individuals*

Interpreters have disagreed over the question of whether the divine hardening of Israel in Rom. 9.18 relates to the final destiny of individuals.[215] There seem to be three related issues here, whether the hardening of 9.18 concerns individuals or groups, whether it has to do with salvation, and whether it is final/irreversible. As for the first aspect of the question, just as we have seen that the election of God's people applies primarily to the Church as a corporate body and secondarily to the individuals who are members of that body, and the mercy of 9.15-16 refers primarily to the mercy of the corporate election of God's people, so here the hardening of Israel is best seen as applying primarily to ethnic Israel as a group and secondarily to individual 'Israelites' as members of the group.[216]

This follows naturally from our view of the hardening as accomplished by means of God making covenant membership contingent on faith in Christ apart from works or ancestry. It is as members of ethnic, Law-observant Israel that Jews of Paul's day might take umbrage at the proclamation that their works and ancestry were useless as a basis of covenant membership and inheritance. This method of hardening aims generally at Jews as a class without necessitating any particular Jew to become hardened nor preventing any particular Jew from believing. But it must be remembered that the hardening would impact individual Jews as it might arise in them as a partial consequence of their identity as Jews. So it is not that the hardening applies to the group to the exclusion of individuals or to individuals to the exclusion of the group, but to the group primarily, and then to individual members of the group as a partial consequence of their membership in it.

As for the second aspect of the question, our exegesis of 9.1-18 strongly favours the hardening of 9.18 as impacting salvation. Paul's whole argument in Romans 9 has related to eschatological covenantal election, which includes salvation as one of its main benefits. (Indeed, salvation is a fair one-word summary of the benefits of the New Covenant election of God's people.) Paul

---

215. See Piper, *Justification*, 175, for a statement of the issue and representatives of the two main views.

216. Contra e.g., Moo, *Romans*, 599; Schreiner, *Romans*, 511; idem, 'Individual', 34. Schreiner attempts to present a nuanced view that recognizes both the corporate and individual concerns in the passage. But he improperly relates the two perspectives. See Abasciano, 'Election', Schreiner's response ('Response'), and my rejoinder of sorts, 'Misconceptions'. Against Schreiner's argument from singular language in Paul's discourse, including 9.18, see Abasciano, 'Election', 358–60.

has referred to this covenantal election as mercy in 9.15-16, 18, and in the current verse he sets hardening in contrast to it.

The case for hardening in 9.18 relating to eternal destiny has been solidly established in my opinion by scholars such as Piper, Moo and Schreiner.[217] In brief, and in addition to what we have already said, the view is supported by Paul's use of mercy language and hardening language elsewhere, including his contrast of 'vessels of wrath prepared for destruction' with 'vessels of mercy which were prepared beforehand for glory' in the closely related 9.22-23, and his discussion of hardening in Romans 11, which is presented as a phenomenon that excludes the hardened from salvation. Earlier we concluded that hardening in 9.18 refers to bringing about resistance to the gospel. For Paul, faith in the gospel is what brings about salvation, and unbelief excludes from salvation. Therefore, hardening does impact the eternal destiny of the hardened.

However, the third aspect of the question under consideration brings perspective and balance to the damning effects of hardening. I would argue that the hardening of 9.18 (and Romans 9–11 generally) is not innately irreversible. As long as a person is hardened, that is, unyielding to the gospel, then he is by definition unbelieving, and hence separate from Christ and excluded from the New Covenant and its salvation. But when Paul considers hardening in more detail in Romans 11, he makes it clear that Jews who have been hardened might yet believe, which would entail them first becoming unhardened.[218]

We have already noted that in 11.7 'the rest' (οἱ λοιποί) are specifically not elect.[219] Indeed, they 'were hardened'. Yet Paul holds out hope that some of 'the rest' will yet come to believe. He magnifies his ministry to the Gentiles in order to provoke his kinsmen to jealousy over Gentile possession of Israel's covenant blessings, and thus to faith in Christ, and so save some of them (11.13-14). Moreover, 11.23 indicates that those who have been hardened and do not believe, and have therefore been cut off from the elect people, can be incorporated into the elect people again *if they come to faith*. Furthermore, in harmony with Paul's efforts to draw some of the hardened Jews of his day to faith *à la* 11.13-14, he speaks of God's purpose for ethnic

217. See Piper, *Justification*, 175–78 (most extensively); Moo, *Romans*, 596–97; Schreiner, *Romans*, 510–12, though I would not agree with all of their reasoning.
218. This is not a reference to the reversal of hardening in a mass conversion of Israel at the end of history, but a claim that Paul clearly believed that hardened Jews could turn from their hardened state now to faith in Christ. This avoids Schreiner's (*Romans*, 511–12) objection to the idea that the eventual removal of hardening for Israel refers to the removal of the hardening of all Israelites throughout history, though Dunn, *Romans*, 555, to whom Schreiner responds, neither says nor implies this. Moo's (*Romans*, 599) attempt to distinguish between the hardening of 9.18 as being individualistic vs the hardening of Romans 11 being corporate fails to account for Paul's hope to win as many Jews as possible in the present time. Moreover, the distinction he makes is invalid according to our exegesis; the hardening of 9.18 is corporate.
219. See note 135 in ch. 5 above.

Israel to receive mercy *now* (νῦν)[220] because of the mercy received by Gentiles in the same present time of Gentile reception of mercy (11.30-31). All of this ties into Paul's main purpose in writing Romans – to obtain support from a church with a Gentile majority for his upcoming mission to Spain, a mission that would be to both Jews and Gentiles, but that would prioritize Jews ('to the Jew first and to the Greek' (1.16)).[221] This is part of Paul's explanation of his controversial missionary practice of going to the Jew first and then to the Gentile, an explanation given as part of the defence of his gospel against its most pressing objection, all with a view toward persuading the church at Rome to support his mission to Spain.

The Old Testament background of Paul's argument also gives some support to the reversibility of the hardening of 9.18. For as we have seen, Exod. 9.16 in its original context exhibits a universalistic concern for all the earth – including Pharaoh and the Egyptians, Israel and all nations – to know God's supreme power, divinity and sovereignty, advancing YHWH's climactic covenant purpose of bringing blessing to the whole world through the seed of Abraham and contributing to Exodus' continuation and development of the story begun in Genesis. Thus, ideally, even the Egyptians, who are viewed by the narrative as in solidarity with their corporate head Pharaoh, could eventually find the blessing of God in Abraham.[222] However, such a meaning-effect could be muted because the text of Exodus shows no particular concern that Pharaoh, the focus of God's hardening judgment, would do so. Still, 'There is even a rabbinic tradition based on Ex 9:15f and 15:11 that Pharaoh was saved from the debacle at the sea and repented (Strack-Billerbeck, I, 647)'.[223]

But more importantly, the immediate context of Exod. 9.16 shows concern for the blessing of the servants of Pharaoh, who suffer God's judgment through his hardening of Pharaoh, and later get hardened themselves (9.34; 10.1). It also reports that some of Pharaoh's servants actually escaped the judgment of God brought on as a result of hardening by trusting in his word (9.18-21). Moreover, the later narrative eventually reports that a mixed multitude – which presumably included some Egyptians – actually joined Israel and left with them in the exodus (12.38). Finally, our analysis of hardening in the exodus narrative discovered that it was not a deterministic phenomenon, leaving open the possibility of a change of heart in the hardened no matter how unlikely given his freely formed proclivities.

All of this hints at the possibility of the reversibility of the hardening of Rom. 9.18. Two further considerations strengthen this subtle impulse of the

---

220.   While some manuscripts omit νῦν in 11.31, most commentators think it original, as Moo, *Romans*, 711 n. 2, observes.

221.   This was not Paul's only purpose in Romans of course. On the purposes of Romans in general and chs 9–11 in particular, and how these purposes relate, see Abasciano, *Romans 9.1-9*, 29–32.

222.   Munck, *Christ and Israel*, 47–49, emphasizes that Pharaoh is regarded as a representative of Egypt.

223.   Piper, *Justification*, 175. But there is also ancient tradition that Pharaoh was killed at the Red Sea (3 Macc. 6.4; 4 Ezra 1.10); see Kugel, *Traditions*, 609–10.

Old Testament context in the Romans context. First, Paul has alluded to more than one Old Testament passage in his argument already that carries the intertextual significance of God's purpose to embrace those whom he had rejected, including apostate Israel.[224] Indeed, this is the case with the previous types Paul has used – apostate Israel, Ishmael and Esau. This intertextual undercurrent in Paul's discourse would increase the volume of the muted note from the exodus narrative, and in any case, push towards construing the hardening of 9.18 as reversible.

Second, Paul goes on to argue explicitly that the divine judgment and hardening of Israel is for the purpose of mercy to both the Gentiles and the Jews (9.22-29; 11.11-32). Romans 9.22-23 is closely related to 9.17-18.[225] We will have to wait for the next volume of our analysis of Romans 9 to present our detailed exegesis of these verses and consideration of alternative views of them. At this point we only have space for limited comments relevant for understanding 9.18 and the reversibility of its hardening. In this vein, the first thing to note is that earlier in the epistle Paul had asked, with some language that is strikingly parallel to 9.22-23, 'Or do you despise the *riches* of his [God's] kindness and toleration and *patience*, not *knowing* that the kindness of God leads you to repentance? But according to your *hardness* and unrepentant heart you are storing up for yourself *wrath* in the day of *wrath* and revelation of the righteous judgment of God' (2.4-5; emphasis mine). As Piper observes, 'From this text it appears that God's long-suffering is an expression of his kindness and has the purpose of leading men to repentance'.[226]

In light of 9.22-23's development of 9.17-18, this suggests that God's bearing with hardened ethnic Israel and forestalling final judgment upon them is partly for the purpose of leading them out of their hardened state to repentance and faith, a conclusion that is strongly substantiated by the fact that Paul says that God's purpose for bearing with them is especially to 'make known the riches of his glory upon vessels of mercy' (9.23).[227] This fits well with the view of hardening that we have advanced as accomplished by the divine establishment of faith in Christ apart from works or ancestry as the basis of reception of the mercy of covenant membership. God sovereignly set faith as the condition of elective mercy in order that he could include

224. See Abasciano, *Romans 9.1-9*, 106 (on Exod. 32–34 in Rom. 9.3), 193–95 (on Gen. 21.12 in Rom. 9.7), and ch. 5.3.f.4. above (on Mal. 1.2-3 in Rom. 9.13).

225. See Piper, *Justification*, 180, 207; Moo, *Romans*, 596; Schreiner, *Romans*, 509–10; cf. Dunn, *Romans*, 558. Cranfield, *Romans*, 489, thinks we have no right to read 9.18 in light of 9.22.

226. Piper, *Justification*, 208. But Piper goes on to argue against the thrust of this observation. However, his argument is based on a view of the hardening and an interpretation of 9.14-23 that our exegesis has found deficient.

227. This purpose holds even if one regards the participle θέλων in 9.22 as causal. In that case, the two purposes are not necessarily inconsistent. God could desire to show his wrath and power against those who will not repent of their hardened condition (and indeed, desire that they store up wrath against themselves) while desiring that as many as would repent, do so, and become vessels of mercy instead. Indeed, God's overarching purpose is 'that he might have mercy on all' (11.32).

both Gentiles and Jews in the covenant and have mercy on all (cf. 11.32), fulfilling his covenant promise to bless the world. Thus, 9.24 continues with a statement that God has called the Church from both Jews and Gentiles with the stress on the calling of Gentiles (using οὐ μόνον/ἀλλά ('not only/but')).

This further fits with Paul's argument in chapter 11 that we looked at above. Paul seeks to win hardened Jews who are resistant to the gospel by making them jealous with the good news of God's mercy to whoever believes it, including Gentiles. Romans 9.23 uses the verb γνωρίζω ('to make known'), which refers to the making known of information and must partly refer in 9.23 to making known God's mercy of covenantal election apart from works or ancestry for all who believe.[228] As Paul says of ethnic Israel in 10.3, 'not knowing about the righteousness of God and seeking to establish their own, they did not submit to the righteousness of God'. Paul hoped that despite the offence of eliminating works or ancestry as a basis of covenantal membership and inheritance, Jews would be provoked to jealousy over Gentiles enjoying by faith the privileges first and foremost meant for Israel (note especially 9.23's references to the covenantal benefit of glory also referred to in 9.3),[229] and would therefore submit to the righteousness of God by faith and receive the mercy of sharing in the covenantal election and blessings of the elect people.

Romans 9.22's reference to God enduring with much patience vessels of wrath is parallel to his allowing Pharaoh to remain alive in 9.17's quotation of Exod. 9.16, where it is phrased as having 'raised up' Pharaoh.[230] But how would allowing hardened ethnic Israel to continue in their stubborn resistance to the gospel rather than destroying them immediately in judgment work toward the accomplishment of the revelation of the riches of God's glory upon the vessels of his mercy? First, it allows them opportunity to repent and so become vessels of mercy themselves, which of course helps to reveal the riches of God's mercy. Second, since God's purpose in covenant and election is to bless all the nations of the earth including Israel, or as 11.32 puts it, to have mercy on all, and his practical goal is to provoke Israel to jealousy and faith through the salvation of the Gentiles, unbelieving ethnic Israel is an essential part of his intended audience for the proclamation of the gospel just as they are for Paul's mission to the Jew first and then to the Gentile.

8.3.e.3. *Hardening as a Means to the Worldwide Revelation of God's Power and Name, and the Accomplishment of the New Covenant Election*

We are now in a position to answer the two questions that we posed before our analysis of the meaning of hardening. These questions emerged from

---

228.   Cf. Paul's use of γνωρίζω in 16.26 to refer to the preaching of the gospel/the mystery to all nations as well as the use in Ephesians of making known the mystery of Gentile inclusion in Israel through Christ/the gospel (1.9; 3.3, 5, 10; 6.19). Cf. also 1 Cor. 15.1; Gal. 1.11; Col. 1.27.

229.   On the covenantal privileges of Israel as an important element of Paul's argument in Rom. 9, see our exegesis of 9.4-5 in Abasciano, *Romans 9.1-9*, 115–42, and specifically on the important privilege of 'glory' (δόξα), 124–27.

230.   See note 38 above.

Paul's use of Exod. 9.16 and its ramifications for the divine purposes in hardening ethnic Israel of Paul's day, which, by way of review, are: (a) for God to choose his people in a new covenant developing and fulfilling the Abrahamic covenant; (b) making his power and name known in all the earth; and (c) fulfilling his climactic covenant purpose of blessing the world. First, how does the hardening of Israel in Paul's day lead to the revelation of God's power and name in all the earth? The answer is multifaceted, with each facet based on the nature of the hardening of Israel as accomplished by God's sovereign act of making elect status conditional on faith in Christ apart from works or ancestry.

Given the nature of hardening, it leads to the revelation of God's saving power because its cause is at one and the same time a central element of the gospel, which is 'the power of God for salvation for all who believe, both to the Jew first and to the Greek' (1.16). On the other hand, in leading to hardening, that same cause also leads to the revelation of God's power in judgment. For the message of God's salvation by faith in Christ apart from works or ancestry provoked the vast majority of Jews to stubborn resistance to Christ and the righteousness of God in him. Such obstinacy brings God's judgment, and in part, God intentionally chose faith as the exclusive basis of covenant membership in order to bring judgment upon Israel for the very ethnocentrism, pride and self-reliance that would lead them to reject Christ and the gospel.

Moreover, hardening fuelled by God's gracious election by faith serves to proclaim God's name in all the earth because faith as the basis of election is the very thing that opens up God's salvation to the Gentiles. It also testifies to God's supreme divinity and sovereignty because it displays his sovereign freedom and Lordship over election, salvation, mercy and judgment. It further demonstrates his merciful character, as it has as its goal to bring God's mercy to the world and ironically to bring the Jews ultimately to faith and salvation as Gentile enjoyment of Israel's privileges provokes Jews to jealousy. Moreover, the very message of the mercy of covenantal election and salvation offered as a free gift to be received by faith is itself the proclamation of God's mercy. That is, the very means of hardening Israel is the proclamation of God's mercy.

Second, how does the manifestation of God's power and name brought about by the hardening of Israel in Paul's day – and God's sovereign establishment of election and covenant inheritance by faith apart from works or ancestry that naturally provokes that hardening – lead to the New Covenant election of God's people and the blessing of the world? The New Covenant election is itself an expression of God's saving power facilitated by the divine establishment of faith in Christ apart from works or ancestry as its condition and naturally accompanied by hardening of ethnic Israel. Moreover, the proclamation of God's name (including his supreme divinity and sovereignty, and his mercy) and his saving power in the gospel are part of the means by which people enter the New Covenant and so come to share in its election and the election of its corporate head, Jesus Christ. At the same time, the proclamation of God's name *in all the earth*, serves the universalistic scope of the New Covenant and the divine purpose for its election to bless the world. Indeed, the proclamation of God's supreme divinity and sovereignty can now be declared in a new way that beckons all nations to come – *as Gentiles* – to this Almighty, supreme, sovereign God by faith in Christ and be welcomed into membership in the New Covenant with its eternal inheritance. Furthermore, just as the New Covenant election is an expression of God's saving power, it is also an expression of his mercy and therefore his name. Consequently, the manifestation of God's name in mercy leads to the New Covenant election, which, based on faith rather than works or ancestry, leads to the blessing of the all the nations of the earth in Abraham.

Thus, Paul's citation of Exod. 9.16 provides strong support for his defence of God's righteousness (in the form of faithfulness to his covenant promises to Israel) in sovereign election. Focusing on hardening as the negative side of God's sovereign election vis-à-vis ethnic Israel of his time, Paul cites an Old Testament text from a context that portrays hardening as a fulfilment of God's covenant promises to Israel.[231] As a natural corollary of the establishment of faith apart from works or ancestry as the sole basis of covenantal election in the New Covenant, Paul's metalepsis created by his quotation of Exod. 9.16 suggests that the hardening of ethnic Israel does not violate his covenant promises to his people, but fulfils them by making his power and name known in all the earth and leading to the New Covenant election of God's people, which brings the Abrahamic covenant promises to realization, especially its climactic promise of blessing all the nations of the earth. Thus Paul supports the righteousness of God in sovereign election by faith apart from works or ancestry.

8.3.e.4. *A Conditional Hardening*

Some interpreters think that 9.18b must refer to unconditional hardening.[232] But this conclusion is chiefly based on their exegesis of Romans 9 up to this point (especially 9.15-16), which takes Paul to be articulating and defending unconditional election. They rightly point out, for example, that the two halves of 9.18 are strictly parallel and must be understood in the same way with respect to the way their contrasting actions are carried out. But since 9.18a basically restates the thrust of 9.15-16, they interpret 'he has mercy on whom he desires' to mean that he bestows his mercy of election for salvation *unconditionally*.

But our exegesis has found that Paul has not been arguing for unconditional election in Romans 9, but for a sovereign one for which God has set the condition according to his own good pleasure and purposes. Indeed, the thrust of 9.15-16 is that God bestows the mercy of covenantal election and blessing on whatever people he chooses based on whatever conditions he chooses. Romans 9.18, therefore, means the same thing. Correspondingly, 9.18b means that God hardens in judgment whatever

---

231. See e.g., our exegesis of Exod. 2.23–4.20 in ch. 6.3.–4. above.
232. For example, Piper, *Justification*, 171–75; Moo, *Romans*, 597–600.

people he chooses based on whatever conditions he chooses. The matter is at his discretion.[233]

The tight parallel between 9.18a and b further implies the conditional nature of hardening, for as we saw, the mercy in view in 9.15-16, and therefore in 9.18a, is the mercy of covenantal election that first required forgiveness of a people that had transgressed grievously. As Murray observes, 'the sin and ill-desert presupposed in hardening is also presupposed in the exercise of mercy. Both parts of this verse rest upon the premise of ill-desert'.[234] This is strongly confirmed by Paul's appeal to the exodus narrative and the hardening of Pharaoh's heart.

Many commentators recognize that God's hardening of Pharaoh's heart was a conditional judgment on Pharaoh for his sin.[235] But some insist that a closer look at the text of the exodus narrative reveals that God's hardening of Pharaoh's heart was actually unconditional, without basis in anything in Pharaoh.[236] However, our exegesis of Exodus 1–15 has found this claim to be incorrect. An even closer examination reveals that the text presents the divine hardening of Pharaoh as a conditional judgment on him for his wickedness and his rebellion against the Lord (see ch. 6 above).[237] Vis-à-vis Paul's application to

233.   Piper, ibid., offers two more arguments. But one is based on his interpretation of 9.11, 13, and our exegesis of those verses in this monograph contradicts Piper's. The other reason he cites is based on his interpretation of Exod. 9.16 and its context of Exod. 4–14. Yet again our exegesis of the same passage in this monograph contradicts Piper's. In our view, this leaves no basis for Piper's position.

234.   Murray, *Romans*, 2.29. Piper, ibid., n. 26, criticizes Murray as being inconsistent with Murray's own interpretation of 9.6-13 as arguing for unconditional salvific election. Murray might be inconsistent here, but in my view the problem is that 9.1-13 does not teach unconditional election. The reason Piper gives to counter Murray's position is that the mercy of election in 9.11f. is unconditional. But as we have seen in our exegesis of those verses, it is debatable whether the election referred to in 9.11f. is unconditional. Nevertheless, as we have also pointed out, even if it is, unconditionality there would apply only to the election of the individual corporate covenant head, not to the election of individuals to become members of the covenant. The election of individual members of the covenant would be conditional on their union with the covenant head and his people. See ch. 5.3.e.1. above.

235.   For example, Fitzmyer, *Romans*, 568; Morris, *Romans*, 361–62; Hendriksen, *Romans*, 326; Murray, *Romans*, 2.29; Forster/Marston, *Strategy*, 64–65, 261; R. H. Mounce, *Romans* (NAC, 27; Nashville: Broadman & Holman, 1995), 200; Leenhardt, *Romans*, 254.

236.   For example, Beale, 'Hardening'; Piper, *Justification*, 159–81; Moo, *Romans*, 597–600; Schreiner, *Romans*, 510.

237.   Moo, *Romans*, 598, offers another reason from the Romans context to question whether Paul would intend for his readers to take God's hardening of Pharaoh to be in any way a response to Pharaoh's wickedness. He argues that we would expect Paul to point out such conditional response on God's part in reply to the objection mentioned in 9.19, which Moo essentially understands to be, 'why does God blame us for doing what he irresistibly causes us to do'? But this misconstrues the sense of the objection in 9.19, which is, as we have already seen (see ch. 3.7.a.2. above), really taking up the question of 3.5, asking why God blames people if their unrighteousness demonstrates his righteousness. But even if Moo's understanding of the question were correct, the OT background would undermine the point he tries to make out of it with its stress on the conditionality of God's treatment of Israel and the nations (Jer. 18). There is much to say about Rom. 9.19ff., but that will have to wait for our next volume and its detailed intertextual exegesis of that passage.

Israel, this coheres with early Christianity's view of contemporary ethnic Israel as sinful and under God's judgment and judicial hardening[238] as well as Paul's view of hardening elsewhere (as discussed earlier) and his view of unbelieving ethnic Israel in Romans 9–11 as under God's judgment, where he cites some of the harshest prophetic judgment passages of Israel's own Scriptures against his own people in the style of the Old Testament prophets.[239] Even in the introduction to his argument, Paul alludes to Exodus 32–34, suggesting the Israel of his day to be idolatrous and apostate, separated from Christ under the deadly curse of the covenant (9.1-3).[240]

Some interpreters think that whether God hardened Pharaoh conditionally or unconditionally in Exodus is irrelevant for Paul's argument, but that Paul's focus is God's initiative and purpose, and that the issue of conditionality plays no role here[241] or that he presents hardening as unconditional whether or not Exodus does.[242] But this fails to appreciate the importance of the Old Testament context for Paul and his argument and that he expects his audience to know that context, to which his quotation of Exod. 9.16 functions as a pointer. It also fails to account for the Pauline and early Christian tradition concerning hardening mentioned above. It further fails to reckon with the fact that early Jewish tradition generally understood the hardening of Pharaoh's heart as a just punishment on him for his severe oppression of God's people (see ch. 7 above) and that Paul could expect his audience naturally to assume this view without indication from him to the contrary.

Nonetheless, there is wisdom in the reminder that Paul's focus is on God's initiative and purpose rather than trying to justify God's treatment of Pharaoh by pointing to his deserving punishment. That would not have been something Paul's audience would have questioned, and Paul is not attempting to justify the idea of divine hardening in the abstract, but of God's hardening of Israel in relation to his covenant promises to her.[243] It has been Paul's intent to argue that God's rejection and hardening of Israel qua ethnic Israel does not violate his covenant promises to his people, but on the contrary, fulfils them by working toward the inclusion of the Gentiles in the covenant in accordance with the climactic covenant promise of blessing all the nations of the earth in Abraham and at the same time allowing for ethnic Jews to possess fully the promises on the same basis as the Gentiles, faith in Jesus Christ. In

238.   See note 197 above.

239.   Cf. Evans, 'Paul', 570.

240.   See our exegesis of 9.1-3 in Abasciano, *Romans 9.1-9*, 89–115.

241.   See e.g., Osborne, *Romans*, 250–51, although he thinks Paul does eventually reveal in 9.30-33 that hardening is conditional on refusal to believe.

242.   See e.g., Dunn, *Romans*, 545–55, although he thinks Paul's limited focus here makes it doubtful that he has eternal reprobation in mind, and that he later expands it to include human responsibility and hardening as partial and temporary.

243.   Still, the consideration that God's hardening of Pharaoh's heart was a just, well-deserved judgment for wicked behaviour largely resolves the theological problem of the matter (see ch. 6.22. above for a brief summary), even if our view of the nature of the hardening as non-deterministic is rejected in favour of a more traditional, deterministic view.

this way Paul supports 9.14's denial of unrighteousness with God with the words of 9.18b, 'he hardens whom he desires', which interpret the quotation of Exod. 9.16 in Rom. 9.17.

While 9.17 can be directly related to 9.14 as a ground, more technically 9.17 and 18b together ground 9.14 with respect to the negative side of God's sovereign election, with 18b carrying the logical stress in its expression of the significance of 9.17. At the same time, 9.18a sums up 9.15-16, and together these two verses ground 9.14 with respect to the positive side of the divine sovereign election. Hence, 9.18 sums up Paul's argument for the righteousness of God in election by faith apart from works or ancestry in 9.14-18. Next, Paul's argument will move to consider an objection to the principle annunciated in 9.18a and b by which he has defended God's righteousness. But we will have to leave that for the next volume in our exegesis of Romans 9.

8.4. *Summary/Conclusion*[244]

Romans 9.17 and the second half of v. 18 together ground 9.14's insistence on God's righteousness vis-à-vis the negative side of God's sovereign election. Verse 18b states the significance of 9.17 and thus bears the logical weight of these two verses. At the same time, 9.18a sums up 9.15-16, which together ground 9.14 with respect to the positive side of the divine sovereign election. Hence, 9.18 sums up Paul's argument for the righteousness of God in election by faith apart from works or ancestry in 9.14-18, which is founded upon Exod. 33.19b and 9.16. Romans 9.14-18, headed by its main point in 9.14 of denying that there is unrighteousness with God, most precisely supports the purpose statement of 9.11c-12b, which maintains that God's purpose to save the world is to be fulfilled not on the basis of works but on the basis of God's faith-based call. Romans 9.11c-12b in turn most precisely supports 9.8, which asserts that all and only those who believe in Christ are regarded as God's covenant people to whom the promises were made. Romans 9.8 in turn most precisely supports 9.6b, which asserts that not all ethnic Israelites are part of the true Israel, to whom the covenant promises were actually made. And 9.6b finally supports 9.6a, the thesis statement of all of Romans 9–11, the insistence that God has been faithful to his promises to Israel.

Focusing in more specifically on 9.14-18, the passage emerges from 9.10-13's contention, in defence of God's election of the Church by faith and rejection of unbelieving ethnic Israel despite their works and ancestry, that God has the right to choose his people according to his own good pleasure, for any reason he deems appropriate (including specifically faith apart from works or ancestry). This leads Paul to consider further the objection that his gospel of justification (which includes elect status and heirship to the

244.   For summaries of our research of interpretive traditions surrounding Paul's OT quotations, see the last paragraph of ch. 7.1. above for Exod. 33.19b, and 7.2.j. above for Exod. 9.16.

covenant promises) by faith apart from works or ancestry makes God out to be unrighteous in the sense of unfaithful to his covenant promises to Israel. Paul vehemently denies that God is unrighteous, and supports his assertion with two quotations of Scripture that point to their original Old Testament contexts. Indeed, as with Paul's other scriptural allusions in Romans 9 so far, we have found that knowledge of their original contexts is essential for fully understanding his argument.

The first quotation comes from Exod. 33.19b, answering the charge of divine unrighteousness from the perspective of God's nature as well as the nature of Israel's election from its beginning. The quotation's original context is remarkably apt for addressing the charge to which Paul responds and for the argument he makes. For the charge he addresses has to do with the justification of God's election of the Church by faith in Christ, the mediator of the New Covenant, apart from works or ancestry, and the concomitant rejection of ethnic Israel from the covenant. In Exodus, the words Paul quotes are a divine pronouncement answering what amounts to Moses' request that God restore covenantal election and its blessings to rejected Israel, from whom the divine election had been withdrawn due to the people's idolatrous apostasy tied up with reliance on a means of mediating the election-bestowing presence of God other than the man the Lord had chosen. Moreover, the pronouncement in its original context means that God has mercy on whomever he chooses based upon whatever conditions he establishes, most specifically referring to the mercy of corporate covenantal election of the people of God. This is exactly the sort of point that Paul needs to make in order to defend his position effectively.

The metalepsis created by Paul's quotation of Exod. 33.19b defends the righteousness of God in sovereign election by pointing to the fact that the fundamental nature of Israel's election involved its subjection to the sovereign will of God. God cannot validly be charged with unfaithfulness to his promises to Israel on the supposition that Israel is to be defined by works and ancestry when God possesses the right to define Israel according to his own good pleasure. Moreover, the covenant itself contained the principle that God would have mercy on those who repent of their sin, maintain covenant relationship with him and who are connected to his righteous and faithful covenant mediator, and that he would reject those who are otherwise. God can hardly be charged with infidelity to his covenant promises for doing just what he said he would do in the covenant.

The transumption of Exod. 33.19b also points to the very nature of God when relating to sinful humanity as revealed in Scripture, to which Jews and Christians of Paul's time would have looked for the standard of righteousness. For Exod. 33.19b is a summary declaration of God's name or character. By showing that Scripture reveals that God's character when interacting with sinful humanity is to determine sovereignly the beneficiaries of his mercy, including any conditions for choosing them, Paul shows that the charge that God would be unrighteous to choose his people apart from works or ancestry is empty. For it would be unthinkable that

God's righteous character according to Scripture would be at odds with his covenant promises to Israel recorded in Scripture. In his use of Exod. 33.19b for application to his own time of inaugurated eschatological fulfilment, Paul has both identified a general principle about how God acts in relation to sinful humanity and invoked salvation-historical considerations about the covenant God has been accused of violating on the granted assumption that Paul's gospel is true.

Romans 9.16 presents Paul's inference from and interpretation of Exod. 33.19b/Rom. 9.15, drawing the logical stress of his argument in 9.15-16 in support of the denial of divine unrighteousness in 9.14. The verse most specifically means that the bestowal of mercy that is the election of God's covenant people is (rightly) at the discretion of the mercy-bestowing God, as are any stipulations he chooses to lay down for the bestowing of his mercy. Election here most precisely refers to the corporate election of a people as God's covenant partner, heir to the covenant promises and blessings, which include salvation. Not even human resolve to keep the Law or works in actual wholehearted and vigorous keeping of the Law can command God's mercy. Since God is rightly free to bestow his mercy as he sees fit, he cannot legitimately be accused of unrighteousness for choosing his people by faith in Christ rather than by works or ancestry, nor for rejecting from his covenant those who do not believe, points that are grounded in the nature of God and the nature of his covenant with Israel, as shown by Exod. 33.19b (Rom. 9.15).

Whereas 9.15-16 took up the positive side of God's sovereignty in election that was articulated in 9.13b by 'Jacob I loved', 9.17-18 proceeds to take up the negative side that was articulated in 9.13c by 'but Esau I hated'. Just as the former offered a supporting Scripture citation (9.15) for God's righteousness in sovereign election followed by an inference stating the Scripture's significance (9.16), so Paul now gives further scriptural support (9.17) followed by an inference stating the Scripture's significance (9.18b), but this time with special reference to the negative side of God's sovereign election – covenantal rejection and hardening. This second quotation that Paul employs for the righteousness of God's sovereign election comes from Exod. 9.16 and is yet another invocation of the Old Testament that is striking in its appropriateness for Paul's argument. In its original context, Exod. 9.16 is part of a statement of God's incomparable power and sovereignty in forestalling fatal judgment on Pharaoh despite his arrogant rebellion against the Lord, a statement formally aimed at bringing Pharaoh to acknowledge YHWH's supremacy and to submit to the divine will. In Romans 9, Paul is arguing for God's rightful absolute sovereignty over election and also aims to bring his hearers to acknowledge it and submit to the divine will. Moreover, Paul's appeal to Pharaoh is apropos for taking up the negative side of God's sovereignty in election – judgment and hardening – for in the exodus narrative, God judges and hardens Pharaoh, and this relates to the election of the people of God and the fulfilment of God's covenant promises.

Specifically, in Exodus the judgment and hardening of Pharaoh facilitates the election of the people of God and the fulfilment of God's covenant promises. Just as Paul has used other figures from salvation history as types of unbelieving and rejected ethnic Israel in his argument in Romans 9, so in 9.17-18 he puts forth Pharaoh as a type of hardened, unbelieving and rejected ethnic Israel. His quotation suggests that just as God hardened Pharaoh to bring about the renewed election of his people and to advance his plan for fulfilling the climactic covenant promise of blessing all the nations in Abraham, so he has hardened unbelieving ethnic Israel in the time of covenant fulfilment to accomplish the same purposes. Paul's typology therefore vindicates God's righteousness consisting in faithfulness to his covenant promises to Israel vis-à-vis God's election of the Church by faith apart from works or ancestry and rejection of unbelieving ethnic Israel despite its works and ancestry. For it conveys that, far from violating God's covenant promises to Israel, the hardening and rejection of ethnic Israel actually contribute to fulfilling them. Even the wording Paul chose for his quotation of Exod. 9.16 highlights God's universal covenantal purpose behind the hardening of Israel, not to mention his own sovereignty and initiative in these matters.

Paul's quotation applies to the revelation of God's power facilitated by forestalling final judgment upon unbelieving ethnic Israel and hardening her, which also facilitates the proclamation of God's name in all the earth. Informed by his intertext in its context, Paul speaks of God's power as Creator in the sense of his supreme divine power and sovereignty with special reference to its exercise in judgment and mercy/salvation. Similarly informed by the Old Testament background of Rom. 9.15-18, he speaks of the proclamation of God's name in the sense of the proclamation of his incomparable sovereignty, supreme divinity, presence, nature, goodness and glory. Notably, this especially includes the proclamation of God's grace and mercy, which for Paul, would undoubtedly involve the proclamation of his sovereign plan for the bestowal of God's grace and mercy in Jesus Christ to all who believe, whether Jew or Gentile.

In harmony with God's non-deterministic means of hardening in the exodus narrative, Paul's invocation of hardening has specific reference to God making ethnic Israel of his day unyielding to the claims of the gospel message by means of God's sovereign act of making elect status conditional on faith in Christ apart from works or ancestry. Just as the hardening of Pharaoh was a judgment on Pharaoh's sin and rebellion against God, so Paul's use of Pharaoh as a type of unbelieving ethnic Israel intimates that God's choice of faith as the exclusive basis of covenant membership was meant partly to bring judgment upon Israel for the very ethnocentrism, pride and self-reliance that would lead them to seek to establish their own righteousness, take offence at Christ and become resistant to accepting the gospel of salvation by faith. Moreover, just as God made Pharaoh's own freely rebellious will to serve as its own punishment in the execution of ironic and poetic justice, so Paul's typology would suggest that God was now making ethnic Israel's own freely formed zeal for establishing their own righteousness by the Law to serve as its own judgment. But even more so, the hardening of ethnic Israel was ironically for the purpose of fulfilling God's covenant promises to his people, most markedly culminating in the blessing of all the nations of the earth by including them in the covenant and its blessings along with Israel. For this cause of hardening – election by faith – is the very means for opening salvation up to the Gentiles while keeping salvation open for the Jews as well.

Indeed, Paul eventually reveals that the salvation of Gentiles, facilitated by the Jewish hardening phenomenon of the establishment of faith apart from works or ancestry as the sole basis of covenant membership/heirship, is intended in part to provoke the Jews to faith. The hardening Paul has in view is corporate, aimed generally at Jews as a class without necessitating any particular Jew to become hardened nor preventing any particular Jew from believing. God and Paul would prefer that every Jew turn from their hardheartedness to faith in Christ and so enter into the covenant inheritance first and foremost meant for them as part of the historic covenant people. That is part of the reason for raising Israel up in the sense of bearing with them patiently in their stubborn obstinacy and foregoing immediate final judgment. Indeed, God's purpose is to have mercy on all people (11.32). But if any will not repent, then it is God's will to pour out his wrath upon them.

Thus, the hardening of Israel that Paul has in view is a phenomenon that excludes the hardened from salvation as long as it is present. But it is not an irreversible state. Both God and Paul are at work to lead non-elect, hardened Jews to faith in Christ, and therefore New Covenant membership/elect status and salvation. Nor is hardening to be construed as an unconditional divine act as is sometimes asserted. Rather, in accordance with the conditional nature of God's hardening judgment upon Pharaoh, the hardening of Israel in Paul's day is to be understood as a conditional judgment, one that draws out ethnic Israel's own freely formed sinful will and makes it serve as its own punishment in the execution of ironic and poetic justice.

Paul shows a remarkable grasp of the original context of his quotation of Exod. 9.16. For it captures the main thrust of the entire exodus narrative. In that context it contributes to a statement of God's incomparable power and sovereignty, forming part of the main point of Exodus 1–15 that YHWH is the supreme, omnipotent God and sovereign who is to be trusted and obeyed above all others, a point intended to encourage the original audience of Exodus to reject idolatry and be loyal to YHWH and his covenant with Israel. Paul cites it partly to encourage his own audience in the time of eschatological fulfilment to reject the idolatry of trusting in a means of mediating God's covenant, presence and blessing other than God had ordained for the present eschatological age, Jesus Christ, and to be loyal to God and his covenant with Israel in its eschatological expression of the gospel and the New Covenant in Christ.

Indeed, Paul laboured, as did Moses in Exodus 32–34, to bring rejected Israel to the restoration of covenantal election and blessing in a new covenant established primarily with the Covenant Mediator and mediated to the people only through connection with him. He did so by going to the Jew first with the gospel of Christ (Rom. 1.16) and also, in the hope of provoking his kinsmen to jealousy and consequent faith, by magnifying his gospel ministry to the Gentiles (11.13-14). In carrying out this gospel ministry he now defends his gospel against its most pressing objection – that its truth would make God unrighteous in the sense of unfaithful to his promises to Israel – as he seeks to win support from the Christians in Rome for his upcoming Jew-prioritizing mission to Spain and the gospel that will stand at its heart. In 9.14-18, he has shown that God's election of the church on the basis of faith apart from works or ancestry and rejection of unbelieving ethnic Israel despite their works and ancestry is not unrighteous, for by virtue of God's sovereign nature as revealed in Scripture, the fundamental nature of his covenant with Israel from its inception, and the covenant promise-fulfilling nature of the divine hardening of Israel, God rightly 'has mercy on whom he desires, and he hardens whom he desires' (9.18). This enables him to pursue his purpose of having mercy on all by making it possible for him to make his mercy conditional on faith in Christ apart from works or ancestry 'so that the promise would be certain to all the seed, not to the one of the Law only, but also to the one of the faith of Abraham, who is the father of all of us' (4.16).

Chapter 9

Concluding Reflections

This investigation has picked up where my previous study of Rom. 9.1-9 left off, bringing our intertextual exegesis of Romans 9 to v. 18 with the intention of completing the exegesis of the chapter in a future volume. I have provided summaries of my exegesis at the end of chapters 5 and 8, so there is no need to retrace my understanding of Paul's argument in detail here. Rather, I would point out that my exegesis of Rom. 9.10-18 has confirmed the conclusions set forth in my first volume, both the general thrust of my exegesis of 9.1-9 and, by and large, the specific conclusions set out in the book's final chapter. Therefore, I would direct readers to those specific conclusions for the conclusions of the present work, bolstered now by further research and exegesis.

Amidst those original conclusions, I expressed the conviction that further intertextual study of Romans 9–11 would confirm our view of the contextual character of Paul's *Schriftgebrauch* and the profound influence of Scripture upon his theology and proclamation in general and his argument in Romans 9–11 in particular.[1] As just mentioned, our exegesis of 9.10-18 has done just that. This only strengthens our conviction that intertextual exegesis of the rest of Romans 9 will further confirm our findings to date. Of course, it remains to be seen how the results of our investigation of 9.19-33 will bear on our findings in vv. 1-18. But the present investigation has strengthened our expectation that further research will confirm the conclusions we have reached.

Two areas mentioned in our former conclusions stand out for having further light shed on them from new information discovered in the course of this investigation. I mention them not because they are necessarily more important than any of the other areas addressed in the conclusions to the first volume of our exegesis of Romans 9, but I single them out simply because the present study has added some new information about them beyond further confirmation.

---

1.   Abasciano, *Romans 9.1-9*, 235. For my response to the objection to this sort of approach represented by the work of Christopher Stanley, see now B. J. Abasciano, 'Diamonds in the Rough: A Reply to Christopher Stanley Concerning the Reader Competency of Paul's Original Audiences', *NovT* 49 (2007), 153–83.

First, in the conclusions to our first volume, I noted that our study of 9.1-9 provided some limited support to the New Perspective on Paul on various points. One of these points is Paul's opposition to Jewish ethnocentrism, obvious in 9.6-9. However, I also noted that observing Paul attack Jewish ethnocentrism in one text in no way suggests that he never attacks a traditional notion of works-righteousness elsewhere. Now in the present investigation we have seen that Paul does bring the idea of 'works' – in the sense of any human deed that could command the divine favour – into his argument.

Specifically, in 9.11c-12b Paul argues that God acted so that his purpose for election would be accomplished not by works, but by God, who names his people by faith. However, we also found that, while Paul speaks of human works of any kind (keeping in mind that faith does not fit into the category of 'works' in Paul's thought), he especially has works of the Law in view.[2] Thus, the traditional perspective that Paul's 'works' language can refer to any meritorious human effort or deed receives some support from our exegesis of 9.12. But the New Perspective also receives support as correctly identifying Paul's specific emphasis, particularly as we observed that the concepts of total Law-keeping and Jewish identity are inextricably linked and that Paul construed the divine purpose in these matters to be set on the blessing of the world facilitated by opening up salvation to the Gentiles. Similarly, we saw that in 9.16 Paul speaks of 'willing' in the sense of human resolve to do the Law, and of 'running' in the sense of actual wholehearted and vigorous keeping of the Law, for the purpose of asserting that these cannot constrain God's mercy, but that the bestowal of God's mercy is at his own discretion. Yet at the same time, Paul's argument makes it clear that no human activity whatsoever can command God's mercy.

All of this is in accord with my view that the New Perspective has identified an important emphasis in Paul's view of the Law and its works, but does not exhaust his view.[3] In some places Paul refers to works understood as human effort or achievement, which is part of the meaning in Rom. 9.12 even if not Paul's focus, and is implicitly excluded as commanding God's mercy in 9.16, though again, this is not Paul's focus. Paul's emphasis often falls upon ethnic

---

2.   We should be careful to remember that there is no *one* New Perspective, but that the New Perspective itself encompasses a variety of viewpoints. With respect to 9.12, Dunn, *Romans*, 543, thinks Paul refers specifically to works of the Law, while Wright, 'Romans', 637, concedes that Paul's 'emphasis is on "works" as the doing of good rather than evil', though he ties this to the rabbinic notion of the patriarchs' obedience to Torah even before it was given to Moses. For relating Romans 9–11 specifically to the New Perspective, see now N. T. Wright, 'Romans 9–11 and the "New Perspective"', in Wilk and Wagner (eds), *Explorations*, 37–54.

3.   First and most fully expressed in Abasciano, 'Romans 9.1-9', 353–55. It is worth noting that leading New Perspective scholar J. D. G. Dunn himself has never restricted 'the works of the Law' solely to circumcision, food laws and Sabbath, but admits that it refers to whatever the Law requires; see his view along with the complaint that he has been repeatedly misunderstood in J. D. G. Dunn, *The Theology of Paul the Apostle* (Grand Rapids/Cambridge: Eerdmans, 1998), 358 and esp. note 97. For balanced scholarship that is appreciative of the New Perspective and wisely adopts some of its insights without wholly embracing it, see the work of Bird (e.g., *Righteousness*).

identity markers in harmony with the covenantal orientation of first-century Judaism and early Christian concerns that the New Perspective has rightfully thrust to the forefront of Pauline scholarship, such as the place of Jews and Gentiles in God's economy of salvation. Such a concern for ethnicity is also present in 9.12, 16, given the context and the observation made above that Law-keeping and Jewish identity are inextricably linked.

On the other hand, it seems likely that Paul would have found the concept of staying in the covenant by obedience, and therefore what Sanders calls covenantal nomism, to be incompatible with God's grace.[4] It also seems likely that some first-century Jews presupposed God's grace on the ideological level in accordance with covenantal nomism while falling into a de facto legalism.[5] Moreover, Richard Bauckham is probably correct to point out that 'the basic and very flexible pattern of covenantal nomism could take forms in which the emphasis is overwhelmingly on meriting salvation by works of obedience to the Law, with the result that human achievement takes centre-stage and God's grace, while presupposed, is effectively marginalized'.[6] But at this point the foundation of the New Perspective is shaken,[7] though it has brought many valuable insights and a welcome corrective to the traditional conception of first-century Judaism as universally a religion of meritorious legalism. The better route is to recognize the complexity of Second Temple Judaism and that Paul sometimes attacked actual Jewish ethnocentrism, sometimes actual works-righteousness and perhaps often a complex mixture of the two, which is probably what Paul has in view in Romans 9.

The second area mentioned in the conclusions to our first volume that deserves further development in light of the findings of this investigation is the question of what text Paul used for his quotations. Our previous study

---

4.   A common point made by critics of the New Perspective; see e.g., Moo, *Romans*, 215–16, and the literature he cites in note 82; Bird, *Righteousness*, 95. It is also important to remember that there is a serious question over the appropriateness of Sanders' categories ('getting in' and 'staying in') for assessing first-century Judaism; see e.g., D. A. Carson, 'Summaries and Conclusions', in D. A. Carson, P. T. O'Brien and M. Seifrid (eds), *Justification and Variegated Nomism, Vol. 1: The Complexities of Second Temple Judaism* (WUNT, 2.140; Grand Rapids: Baker, 2001), 505–48 (543–47); Bird, *Righteousness*, 92.

5.   Another common observation; see e.g., D. A. Hagner, 'Paul and Judaism: Testing the New Perspective', in P. Stuhlmacher, *Revisiting Paul's Doctrine of Justification: A Challenge to the New Perspective* (Downers Grove: IVP, 2001), 75–105 (84–88); C. G. Kruse, *Paul, the Law, and Justification* (Peabody: Hendrickson, 1996), 296; Moo, 216–17.

6.   R. Bauckham, 'Apocalypses', in Carson, O'Brien and Seifrid (eds), *Justification*, 135–87 (174). I would hasten to add that bold advocacy of attempting to earn merit before God appears to be relatively rare in the literature of Second Temple Judaism. For characterizing the variation within Judaism in general based on the relevant texts, Kruse, ibid., helpfully speaks of texts which stress observing the Law and texts which stress God's election and grace. It does seem that covenant and the Law figured prominently in Judaism generally, though there could be exceptions even to this rule, at least in relation to covenant (see e.g., P. Spilsbury, 'Josephus', 241–60; D. M. Hay, 'Philo of Alexandria', 357–79 (370), both in Carson, O'Brien and Seifrid (eds), *Justification*).

7.   Cf. Bird, *Righteousness*, 93–94 n. 14, who even wonders if the term 'covenantal nomism' has become 'so broad as to be meaningless' when it can be thought of as accommodating merit theology.

supported the scholarly consensus that Paul generally relied on the Septuagint for the text form of his scriptural quotations. But I noted that this in no way argues against the possibility that Paul sometimes made use of Hebrew. The present investigation has now found that Paul did make use of Hebrew in his quotation of Exod. 9.16 in Rom. 9.17. At the same time, we have found that Paul used the LXX for his quotation of Gen. 25.23 in Rom. 9.12, Mal. 1.2-3 in Rom. 9.13, and Exod. 33.19b in Rom. 9.15. Thus, this investigation continues to support the position that Paul generally relied on the Septuagint for the text form of his scriptural quotations. Yet it adds the additional point that he did sometimes make use of Hebrew, at least in the case of Rom. 9.17. Still, even in this case he appears to have made some use of the LXX as well. It appears that Paul was aware of both the Hebrew and the LXX of Exod. 9.16, and that he made use of both in his quotation in Rom. 9.17 in a way that would best apply his understanding of the passage to his context and make his point most effectively.

Of the various contributions this study makes to current scholarship, the most significant is perhaps its exegesis of the specific text under consideration (Rom. 9.10-18) based upon an analysis of Paul's use of the Old Testament in its socio-cultural milieu. Its other contributions are founded on this rigorously exegetical approach, whether judgments about Paul's use of Scripture or identifying the content of his theology. By way of summary, in support of God's election of those who believe in Christ (the Church) as his covenant people/ heirs rather than ethnic Israel (9.8), the passage argues, often intertextually, that God's covenant promises and purpose for election are fulfilled not by works or ancestry, but by the sovereign call/naming of God, which he bestows on the basis of faith in Christ. God, Paul suggests, is righteous (in the sense of faithful to his covenant promises) to do so because (1) the election of God's people depended wholly on his sovereign will from the beginning and therefore remained subject to the dictates of his own will; (2) the fundamental nature of his covenant with Israel from its inception allowed for the rejection of the unfaithful and covenant blessing for those who trust in God's chosen means of mediating it; (3) the bestowing of covenantal election by faith rather than works or ancestry, which hardened ethnic Israel, enables God to fulfil his covenant promises by allowing him to include all the nations of the earth in the covenant, which is the climactic covenant promise representative of them all; and (4) God's nature when relating to sinful humanity is both merciful and sovereign in the determination of the beneficiaries of his mercy, including any conditions for choosing them.

We can sum these matters up from the text most succinctly by saying that 'the purpose of God in election' is fulfilled 'not by works, but by the one who calls' (9.11c-12b), for God rightly 'has mercy on whom he desires, and he hardens whom he desires' (9.18). Next, Paul's argument will move to consider an objection to Paul's justification for the faith-based call of God represented by 9.18. It is to that next stage of Paul's argument that we intend to turn in our next volume as we forge ahead in the intertextual exegesis of Romans 9.

BIBLIOGRAPHY

Aalders, G. C., *Genesis*, II (trans. W. Heynen; BSC; Grand Rapids: Zondervan, 1981).

Abasciano, B. J., 'Clearing Up Misconceptions about Corporate Election', *ATJ* 41 (2009), 59–90.

— 'Corporate Election in Romans 9: A Reply to Thomas Schreiner', *JETS* 49/2 (June 2006), 351–71.

— 'Diamonds in the Rough: A Reply to Christopher Stanley Concerning the Reader Competency of Paul's Original Audiences', *NovT* 49 (2007), 153–83.

— *Paul's Use of the Old Testament in Romans 9.1-9: An Intertextual and Theological Exegesis* (JSNTSup/LNTS, 301; London: T&T Clark, 2005).

— 'Paul's Use of the Old Testament in Romans 9:1-9: An Intertextual and Theological Exegesis' (PhD thesis; University of Aberdeen, 2004).

Achtemeier, P. J., *Romans* (IBC; Atlanta: John Knox, 1985).

Allis, O. T., 'The Birth-Oracle to Rebekah (Gen. XXV.23): A Study in the Interpretation of Prophecy', *EvQ* 11.2 (1939), 97–117.

Arnold, B. T. and J. H. Choi, *A Guide to Biblical Hebrew Syntax* (New York: CUP, 2003).

Aschoff, D., 'Maior Minori Serviet: Zur Wirkungsgeschichte eines Genesisverses (Gen 25,23)', in M. Becker and W. Fenske (eds), *Das Ende der Tage und die Gegenwart des Heils: Begegnungen mit dem Neuen Testament und seiner Umwelt* (FS H.-W. Kuhn; AGJU, 44; Leiden: Brill, 1999), 281–304.

Ashby, G., *Go Out and Meet with God: A Commentary on the Book of Exodus* (ITC; Grand Rapids: Eerdmans, 1998).

Badenas, R., *Christ the End of the Law: Romans 10.4 in Pauline Perspective* (JSNTSup, 10; Sheffield: JSOT, 1985).

Bailey, R. C., *Exodus* (The College Press NIV Commentary; Joplin, MO: College Press, 2007).

Baker, D. W., 'Source Criticism', *DOTP*, 798–805.

Baldwin, J. G., *Haggai, Zechariah, Malachi: An Introduction and Commentary* (TOTC, 24; Leicester: IVP, 1972).

Barclay, J. G. M., '"By the grace of God I am what I am": Grace and Agency in Philo and Paul', in J. M. G. Barclay and S. Gathercole (eds), *Divine and Human Agency in Paul and His Cultural Environment* (LNTS, 335; London: T&T Clark, 2006), 140–57.

— 'Unnerving Grace: Approaching Romans 9–11 from the Wisdom of Solomon', in Wilk and Wagner (eds), *Explorations*, 91–109.

Barrett, C. K., *A Commentary on the Epistle to the Romans* (BNTC; London: A & C Black, 2nd edn, 1991).

Bauckham, R., 'Apocalypses', in Carson, O'Brien and Seifrid (eds), *Justification*, 135–87.

Bauernfeind, O., 'τρέχω', *TDNT*, 226–33.

Beale, G. K., 'An Exegetical and Theological Consideration of the Hardening of Pharaoh's Heart in Exodus 4–14 and Romans 9', *TJ* 5 NS (1984), 129–54.

— 'Isaiah VI 9-13: A Retributive Taunt against Idolatry', *VT* 41/3 (1991), 257–78.

— Review of J. Piper, *The Justification of God: An Exegetical and Theological Study of Romans 9:1-23*, *WTJ* 46 (1984), 190–97.

— *We Become What We Worship: A Biblical Theology of Idolatry* (Downer's Grove: IVP, 2008).

Bell, R. H., *The Irrevocable Call of God* (WUNT, 184; Tübingen: Mohr Siebeck, 2005).

— *Provoked to Jealousy: The Origin and Purpose of the Jealousy Motif in Romans 9–11* (WUNT, 2.63; Tübingen: Mohr Siebeck, 1994).

Belli, F., *Argumentation and Use of Scripture in Romans 9–11* (AnBib, 183; Roma: Gregorian and Biblical Press, 2010).

Berger, K., 'Abraham in den paulinischen Hauptbriefen', *MTZ* 17 (1966), 47–89.

Berkley, T. W., *From a Broken Covenant to Circumcision of the Heart: Pauline Intertextual Exegesis in Romans 2:17-29* (SBLDS, 175; Atlanta: SBL, 2000).

Best, E., *The First and Second Epistles to the Thessalonians* (BNTC; Peabody: Hendrickson, 1986).

Bird, M. F., *The Saving Righteousness of God: Studies on Paul, Justification, and the New Perspective* (PBM; Milton Keynes: Paternoster, 2006).

Black, M., *Romans* (NCB; London: Marshall Morgan and Scott, 1973).

Borgen, P., *Philo of Alexandria: An Exegete for His Time* (NovTSup, 86; Leiden: Brill, 1997).

Botha, A. J., 'Die belang van Maleagi 1:2-5 vir die verstaan van die boek', *Skrif en Kerk* 21 (2000), 495–506.

Brandenburger, E., 'Paulinische Schriftauslegung in der Kontroverse um das Verheissungswort Gottes (Röm 9)', *ZTK* 82 (1985), 1–47.

Brown, A. P., II, 'Does God Harden People's Hearts?', *God's Revivalist and Bible Advocate* 121.3 (April 2009), 14.

Bruce, F. F., *The Epistle to the Hebrews* (NICNT; Grand Rapids: Eerdmans, 1964).

Bruckner, J. K., *Exodus* (NIBCOT, 2; Peabody: Hendrickson, 2008).

Brueggemann, W., 'The Book of Exodus: Introduction, Commentary, and Reflections', in L. E. Keck et al. (eds), *The New Interpreter's Bible*, I (NIB, 1; Nashville: Abingdon, 1994), 675–982.

— *Genesis* (IBC; Atlanta: John Knox, 1982).

Bultmann, R., 'γινώσκω, κτλ.', *TDNT*, 1.689–719.

Bush, G., *Notes, Critical and Practical on the Book of Exodus* (2 vols in 1; Boston: Henry A. Young & Co., 1870).

Butler, T. C., *Joshua* (WBC, 7; Dallas: Word, 1983).

Byrne, B., *Romans* (Sacra Pagina, 6; Collegeville, MN: Liturgical Press, 1996).

Calvin, J., *Commentary on Philippians, Colossians, and Thessalonians* (http://www.ccel.org/: CCEL, n.d).

— *Genesis* (ed./trans. J. K. King; Geneva Commentary; 2 vols in 1; repr., Edinburgh: Banner of Truth, 1965).

Campbell, D. A., *The Deliverance of God: An Apocalyptic Rereading of Justification in Paul* (Grand Rapids: Eerdmans, 2009).

Carson, D. A., 'Summaries and Conclusions', in Carson, O'Brien and Seifrid (eds), *Justification*, 505–48.

Carson, D. A., P. T. O'Brien and M. Seifrid (eds), *Justification and Variegated Nomism. Vol. 1: The Complexities of Second Temple Judaism* (WUNT, 2.140; Grand Rapids: Baker, 2001).

Cassuto, U., *A Commentary on the Book of Exodus* (trans. I. Abrahams; Jerusalem: Magnes, 1967).

Chae, D. J.-S., *Paul as Apostle to the Gentiles: His Apostolic Self-Awareness and Its Influence on the Soteriological Argument in Romans* (PBTM; Carlisle: Paternoster, 1997).

Charles, B. C., *The Book of Jubilees or the Little Genesis* (London: Adam and Charles Black, 1902).

Cheon, S., *The Exodus Story in the Wisdom of Solomon: A Study in Biblical Interpretation* (JSPSup, 23; Sheffield: SAP, 1997).

Childs, B. S., *The Book of Exodus: A Critical, Theological Commentary* (OTL; Philadelphia: Westminster, 1974).

Chilton, B. D., 'Romans 9–11 as Scriptural Interpretation and Dialogue with Judaism', *Ex Auditu* 4 (1988), 27–37.

Chisholm Jr, R. B., 'Divine Hardening in the Old Testament', *Bsac* 153 (Oct.–Dec. 1996), 410–34.

Clements, R. E., *Exodus* (CBC; Cambridge: CUP, 1972).

Clendenen, E. R., 'Malachi', in R. A. Taylor and E. R. Clendenen, *Haggai, Malachi* (NAC, 21A; Nashville: Broadman & Holman, 2004), 203–464.

Clines, D. J. A., D. M. Gunn and A. J. Hauser (eds), *Art and Meaning: Rhetoric in Biblical Literature* (JSOTSup, 19; Sheffield: JSOT, 1982).

Coats, G. W., *Exodus 1–18* (FOTL, 2A; Grand Rapids: Eerdmans, 1999).

— *Genesis with an Introduction to Narrative Literature* (FOTL, 1; Grand Rapids: Eerdmans, 1983).

Cole, R. A., *Exodus: An Introduction and Commentary* (TOTC, 2; Leicester; Downer's Grove: IVP, 1973).

Collins, C. J., 'כבד', *NIDOTTE*, 2.577–87.

Coover Cox, D. G., 'The Hardening of Pharaoh's Heart in its Literary and Cultural Contexts', *Bsac* 163 (July–Sept. 2006), 292–311.

Cottrell, J., *Romans*, II (CPNIVC; Joplin: College Press, 1998).

Cranfield, C. E. B., *A Critical and Exegetical Commentary on the Epistle to the Romans* (ICC; 2 vols; Edinburgh: T&T Clark, 1975–79).

Cranford, M., 'Election and Ethnicity: Paul's View of Israel in Romans 9.1-13', *JSNT* 50 (1993), 27–41.

Cresson, B. C., 'The Condemnation of Edom in Postexilic Judaism', in J. M. Efird (ed.), *The Use of the Old Testament in the New and Other Essays* (FS W. F. Stinespring; Durham: Duke University Press, 1972), 125–48.

Croy, N. C., *3 Maccabees* (SCS; Leiden: Brill, 2006).

Currid, J. E., *Ancient Egypt and the Old Testament* (Grand Rapids: Baker, 1997).

— 'Why Did God Harden Pharaoh's Heart?', *BRev* 9 (1993), 46–51.

Davies, W. D., 'Paul from the Jewish Point of View', in W. Horbury, W. D. Davies and J. Sturdy (eds), *Cambridge History of Judaism III: The Early Roman Period* (Cambridge: CUP, 1999), 678–730.

Delitzsch, F., *Psalms* (trans. J. Martin; Commentary on the Old Testament, 5; 3 vols in 1; repr., Grand Rapids: Eerdmans, 1973).

Derrett, J. D. M., '"Running" in Paul: the Midrashic Potential of Hab 2,2', *Bib* 66 (1985), 560–67.

Dicou, B., *Edom, Israel's Brother and Antagonist: The Role of Edom in Biblical Prophecy and Story* (JSOTSup, 169; Sheffield: SAP, 1994).

Di Lella, A. A., 'Tobit 4,19 and Romans 9,18: An Intertextual Study', *Bib* 90 (2009), 260–63.

Dohmen, C. and P. Stenmans, 'כָּבֵד', *TDOT*, 7.13–22.

Donfried, K. P. 'False Presuppositions in the Study of Romans', in Donfried (ed.), *Debate*, 102–25.

— (ed.), *The Romans Debate* (Peabody: Hendrickson, rev. edn, 1991).

Duling, D. C., 'Testament of Solomon: A New Translation and Introduction', *OTP*, 1.935–87.

Dunn, J. D. G., *Romans* (WBC, 38; 2 vols; Dallas: Word, 1988).

— *The Theology of Paul the Apostle* (Grand Rapids/Cambridge: Eerdmans, 1998).

Dunn, J. D. G. (ed.), *Paul and the Mosaic Law* (WUNT, 89; Tübingen: Mohr-Siebeck, 1996).

Durham, J. I., *Exodus* (WBC, 3; Waco: Word, 1987).

Du Toit, A. B., 'A Tale of Two Cities: "Tarsus or Jerusalem" Revisited', *NTS* 46 (2000), 375–402.

Ebel, G., 'τρέχω', *NIDNTT*, 3.947.

Edwards, J. R., *Romans* (NIBCNT; Peabody: Hendrickson, 1992).

Ellis, E. E., *Paul's Use of the Old Testament* (Grand Rapids: Baker, 1957).

Ellison, H. L., *Exodus* (DSB; Philadephia: Westminster, 1982).

— *The Mystery of Israel: An Exposition of Romans 9–11* (Exeter: Paternoster, 3rd edn, rev. and enl., 1976).

Endres, J. C., *Biblical Interpretation in the Book of Jubilees* (CBQMS, 18; Washington, DC: CBAA, 1987).

Enns, P., *Exodus* (NIVAC; Grand Rapids: Zondervan, 2000).

— *Exodus Retold: Ancient Exegesis of the Departure from Egypt in Wis 10:15-21 and 19:1-9* (HSMM, 57; Atlanta: Scholars Press, 1997).

Eslinger, L., 'Freedom or Knowledge? Perspective and Purpose in the Exodus Narrative (Exodus 1–15)', *JSOT* 52 (1991), 43–60.

Evans, C. A., 'Paul and the Hermeneutics of "True Prophecy": A Study of Rom 9–11', *Bib* 65 (1984), 560–70.

Fabry, H.-J., 'לֵב', *TDOT*, 7.399–437.

Fee, G. D., *The First Epistle to the Corinthians* (NICNT; Grand Rapids: Eerdmans, 1987).

Fitzmyer, J. A., *Romans: A New Translation with Introduction and Commentary* (AB, 33; New York: Doubleday, 1993).

Fokkelman, J. P., *Narrative Art in Genesis: Specimens of Stylistic and Structural Analysis* (Assen/Amsterdam: Van Gorcum, 1975).

Ford, W. A., *God, Pharaoh and Moses: Explaining the Lord's Actions in the Exodus Plagues Narrative* (PBM; Milton Keynes: Paternoster, 2006).

Forlines, F. L., *Romans* (RHBC; Nashville: Randall House, 1987).

Forster, R. T. and V. P. Marston, *God's Strategy in Human History* (Eugene, OR: Wipf and Stock, 2nd edn, 2000).

Freedman, H. and M. Simon (eds), *The Midrash Rabbah* (5 vols; London/Jerusalem/New York: Soncino, new edn, 1977).

Fretheim, T. E., *Exodus* (IBC; Louisville: John Knox, 1991).

Garland, D. E., *1 Corinthians* (BECNT; Grand Rapids: Baker Academic, 2003).

Gaston, L., 'Israel's Enemies in Pauline Theology', in L. Gaston, *Paul and the Torah* (Vancouver: University of British Columbia Press, 1987), 80–99.

Gaventa, B. R., 'On the Calling-Into-Being of Israel: Romans 9:6-29', in Wilk and Wagner (eds), *Explorations*, 255–69.

Gibson, J. C. L., *Genesis*, II (DSB; Philadelphia: Westminster, 1982).

Gilbert, P., 'Libre arbitre et déterminisme: Une réflexion sur la figure de Pharaon', *Theoforum* 32 (2001), 5–21.

Gilchrist, P. R., 'יָדַע', *TWOT*, 1.366–67.

Ginzberg, L., *The Legends of the Jews* (7 vols; Philadelphia: Jewish Publication Society, 1909–38).

Glazier-McDonald, B., 'Edom in the Prophetical Corpus', in D. V. Edelman (ed.), *You Shall Not Abhor an Edomite for He is Your Brother: Edom and Seir in History and Tradition* (ABS, 3; Atlanta: Scholars Press, 1995).

— *Malachi: The Divine Messenger* (SBLDS, 98; Atlanta: Scholar's Press, 1987).

Godet, F., *Commentary on St. Paul's Epistle to the Romans* (trans. A. Cusin and T. W. Chambers; New York: Funk & Wagnalls, 1883).

Goodwin, J., *An Exposition of the Ninth Chapter of the Epistle to the Romans* (London, c. 1652).

Gowan, D. E., *Theology in Exodus: Biblical Theology in the Form of a Commentary* (Louisville: Westminster/John Knox, 1994).

Green, G. L., *The Letters to the Thessalonians* (PNTC; Grand Rapids: Eerdmans, 2002).

Greenspoon, L. J., 'Old Testament Versions, Ancient', *DNTB*, 752–55.

Grindheim, S., *The Crux of Election* (WUNT, 2.202; Tübingen: Mohr Siebeck, 2005).

Gunn, D. M., 'The "Hardening of Pharaoh's Heart": Plot, Character and Theology in Exodus 1–14', in Clines, Gunn and Hauser (eds), *Art and Meaning*, 72–96.

Haacker, K., 'Die Geschichtstheologie von Röm 9–11 im Lichte philonischer Schriftauslegung', *NTS* 43 (1997), 209–22.

Haag, H., 'סֶלַע', *TDOT*, 10.270–77.

Hafemann, S. J., *Paul, Moses, and the History of Israel: The Letter/Spirit Contrast and the Argument from Scripture in 2 Corinthians 3* (Peabody, MA: Hendrickson, 1995).

Hagner, D. A., 'Paul and Judaism: Testing the New Perspective', in P. Stuhlmacher, *Revisiting Paul's Doctrine of Justification: A Challenge to the New Perspective* (Downers Grove: IVP, 2001), 75–105.

Hamilton, V. P., *The Book of Genesis* (NICOT; 2 vols; Grand Rapids: Eerdmans, 1990/1995).

Hanson, A. T., *Studies in Paul's Technique and Theology* (London: SPCK, 1974).

Harrington, D. J., 'Pseudo-Philo: A New Translation and Introduction', *OTP*, 2.297–377.

Hartley, J. E., 'צוּר', *TWOT*, 2.762.

Hay, D. M., 'Philo of Alexandria', in Carson, O'Brien and Seifrid (eds), *Justification*, 357–79.

Hay, D. M. and E. E. Johnson (eds), *Pauline Theology III: Romans* (Minneapolis: Fortress, 1995).

Hays, R. B., *Echoes of Scripture in the Letters of Paul* (New Haven/London: Yale University Press, 1989).

Heard, R. C., *Dynamics of Diselection: Ambiguity in Genesis 12–36 and Ethnic Boundaries in Post-Exilic Judah* (SBLSS, 39; Atlanta: SBL, 2001).

Hendriksen, W., *Exposition of Paul's Epistle to the Romans* (NTC; Grand Rapids: Baker Book House, 1980–81).

Hengel, M. with R. Deines, *The Pre-Christian Paul* (Philadelphia: TPI, 1991).

Hess, R. S., *Joshua: An Introduction and Commentary* (TOTC, 6; Downer's Grove: IVP, 1996).

Hesse, F., 'חָזַק', *TDOT*, 4.301–08.

Hill, A. E., *Malachi: A New Translation with Introduction and Commentary* (AB, 25D; New York: Doubleday, 1998).

Hock, R. F., 'Paul and Greco-Roman Education', in J. P. Sampley (ed.), *Paul in the Greco-Roman World* (Harrisburg: TPI, 2003), 198–227.

Hodge, C., *Commentary on the Epistle to the Romans* (Grand Rapids: Eerdmans, rev. edn, 1886).

Houtman, C., *Exodus* (trans. J. Rebel and S. Woudstra; Historical Commentary on the Old Testament; 3 vols; Kampen: Kok, 1993–96).

Hübner, H., *Gottes Ich und Israel: Zum Schriftgebrauch des Paulus in Römer 9–11* (Göttingen: Vandenhoeck & Ruprecht, 1984).

— *Vetus Testamentum in Novo, II, Corpus Paulinum* (Göttingen: Vandenhoeck & Ruprecht, 1997).

Hyatt, J. P., *Exodus* (NCB; London: Marshall Morgan and Scott, 1971).

Irwin, B. P., 'Yahweh's Suspension of Free Will in the Old Testament: Divine Immorality or Sign-Act?', *TynBul* 54.2 (2003), 55–62.

Isbell, C. D., 'Exodus 1–2 in the Context of Exodus 1–14: Story Lines and Key Words', in Clines, Gunn and Hauser (eds), *Art and Meaning*, 37–61.

— *The Function of Exodus Motifs in Biblical Narratives: Theological Didactic Drama* (SBEC, 52; Lewiston: Mellen, 1992).

Jacob, B. *The Second Book of the Bible: Exodus* (trans. W. Jacob; Hoboken: KTAV, 1992).

Janzen, J. G., *Abraham and All the Families of the Earth: A Commentary on the Book of Genesis 12–50* (ITC; Grand Rapids/Edinburgh: Eerdmans/Handsel, 1993).

Jewett, R., *Romans: A Commentary* (Hermeneia; Minneapolis: Fortress, 2007).

Johnson, L. T., *Reading Romans: A Literary and Theological Commentary* (New York: Crossword, 1997).

Joüon, P. and T. Muraoka, *A Grammar of Biblical Hebrew* (SB 14/1–14/2; 2 vols; repr. with corrections, Rome: Editrice Pontifico Istituto Biblico, (1991) 1993).

Kaiser, W. C., 'Exodus', in F. E. Gaebelein (ed.), *The Expositor's Bible Commentary*, II (Grand Rapids: Zondervan, 1990), 285–498.

Käsemann, E., *Commentary on Romans* (trans. G. W. Bromiley; Grand Rapids: Eerdmans, 1980).

Keck, L. E., *Romans* (ANTC; Nashville: Abingdon, 2005).

Keil, C. F., *The Pentateuch* (trans. J. Martin; Commentary on the Old Testament, 1; 3 vols in 1; repr., Grand Rapids: Eerdmans, 1973).

Kellenberger, E., *Die Verstockung Pharaos: Exegetische und auslegungsgeschichtliche Untersuchungen zu Exodus 1–15* (BWANT, 171; Stuttgart: Kohlhammer, 2006).

Kidner, D., *Genesis: An Introduction and Commentary* (TOTC, 1; London: Tyndale, 1967).

Kitchen, K. A., 'Magic and Sorcery: Egyptian and Assyro-Babylonian', *NBD2*, 724–26.

Klein, W. W., 'Paul's Use of *KALEIN*: A Proposal', *JETS* 27/1 (March 1984), 53–64.

Knauth, R. J. D., 'Esau, Edomites', *DOTP*, 219–24.

Koch, D.-A., *Die Schrift als Zeuge des Evangeliums: Untersuchungen zur Verwendung und zum Verständnis der Schrift bei Paulus* (BHT, 69; Tübingen: Mohr Siebeck, 1986).

Kruse, C. G., *Paul, the Law, and Justification* (Peabody: Hendrickson, 1996).

Kugel, J. L., *Traditions of the Bible: A Guide to the Bible as It Was at the Start of the Common Era* (Cambridge, MA/London: Harvard University Press, 1998).

Kuss, O., *Der Römerbrief*, III (Regensburg: Pustet, 1978).

Lambdin, T. O., *Introduction to Biblical Hebrew* (New York: Charles Scribner's Sons, 1971).

LaSor, W. S., 'Poetry, Hebrew', *ISBE*, 3.891–98.

Leenhardt, F. J., *The Epistle to the Romans: A Commentary* (London: Lutterworth, 1961).

Leupold, H. C., *Exposition of Genesis*, II (Grand Rapids: Baker Book House, 1942).

Lim, T. M., *Holy Scripture in the Qumran Commentaries and Pauline Letters* (Oxford: OUP, 1997).

Lodge, J. G., *Romans 9–11: A Reader-Response Analysis* (ISFCJ, 6; Atlanta: Scholars Press, 1996).

Longenecker, B. W., *Eschatology and the Covenant: A Comparison of 4 Ezra and Romans 1–11* (JSNTSup, 57; Sheffield: JSOT, 1991).

Lübking, H.-M., *Paulus und Israel im Römerbrief: Eine Untersuchung zu Römer 9–11* (Frankfurt: Lang, 1986).

Luc, A., 'לֵב', *NIDOTTE*, 2.749–54.

Luz, U., *Das Geschichtsverständnis des Paulus* (BevT, 49; Munich: Kaiser, 1968).

Lyonnet, S., 'Le rôle d'Israël dans l'histoire du salut selon Rom 9–11' in S. Lyonnet, *Etudes sur l'Epître aux Romains* (AnBib, 120; Rome: Editrice Pontifico Istituto Biblico, 1989), 264–73.

Mackay, J. L., *Exodus* (Fearn, Ross-shire: Mentor, 2001).

Maher, M., *Targum Pseudo-Jonathan: Genesis: Translated, with Introduction and Notes* (TAB, 1b; Collegeville, MN: The Liturgical Press, 1992).

Maier, G., *Mensch und freier Wille nach den jüdischen Religionspartien zwischen Ben Sira und Paulus* (WUNT, 12; Tübingen: Mohr Siebeck, 1971).

Maillot, A. 'Essai sur les citations vétérotestamentaires continues dans Romains 9 à 11, ou comment se servir de la Torah pour montrer que le "Christ est la fin de la Torah"', *ETR* 57 (1982), 55–73.

Mathews, K. A., *Genesis 11:27–50:26* (NAC, 1B; Nashville: Broadman & Holman, 2005).

Mayer, B., *Unter Gottes Heilsratschluss: Prädestinationsaussagen bei Paulus* (Würzburg: Echter, 1974).

McCall, T. H., 'I Believe in Divine Sovereignty', *TJ* 29/2 (2008), 205–26.

— 'We Believe in God's Sovereign Goodness: A Rejoinder to John Piper', *TJ* 29/2 (Fall 2008), 235–46.

McNamara, M. and R. Hayward, *Targum Neofiti 1: Exodus* (TAB, 2; Collegeville, MN: Liturgical Press, 1994).

Meadors, E. P., *Idolatry and the Hardening of the Heart: A Study in Biblical Theology* (New York/London: T&T Clark, 2006).

Metzger, B. M., 'The Fourth Book of Ezra: A New Translation and Introduction', *OTP*, 1.517–59.

Michaels, J. R., *1 Peter* (WBC, 49; Waco: Word, 1988).

Millard, A. R., 'Jacob', *ISBE*, 4.948–55.

Moberly, R. W. L., *At the Mountain of God: Story and Theology in Exodus 32–34* (JSOTSup, 22; Sheffield: JSOT, 1983).

Mohrmann, D. C., 'Semantic Collisions at the Intertextual Crossroads: A Diachronic and Synchronic Study of Romans 9:30–10:13' (unpublished PhD thesis; University of Durham, 2001).

Moo, D. J., *The Epistle to the Romans* (NICNT; Grand Rapids: Eerdmans, 1996).

— 'The Theology of Romans 9–11: A Response to E. Elizabeth Johnson', in Hay and Johnson (eds), *Pauline*, 240–58.

Morison, J., *Exposition of the Ninth Chapter of the Epistle to the Romans: A New Edition, Re-written, to which is Added an Exposition of the Tenth Chapter* (London: Hodder and Stoughton, 1888).

Morris, L., *The Epistle to the Romans* (Grand Rapids: Eerdmans, 1988).

Mounce, R. H., *Romans* (NAC, 27; Nashville: Broadman & Holman, 1995).

Müller, C., *Gottes Gerechtigkeit und Gottes Volk: Eine Untersuchung zu Römer 9–11* (FRLANT, 86; Göttingen: Vandenhoeck & Ruprecht, 1964).

Munck, J., *Christ and Israel: An Interpretation of Romans 9–11* (Philadelphia: Fortress, 1967).

Murphy-O'Connor, J., *Paul: A Critical Life* (Oxford: OUP, 1996).

Murray, J., *The Epistle to the Romans* (NICNT; 2 vols in 1; Grand Rapids: Eerdmans, 1959–65).

Neufeld, E., 'In Defense of Esau', *JBQ* 20.1 (Fall 1991), 43–49.

Oden, T. C., *The Transforming Power of Grace* (Nashville: Abingdon, 1993).

Oepke, A., 'ἐξεγείρω', *TDNT*, 2.338.

Ogden, G. S., 'Idem per Idem: Its Use and Meaning', *JSOT* 53 (1992), 107–20.

Oropeza, B. J., 'Paul and Theodicy: Intertextual Thoughts on God's Justice and Faithfulness to Israel in Romans 9–11', *NTS* 53 (2007), 57–80.

Osborne, G. R., *Romans* (IVPNTC; Downer's Grove: IVP, 2004).

Oswalt, J. N., 'Theology of the Pentateuch', *DOTP*, 845–59.

Park, B. K.-H., 'God's Sovereign Election and Rejection: Paul's Use of the Old Testament in Romans 9:10-13' (unpublished masters thesis; Gordon-Conwell Theological Seminary, 1992).

Patterson, R. D., 'סלע', *TWOT*, 2.627.

Petter, D., 'Exodus 34:6-7: The Function and Meaning of the Declaration' (MTh thesis; Gordon-Conwell Theological Seminary, 1997).

Pfitzner, V. C., *Paul and the Agon Motif* (NovTSup, 16; Leiden: Brill, 1967).

Piper, J., 'I Believe in God's Self-Sufficiency: A Response to Thomas McCall', *TJ* 29/2 (Fall 2008), 227–34.

— *The Justification of God: An Exegetical and Theological Study of Romans 9:1–23* (Grand Rapids: Baker, 2nd edn, 1993).

Pohlig, J. N., *An Exegetical Summary of Malachi* (Dallas: Summer Institute of Linguistics, 1998).

Porter, S. E., 'Diatribe', *DNTB*, 296–98.

Propp, W. H. C., *Exodus 1–18: A New Translation with Introduction and Commentary* (AB, 2; New York: Doubleday, 1999).

Räisänen, H., 'Faith, Works and Election in Romans 9: A Response to Stephen Westerholm', in Dunn (ed.), *Law*, 239–46.

— 'Römer 9–11: Analyse eines geistigen Ringens', *ANRW* 2.25.4 (1987), 2891–939.

Refoulé, F., 'Unité de l'Épître aux Romains et histoire du salut', *RSPT* 71 (1987), 219–42.

Reichert, A., *Der Römerbrief als Gratwanderung: Eine Untersuchung zur Abfassungsproblematik* (FRLANT, 194; Göttingen: Vandenhoeck & Ruprecht, 2001).

Rigsby, R. O., 'Jacob', *DOTP*, 461–67.

Ringgren, H., 'דמע', *TDOT*, 11.178–87.

Robertson, A. T., *Word Pictures in the New Testament* (Nashville: Broadman Press, 1932–33, 1960), accessed at http://www.biblestudytools.com/commentaries/robertsons-word-pictures/.

Robertson, R. G., 'Ezekiel the Tragedian: A New Translation and Introduction', *OTP*, 2.803–19.

Sailhamer, J. H., 'Genesis', in F. E. Gaebelein (ed.), *The Expositor's Bible Commentary*, II (Grand Rapids: Zondervan, 1990), 1–284.

— *The Pentateuch as Narrative: A Biblical-Theological Commentary* (Library of Biblical Interpretation; Grand Rapids: Zondervan, 1992).

Salveson, A., *Symmachus in the Pentateuch* (JSS Monograph, 15; Manchester: University of Manchester Press, 1991).

Sanday, W. and A. C. Headlam, *A Critical and Exegetical Commentary on the Epistle to the Romans* (ICC; New York: Charles Scribner's Sons, 10th edn, 1905).

Sarna, N. M., *Exploring Exodus: The Heritage of Biblical Israel* (New York: Schocken, 1986).

— *Genesis* (JPSTC; Philadelphia: JPS, 1989).

Schmithals, W., *Der Römerbrief: Ein Kommentar* (Gütersloh: Gütersloher, 1988).

Schmitt, R., *Gottesgerechtigkeit-Heilsgeschichte-Israel in der Theologie des Paulus* (Frankfurt: Lang, 1984).

Schnelle, U., *Apostle Paul: His Life and Theology* (trans. M. E. Boring; Grand Rapids: Baker Academic, 2005).

Schreiner, T. R., 'Corporate and Individual Election in Romans 9: A Response to Brian Abasciano', *JETS* 49/2 (June 2006), 373–86.

— 'Did Paul Believe in Justification by Works? Another Look at Romans 2', *BBR* 3 (1993), 131–58.

— 'Does Romans 9 Teach Individual Election unto Salvation? Some Exegetical and Theological Reflections', *JETS* 36 (1993), 25–40.

— *Romans* (BECNT, 6; Grand Rapids: Baker, 1998).

Segal, M., *The Book of Jubilees: Rewritten Bible, Redaction, Ideology and Theology* (JSJSup, 117; Leiden: Brill, 2007).

Seifrid, M. A., 'Romans', in G. K. Beale and D. A. Carson (eds), *Commentary on the New Testament Use of the Old Testament* (Grand Rapids: Baker Academic, 2007), 607–94.

Shellrude, G., 'The Freedom of God in Mercy and Judgment: A Libertarian Reading of Romans 9:6-29', *EvQ* 81.4 (2009), 306–18.

Shum, S.-L., *Paul's Use of Isaiah in Romans: A Comparative Study of Paul's Letter to the Romans and the Sybilline and Qumran Sectarian Texts* (WUNT, 2.156; Tübingen: Mohr Siebeck, 2002).

Shupak, N., 'ḤZQ, KBD, QŠH LĒB: The Hardening of Pharaoh's Heart in Exodus 4:1–15:21 – Seen Negatively in the Bible but Favorably in Egyptian Sources', in G. N. Knoppers and A. Hirsch (eds), *Egypt, Israel and the Mediterranean Worlds: Studies in Honor of Donald B. Redford (Probleme der Ägyptologie*, 20; Leiden: Brill, 2004), 389–403.

— *Where Can Wisdom Be Found?: The Sage's Language in the Bible and in Ancient Egyptian Literature* (OBO, 130; Fribourg/Göttingen: University Press/Vandenhoeck & Ruprecht, 1993).

Siegert, F., *Argumentation bei Paulus: gezeigt an Röm 9–11* (WUNT, 34; Tübingen: Mohr Siebeck, 1985).

Silva, M., 'Old Testament in Paul', *DPL*, 630–42.

Sim, M. G., 'A Relevance Theoretic Approach to the Particle ἵνα in Koine Greek' (PhD thesis; University of Edinburgh, 2006).

Skehan, P. W. and A. A. Di Lella, *The Wisdom of Ben Sira* (AB, 39; New York: Doubleday, 1987).

Smith, D. M., 'The Pauline Literature', in D. A. Carson and H. G. M. Williamson (eds), *It is Written: Scripture Citing Scripture: Essays in Honour of Barnabas Lindars* (Cambridge: CUP, 1988), 265–91.

Smith, R. L., *Micah–Malachi* (WBC, 32; Waco: Word Books, 1984).

Speiser, E. A., *Genesis* (AB, 1; New York: Doubleday, 1964).

Spilsbury, P., 'Josephus', in Carson, O'Brien and Seifrid (eds), *Justification*, 241–60.

Stanley, C. D., *Paul and the Language of Scripture: Citation Technique in the Pauline Epistles and Contemporary Literature* (SNTSMS, 69; Cambridge: CUP, 1992).

Stegner, W. R., 'Jew, Paul the', *DPL*, 503–11.

Steinmann, A. E., 'Hardness of Heart', *DOTP*, 381–83.

Stiebert, J., 'The Maligned Patriarch: Prophetic Ideology and the "Bad Press" of Esau', in A. G. Hunter and P. R. Davies (eds), *Sense and Sensitivity: Essays on Reading the Bible in Memory of Robert Carroll* (FS Robert Carroll; JSOTSup, 348; London/New York: SAP, 2002), 33–48.

Stone, M. E., *Fourth Ezra: A Commentary on the Book of Fourth Ezra* (Hermeneia; Minneapolis: Fortress, 1990).

Stowers, S. K., *The Diatribe and Paul's Letter to the Romans* (SBLDS, 57; Chico, CA: Scholars Press, 1981).

Strawn, B. A., 'Pharaoh', *DOTP*, 631–36.

Stuart, D. K., *Exodus* (NAC, 2; Nashville: Broadman & Holman, 2006).

— 'Malachi', in T. E. McComiskey (ed.), *The Minor Prophets: An Exegetical and Expository Commentary*, III (Grand Rapids: Baker, 1998), 1245–396.

Syrén, R., *The Forsaken First-Born: A Study of a Recurrent Motif in the Patriarchal Narratives* (JSOTSup, 133; Sheffield: SAP, 1993).

Thielman, F., 'Unexpected Mercy: Echoes of a Biblical Motif in Romans 9–11', *SJT* 47 (1994), 169–81.

Tobin, T. H., *Paul's Rhetoric in Its Contexts: The Argument of Romans* (Peabody: Hendrickson, 2004).

Tozer, A. W., *The Knowledge of the Holy: The Attributes of God: Their Meaning in the Christian Life* (New York: HarperSanFrancisco, 1961).

Travis, S. H., 'Judgment', *DJG*, 408–11.

Turner, L. A., 'Genesis, Book of', *DOTP*, 350–59.

Verhoef, P. A., *The Books of Haggai and Malachi* (NICOT; Grand Rapids: Eerdmans, 1987).

Wagner, J. R., *Heralds of the Good News: Isaiah and Paul 'in Concert' in the Letter to the Romans* (NovTSup, 101; Leiden: Brill, 2002).

Wallace, D. B., *Greek Grammar Beyond the Basics: An Exegetical Syntax of the New Testament* (Grand Rapids: Zondervan, 1996).

Waltke, B. K. and M. O'Connor, *An Introduction to Biblical Hebrew Syntax* (Winona Lake: Eisenbrauns, 1990).

Walton, J. H., *Genesis* (NIVAC; Grand Rapids: Zondervan, 2001).

Walton, K., *Thou Traveller Unknown: The Presence and Absence of God in the Jacob Narrative* (PBTM; Carlisle: Paternoster, 2003).

Wanamaker, C. A., *The Epistles to the Thessalonians: A Commentary on the Greek Text* (NIGTC; Grand Rapids: Eerdmans, 1990).

Watson, D. F., 'Diatribe', *DPL*, 213–14.

Wenham, G. J., *Genesis 16–50* (WBC, 2; Dallas: Word, 1994).

Westermann, C., *Genesis 12–36: A Commentary* (trans. J. J. Scullion; Minneapolis: Augsburg, 1985).

Wevers, J. W., *Notes on the Greek Text of Exodus* (SBLSCS, 30; Atlanta: Scholars Press, 1990).

— *Notes on the Greek Text of Genesis* (SBLSCS, 35; Atlanta: Scholars Press, 1993).

Whiston, W. (trans.), *The Works of Josephus: New Updated Edition Complete and Unabridged in One Volume* (Peabody, MA: Hendrickson, 1987).

Wilckens, U., *Der Brief an die Römer*, II: Röm 6–11 (EKKNT, 2; Zürich: Benziger/ Neukirchen: Neukirchener Verlag, 1980).

Wilk, F. and J. R. Wagner (eds), *Between Gospel and Election: Explorations in the Interpretation of Romans 9–11* (WUNT, 257; Tübingen: Mohr Siebeck, 2010).

Wilson, J. M. and R. K. Harrison, 'Birthright', *ISBE*, 1.515–16.

Wilson, R. R., 'The Hardening of Pharaoh's Heart', *CBQ* 41 (1979), 18–36.

Wintermute, O. S., 'Jubilees: A New Translation and Introduction', *OTP*, 2.35–142.

Witherington III, B. with D. Hyatt, *Paul's Letter to the Romans: A Socio-Rhetorical Commentary* (Grand Rapids: Eerdmans, 2004).

Wright, N. T., *The Climax of the Covenant: Christ and the Law in Pauline Theology* (Edinburgh: T&T Clark, 1991).

— 'Romans', in L. E. Keck (ed.), *The New Interpreter's Bible*, X (NIB, 10; Nashville: Abingdon, 2002), 393–770.

— 'Romans 9–11 and the "New Perspective"', in Wilk and Wagner (eds), *Explorations*, 37–54.

Yonge, C. D. (trans.), *The Works of Philo: New Updated Edition Complete and Unabridged in One Volume* (Peabody, MA: Hendrickson, 1993).

Young, B. H., *Paul The Jewish Theologian: A Pharisee among Christians, Jews, and Gentiles* (Peabody: Hendrickson, 1997).

Zerwick, M., *Biblical Greek: Illustrated by Examples* (ed./trans. J. Smith; SPIB, 114; Rome: SPIB, 1963).

Zipor, M., 'קשה', *TDOT*, 13.189–95.

Index of References

Index of Modern Authors